Happiness for Humans

Happiness for Humans

Daniel C. Russell

OXFORD
UNIVERSITY PRESS

OXFORD
UNIVERSITY PRESS

Great Clarendon Street, Oxford, OX2 6DP,
United Kingdom

Oxford University Press is a department of the University of Oxford.
It furthers the University's objective of excellence in research, scholarship,
and education by publishing worldwide. Oxford is a registered trade mark of
Oxford University Press in the UK and in certain other countries

British Library Cataloguing in Publication Data
Data available

Library of Congress Cataloging in Publication Data
Data available

ISBN 978–0–19–958368–3

Printed in Great Britain by
MPG Books Group, Bodmin and King's lynn

To the memory of Jean Hampton

Acknowledgments

It was in 2005 that I first realized that this book was one I wanted to write, during an Arizona Current Research Workshop on a paper of mine about the Stoics. The workshop was organized by David Schmidtz and made possible by the Arizona Center for the Philosophy of Freedom, with the generous support of Randy Kendrick and the Institute for Humane Studies. During that workshop I received formal comments from Tony Long and Nancy Sherman, and though it will sound like an exaggeration, these comments really did change forever how I think about ancient debates over the relation of virtue to happiness. This book is the result of my coming to terms with that change, that new appreciation of how and why those debates still matter. I wish to extend my deepest gratitude to everyone involved with the workshop. This book would have been impossible without it.

A précis of the basic plot of this book was first presented at the 2007 Philosophy in Assos conference, organized by Örsan Öymen, and later as part of the 2007 Boston Area Colloquium in Ancient Philosophy, organized by the late John Cleary and with comments from Tim Roche. I thank the organizers and participants at both meetings. The précis subsequently appeared as "Happiness and Agency in the Stoics and Aristotle," *Proceedings of the Boston Area Colloquium in Ancient Philosophy* 24 (2008), 83–112, along with Tim Roche's excellent comments.

I wrote the first draft of this book in the 2008 fall semester while I was a visiting scholar at the Social Philosophy and Policy Center at Bowling Green State University; I also prepared the penultimate draft there during a visiting scholarship in summer 2011. I am greatly indebted to the Social Philosophy and Policy Center for this most generous support, especially Fred Miller, Ellen Paul, and Jeffrey Paul. I also thank the Department of Philosophy and the Fairmount College of Liberal Arts and Sciences at Wichita State University for a leave of absence during the 2008 fall semester, as well as for subsequent support of my further work on the manuscript. Those preparations were also aided greatly by Mark LeBar's comments on the entire first draft; his comments were, as usual, invaluable to me. Thanks also to several anonymous commentators on the first draft; indeed, in one case I was prompted to think through ancient debates about the nature of the self that changed the final manuscript in very substantial ways. Likewise, thanks to Peter Momtchiloff and Sarah Parker at Oxford University Press.

I also wish to thank those who participated in discussions of the penultimate draft at the University of Arizona: Julia Annas, Sameer Bajaj, Michael Bukoski, Laura Lenhart, David Owen, Liz Phillips, Daniel Silvermint, and especially Guido Pincione, with whom I discussed the entire manuscript. Preparation of the final draft was made possible by the support of the Arizona Center for the Philosophy of Freedom, so I am once again indebted to David Schmidtz, the Freedom Center's director, for his support of my work. Thanks for the vote of confidence, Dave.

Most of the central ideas in Chapters 1–3 have been distilled for publication as "Happiness and the Virtues," in D. Russell, ed., *The Cambridge Companion to Virtue Ethics* (Cambridge, forthcoming in 2012). I thank Hilary Gaskin of Cambridge University Press for the invitation to contribute the paper, and Tim Chappell and Mark LeBar for their comments. A large portion of Chapter 2 has been adapted from a paper that I co-authored with Mark LeBar, entitled "Well-Being and Eudaimonia: A Reply to Haybron" (forthcoming at the time of this writing in a collection edited by Julia Peters); I thank Mark for his kind permission to adapt that material here, and we would both thank Dan Haybron for his generous and helpful feedback on an earlier draft. A few small alterations aside, Chapter 5 was originally published as "Virtue and Happiness in the Lyceum and Beyond," *Oxford Studies in Ancient Philosophy* 38 (2010), 143–85. I thank Brad Inwood, the journal's editor, for permission to use that paper here. A version of Chapter 6 was presented at the 16th Annual Arizona Colloquium in Ancient Philosophy; I thank Mark McPherran for the opportunity to participate, my fellow participants for useful discussion, and especially Robbie Waggoner for his prepared comments. Finally, some central arguments of Chapters 7, 8, and 11 were presented (and are forthcoming) under the title "Two Mistakes about Stoic Ethics" as part of the 2011 Keeling Colloquium in Ancient Philosophy. I thank Fiona Leigh for the opportunity to participate, as well as the other participants, especially David Sedley for his prepared comments. Thanks also to the Freedom Center for hosting a brown-bag workshop on this paper.

I have dedicated this book to the memory of Jean Hampton. I first met Jean when I was an undergraduate student in her classes in ethics and political philosophy, classes that focused very heavily on the historical background of these fields. The study of the history of philosophy is many things, but for Jean it was most exciting as a way into a world of ideas that still need to be reckoned with, ideas that are still fresh and invigorating and have no expiration date. To study Hobbes, say, with Jean, was not just to learn what Hobbes said, but to wrestle with the philosophical problems that prompted him to say it; she didn't just pull his view out of the coat closet, but told you to try it on. This book finds me wrestling in that spirit with some of the ideas that have captivated me the most for as long as I have been a philosopher. How happy I am that I get to spend my time doing that! I thank Jean, in what way I can, for passing that sense of excitement on to me.

My greatest debt, as always, is to my wife Gina Russell, and to our daughters Jocelyn, Grace, and Julia Russell, for their unfailing love and support over the years it took me to write this book.

D. C. R.

Tucson, Arizona, 2012

Contents

Abbreviations and translations of texts used

Acad.	Cicero, *Academics*
AD	Arius Didymus, *Epitome of Stoic Ethics* (in Stobaeus, *Anthology* II) Inwood and Gerson 1997
Ap.	Plato, *Apology* G. M. A. Grube, in Cooper 1997
Contrad.	Plutarch, *On Stoic Self-Contradictions*
Diss.	Epictetus, *Discourses* (*Dissertationes*) Gill and Hard 1995
DL	Diogenes Laertius, *Lives of Eminent Philosophers* Inwood and Gerson 1997
Doctrines	Galen, *On the Doctrines of Hippocrates and Plato*
EE	Aristotle, *Eudemian Ethics*
Ep.	Seneca, *Letters* (*Epistulae*) Gummere 1917
Euthd.	Plato, *Euthydemus* R. K. Sprague, in Cooper 1997
F + number	Text in Fortenbaugh et al. 1992
Fin.	Cicero, *On Goals* (*de Finibus*) Annas and Woolf 2001
FW + number	Text in Fortenbaugh and White 2004
Gorg.	Plato, *Gorgias* D. J. Zeyl, in Cooper 1997
IG + number	Text in Inwood and Gerson 1997
In NE	Aspasius, *Commentary on the Nicomachean Ethics*
LS + number	Text in Long and Sedley 1987
M	Sextus Empiricus, *Against the Professors* (*Adversus Mathematicos*) Inwood and Gerson 1997
Med.	Marcus Aurelius, Meditations Farquharson 1989
Misc.	Clement, *Miscellanies*
MM	Uncertain Aristotelian author,[*] *Magna Moralia*

---

[*] Although scholars generally agree that Aristotle did not author the *MM*, it is nonetheless widely regarded as a good indication of how early Aristotelians interpreted Aristotle's ethical thought.

NE	Aristotle, *Nicomachean Ethics* Broadie and Rowe 2002
Off.	Cicero, *On Obligations* (*de Officiis*)
Phd.	Plato, *Phaedo*
Pol.	Aristotle, *Politics*
PS	Cicero, *Stoic Paradoxes* (*Paradoxa Stoicorum*) Rackham 1942
Rep.	Plato, *Republic*
TD	Cicero, *Tusculan Disputations* King 1927

On some occasions I have made minor modifications to the translations. Other translations have been used where noted.

Introduction

1 Happiness: a practical perspective

The towering figure in John Steinbeck's *East of Eden* is Samuel Hamilton, Steinbeck's own maternal grandfather and the novel's great patriarch. Steinbeck himself was only a boy when the real Samuel Hamilton died, so he introduces the reader to Samuel through the eyes of another character, Adam Trask. The first time he meets Samuel, Adam comes upon him working at his forge on his ranch, pounding out some angle-irons for a neighbor. Such a visit means being invited to stay for supper, so the neighbor has brought a side of venison to share with Samuel's family. For his part, Adam brings a bottle of whiskey to share in friendly conversation at the forge, careful to keep Samuel's tea-totaling wife Liza innocent of this honored custom. Adam himself is a newcomer to the area and has come for Samuel's advice on choosing a homestead; later he will hire Samuel and his sons to engineer and construct wells for him. For this, Adam will pay Samuel generously, but it is the work itself—designing some new contraption and then building it—that Samuel really loves.

Samuel's life is one of many loves, actually. He loves engineering and patenting his designs, and he loves being busy on his ranch too, dry, flinty patch of earth that it is. He loves his work and the opportunity it often gives to spend time with neighbors. He loves the home where he and Liza raise their children, the next boisterous generation of Hamiltons. And of course he loves those children and Liza too, hard woman though she is. All of this Adam sees when he first meets Samuel, who is busy outdoors, his wife busy indoors, and their children off to a dance and raising a customary degree of hell; all is well in Samuel's universe. Samuel has a happy life, and Samuel knows it.

That's not to say that Samuel has everything he might want. Although he is a respected man, even cherished, in the valley where he lives, he is far from being a wealthy man. His parched ranch is not terribly bountiful; his designs, though ingenious, cost a lot to patent but never pay; and his labors make him rich only in promissory notes. Still, he has plenty for the life that he is living, and it is a happy life.

Surely there's a lesson here. We don't all want the same life that Samuel has, of course, but we *do* all want to have a happy life, each of us in his own way. So, what is Samuel's secret?

That's the sort of question that philosophers have considered for several thousand years. More recently—in the past few hundred years—the most common approach has been to try to find that thing in a life like Samuel's that is its happiness: perhaps it is how pleasant and joyful his life is, at least on balance; perhaps it's the fact that Samuel has so much of what he wants; perhaps it's the fact that there are so many things in his life that would be good for everyone, like friendship, whether everyone thinks so or not. More recently still, in the past few decades, this focus has tended to narrow even further, from Samuel's well-being overall to something like a specific sort of feeling or sense of satisfaction with his life. (This shift has sometimes been paired with assurances that this is all that "happiness" ever meant in the first place—no shift after all, then.)

But as much as there is to be learned from focused thinking about this or that part of what makes our lives go well, the millennia-old perspective of a happy *life* as a whole is one that has never gone away. It hasn't gone away because it is above all a very *practical* perspective, one that we take when we think about what to make of our lives. To see this, imagine Samuel Hamilton not as he appears in the novel, an old man who has already lived a full, happy life, but instead as a young man with his whole life still ahead of him and wondering what to do with that magnificent opportunity. From that perspective, a "happy life" is a goal, something that can make sense of the plans that he then makes and the more concrete aims that he adopts. In time, those plans and aims turn into a life with a loving partner and sharing with friends and productive work and cherished pastimes and, in a word, a person's whole life. And if all goes well, that life will be that person's happiness. That is what happiness looks like from the perspective of someone planning for his future, because from that perspective "happiness" is not the name of a concept to be analyzed or a quantum to be maximized. Here, "happiness" is the name of a solution to the very practical problem of how to give oneself a good life. Having that wonderful problem is part of being human. That is why the view of happiness as a good life as a whole has never gone away—because it *can't* go away. Whatever gains we might make through conceptual analysis, in the end we must come to understand what happiness is by asking what it would have to be in order to play the role in our practical economies that it actually does play.

Unfortunately, taking this perspective on happiness does not tell us what happiness is, just like that. Still, it does make a few things clear already. For one thing, it is clear that happiness is not just a good, but a good *for* the person who has it. For instance, being a perfected specimen of humanity may be some sort of good, but it is not the sort of good that happiness is. After all, when I ask how I might live so as to give myself the gift of happiness, the gift of a good life, I am asking about something that will be good for me; I'm not asking how I might give a gift to my species, or to history, or to the universe. For another, it is clear that giving myself that gift means finding things to live for. It's not enough just to have a reason to get out of bed every morning, as important as that is. More than that, I need to find things that I find fulfilling to devote myself to and that make my life identifiable as uniquely mine. And even though living for those things is to give myself the gift of a good life, a moment's thought reveals that the things I live for don't have to be selfish aims—in fact, making those aims selfish, I think, would be a particularly ineffective way of trying to give myself a good life.

From this perspective, it is also clear why we think that a good like pleasure or enjoyment is such an important part of happiness. None of us wants a future he doesn't enjoy, or finds frustrating or tedious: that would not be a life of fulfillment, and not much of a gift. It is also clear why satisfying our desires is so important, since the desires that matter most for happiness are those that are ushered into our lives by the things we have made our lives about.[1] Those things make our life ours, and that's what makes our desires about them so salient. And it's clear too why there are some good things—such as love, and knowledge—that should be part of every good life, whether one presently desires them or not. After all, it is possible to make mistakes about how best to give oneself the gift of a happy life.

However, this practical, forward-looking perspective on happiness also reveals why none of these things, important for happiness as they all are, can be the same thing as a happy life. The problem of deciding what to do with one's life is the problem of deciding what to live for and what things to make one's life about. That is to ask, for one thing, what things one might become the sort of person to enjoy in the first place. It's good advice to tell a young Samuel Hamilton that, whatever he does with his life, it should be a life that he can enjoy. But it's not as if what things he will enjoy in life is something he already knows; it's not even as if there is already a fact of the matter for him to know in the first place, in advance of making his choices. Ultimately he has to make choices about finding things to live for so as to live a happy life, and telling him that happiness is the same thing as, say, pleasure is either to tell him that pleasure is all there is to live for, or to tell him that happiness isn't about finding anything to live for. Either way, happiness would then have little role to play in his thinking about what life to give himself.

The same point applies to desire satisfaction. It's useful to be told that one should avoid living for things that will probably end in frustration, but if happiness is just the same thing as desire satisfaction, then either desire satisfaction is all there is to live for, or happiness isn't about finding things to live for. Likewise for the idea that happiness is a life full of good things. That is surely true, and it's good advice to tell a young Samuel Hamilton that there are certain goods he should be careful not to leave out as he puts his life together. But making sure to pursue some things falls well short of finding things to live for and commit himself to. We do no better by thinking of happiness as a conglomeration of ingredients, as if a life is happy insofar as it has X, Y, and Z, since each of these has a certain power to make life better. As James Griffin complains, this is as inapt when thinking about happiness as it is in the case of cooking:

We can measure the quantities of wine and beef and onions separately, but we can only measure their value to the dish by considering them in various combinations. With our different ends, too, the important estimate of how valuable they are is their contribution to a whole life.... So

---

[1] Cf. Griffin 1986 and 2000.

the amount of value cannot be decided by attaching a value to each separately and then adding. (1986, 36)

My aim has not been to show that these other ways of thinking about happiness are all *wrong*, but to show that they are about the nature of a sort of good that is *different* from, and narrower than, a good life as a whole. There are goods of that narrower sort that are important to think about carefully, and obviously there is nothing wrong with calling those goods "happiness." My point is that it is also worthwhile—more than that, indispensable—to think about happiness in another way as well, happiness that is one's life as a whole, the sort of happiness that we have in view when we think about what to make of our futures. This book is about happiness understood from that perspective.

Let me put the point another way. The question naturally arises how my discussion of happiness in this book fits into the current philosophical terrain of philosophical thought about happiness; and my answer, in short, is that it doesn't, except at a fairly broad level. The current philosophical literature on happiness divides into two broad camps.[2] One, there are theories of happiness understood strictly as a psychological phenomenon, which attempt to describe the various cognitive and affective dimensions of, say, a sense of satisfaction with one's life. And two, there are theories that treat happiness in normative terms, the sort of good that is often called welfare or well-being, and which we can think of as a source of reasons to act.[3] It is clear, I trust, that happiness as I have been discussing it here is of the normative rather than descriptive variety. In this very broad respect, it is like other modern accounts of happiness to which I have alluded: what Derek Parfit has called hedonist, desire-satisfaction, and objective list theories of happiness.[4] Beyond that, however, my theory and these others are about importantly different things.

To see that difference more sharply, shift from the perspective of someone thinking about his future to the perspective of a policy-maker whose aim is to make people happier through the policies he creates. (Not coincidentally, this has been the main perspective on happiness that philosophers have taken over the past few centuries.)[5] Obviously, a policy-maker cannot pursue the happiness of others by living their lives for them, so happiness, in this context, must necessarily be something narrower than that. Rather, the policy-maker must think about happiness as some more specific good in persons' lives, one that the policy-maker can do something about. For instance, in

---

[2] For discussion of this taxonomy, see Crisp 2008, § 1; Haybron 2011, § 1.
[3] For a good overview of these, see Crisp 2008, § 4; Feldman 2010.
[4] Parfit 1984, 493–502.
[5] See Sumner 2002, 21, who notes the influence that this perspective in utilitarian ethics has had on modern thinking about happiness. (This is important: moral philosophers often seem to forget that Bentham's philosophy was above all about public policy.) He also notes that such a perspective is reinforced by social scientific aspirations to render happiness measurable (pp. 24–5). See also Tiberius 2006, and Tiberius and Plakias 2010, who suggest that any adequate philosophical account of happiness must be such as to guarantee that social scientists can keep on measuring it.

deciding between one policy and another, the policy-maker might look for the policy that will create more happiness by bringing people more (or superior) pleasure, say, or by satisfying more of their desires (or some special subset of their desires), or by increasing access to objectively valuable resources. Very simply put, most modern theories of happiness are about happiness as we see it from a policy-maker's perspective. By contrast, I intend to consider it from the perspective of one reflecting on his life as a whole, one who means to do something about his happiness by living a happy life.

2 Happiness for humans

Happiness, as I shall discuss it in this book, is a happy life, understood as a life composed of activities that give it shape as a life of one's own. When I talk about happiness in this book, then, the subject matter is a happy *life* in this sense. But to say what 'happy' is to be predicated *of* is not to say under what conditions that predicate *holds*. Let me offer a brief preview of what I mean to say about that in this book. Four main points will suffice for now.

First of all, I argue that happiness is a life of *activity*. Living a happy human life means actively living, engaging the world, finding things to live for and then living for them. Furthermore, by "activity" in this context I don't really have in mind day-to-day errands so much as the major areas of pursuit that make one's life the life it is. Put another way, if we were to individuate the various things that Samuel Hamilton lived for, we would have a list of the main "activities" of his life in this sense.

Second, I argue that a happy life is a life that is *fulfilling* for the one living it. Part of this fulfillment is the sense or experience of fulfillment: it is obvious that a happy life must be one that one *finds* fulfilling. Another part of it, though, is the idea that a happy life must really *be* fulfilling. Someone incapable of loving others, for instance, might have a life that is as fulfilling for him as it can be, given that unique make-up of his, but we would not point to his life as a good example of happiness. (It's certainly no life one would wish on a friend.) If that is so, then we can understand happiness only by keeping in view that it is *happiness for humans* that we are talking about. An adult who is incapable of love, or emotionally childish, might have a life that is as good as it gets for someone like that, but that is not the same as having a happy human life. This is not to confuse human happiness with human perfection, or what we might call good human specimen-hood. Human fulfillment enters the picture as helping us make sense of what is good for someone given that he is a human (rather than some other creature), not as depicting the goodness of good human specimens.

Moreover—and for that very reason—a happy human life must be one that is fulfilling for the one living it, as the unique individual one is. By this I mean being fulfilled in those things that one is such as to find fulfilling, and that are capable of giving one things one can live for. This too is part of what it is for a human life to be a happy life.

Third, I argue that a happy human life is one that is *lived well*. Humans are a complex and wonderful combination of reason and emotion, and crucial to human happiness is fulfillment as such a wonderful combination. A human life is something for the one living it to construct, by finding ends to live for and then living for them. Part of human fulfillment is exercising practical wisdom in putting one's life together. Part of it too, though, is emotional well-being, in the form of both satisfaction with one's life and harmony with practical wisdom. These two parts of human fulfillment I shall call "practical wisdom" and "emotional soundness," respectively. Furthermore, practical wisdom and emotional soundness, taken together, are what I have in mind when I speak of "virtue." Activity in accordance with virtue—or virtuous activity, for short— is therefore just activity that is characterized by practical wisdom and emotional soundness.

Now, I do not think of virtuous activity as some special category of activity, distinct from activities like doing one's job, say, or practicing a hobby. Rather, activities like these just *are* virtuous activities, provided they are done with wisdom and sound emotions. It is this that I shall have in mind when I say, as I do in this book, that a happy human life is (among other things) a life of virtuous activity. It should be clear, then, that by this I do not have in mind a do-gooder's life, or a life of philosophical sophistication, or what have you. In fact, much of the point of taking Samuel Hamilton's life—a life of a simple and in many ways ordinary man—as an example of human happiness was to head off just such a misunderstanding from the outset. Likewise, I do not take the substance of "virtue" to be fixed already, as if I meant to show how being a do-gooder (say) must be important for human happiness (surprise!). On the contrary, on my view what counts as a "virtue"—literally, an "excellence"—in a human being depends on what humans must be like in order to live happy, fulfilled human lives. The idea that a happy life is a life of virtuous activity, then, is simply the idea that there are forms of rational and emotional fulfillment crucial to human happiness. Very simply, it is a way of giving more detail to the notion that human happiness is after all something *human*.

Fourth and finally, I argue that human happiness is a life of activity that is *inextricable* from the particular ends that one lives for. Here I have in mind one side of the following contrast between Samuel and his wife Liza. When Samuel and Liza become too old to maintain the ranch and go instead to live with their children in town, Liza's life remains the same in a way that Samuel's does not. Before the move, Liza's life had the ranch and its activities as its circumstances, but the activity that defined Liza was really a certain pattern of the exercise of her will—roughly, the more "formal" activity of conducting herself well with respect to ranch life when ranch life was what presented itself to her. Consequently, the move from the ranch to town leaves Liza's life surprisingly uninterrupted.

Not so with Samuel. Samuel's life, his activity, was not just his exercising choice with respect to whatever presented itself. His life, his activity, his happiness just *was* ranch life: his happiness was his activi*ties*, in the plural, namely his unique relationship with Liza, his keeping of his ranch, the things he did to earn his living, the friendships that he had—*these* things were his life, and his happiness. It was within those activities that Samuel experienced his life as his own, and took himself to be Samuel Hamilton.[6] Put another way, Samuel's activities were not simply *in relation to* the things and people around him but were "embodied" in his relations to them. In my view, it was Samuel rather than Liza who was right about happiness. (It seems to have been so in Steinbeck's view, too: Samuel's death is the loss of a force of nature; Liza's is just one of the events in the life of a busy town.)

To summarize, the view I develop in this book is that happiness is a life of activity. That activity has two main features: it is having ends we can live for, and living for them wisely; and it is embodied in our connections with the particular persons, projects, and places that make those ends meaningful to us. In a word, and in the terms I have briefly introduced here, I shall say that happiness is *a life of embodied virtuous activity*.

3 Overview of the book

My account of happiness shares its perspective with ancient accounts, which all begin from deliberating about one's life. For that reason, I develop my account in this book by drawing on ancient theories of happiness, and that in two main ways. First, I draw on Aristotle's seminal discussion of the role of happiness in practical reasoning, and show how such a perspective casts light both on practical reasoning as oriented towards pursuing a good life, and on the nature of the good life itself. Second, I make my own account of happiness—and especially the notion of "embodied" activity—more precise by confronting some controversial questions that were at the center of ancient debates about happiness. My hope is that by returning to this ancient perspective on happiness, I might find new directions for our own thinking about the good lives we want for ourselves.

My discussion breaks into three main parts. The first part sets out the main outlines of my view of happiness for humans. The second part develops a major challenge for that view—a challenge concerning the notion of "embodied" activity—and the third attempts to come to grips with that challenge. Let me say a bit more about each of these three parts.

3.1 Part 1: happiness, then and now

My view of happiness falls within a tradition going back to early Greek and Roman philosophers that we now call "eudaimonism." That label has been used in many ways, though, so I should begin by clarifying what I mean by it.[7] Simply put, by "eudaimonism" I mean the following three things:

---

[6] It is therefore interesting that Samuel advises his son Tom, whose life is failing to launch, to find things to live for by telling him, "Be Tom Hamilton!"

[7] E.g., Fred Feldman takes eudaimonism to be the view that well-being or (what I am calling) happiness is determined by "garden-variety happiness," that is, "the ordinary sort of happiness that non-philosophers

1) An account of practical reasoning on which eudaimonia is the final end for deliberation,

2) where eudaimonia is a good life for the one living it—that is, happiness—and as such

3) a starting-point for thinking about the nature of human fulfillment, or virtue.

In developing my eudaimonist approach, I focus on Aristotle's seminal account of eudaimonia in the first book of the *Nicomachean Ethics*. This is not because my interests are particularly historical but because I think that his account is still the best place to begin.

It is an important question whether one thing can play both of the roles described in (1) and (2) above. Chapter 1 takes up the very idea of a final end for deliberation, and then asks whether the sort of good that eudaimonia is supposed to be—a good life for the one living it—could also serve as that final end. Chapter 2 then turns that question around, asking whether eudaimonia is the same good that happiness is. It is there that I take up the notion of happiness as a kind of fulfillment, paying special attention to the idea that happiness requires our fulfillment as humans (and not just as individuals), and distinguish this from an idea that I reject, namely that happiness is a sort of human perfection.

In Chapter 3, I argue that eudaimonia affords us a place to begin in thinking about what counts as an excellence or virtue in a human being. In doing so, I explain why I think that human happiness is a life of virtuous activity. Finally, in Chapter 4, I develop the contrast I sketched above between Liza and Samuel Hamilton: activity as something that goes on in relation to one's particular surroundings (what I shall call "formalized" activity), versus something that is inextricable from those very surroundings ("embodied" activity). This contrast, I argue, is crucial for thinking about the vulnerability of our happiness to fortune, since on the former view the continuity of the activity that is one's happiness is much less hostage to fortune than it is on the latter.

---

mean to indicate when they speak of happiness," namely "some sort of psychological phenomenon" (2010, 181). (Surprisingly, on this usage Plato and Aristotle turn out not to be eudaimonists.) Daniel Haybron (2008) takes eudaimonism to be the view that happiness lies in fulfillment of one's nature, where this might be one's individual nature *as opposed to* one's human nature. And so on.

Furthermore, eudaimonist accounts are often characterized as types of objective list accounts, but I don't find that a very helpful way to look at it. For one thing, my account starts, not with a list of putatively worthwhile ends, but with what it takes for our ends to add up to a happy life: one, we need to have not just ends but ends that we live for, and two, we need to live for them in a good human way, with wisdom and sound emotions. For another thing, my account begins not by pumping our intuitions about the sources of happiness but by thinking about the nature of practical reasoning about our lives as wholes, and the role that happiness plays in such reasoning.

3.2 Part 2: happiness then

Although I think that happiness is a life of virtuous activity, I do not think that virtuous activity is sufficient for happiness. The question of the vulnerability of happiness to fortune was the central question in ancient ethics for several centuries (or so Cicero tells us, anyway), and in this part of the book I argue that the key to unlocking this debate is making explicit the choice we have to make between the two conceptions of activity that I distinguished in Chapter 4. On my view, happiness depends not only on virtuous activity but on good luck, too. However, this is not because happiness also requires other goods *besides* virtuous activity, but because the virtuous activity that happiness consists in is inextricable from goods that we ultimately cannot control.

In ancient ethics, this issue is discussed as the question whether virtue is sufficient for happiness. This part of the book focuses on the main players in the ancient debate over that question, again not because my interests are purely historical but because I think that this approach gives us a particularly vivid perspective on just why the distinction between conceptions of activity matters and how much is at stake. Chapter 5 focuses on the Aristotelian side of the debate, which held that human happiness is indeed vulnerable to fortune. Unfortunately—and surprisingly—their defense of that position was never fully successful in the ancient world, and I argue that this is because neither Aristotle nor his followers brought the notion of "embodied" activity to bear on the debate.

What I shall call the "formalized" notion of activity, however, was central to the other side of the debate, represented primarily by the Stoics, who argued that virtuous activity is invulnerable to fortune and indeed sufficient for happiness (call this the "sufficiency thesis" for short). Chapter 6 explores the origins of this view of activity in Socrates' defense of the sufficiency thesis in several of Plato's dialogues that were of particular importance among the Stoics. Chapter 7 sets out the Stoics' formalized conception of activity, as it was developed explicitly by Epictetus, and in Chapter 8 I explain how that conception of activity was crucial to Stoic ethics and in particular to their case for the sufficiency thesis. For the Stoics, the sufficiency thesis stems not simply from their belief that virtuous activity is the only good, but from that belief *plus* their view of virtuous activity as formalized rather than embodied. My view accepts their thesis about what kind of *good* virtuous activity is, but puts forward a very different view of what kind of *activity* it is.

3.3 Part 3: happiness now

In the last part of the book I do two things. First, in Chapter 9, I flesh out the embodied conception of activity that is central to my own view of human happiness. Second, I take up a serious normative challenge for that way of thinking about activity, a challenge that I think motivated the Stoics to reject my way of thinking about virtuous activity as embodied in worldly attachments.

This challenge is also present in the contrast between Samuel and Liza Hamilton. Although Samuel's is a happy life, its later years are very difficult for Samuel. The death of one of his adult children strikes Samuel very hard, and soon his other children notice that their once-vibrant father is now growing old very quickly. His children and their spouses agree that it is time for their parents to leave the hardships of ranch life behind, and they devise to take turns hosting their parents for a series of long holidays. Samuel is still sharp enough to see that the children's invitation to visit them in town is really a ruse to retire their parents from the ranch, but he accepts their invitation anyway and, with it, the end of his life. That end comes quickly for Samuel; leaving his life on the ranch means leaving behind what had made him Samuel Hamilton, and before long Samuel stops living altogether. Not so with Liza, though, who lives for many more years, and that largely as she always had, and largely with equanimity. All along, her life was not about being tied to any particular place or pursuit but about the choices she made wherever she happened to be.

This difference between Samuel and Liza raises an important question about what I am calling embodied activity: does such a conception of happiness make one too vulnerable to circumstances beyond one's control, vulnerable in a way that could actually undermine one's happiness, even one's very humanity? This is a question about coping with loss, so, in Chapter 10, I examine some recent psychological literature on bereavement and grief. There I argue that our best current understanding of healthy grief resolution suggests that significant losses need not be psychologically damaging, by common-sense standards, for those whose identity is wrapped up in vulnerable things. Nonetheless, in Chapter 11, I give the last word to the Stoics, who argue that our commitment to protect our happiness is the main source of our degradation and wrongdoing, for those whose happiness depends on things they cannot themselves control. As I said above, I would rather have a life like Samuel's than one like Liza's. However, the Stoics warn that such a life would put me too much at the mercy of circumstances, and this may lead me to abandon practical wisdom in trying to preserve what I have staked my happiness on. If the Stoics have a point that we should take seriously—and I argue that they do—then whether we take Samuel's outlook on happiness or Liza's, there is no outlook that comes without cost. This does not move me to reject my view of happiness as embodied activity, but it does make me soberly appreciate how risky a proposition that is.

3.4 Who is this book for?

I hope that this book will be useful for scholars and other specialists. But I hope at least as much that it will be of use to a wide group of philosophical readers interested in exploring the nature of virtue and happiness. Although I have situated this book in the history of philosophy, this is not because of any antiquarian leanings—quite the contrary, actually. Perhaps my overarching hope is to bridge two discussions of virtue and happiness that are separated by time, but not by vigor, importance, or interest. I encourage you to think of the ancient eudaimonists not as distant forebears but as fellow-travelers.

PART 1

Happiness, then and now

1

Happiness, Eudaimonia, and Practical Reasoning

In an early scene in the musical *Fiddler on the Roof*, two young girls wonder, starry-eyed, what sort of husband the matchmaker will one day bring for them—someone interesting, someone important, perhaps rich, maybe intelligent, but in any case hopefully "as handsome as anything." Their older sister is more cynical about how these matches can turn out, though, and she teases her naïve younger sisters by imitating the village's old matchmaker lady, offering the sorts of matches that come to poor girls without dowries: fat, old men with foul, abusive tempers, whose only saving grace is that most of the time they're too drunk to fight anyway. But such a man is still "a good catch," the make-believe matchmaker assures them:

> I promise you'll be happy,
> And even if you're not,
> There's more to life than that—
> Don't ask me what!

The scene is a comical one, but as Mel Brooks is often quoted as saying, "Tragedy is when I cut my finger; comedy is when you walk into an open sewer and die." A moment's thought later, and the prospects imagined for these girls fill us not just with dismay but despair: wives who neither love nor are loved, who spend days in servitude instead of fulfilling work, who know fear and loneliness and neglect, and who find themselves locked into all of it without ever having a say about it. The taunt about their happiness is grim, because we see full well that "happiness" and "unhappiness" here are the names, not of feelings, but of *futures*, and the difference between those futures is whether one is genuinely living one's life or just getting through it. To say that there's more to life than happiness is a joke precisely because it's to say there's more to life than genuinely living. "There's more to life than that"—more to *what life*?

None of us could envy these girls' prospects, but all hope may not be lost. Even with an unlucky match, each girl might still be able to make her life, or at least some corner of it, really her own, by finding things to live for, things *she* can choose to devote herself to and make her life about. Of course, choosing to live for those things will go towards reclaiming her life only if the choosing is genuinely *hers*, so her first choice must be to commit to her own needs and interests, to commit enough to herself to give herself the best life she can by finding people and pursuits to love. This is not to say she needs to be more selfish—perhaps just the opposite. For instance, she might reclaim her life through serving others—raising her children, say—provided she does so out of a love for others that she has chosen to make part of the good life she wants to give herself. Jean Hampton (1993) has called this way of living and loving "authentic," and the idea is that for creatures like us, genuinely living one's life means being committed to giving oneself a good life, by living for things in which one will find fulfillment, both as a human being and as the unique individual one is. I would say: committing to giving oneself such a life just is committing to one's *happiness*.

This is a book about happiness in exactly that sense. By the end of it, I shall try to say what I think happiness is, so understood. Although philosophers have no monopoly on good insights about happiness, they do bring methods and analytical skills to bear in order to expand our understanding in ways we might have otherwise missed. However, while philosophy might promise its own kind of insight, it also risks its own kind of blindness by treating happiness as yet another concept to be analyzed, yet another thing about which to adjudicate between our "conflicting intuitions." There is a place for that too, but my story about the "Matchmaker" song suggests that what we say about happiness will be worth hearing outside the seminar room only if we begin with the very great, very practical role that happiness actually plays in our lives. Happiness is what we want for our children and what we try to raise them to find. It is what we want for our friends, and what we hope that we and our friends will bring each other. It is what we want for our neighbors, and guides the help and concern (and at times the wide berth) we extend to them. It is why we share our lives and our communities with each other. The freedom to pursue it is one of the first things that people will live and indeed die for. And without committing to it, there is nothing else we can commit to with authenticity. We cannot know what happiness is except by knowing what sort of good could be all of the things that happiness really is to us.

For that reason, I want to think of happiness in terms of what ancient Greek philosophers called eudaimonia. As will become clear, eudaimonia—like happiness as I have spoken of it here—is also the name, not of a feeling, but of a future. That is, eudaimonia is about one's life as a whole, both through the whole time-span of one's life and across all of its various dimensions. It is the sort of good life that is good for the one living it, a life experienced as rewarding and rich, and in which one finds one's existence meaningful. Eudaimonia is also a life of completion and fulfillment, both in one's nature as a human being and as a unique individual. Eudaimonia, I believe—and shall argue—is just the right sort of good to play the roles in our practical lives that we know happiness plays. And crucially, the ancient Greek philosophical tradition of thinking of our lives in terms of eudaimonia is one that has always begun from the significance of eudaimonia in our practical economies—our decision-making, goal-setting, and deliberation. In this tradition, the practical importance of happiness isn't just background to the story about what happiness is. It *is* the story. That, I think, is exactly as it should be.

The place for us to begin, therefore, is with a much closer look at the role of eudaimonia in deliberation and practical reasoning. This will give us a much better sense of the sort of goal or end that eudaimonia is, and in the next chapter I shall argue that thinking of happiness in terms of eudaimonia is a plausible and helpful way of trying to understand happiness.[1]

1 Eudaimonism: an overview

I have mentioned the ancient Greek philosophical tradition of thinking of practical reasoning in terms of the practical centrality of eudaimonia, a kind of complete, fulfilled, good life. This tradition is commonly known as eudaimonism.[2] More specifically, "eudaimonism" can refer to theories about practical reasoning, or the nature of happiness, or the virtues of character; I shall discuss these three approaches in the first three chapters of this book, respectively.

Eudaimonism as a theory of practical reasoning focuses on the role of ends or goals in deliberation, and it consists of two main ideas. The first of these is that *deliberation requires a "final end"*: an end that we pursue for its own sake and nothing further, and for the sake of which we pursue all of our other ends. This is because deliberation takes place within a hierarchy of ends, and this hierarchy must be organized in a way that enables one to make sense of one's life as a unified whole. The other main idea is that *this final end is eudaimonia*—a good life, or more precisely a happy life in the sense of happiness that we have been discussing. Taken together, these two ideas have it that happiness is the fundamental end or goal of one's life as a whole, on the basis of which one can deliberate about what to make of one's life and what person to be. We need to look more closely at each of these two ideas (this section), and then we can think about the upshot of them (the rest of the chapter).

1.1 Practical reasoning and the final end

The seminal eudaimonist account of practical reasoning is the first book of Aristotle's *Nicomachean Ethics*. My remarks on eudaimonism will focus on Aristotle's account, since it is that account that set the terms of subsequent eudaimonist discourse in the ancient world, a discourse from which I argue in this book we still have much to learn, and which I find especially promising as a way of thinking about practical reasoning and happiness. Fair warning: I shall also argue in the second part of the book (and especially Chapter 5) that Aristotle's account is ultimately doomed without some serious changes.

---

[1] So for the moment I shall speak of "eudaimonia," not "happiness," to avoid prejudging whether we should think that these are the same.

[2] The seminal modern work on ancient Greek and Roman eudaimonism is still Annas 1993a.

But it's still the best place to start, and the changes that need to be made can be safely kept to one side for now.[3]

Aristotle begins by considering a general feature of ends, namely how our various endeavors are arranged with respect to ends (NE I.1). For a start, we can distinguish various spheres of action in terms of their respective immediate ends: to take an example of Aristotle's, horse training is one such sphere, which consists of all the things done so as to make horses fit for military service; weapons-making is another, consisting of the things done to produce spears, shields, and the like, and so on. Furthermore, several spheres of action can be grouped together insofar as the whole group of them has a further end—in these examples, the waging of war. The process can then be repeated, as we can look for the ends for the sake of which war is waged— the end of protecting the citizenry, say—and so on again until we arrive at a more basic and unifying end for all such social endeavors generally, such as the peaceful cohabitation of citizens. The process can also be repeated in the direction of even more ancillary spheres: iron-smithing is for the sake of weapons-making, ore-refining for the sake of iron-smithing, and so on. Of course, the ends and actions in these examples belong to social groups and even whole societies, not to individuals. Nonetheless, the observations about these ends are perfectly general observations about ends just as such, so they will be as true of an individual person's ends and endeavors as they are of the broader societal ones in Aristotle's own examples. And the main observation is this: we understand what people are doing in terms of their ends, and together these ends form a hierarchy in which each is explained by the next end in this "chain" of ends.

What might it mean to say that something is done "for the sake of" an end? Take the case of the horse-trainer who prepares horses for the cavalry: training the horse is for the sake of that end in the sense that it is a means to it, so here the for-the-sake-of relation is a means-end or instrumental relation. But that is just one kind of for-the-sake-of relation, and clearly we do many things for their own sake—some people might train horses just to be out there with the horses—either instead of or in addition to doing them as means to something else.

However, it is also possible to do something for the sake of another end *without* doing it as a *means* to anything at all. On this point, J. L. Ackrill once offered an analogy that I have always found helpful. Consider a golf-lover who wants to have a nice holiday and so chooses to spend some days of his holiday playing golf. While he does spend the day playing golf for the sake of having a nice holiday, it would surely be a mistake to think that he is playing golf as a *means* to having a nice holiday. Holidays aren't like that, as if you do some golfing, or go fishing, or visit some museums—and then, *voilà!* Now this *other* thing happens: in *addition* to all of this, you *also* have a good

---

[3] As my aims at the moment are not primarily scholarly, I shall try to be faithful to Aristotle's account while nonetheless avoiding as many technical and scholarly quandaries as possible. Also, I shall not be shy about trying to extend the account beyond Aristotle's original where I think it can be usefully extended (and I shall try to make it clear when I am doing so).

holiday. No, if you like golfing, then golfing during your holiday is not a means to having a good holiday but a *way of having* a good holiday.[4]

Furthermore, and importantly, sometimes we find that succeeding with respect to one end amounts to choosing another end to pursue for its own sake. Consider an end like having a satisfying career: that just is the end of finding another end—like being a doctor or engineer—that one can pursue for its own sake. (Notice how common such ends are among university students, for instance.) Following David Schmidtz (1994), we can call such ends "maieutic" ends, from the Greek word for childbirth (*maieusis*), since these ends "give birth" to other ends. In such cases, one end is chosen for the sake of another, maieutic end, but clearly not as a means to it. Someone who chooses a career as an engineer does not then think about how to build the next bridge so as to make his career more satisfying. Not only would that be ridiculous, it would defeat the purpose: the whole point of making a satisfying career of engineering, after all, is to immerse oneself in that kind of work on its own terms.

Aristotle says little about for-the-sake-of relations in his overview of practical reasoning in *NE* I, but he has more to say elsewhere. For instance, in his discussion of phronesis or practical wisdom, the virtue of the practical intellect concerned with deliberation, Aristotle suggests that before we can look for the means to an end, we must first deliberate about what it would mean for that end to be achieved in the first place.[5] For instance, a physician deliberates about how to heal his patient, but before he can know what means to employ (e.g. cutting or cautery, on this or that part of the body, etc.) he must specify just what would *constitute* healing—just what healing would look like—here and now in this patient. This is because the end of healing a patient—like persuading an audience, or governing well[6]—is a determinable but as yet indeterminate end; in this respect, it is like the ends of having a good holiday, or having a satisfying career. And of course, so too is the end of having a good life, about which Aristotle says it takes phronesis to deliberate properly (*NE* VI.5, 1140a24–8). This end, like the end of having a satisfying career, is such that we can determine what to do for the sake of that end only by deliberating about what other ends to pursue for their own sake.[7]

---

[4] Ackrill 1999, 67. Con. Rist 1969, 4–5, 12–13, who takes all for-the-sake-of-relations here to be means/end relations.

[5] *NE* VI.12, 1144a6–9, 20–6. Virtue, he says, makes one's goal correct (e.g. to act generously); cleverness works out the correct means; and phronesis determines what one's goal actually comes to (e.g. what it would actually be generous to do, here and now). For discussion, see McDowell 1998 and Russell 2009, chap. 1. Deliberative virtue is also the topic of Tiberius 2008.

[6] For these examples, see *NE* III.3, 1112b11–20.

[7] To be sure, Aristotle says that we don't deliberate about ends, but about things for the sake of (literally, "towards") ends (III.3, 1112b11–12). However, many scholars now agree that Aristotle means only that when one deliberates *now*, some end has to be taken as given now (e.g. to deliberate about how to heal is not also to deliberate about whether to heal), which of course doesn't rule out deliberating about that end at some *other* time. See Russell 2009, 5–11 and references.

The point of all this is that we should interpret the for-the-sake-of relation within our various "chains" as broadly as the variety of our reasons demands.[8] This is important to appreciate, especially since eudaimonism is sometimes thought to involve the idea that our lives are or ought to be organized around some "grand end" or theme, and that one must deliberate about everything one does as fitting into a sort of blueprint of a life organized around that grand end. The notion of such a blueprint also suggests a kind of fixity, laying out a master plan for the rest of one's days. However, that should strike us as an odd way of thinking about doing things for the sake of a good life; at the very least, it would be odd to suppose that that is generally how practical reasoning works. People find all sorts of things to live for—a loving relationship, raising a child, pursuing a career, enjoying pastimes—but usually not as part of any master plan, and not for the sake of any grand end. One does not deliberate about how to pursue a career or raise a child so that doing so will lead to a grand end. One deliberates about them on their own terms. That is, one lives one's life.[9]

Now, Aristotle observes (NE I.2) that, because there is a point to the endeavors within these chains of for-the-sake-of relations, the chains can neither be infinitely long (as if there were no answer to the question what the point of the endeavors is) nor loop back on themselves (as if we were to go to war so that smiths can produce sword-blanks, say). There must therefore be such things as *ultimate* or *final* ends (Greek *telos*; plural, *telē*), that is, ends for the sake of which we do other things but which we do not pursue for the sake of anything further. A person's life, then, must have final ends; otherwise there would be no point to any of the things he does, in which case his deliberation about what to do couldn't even get started.[10] For Aristotle, then, our need for final ends stems from the very fact that we deliberate.[11]

However, Aristotle goes on to claim, surprisingly, that there must be exactly *one* final end per life (NE I.2, 1094a21–2), and what is more, he takes it for granted that every life has the *same* final end. Consider the first point first. Initially this is puzzling: surely it is one thing to say that every sphere of action aims at some end, and another that there is some end at which every sphere aims![12] Even more strangely, Aristotle does not explain this move, and it does not follow from anything he says in these passages. Nonetheless, I think that there are good reasons to say just what Aristotle says here, and these reasons are worth pausing over.[13]

For one thing, each *life* is only one, and so cannot be organized around conflicting ends, whereas multiple final ends would set the stage for just such conflicts—and such

---

[8]   Cf. Richardson 1994, 201, 213.

[9]   For critique of the "grand end" view, and for discussion of eudaimonist deliberation in general, see Broadie 1991, chap. 4; see also Jacobs 2004, 105; Russell 2009, chap. 1.

[10]   I discuss Aristotle's account of deliberation and deliberative virtues in 2009, chap. 1.

[11]   People sometimes say that for Aristotle, this human *telos* is an inner essence or purpose or nisus of the species (e.g. Williams 1985). I trust it is clear already that this is not at all what Aristotle has in mind *here*.

[12]   See Richardson 1994, 197–8, for discussion of a similar move in contemporary philosophy.

[13]   See Broadie 1991, 8–17, for discussion.

conflicts are precisely the sorts of problems that we engage in deliberation to address in the first place.[14] For the same reason, we cannot understand the final end as merely elliptical for some bundle of ends, as if one were to aim at several ends and call the achieving of all of them the "final" end.[15] In both of these ways, then, the nature *of the very end in question* pushes forward the idea that there is only one of its kind.

Furthermore, I think there is an even deeper reason why the final end is only one per life: quite simply, for the kinds of creatures we are there *is* in fact exactly one place where the deliberative buck must stop. We are practically rational creatures, and one very weak sense in which our rationality is practical is that it is about practical as opposed to theoretical things. Rationality that is practical in this weak sense is such that someone who has ends and is acting for the sake of them—in a word, "practical things"—can bring rational thought to bear on those things. However, if rationality were practical only in this weak sense, it would offer guidance only in the event that one happened to have ends to act for; it would not guide us as to *whether* we should have any ends in the first place. Clearly, then, our rationality is practical in a stronger sense as well: it doesn't just tell us what to do *if* we have ends, it also tells us to *have* ends. This point was not lost on Kant, for one, who held that part of possessing practical rationality is to give oneself imperatives to have certain ends, such as to be productive instead of wasting one's potential (*Metaphysics of Morals* 6: 386–7, 391–3).

But I think that our rationality is practical in an even stronger sense than that: it doesn't just tell us to be sure to get out of bed and be productive every day: what it tells us is to be sure to have something to get out of bed and be productive *for*. Telling me not to waste my time and potential is good advice, and it tells me to have ends to act for, but it doesn't tell me whether I should have any ends to give purpose to my life as a whole. Our fear for the girls in the "Matchmaker" scene is not merely that there are some ends they might end up neglecting, but that they might miss out on having ends that give them a life genuinely of their own. It is because our rationality is practical in *this* way that not having such ends is a kind of starvation. There are ends we act for, and then there are ends we *live* for: ends that give our existence direction and purpose, that make the difference between a shapeless existence and a complete *life*. In a word, practical rationality tells us to find ends to live for and then live for them.

And that, I think, is why there is only one final end: ultimately what practical reasoning seeks is to fulfill the end of finding other ends to live for, and in living for those ends to live a good life. As we saw above, there are some ends—maieutic ends—that we seek only by coming to have *other* ends we seek for their own sake. Having a good life is the ultimate case of that sort of end. Ultimately, one's end in life is to give

---

[14] See S. White 1992, 13–15; Annas 1993a, 32–3. See also N. White 2006, 19–20, for discussion of a similar point in Plato's *Rep*. This point should be taken with the point made earlier, namely that resolving conflict need not be restricted to choosing between conflicting means; as Richardson (1994, 213) observes, such conflicts are often between ends pursued for their own sakes.

[15] Irwin 1986, 207–13, reads Aristotle this way. For critique, see Annas 1993a, 36, 45.

one's life meaning and to make it about something. When that process succeeds, one has several ends to pursue for their own sake and the life one lives in living for these ends is a good life.[16]

Furthermore, this way of reading the first oddity of Aristotle's discussion also helps to clarify the second, since the reason that every life has only *one* final end is also the reason that every life has the *same* final end. To have an end as practically *rational* creatures do, one must be able to step back from one's life and ask, not only whether one does in fact have ends to live for, but also whether one has good reasons to live for the ends one has or might adopt. It is more correct, then, to say that practical rationality tells us to find *good* ends to live for and then live for them. Very simply put, practical rationality tells us to get up and have a good life. But again, that is a deliberative buck-stopper: insofar as I deliberate about what to do with my life, what cannot be in question is *whether* to have a life arranged around ends that I find reason-giving. The deliberative buck must stop somewhere, and if it stops anywhere, then it must surely stop when one realizes that pursuing a certain end is a waste of a life, and a life poorly lived is a life wasted, the waste of the only opportunity that ultimately matters. So the end of having good ends to live for is, for creatures with our sort of practical rationality, the *sine qua non* of having any other ends at all. It is *that* end, I think, that is the final end—the *only* final end—for practical reasoning. And clearly, the broadness of this final end shows again that we can all share it without ever supposing that we all have to live the same way and want the same things. The point is not that everyone should live the same life, only that everyone needs to find a good life.[17]

Of course, it would go too far to suggest that this is Aristotle's view—we are, after all, discussing a *gap* in his argument. But I find it plausible in its own right, and at the very least it illustrates the kind of flexibility that the notion of a final end can have. Furthermore, this way of thinking about the final end does fit precisely with Aristotle's broader discussion, in two main ways. One, it becomes clear as Aristotle goes on that a central concern in his thinking about the final end is our need to have ends that we can live for. Aristotle says repeatedly that the human mode of life is a life of activity (e.g. *NE* I.5), and he maintains that all activity is for the sake of some good or end (*NE* I.1); to live a human life, it seems, means first of all finding things to live for. Likewise, Aristotle argues that many views of the final end—taken as eudaimonia—fail on just this point: for instance, some think consumption is the final end and eudaimonia, but while cows may live for filling their bellies, that is no life for us; nor is it just being a

---

[16] Cf. Richardson 1994, 202: Aristotle "does not try to prove that there must be exactly one unqualifiedly final end; rather, he locates one such end, happiness or eudaimonia, and provides grounds for doubting that there is any other such end." From these considerations it follows that it is not true, as Hume thought it was, that practical reasoning concerns means to ends but never the ends themselves. After all, in order to pursue the end of having a satisfying career, one must choose a career to pursue not as a means but as an end.

[17] On this point cp. Annas 1988, 157–8; Hursthouse 1999, 214–16, 227–8; McDowell 1980, 360. The importance of individuality and diversity in our lives has been a constant theme in the writings of John Kekes; see esp. Kekes 2002.

"good person," since such a life could just as well be inactive;[18] living for prestige or honor is better, since it is at least living for something, but really the excellence of which prestige is supposed to be the sign is more important than prestige itself (I.5, 1095b19–1096a2). Furthermore, Aristotle goes on to describe human life as "practical" (*praktikē*), not merely in the sense that we can obey reason, but in the deeper or "more proper sense" (*kyriōteron*) that we possess reason of our own that initiates action; it is in this sense that our life is properly called "active" (*kat' energeian*; I.7, 1098a3–7).

And two, when Aristotle does say what he thinks our final end is, he identifies it not as some specific pursuit but as a way of engaging in pursuits: it is the life of activity of a creature that possesses practical reason, insofar as that activity is in accordance with good practical reasoning (*NE* I.7, 1098a7–20).[19] It seems, then, that there is one final end for everyone, not because we should all pursue the same thing, but because we all have the same basic need to find things to live for and to live for them wisely.

Be that as it may, at this point we will surely suspect that Aristotle's claims about this one final end all have the air of platitudes about them. That is because they do, as Aristotle is fully aware:

> If then there is some end in our practical projects that we wish for because of itself, while wishing for the other things we wish for because of it, and we do not choose everything because of something else (for if that is the case, the sequence will go on to infinity, making our desire empty and vain), it is clear that this will be the good, i.e. the chief good. So in relation to life, too, will knowing it have great weight, and like archers with a target would we be more successful in hitting the point we need to hit if we had this knowledge? If so, then one must try to grasp it at least in outline, that is, what it might be, and to which sort of expertise or productive capacity it belongs. (*NE* I.2, 1094a18–26)

I find the analogy of the archers helpful: telling us that there is some end that is our final end is a lot like telling an archer that there is some target that is his target—in both cases we need to know *which* one it is. Now, I have argued that there is already more that we can plausibly say about our final end than that, namely that practical rationality is ultimately about achieving the final end of having a life organized around other reason-giving ends. But even so, this does not tell us what kind of good that final end is or in just what manner it gives us reasons to find other ends to live for. So far, then, the breadth of this statement of the final end leaves us with the task of trying to say more specifically just what it is that a good life would amount to. This of course is why eudaimonism brings in its second main idea: the final end, the one that keeps deliberation from being empty, is eudaimonia.

---

[18] Aristotle characterizes what we have called "being a good person" as being "virtuous." However, "virtue" as it is conceived here differs from how he himself thinks of it, since Aristotle objects that being "virtuous" in the popular sense is compatible with being chronically inactive, whereas Aristotle himself takes virtue to be inseparable from virtuous *activity*.

[19] Aristotle calls this "activity of soul in accordance with excellence . . . in a complete life" (I.7, 1098a16–18). By "soul" here, Aristotle explains in I.13 that he means a person insofar as he possesses practical reason.

1.2 The final end as eudaimonia

Anyone looking for Aristotle's proof from first principles that eudaimonia is our final end will be sadly disappointed. Here is what he says when he moves from the idea that there is a final end to the idea that it is eudaimonia:

> Let us then resume the argument: since every sort of knowledge, and every undertaking, seeks after some good, let us say . . . what the topmost of all achievable goods is. Pretty well most people are agreed about what to call it: both ordinary people and people of quality say eudaimonia, and suppose that living well (*eu zēn*) and faring well (*eu prattein*)[20] are the same thing as having eudaimonia (*eudaimonein*). (*NE* I.4, 1095a14–20)

The way that Aristotle introduces eudaimonia into the discussion is significant: the final end would have to be the greatest good of all, and the conversation about the greatest good, he says, is one that is already familiar—it is the conversation about eudaimonia. Instead of a proof, Aristotle tries to demonstrate the greater practical significance of ideas that are already part of our thought and discourse about our lives.

But why does Aristotle think that the conversation about the final end and the conversation about eudaimonia are conversations about the very same thing? His answer, apparently, is that each is a conversation about the greatest good; but this seems unsatisfying. In each of these two cases, we might object, "greatest good" stands as a placeholder for the target of the discourse: whatever the final end is, in the one discourse, and whatever eudaimonia is in the other. However, if these are two different discourses growing out of very different concerns over different kinds of goods, then there is no reason to suppose that their targets should be the same—surely not just because we can find a common name for both targets.

However, Aristotle's point seems to be a different one, namely that the two discourses are *in fact* the same, if we take a closer look at them. Everyone calls the greatest good the same thing ("eudaimonia"), Aristotle says, but they disagree about what it is: for instance, a lot of people say that it is pleasure or prestige (*NE* I.4, 1095a22–3; I.5, 1095b14–17, 23–6); people who are either physically or financially down on their luck might say it is health or wealth (I.4, 1095a24–5); and so on. Now, Aristotle thinks that these are poor answers to questions about the greatest good,[21] and he thinks a better answer will require more sophistication (I.5, 1095b19–22). Even so, he does consider all of these answers to be attempts, even if failed attempts, to say what it is that our lives should be *about*, what it is that should give our lives direction, and what is such a great good for us that we should go for it above anything else. In this respect, Aristotle's critique of the idea that prestige is the greatest good is especially telling: as we saw above, Aristotle thinks that prestige is valuable only because it signifies something else, namely excellence (1095b22–31); in that case, it is silly to

---

[20] Broadie and Rowe (2002) render this "doing well," but I think "faring well" gets closer to what Aristotle seems to mean here.

[21] We shall see why in Chapter 3.

think that prestige *itself* could be the kind of good for the sake of which one should organize his life.

This brings us to another reason why Aristotle would reasonably think that eudaimonia was the final end he was looking for: like the final end, eudaimonia is an end that is largely indeterminate and malleable, and yet it also has enough shape to be recognizable as what we all agree we want above all from life. Its shape is such that to have eudaimonia (whatever that is) is to have succeeded at living in all the ways that count (whatever those are), that looks like exactly the right shape to be the sort of good for the sake of which we could ultimately do everything else. And yet, also like the final end, eudaimonia is indeterminate enough to allow for disagreement about what this greatest good in life could be. Taken together, these two features of eudaimonia make it look exactly like the sort of good that the final end is supposed to be.

To these two arguments I would add one that I sketched at the beginning of this chapter. Whatever the various ends that we adopt for our lives, one thing that we must surely want is for our ends to be genuinely *our own*—"authentic" ends, in Hampton's sense. This authenticity means adopting ends not in a self-abnegating way, but out of a commitment to one's interests, a commitment to giving oneself a good life. This for Aristotle is the sort of life that eudaimonia is, and in that case, the ends one adopts must stem from a deliberation-halting commitment to one's own eudaimonia. For creatures like us, therefore, eudaimonia looks like the sort of thing for the sake of which to adopt all other ends.

1.3 Having more to say: a strategy and a problem

In spite of all of this, however, eudaimonia still seems so indeterminate an end that, as Aristotle himself says, it seems somewhat platitudinous to say that eudaimonia is the greatest good, "and a more distinct statement of what it is is still required" (*NE* I.7, 1097b22–4). To be fair, the approach actually has more substance to it than Aristotle's concession makes it seem. This is because Aristotle's discussion puts us in position to work towards the "more distinct statement" about eudaimonia we need by approaching it from a pair of directions. These two directions correspond to the two discourses about the "greatest good" that we explored above: on the one side, the idea is that eudaimonia is the final end, *a good that halts deliberation* by being the final source of reasons for our other ends; on the other side, eudaimonia is *a good human life*, good for the one whose life it is.[22] The strategy, then, is to proceed from each of these directions until we find some good that is the good we are looking for *on both sides*—a good that *both* is a good human life *and* brings deliberation to a halt. This twofold approach would thus yield a "more distinct statement" of just what eudaimonia is.

What is more, the pay-off of that "more distinct statement" would be twofold as well. On the one hand, by identifying the final end with a life that is good for the one

---

[22] I discuss these two features of eudaimonia—namely that it is beneficial for the one who has it and beneficial for him in a distinctly human way—in Chapter 2.

living it—that is, by identifying the final end with eudaimonia—we illuminate the nature of the final end for deliberation and thus also what kinds of reasons are in play at the termini of the various chains of for-the-sake-of relations. In a word, the approach would reveal that we succeed in having reasons for our various ends insofar as we can pursue them as part of a good life; and that is indeed a substantial and "distinct statement" about the final end. On the other hand, by identifying eudaimonia with the final end, we also sharpen our understanding of what kind of good life eudaimonia must be: in order for eudaimonia to be the final end for practical reasoning, it must be a good that halts deliberation by being that for the sake of which we have our other ends. The approach from this direction would rule out many candidates for the good life on the grounds that they cannot halt deliberation; in fact, we have already seen this in the case of prestige, which Aristotle says is good only on account of something else. But not only would this approach direct us away from goods like prestige in our search for the good that eudaimonia is, it would also direct our attention towards a good that is a life in which we succeed in finding other ends to live for, succeed both as humans and as unique individuals.

So the approach would give us something substantive and "distinct" to say both about the final end and about eudaimonia. The big question, therefore, is whether there really *is* any good that can be plausibly identified with *both* the final end for deliberation *and* the sort of life that is good for the one living it. We cannot take it on faith that there is; on the contrary, it probably looks as if these two directions of inquiry are really *opposite* directions. In the one direction, we look for a good that could make sense of all the ends we have reason to pursue; but surely, the worry goes, many of these ends cannot plausibly be understood as being for the sake of one's own good life. Perhaps we could address this worry by broadening our notion of a "good life" to suit, but doing so would just make that notion less recognizable as eudaimonia. Indeed, we might suspect that this is exactly Aristotle's pitfall when he goes on, famously, to describe the "good life" as above all else a life of virtuous activity (*NE* I.7, 1098a7–20; I.10, 1100b7–1101a21). In that case, we might conclude, no good we found by looking in the one direction could be the same good we found in the other direction. The problem we saw above has now resurfaced: each direction of inquiry may lead to something that can plausibly be called "the greatest good," but that's no reason to assume that they each lead to the *same* good. Put another way, all that this approach shows is that "greatest good" is said in many ways. That point hardly ought to have been lost on Aristotle, of all people; perhaps that is just the sort of mistake that eudaimonism dooms one to make.

But I don't think so. In the rest of this chapter, I examine the first horn of this dilemma, arguing that it is not just plausible but downright attractive to understand the final end in terms of eudaimonia, a good life for the one living it. In the next two chapters I address the second horn, arguing that eudaimonia offers us an attractive way of thinking about happiness (Chapter 2), and that the sort of human fulfillment involved in happiness leads naturally to a focus on virtuous activity, which I shall understand as any activity whatsoever insofar as it is practically wise and emotionally sound (Chapter 3).

Eudaimonism gives us a lot to hope for. For one thing, the idea that there is a final end for deliberation offers the hope of a unified view of practical reasoning. For another, the identification of that final end with eudaimonia would hopefully unify practical reasoning through a particularly attractive understanding of human happiness. Whether the second hope can be realized is the question I take up in the next chapter. For the remainder of this one, I want to focus on the first one. There are, in particular, four issues about practical reasoning for us to consider now: reasons to act for the benefit of others (section 2); reasons to sacrifice for others (section 3); and reasons that we are obligated to act for (section 4).

2 Eudaimonia and other-regarding ends

If the final end for the sake of which one does everything else is one's own eudaimonia, does that mean that all one really has reason to do is to look out for one's own interests? One might think so, given the characterization of eudaimonia as a good life for the one living it. It seems clear that, at minimum, that sort of life would be one in which one's needs as a human were met, but, as Hampton observes (1993, 153), one very important need that humans have is the need to have one's life reflect the unique individual that one is, because "flourishing human beings are interested in and capable of defining themselves in distinctive and original ways." This fact about good lives has important implications for the sorts of ends that structure them: they will be ends that one chooses to live for because they are the ends one *wants* to live for, ends the pursuit of which is a way of giving oneself a good life. And we might suppose that since based on this view all of one's ends are for the sake of the good life one wants to give oneself, this means that one's ends are really about serving one's own interests. But how then can we make sense of the obvious fact that it can be rational to serve the interests of others?

Consider the following example that Hampton offers:

I have a friend whom I consider to have made an authentic choice to be a housewife and mother . . . She stayed home to care for her children because she adored them, and she genuinely liked the control over her own time that the life of a housewife gave her. Moreover, she has been quite capable of limiting her care to her family over the years whenever she thought they were demanding too much, by using a kind of prickly sarcasm they have been loath to experience. Her life has always included all sorts of projects and plans (e.g., involvement in art organizations and women's organizations' self-study projects that have made her an expert in the flora and fauna of her region) that she greatly enjoys and that have helped to make her a fascinating individual to know. So she is a richly developed person, and her care of others is a natural result of what she has chosen to love in her life. (Hampton 1993, 157)

There are several things to notice about the woman described here. For one thing, it seems clear that she lives in a way that reflects her individuality and allows her to continue developing it. For another, much of her life is devoted to serving others: raising her children and keeping her family's home. But most significant for our purposes is how these points are actually connected: "her care of others is a natural result of what she has chosen to love in her life." Indeed, she seems to have chosen to make caring for her family one of the loves of her life as a way of giving herself a good life, a life in which she can grow into a unique individual that she likes to be. And it is this fact about her that makes her choice rational and, as Hampton says, authentic, the choice of someone authoring her own life. Although Hampton does not put the point this way, I would say that her friend has the end of caring for others as part of her own eudaimonia.

So return to our opening question: does the fact that her choice to care for others was for the sake of her eudaimonia make it difficult to see how she might care for them for their own sake? Of course not. On the contrary, her case illustrates that some of the most rewarding ends that humans can have for the sake of their eudaimonia are ends of caring about others for their own sake. More generally, even if the reason for having ends is for the sake of eudaimonia, there is no reason to suppose that those ends would be focused exclusively on oneself. Put another way, eudaimonism is a view about how we *adopt* our ends—for the sake of a good life—but it does not say that the *ends* we adopt should be self-serving. On the contrary, what we know about the sorts of lives that benefit us really suggests that living a purely self-serving life would be a particularly *poor* substitute for giving oneself the gift of a good life.

Now, in effect I have just distinguished two levels of reasons: one, reasons for acting in virtue of the ends one has, and two, reasons to have those ends in the first place. (This distinction is also operative in many "for the sake of" relations, and especially in the case of maieutic ends, as we saw above.) And what I have just argued is that if the question is whether identifying the final end with eudaimonia means that reasons of the first sort must be self-interested, then the answer is clearly no. But perhaps the question will turn to the second sort of reasons, reasons for adopting the ends one has—for *those* reasons clearly *are* all for one's own sake, if the final end is eudaimonia. So we now might ask, if the ends themselves need not be self-serving, then what could be gained by the further thought that those ends are for the sake of eudaimonia?

Actually, I think rather a lot is gained; I'll mention the two gains I think are most significant. For one, such an approach builds in the proper perspective on one's close relationships, precisely for the sake of preserving that closeness. This, I argue, is because each person in a close relationship needs to be sure that the relationship occupies a place in his life that he can live with.

Begin by thinking about closeness in relationships, and consider again the woman in the example above. She cares for her family out of love for them, and that love for them she has chosen as part of her good life. This suggests that to ask whether that love is in her life for her sake *or* for theirs would be too simplistic. "Those who experience such love," Hampton writes, "are so unified with those whom their acts are attempting to benefit that what they regard as good for themselves is what will be good for those with whom they are unified" (1993, 158). When a very close relationship thrives, the difference between acting for one's own sake or one's partner's sake begins to break down: acting for each other's sake just is part of the good life each has chosen to give himself by joining lives with the other person.

However—and this is the point—in order for that kind of closeness and devotion to another to continue as that kind of good, one must also remember that the point of devoting oneself to another *is* for the sake of giving oneself a good life. When that perspective is lost, devotion becomes "selfless" in the pejorative sense of self-abnegating, losing perspective on one's life as a whole. The closeness that makes such relationships the goods that they are is destroyed when one partner becomes too demanding, and that means that each partner must maintain a perspective from which to see when the demands threaten to rob the relationship of its purpose in his life. We see this in the woman in Hampton's example, too, who can still tell, after all, when her family demands too much of her; she has not lost herself to the relationship. That is, she can still ask whether the relationship she has chosen is holding the right sort of place in her life. Indeed, even when she reasserts her interests against too-demanding family members, her aim is to readjust the terms of the relationship so as to restore it to a place where differences between what is for *her* sake and what is for *their* sake can once again cease to matter. After all, eliminating such differences is the whole point of getting into that kind of relationship. Each partner must be ready to assert his interests, precisely so that the difference between their interests can once again be happily effaced and the relationship can thrive as the sort of good it ought to be. Choosing a relationship for the sake of eudaimonia, therefore, builds in the very sort of perspective that it takes for close relationships to be the sorts of goods that they are for humans.

The other thing gained by this perspective on one's ends is the very rationality of adopting them in the first place. This is because committing to an end means committing *oneself* to it, in a couple of ways. First, one must judge whether the end in question is worth making part of one's life, devoting the necessary resources to live up to that end. Indeed, every choice to do one thing is also a choice not to do all of the other things one might have done instead—that is, a choice to bear certain opportunity costs. Part of choosing an end for a reason is to assess its merits *taken with* its opportunity costs, so it is unclear what it would be to choose an end on its merits without first looking at that end from the broader perspective of one's life. And second, one must also judge whether one's life is worth investing in by making that end a part of it. After all, a person may believe that such-and-such an end would be worthwhile for him to live for *if* his life were worth giving himself an end to live for, without also believing that his life really is worth that trouble. Improving one's life by finding ends to live for is to give oneself a gift—and like any gift, it represents an investment. Finding ends to live for requires the more basic conviction that such an investment in one's eudaimonia is a worthwhile investment to make.

3 Eudaimonism and sacrifice

In the previous section I argued that having eudaimonia as one's final end allows one to preserve one's individuality by readying one to reassert one's interests when relationships get out of balance (too demanding, exploitative, etc.). Now, it is no surprise that such a final end can warrant the *assertion* of one's interests—but could it ever warrant their *sacrifice*? If one's final end is to give oneself a good life, then the following dilemma seems to arise: what appear to be acts of rational self-sacrifice must in truth be either not really *rational* (because not for the sake of eudaimonia) or not really *sacrifices* (because somehow for the sake of eudaimonia after all). And yet isn't it clear that in truth there *are* such things as acts of rational self-sacrifice?

In order to sharpen this query, we need to be clear about what we mean by "rational self-sacrifice." To be sure, some acts of self-sacrifice are not rational: if one accepts a loss to oneself because one thinks that one's interests, just being *one's own*, count for little or nothing, then such sacrifices are "selfless" in the pejorative sense of being self-abnegating—losing touch with oneself.[23] In such cases, we onlookers are right to ask, "The rest of us could see that there was a cost to him, and that that mattered; so why couldn't *he*?" Yet rational choices, unlike compulsions, say, are made on their merits, and again, part of really seeing those merits as reason-giving in the first place is seeing them *with* their costs. There is, after all, some merit to jumping off a bridge—what a rush!—but that hardly settles the question whether one has reason to do it. The importance of appreciating merits as taken with the costs means that in order for a choice to be *for a reason*, the one choosing must be persuadable in principle by taking countervailing considerations into account. As Robert Audi has put the point, reasons are "contrastive" in the sense that other considerations can be brought to bear on one's assessment of whether one does in fact have a reason.[24] (Think of the way in which a compulsion is *not* contrastive.) The costs of a choice, therefore, matter for the reasonability of making that choice. Consequently, *rational* self-sacrifices are those that have significant costs for the agent but are nonetheless worth doing for the sake of someone or something else. For instance, jumping off a bridge may be rational if it is one's best hope of drawing an assailant's gunfire away from his loved ones.

Our question, then, is whether self-sacrifice, so understood, could be rational on the assumption that eudaimonia is the final end. Stephen Darwall (2002, 22–7) has argued that it could not, and it will be worthwhile to think about his argument. Consider, with Darwall, a case from Edgar Rice Burroughs' *The Return of Tarzan*. Tarzan discovers that he is the rightful Lord Greystoke, a title illegitimately held by another man. However, Tarzan also cares deeply for the future of his beloved Jane, who as it happens is betrothed to the man who has usurped his title. Tarzan therefore has a

---

[23] This, of course, is Hampton's whole point in her 1993 paper.
[24] See Audi 1997, 93–5. See also Smith 1997, 307–8; Wallace 1997, 324. I discuss this point further in Russell 2009, chap. 11.

difficult choice to make: he can take his title and all the benefits that it entails, but jeopardize Jane's future in the process, or else he can protect Jane at the cost of forgoing the title that is rightfully his. Tarzan chooses the latter, sacrificing an interest of his own for the sake of another's interest. Tarzan's choice (I shall agree) seems to be a rational one, and yet how could it be if Tarzan's final end were his own eudaimonia?

Darwall argues that such a case is therefore fatal for eudaimonism. If Tarzan's act is one of rational self-sacrifice, then his act is one of fully appreciating the costs in terms of his interests and then choosing to put Jane's interests ahead of his own. Now, if Tarzan's final end were his own eudaimonia, then his choice to forgo his title ultimately would have to be a choice for the sake of his eudaimonia; but in that case, his choice could not be a sacrifice; and yet if it *is* a sacrifice, and thus not for the sake of his eudaimonia, then his choice cannot be rational. Therefore, Darwall concludes, eudaimonism cannot make sense of the possibility of acts that are both self-sacrificial and rational, and yet such a possibility clearly does exist.

My reply is not to deny that acts of self-sacrifice can be rational—of course they can. (Nor is it easy to suppose Greek eudaimonists would have denied this, who knew only too well the history of Socrates' ultimate sacrifice for the sake of philosophy.) Rather, I argue that one *can* choose an act of real self-sacrifice for the sake of eudaimonia, in which case such a self-sacrificial act can also be rational. In fact, I think this is exactly what the Tarzan case shows. Obviously, Darwall is correct to say that Tarzan's choice to forgo his title means giving up something that matters deeply to him. However, so too would the choice of taking up that title, since Jane's interests matter deeply to him as well. Either way, then, Tarzan must accept some sacrifice or other. Now, I don't suppose that Darwall would deny this point, but I do think he would hasten to add that the sacrifice that Tarzan would have incurred by taking up his title would not have been a sacrifice *with respect to eudaimonia*. According to Darwall, to think otherwise would be to conflate Tarzan's values with Tarzan's good.

I disagree: Tarzan's sacrifice in taking up his title is plausibly seen as a sacrifice with respect to eudaimonia, without making any such conflation. It is tempting to view Tarzan's eudaimonia as something fixed independently of his choice, and his choice as a choice between that fixed eudaimonia and something else. However, that would be a mistake. Tarzan is deliberating not merely about whether to take up his title or not. He is deliberating about a pair of futures, and whatever choice he makes, that future will be the future of the one who made that very choice. After all, if we think of eudaimonia as lying in activity, then we should also think of how one chooses and constructs a life for oneself as *itself* among the activities in which eudaimonia lies. Our picture of Tarzan's choice now changes: we can no longer take his eudaimonia to be something fixed and independent of the choice he makes between his two options. That is, we can no longer think of Tarzan as choosing between his eudaimonia, taken as fixed whatever he chooses, and something else. Rather, we now think of Tarzan's eudaimonia not as one of the two options before him (namely taking up the title) but as his life as a whole, of which his very act of choosing between his options will remain an important part.

Notice that in that case, even the choice to take up his title could be a great loss to Tarzan in terms of his own eudaimonia. Tarzan's question is this: which of these futures holds the best hopes for my giving myself a good life? And there is no reason to assume that it would have to be a future as Greystoke, letting Jane fare as she may. Where one's eudaimonia is concerned, there is all the difference in the world between taking up some good thing and taking it up at all costs. Indeed, there are likely to be costs in terms of eudaimonia for Tarzan, whichever way he chooses. But the point is that one way of making that choice—one way of choosing which cost to bear—can be better than the other for Tarzan, better with respect to his own eudaimonia. In that case, rational self-sacrifice is possible after all, since in cases such as this one some sacrifice will be made either way, and one sacrifice can make more sense than another with respect to eudaimonia.

Does this conflate Tarzan's values with his good? It might seem that way: unquestionably, Tarzan values Jane's well-being and therefore values making sacrifices for her well-being, but surely that does not mean that those sacrifices would be part of Tarzan's good. So how could it be that Tarzan could be better off making such sacrifices?

To answer that question, I want to broaden our scope from self-sacrifice to reflect more generally on choices by which we stand to suffer loss, and know it. One of these is the choice to love. In the film *Shadowlands*, C. S. ("Jack") Lewis struggles to cope with the impending death of his beloved wife, Joy. Jack's life before meeting Joy had been comfortable, safe, and always familiar; in fact, something that initially attracted him to Joy was that she was unafraid to point out how comfortable he had become and that some real challenges would do him a lot of good. And she was right: his life with Joy was filled with passion, closeness, and the real challenge of reckoning with a formidable equal. But now that Joy is about to die, Jack curses the sorrow to come. What Joy tells him is significant: "We can't have the happiness of yesterday without the pain of today. That's the deal." Question: why do we take the deal?

Perhaps it is a matter of cost-benefit analysis: we subtract the pain of tomorrow from the happiness of today and see whether we come out at a gain or a loss. There is something to that, although I think it better explains the times when we *don't* take the deal. When we *do* take the deal, I think the deal we are taking is committing to care and desire and cherish *in such a way that* there is something *to be lost*. That certainly was the point for Jack. Joy had been close to death once before, when she and Jack were not yet married, and the first time Jack realized he loved Joy was when he imagined how he would feel if this dying woman were his wife. If she were his wife, he said, he would love her, she would be the most important thing to him in the world, and the thought of her dying would be utter torment—and that was when Jack admitted to himself that that was exactly how he did feel. For Jack, the point of being Joy's lover was to have her in his life precisely *because* her loss could touch him that deeply. Before Joy, Jack's life was so comfortable that there wasn't much he could lose—but that was the problem. Solving that problem by loving Joy was a way of giving himself a good life, and the vulnerability he brought upon himself was not the *cost* of that solution but part of what made it a *solution* at all.

What does this have to do with acts of self-sacrifice—giving up a title, rushing into a burning building, falling on a grenade? As in love, the losses sustained here really are losses: these acts are indeed sacrifices. But it is important to understand what kinds of sacrifices they are. No one ever wants to fall on the grenade, but that does not mean that the necessity of doing so is external to one's ends, or one's eudaimonia. Sometimes even dying can be the best way of getting on with the business of one's life: for the sake of giving ourselves a good life, some of our ends need to be ends we find worth dying for in order to find them worth living for in the first place. Why make a sacrifice? Because being prepared to make a sacrifice is part of what it means to care deeply about things that matter, and caring about things in that way can be part of the good life one chooses to give oneself. Of course, there is always the option of caring only about saving one's skin; but then, what kind of life is that?

Identifying the final end with eudaimonia yields a way of understanding what is rational about rational self-sacrifice. Even when our ends can cost us something, it can make sense to adopt those ends for the sake of eudaimonia. Those costs are real, and they are real sacrifices, but the point is that the costs grow out of the ends that make one's life a good life in the first place. To be sure, this is not to say that rational self-sacrifice involves choosing another's interests *instead of* one's own eudaimonia, since that way of thinking about self-sacrifice assumes that eudaimonia is independent of how one treats others' interests and the ends for which one lives. But if the question is whether it can be rational to act for the sake of others at significant cost to oneself, then the answer is clearly yes.

4 Eudaimonia and the right kinds of reasons

Even if a person whose final end is eudaimonia *might* act for the good of others (section 2) and *might* even make sacrifices for others (section 3), could that final end really make sense of an *obligation* to act in those kinds of ways? Since reasons for acting are ultimately for the sake of the agent's own eudaimonia, the worry goes, eudaimonism cannot make sense of reasons to treat others morally for the sake of those others. Simply put, eudaimonist reasons for pursuing morally good ends are the wrong kinds of reasons to be genuine moral reasons, in a couple of ways. First, we might worry that such reasons would be too "optional" or contingent to be moral reasons: whether or not I have a reason to treat others well turns out to depend on whether my idea of a good life happens to make such a thing important to me. Second, even if I were to decide that treating others well is important to me, any reason this consideration gives me to treat others well seems unlike a moral reason. If I were to treat another poorly in spite of such a reason to treat him well, this would seem to be none of his business: I have gone against one of the things I happen to find important, but that is my business, not his.[25] Perhaps in going against something I hold important in this way I have harmed myself, but that surely does not capture the relevant nature of the wrong I do in treating another poorly.[26]

However, if the first problem is that reasons to treat others well might be too contingent, then the solution would be that they are not. That solution will depend on the relation between eudaimonia and human sociality: if human sociality is such an important part of our nature that one cannot have a good, rewarding human life without respecting that sociality, and if respecting that sociality means treating others well, then the end of giving oneself a good life necessarily gives one a reason to commit to the end of treating others well, whether one realizes it or not. Taking such reasons seriously would not be just one option, but the only one.

Likewise, if the second problem is that committing to morally good ends for the sake of eudaimonia makes those ends strictly one's own business, then the solution would be that it does not. Whatever else it is to regard others as having claims against me that I treat them well, it must surely be to regard it as the business of others that I do so. In this fashion, Mark LeBar (2009) argues that eudaimonism can account for moral reasons and constraints that focus on the effects for victims of violations of those constraints, and not on the effects for the perpetrator. Here LeBar draws on Darwall's (2006) work on "second-personal reasons." To illustrate such reasons, LeBar and Darwall imagine two different ways in which you might respond to me when I am standing on your foot and causing you pain. One way is to point out to me that you are in pain, and hope that I will see that pain as something there are reasons to alleviate. Here the reason you give is a reason for *someone* to alleviate that pain, and you point out that reason to *me* only because I happen to be in the most fortuitous position to do something about that pain (namely, by standing somewhere else).

Another way to respond is to address me

with a moral claim or demand, asserting that you have the moral standing or authority to demand that [I] move. In this sort of appeal, you are addressing [me] as someone in a second-personal moral relation with you—as one rational agent standing in a moral relation with another, each capable of making and responding to claims upon the other. (LeBar 2009, 647)

To address me in this way is to give me the sort of reason that Darwall calls a second-personal reason. When you address me in this way, you simultaneously recognize your obligation to move me to act only by appealing to me as a rational agent—it is my claim against you that you do so—and make your claim against me insofar as you have the authority to make that claim and I am capable of recognizing and respecting your authority.

To address each other in this way is to adopt the "second-person standpoint," and to adopt that standpoint is to view oneself as a member of a community of rational agents and to take oneself to have reasons to do what such membership entails. For our

---

[25] See Korsgaard 1993.   [26] See Scheffler 1988 and 1992.

purposes, then, there are two questions: whether there are reasons to adopt the second-personal standpoint if the final end is eudaimonia, and whether those reasons are of the right sort to be moral reasons.

Let's take the first question first. LeBar asks us to imagine a pill that causes one to regard others not from the second-personal standpoint, but only strategically, as so many catalysts and obstacles in the pursuit of one's goals (as Hobbes seems to think people do in the state of nature; LeBar 2009, 653, 659). Darwall himself finds such a life unrecognizable as a really human life (2006, 278), and as LeBar points out, this point is of enormous importance for the eudaimonist: people who occupy the second-person standpoint live better, richer human lives than those who do not (2009, 652):

> The ways we see each other as capable of responding to reasons and as accountable to each other for doing so interpenetrate virtually every dimension of our social lives. Life stripped of such relationships is almost inconceivable; certainly it would bear no resemblance to anything like the lives we think we have reason to lead. [W]e can make the case for counting this disposition part of virtue by pointing out that a life without it rather spectacularly fails to satisfy the constraints on what can count as a good human life. (LeBar 2009, 654)

Indeed, while taking the "Hobbesian pill" is a conceptual possibility, to do so is also to become a seriously damaged human (2009, 661–2).

So if the final end is eudaimonia, then there is a reason to occupy the second-person standpoint and thus to be responsive to second-personal reasons. But are these the right kinds of reasons to be moral reasons? We might think that they are not: because I adopt the second-person standpoint for the sake of my eudaimonia, when I move off your foot at your second-personal request I must do so ultimately, not for your sake, but for my own. However, that thought would be mistaken, because it would conflate two very different levels of justification (see LeBar 2009, 663–4). We must distinguish (a) my reasons for according you second-personal respect (e.g. by getting off your foot), given that I occupy the second-person standpoint, from (b) my reasons for being someone who occupies the second-person standpoint with persons like you in the first place. (Of course, these correspond to the two levels of reasons for other-regarding acts that I outlined in section 2.) If the final end is eudaimonia, then (b)-level reasons are ultimately for the sake of the agent's eudaimonia, but (a)-level reasons are second-personal reasons to act out of respect for you, for your sake rather than mine. In that case, I need a reason (at level [a]) to get off your foot, and that reason is the fact that I owe it to *you* not to cause *you* that pain—it is not that I owe it to myself, but that I owe it to *you*. That is consistent with the fact that, when we ask what reasons I may have to relate to others in terms of what we owe each other within a second-person standpoint (at level [b]), the answer is that there can be no living a good human life otherwise.

I am persuaded by LeBar's argument, but obviously it would go far beyond my present scope, and be foolishly heroic, for me to try to offer a full-blown discussion of this very thorny theoretical issue here. But I will pause to note three important features of this approach. One is that such an approach supplements ancient accounts of eudaimonism, addressing questions that ancient accounts do not address directly (see LeBar 2009, 652n). Another point is that the approach makes important assumptions about the importance of sociality in human life, and thus about human nature. Differences in thinking about human nature make for crucial differences between one sort of eudaimonism and another; I take up this point in Chapter 3. And third, this approach highlights a crucial general feature of eudaimonism: its emphasis on the *humanity* of human happiness, something I address in Chapter 2.

Now, lastly, many philosophers will object to the very idea of being *obligated* to stand in reciprocal relations with others, *if* the obligation is to stand in such relations *for the sake of* one's own eudaimonia or happiness. This objection goes back to Immanuel Kant, who famously argued that there is no obligation at all to seek one's own happiness, and Kant's claim has led to a widespread dogma among philosophers that we just cannot make sense of obligations to pursue one's own happiness—that morality just is not about reasons of that sort. Clearly, it would take a lot to respond to such a claim adequately, and this book is not the place for that response. But for the present, it is crucial to appreciate that Kant's claim gets off the ground only with the support of assumptions about the nature of happiness that I mean to reject. Let me explain, briefly, what I mean.

Note that Kant does not deny an obligation to seek one's own happiness on the grounds that it concerns *happiness*; on the contrary, he says that one is obligated to promote the happiness of others (*Metaphysics of Morals* 6:387–8, 393–4). Nor does he deny such an obligation on the grounds that it is concerned with *oneself*, since one is obligated to develop one's talents (6:386–7, 391–3). Why, then, is there for Kant no obligation to seek *one's own happiness*?

Two answers suggest themselves. First, Kant thinks of happiness as the satisfaction of desires (see *Groundwork* 4:399), and so perhaps he believes that we all seek our own happiness anyway, without having to be directed to do so by practical reason.[27] In that case, the very idea of an *obligation* to seek our happiness would be inapt. However, it should be clear already that the same cannot be said about eudaimonia. As I argued in section 1, it is part of our practical rationality to need not just ends but ends to live for, and eudaimonia is the end of living for such other ends in a way that amounts to a good life. Now, it is obvious that people regularly fail to seek the end that eudaimonia is, understood in this way; that is why Aristotle points out the mistake of those who think that eudaimonia is something like prestige or indulgence. Consequently, if *that* is the

---

[27] However, elsewhere Kant characterizes happiness as a mental state of contentment, *Critique of Practical Reason* 5:22. See Denis 2011 for an excellent discussion and construction of a Kantian view of happiness. On the inevitability of seeking one's happiness, see *Groundwork* 4:414–15; *Metaphysics of Morals* 6:386. Kant does say that there is an "indirect" obligation to preserve one's happiness, but only because dejection can lead to temptation, and it's really just temptation that he finds problematic (*Groundwork* 4:399).

sort of end that eudaimonia is, and if eudaimonia is happiness, then there is every reason to think that practical reason obligates us to seek happiness after all.

Second, according to eudaimonism, reasons to act morally are, like all reasons, reasons we have ultimately for the sake of the final end of eudaimonia or a life that is good for the one living it. By contrast, Kant says that reasons for acting morally cannot be based on any other end at all; to think otherwise would be to base our reasons for acting morally on our mere inclinations, so that those reasons or imperatives would be hypothetical rather than categorical (*Critique of Practical Reason* 5:109). The question, though, is whether basing reasons to act morally on eudaimonia really is to base them on inclination, and as we have just seen, there is good reason to think that it is not. As Terence Irwin has pointed out, "In objecting to an account of morality that treats the highest good [namely eudaimonia] 'as the determining ground of the will prior to the moral law,' Kant assumes that the highest good is an object of inclination if it is taken to be prior to the moral law" (Irwin 1996, 81). But we should not accept that assumption. On the contrary, I have suggested that it is practical reason itself, not mere inclination, that pushes us on to give ourselves the gift of a good life, to find things to live for and then live for them.

Again, the issues involved here are too big for me to address them adequately here.[28] But I do hope to have shown that there is a very strong case to be made for the idea that eudaimonia is the final end for practical reasoning. In that case, the place for us to turn now is to happiness: *is* it actually plausible to think that happiness is eudaimonia?

---

[28] E.g., I have not mentioned Kant's view that no account of morality can start from anything that is a matter of our humanity as opposed to our pure personhood. See Denis 2011, 168–9, 172.

2

Happiness as Eudaimonia

In the previous chapter I argued that the final end for deliberation can be plausibly understood in terms of eudaimonia, that is, the notion in ancient Greek philosophy of a good life for the one living it. There I had to take it for granted that eudaimonia is the sort of good that happiness is. But no more: in this chapter I argue that eudaimonia does indeed provide an excellent platform for thinking about happiness. As some readers will know, this is a controversial claim that has come under attack in the philosophical literature on happiness and welfare over the past couple of decades. However, I believe that there is a lot for us to learn about happiness by thinking about eudaimonia, and if (as I also believe) a lot of the resistance to doing so is misguided, then there is a serious risk of our missing out.

There are two main sets of questions about eudaimonia that I shall consider. One has to do with whether happiness occupies the same kind of conceptual space in our thinking as eudaimonia does in ancient Greek thought (section 1). The other concerns a feature of eudaimonia that we saw in the previous chapter, namely the idea that eudaimonia involves one's fulfillment, not only as an individual, but also as a member of humanity (sections 2–4). These are the two fronts on which views of happiness like mine have encountered the most resistance, so it makes sense for us to focus our attention on them.

1 Sharing space

The Greek word 'eudaimonia' is notoriously difficult to translate into English. It is most commonly rendered "happiness," but of course this always has to be accompanied by some caveats: "happiness" can easily sound to our ears like the name of a mood or emotion, the opposite of sadness, but of course ancient Greek philosophers were not trying to say that the emotion opposite of sadness was the final end for practical reasoning. Arguably, the main reason the translation "happiness" is so common is merely that other candidate words fit as badly or worse (e.g. "flourishing" works fairly well, but if left unqualified it can also be applied to animals and even plants; "welfare" and "well-being" lack straightforward cognate adjectives; etc.). However, we may suspect that a far more serious problem underlies this annoying practical one: perhaps the word 'eudaimonia' is so difficult to translate into English because the Greeks used it to talk about something we don't, or at least something we don't talk about when we are talking about happiness.

There are two worries of this latter sort that I want to consider before going any farther. One is that we and the ancient Greeks are involved in such deeply different discourses about "the good life" that there is no point trying to import their notion of eudaimonia into our discourse. The other is, more specifically, that eudaimonia is plausibly treated as an "objective" good (in a sense I'll explain) in ways in which happiness is not.

1.1 Did they mean what we mean?

A familiar feature of Greek ethics is its emphasis on human fulfillment, and especially virtuous activity, as important for eudaimonia. It might be tempting to suppose that eudaimonia and happiness are therefore different concepts: in particular, that eudaimonia as we find it in the Greek philosophers is, first, a specific part of Greek thought, and second, one that we do not have, at least not in any straightforward way. But I think that this assumption would be mistaken on both counts. Take the first point first. Without a doubt, Greek philosophers use the notion of eudaimonia as a kind of good human life that potentially has rather a lot to do with the virtues and the fulfillment of one's human nature. However, this focus does not stem from some peculiar element of an ancient Greek perspective on the good life. Aristotle himself makes this very clear, reporting that most people in his culture identify eudaimonia with something like pleasure or being famous or having a lot of money (NE I.4–5; cp. EE I.3, 1214b34–1215a3; I.4). In fact, the Greek word 'eudaimonia' originally derived from the idea of having a favorable (eu-) guardian spirit (daimōn), which suggests having good fortune in a simple and conventional sense.[1] So it is not surprising that, as Aristotle also reports, many Greeks in his own time still just took eudaimonia and good luck to be the same thing (EE I.1, 1214a21–25). Evidently, ancient Greeks did not differ too much in their thinking about eudaimonia from our own thinking about happiness. No, if 'eudaimonia' in Greek ethics takes on a sense of living one's life well, it can only be because philosophical reflection turns out to lead in that direction.

Furthermore, among Greek philosophers, eudaimonia could play a role in philosophical thought about living wisely, not because the Greek word 'eudaimonia' was already specific in that way but, on the contrary, precisely because it was malleable enough to be ascribed such a meaning in philosophical discussion. For reasons I don't fully understand, people often find it tempting to think that a word that is assigned a specific meaning is so used because it already had that specific meaning. For instance, people often say that when St Paul wrote of "unconditional love," he was referring to a specific Greek concept for which the Greek language even had a special word, 'agapē.' That is of course how Paul used the word, but that is not what the Greek word meant:

---

[1] The etymology of English "happiness" is similar, deriving from "hap": "chance" or "fortune." See also Bett 2005, 47–8, on the affinity in this regard between 'eudaimonia' and the German 'Glück.'

on the contrary, it was a fairly generic Greek word for loving or even just liking. Paul used the word 'agapē' not because its meaning was already in place, but precisely because its usage was broad and malleable enough to allow him to assign it the meaning that interested him (as, e.g. neither 'philia' nor 'erōs' would have done, being far more rigid in meaning). And this is just what happened when ancient Greek philosophers used the word 'eudaimonia'—they exploited its malleability and assigned it a theoretical usage.

Still—and this is the second point—perhaps it is just that sort of malleability that our concept of happiness lacks. Perhaps, that is, happiness for us just *is* a matter of subjective satisfaction, say, and any use of it to refer to things like living wisely or human fulfillment is just an abuse of the term (see, e.g. Sumner 1996, 2002). But I do not think so. For instance, Richard Kraut (1979) has argued persuasively that we often speak of happiness in such a way that, while feelings of satisfaction may be a necessary condition for happiness, still they are not sufficient for it, such as when we wish a newborn child or newlywed couple "every happiness." Surely we do not have in mind anything as cruel as that they should merely feel satisfied with their lot in life, however horrid that life should otherwise prove to be.[2]

Of course, there is no denying that we *do* often use the word 'happiness' for a kind of emotion or good feeling, and obviously there is nothing wrong with using the word that way.[3] The point is that we can speak of happiness in other ways, too, and in particular in ways that have a lot more to do with leading a good human life. To appreciate this, I think one need only watch the engrossing documentary series that began in 1964 with the film *Seven Up!* The original film profiled a number of 7-year-old English children from all walks of life, and the series follows up on them every seven years (the most recent installment at the time of this writing is *Forty-Nine Up*). It is interesting to see how the children change (or not!) as they become 14-year-olds, but by the time one watches the films at 21 and 28, one's interest takes a marked turn: these are the years when we first glimpse how their adult lives are starting to take shape and how their hopes may or may not start coming to fruition. These are the years, that is, in which thinking about life as a whole begins to be a serious issue. It is surprising how much interest one can take in how things go for a stranger seen only in a film, yet as we watch these changes occur in them, we find that there is something we do wish for them. Let's focus on that wish for a moment.

For me, this wish was most pronounced in two cases. One was Tony, whose dream as a boy and a young man was to become a jockey, which he did. However, by the age of 21 he had already realized that he had no future as a jockey, and was working as a

---

[2] What is more, ancient Greek philosophers also generally agreed that pleasure or subjective satisfaction was a necessary condition for eudaimonia. See Gosling and Taylor 1982.

[3] And even here we do not mean just one thing. As Haybron (2008, 30–2) notes, "happiness" in the sense of an emotion sometimes refers to a broad and long-lasting state of mind, sometimes to a certain elated feeling or mood, etc.

bet-setter at a racecourse while trying to earn his credentials as a taxi driver (which is more like a skilled trade in England than in most other countries). These were very uncertain times for Tony, and I found myself with strong wishes for him as his life unfolded during the years between 21 and 28. The other case was Susie, the daughter of a very wealthy (but, one suspects, somewhat dysfunctional) family who had become a rather sullen 14-year-old and very anxious and cynical by 21. I confess that my hopes for Susie were low by that time, although I also wished for her what I wished for Tony. And to my delight, when they were 28 I found that my wishes for each of them had started coming true. Tony was married to a woman he loved, raising a family he adored, and doing well as a taxi driver. Over all, his life was working out and he seemed to be genuinely delighted about it. Susie had an even more remarkable transformation: she too had married and started a family, but more than that she had become a radiant young woman who now loved her life, no longer that sullen, cynical girl. One could see it in her very face. So far anyway, Tony and Susie were each a real success, and their success was a joy to see.

What is it that we wish for people like Tony and Susie as we watch their lives take shape? I trust that the most natural thing to say we wish for them is their *happiness*. Viewing a life in seven-year chunks gets us away from thinking about happiness as something episodic or temporary, like a way that one feels at one time or another, and towards thinking of it instead as a way that a life *goes*, although of course this includes one's attitude about how one's life is going. I think that an "episodic" focus on the good life seems attractive only as long as we direct our attention away from our lives as wholes, and this can be made easier by the fact that the progression of one's life is spread out over long periods of time. It is that deceptive spread that falls away in the *Up* series, and makes it more apparent that we are in firm possession of a decidedly non-episodic conception of happiness after all.

It is happiness in *that* sense that we need to think about when we consider deliberation and final ends. Now, it still remains to be seen *what* happiness is, more precisely; nothing I have said here suggests that it does or does not consist in virtuous activity or money-making or what have you. But what matters is that we seem to be able to think of happiness in a way that *both* casts light on deliberating about one's life as a whole *and* is indeterminate enough to be specified in many different ways. In other words, our notion of happiness seems to be malleable enough to serve our purposes in precisely the way that Aristotle's notion of eudaimonia served his. In this way, happiness is rather a lot like eudaimonia, as Greek philosophers thought of it. If we can use the notion of happiness in this way, then it would seem to be about as malleable as we need it to be, as long as we remember that it *is* the malleability that we are exploiting.

1.2 Eudaimonia, happiness, and objective goods

However, it is often said that eudaimonia is an "objective" notion, and this might lead us to think that whatever eudaimonia is, it cannot be happiness. In this context, by "objective" I do not mean "lacking any subjective elements," such as one's feelings or emotions. It should be clear enough already that eudaimonia can be regarded as including any number of positive attitudes and feelings of satisfaction. After all, eudaimonia is the flourishing of a human *as a whole*, and that whole includes how one judges and feels about one's life; after all, humans are also affective creatures, so satisfaction with one's life should be part of eudaimonia.[4] Furthermore, part of being human just is a deep need to develop as a unique individual, and thus to have a life that is experienced as expressing one's individuality (see Hampton 1993, 149–50). So it should come as no surprise that all of the ancient eudaimonists held that subjective satisfaction and enjoyment of one's life are important and indeed necessary parts of eudaimonia. It is also important to recognize that this idea is not in competition with the centrality of practical reason in those accounts. This can be easy for us to miss, however, especially if we begin from familiar views of emotion on which it is far more sharply distinguished from practical reason than it is in ancient moral psychology.[5]

So eudaimonia is *not* "objective" in the sense of involving no subjective elements, such as satisfaction, pleasure, and emotional fulfillment generally. Rather, the sense in which eudaimonia is "objective" is that the agent is not the final authority on whether his life has it. This is because even though eudaimonia requires subjective satisfaction and the judgment that one is happy, it depends also on one's doing well as a human all around, about which it is possible to be mistaken. Simply put, something can be important for one's eudaimonia even if one does not think it is. In fact, even the requirement that eudaimonia include such things as emotional well-being and subjective satisfaction is itself an objective requirement—that is, one's eudaimonia may require such things even if one doesn't think so.[6]

Is this sort of objectivity appropriate at all in a conception of *happiness*? If I think I'm happy, what sense can it make to tell me that I'm not? Now, if by "happiness" we just mean something like a sense of subjective satisfaction, then of course I cannot fail to be happy if I think I am.[7] Again, I do not want to deny that this is a legitimate way of using the word "happiness"—clearly, in many cases all that we mean in describing someone as happy is that he feels satisfied and believes that things are going well for him. It is clear, of course, that eudaimonia in Greek philosophy is not this sort of happiness—if it

---

[4] Kraut 1979, 170–4; LeBar 2004, 207–8; Toner 2006, 225–9. See Aristotle, *NE* VII.13, X.5; *EE* I.1, 1214a7–8.

[5] I discuss the place of subjective well-being in Plato's eudaimonism in 2005. It is sometimes said that the Stoics hold that eudaimonia should be totally devoid of emotion, but this is a terribly misleading way of describing their view; in fact, it is simply false, as I argue in later chapters.

[6] See e.g. Foot 2001, 85–6; LeBar 2004. See also Haybron 2008, chap. 9, for an excellent defense of a similar point. See also Tiberius 2006, 497–500, who suggests that theories of happiness should not be objective in this sense, because such objectivity would make happiness more difficult for social scientists to measure; the demands of measurability make it much more attractive to give subjects the final authority on how happy they are. However, although Tiberius opens her paper by locating the concept of happiness via its central role in practical reasoning (p. 493), she does not explain why the things that could play that role must be confined to those that can be ascertained from self-reports, for instance. Cf. Tiberius and Plakias 2010, 402.

[7] See e.g. Telfer 1980, 9–10, 37–8.

were, it could hardly be the final end. When I speak of eudaimonia as happiness, then, I mean something like what Philippa Foot (2001, 85) has called "happiness that could convincingly be called humanity's good."

But is there any use for a conception of happiness in this sense anyway? I think there is. As many philosophers have seen, there must be some sense of happiness that is more than a feeling, because feelings can be mistaken, even manipulated. Amartya Sen (1987) has made this point very forcefully: if feeling happy were all there is to being happy or well off, then someone who has been manipulated into feeling satisfied, despite being the victim of exploitation, should be as happy or as well off as anyone can be—which of course is outrageous. So it seems that autonomy—living a life that is really your own—must be an important part of happiness, and so there must be more to having a happy life than just feeling happy with it.[8]

But does this point get us all the way to objectivity? L. W. Sumner says no. Sumner uses different terminology from mine: he distinguishes "happiness," which he defines as a purely subjective sense of satisfaction, from "well-being," or really having a good life (what I am calling "happiness"). Sumner then argues that feeling happy and sincerely judging that one is happy (in his sense) is all that well-being requires, provided that such judgments really are one's own. This means that such judgments must be *informed* (not made in the absence of information which, if known, would significantly change one's judgment) and also *autonomous*, that is, not the result of manipulation (1996, 160–71). But, Sumner insists, this is *not* to say that well-being is an objective good—on the contrary, it still depends solely on one's own assessment of one's happiness; the information and autonomy conditions require only that that assessment actually *be* one's own. Therefore, Sumner concludes, a theory of well-being as a thoroughly subjective good can also agree that there is more to being well off than just thinking that one is.[9]

However, while Sumner may be able to countenance an observation like Sen's, I agree with Mark LeBar (2004) that he cannot explain *why* that observation ever should have mattered in the first place.[10] As Sumner himself acknowledges (1996, 179), the autonomy condition is not a requirement on well-being as such, but only on *human* well-being in particular. Other sentient creatures are subjects of well-being—dogs and cats can be well or badly off, say—but there is no need that their feelings or judgments (such as they may be) must be autonomous. Autonomy conditions therefore attach to us not merely as *subjects* of well-being, but as specifically *human* subjects

---

[8] For any two philosophers there are probably three conceptions of "autonomy," but I am thinking of it here just in Sen's very broad sense of not being the victim of manipulation.

[9] Cf. Tiberius and Plakias 2010, 410–11, who say that any norms on happiness other than the subject's own norms are simply "arbitrary." Their reason for saying this seems to be their assumption that if happiness is good for the subject, then any norms other than the subject's norms are "suspect." However, surely it is one thing to say that happiness is good for the person who has it (i.e. what *kind* of good it is), and another to say that the person whose happiness is in question is the final authority on what has that kind of goodness. I say more about "good for" below.

[10] See also Haybron 2008, 189–92.

of well-being.[11] A subjectivist about well-being is of course free to *agree* that autonomy is necessary for well-being, but what he cannot do is *explain why* it should be necessary. In that case, such an approach smuggles in a way of thinking about well-being that it takes a more objective approach to motivate in the first place. Eudaimonism, by contrast, is objective in just that way: human well-being must be autonomous because self-direction is part of human nature, and human well-being involves flourishing in one's nature as a human. Therefore, taking the autonomy condition seriously means that our conception of human happiness requires a conception of human nature after all.

2 Human nature

However, it is that very idea—namely, that eudaimonia and happiness involve human fulfillment—that turns out to be more difficult than it may seem at first, so it is that idea that we need to examine in the rest of this chapter. I begin by arguing in this section that the conception of human nature at work here should be understood as a normative one rather than a strictly empirical or biological one. Here I have in mind a distinction that John McDowell draws between two broad forms of thinking about human nature in evaluative contexts. One way of thinking about human nature aims at deriving ethical facts from ethically neutral facts about our nature (call this our "first nature"). For instance, such a view might hold that fidelity is a virtue on the grounds that human life is such that we need to be able to make and accept promises. Here the facts about our nature are the ethically neutral facts that in everyday life we need to get people to do things for us, and that using a convention of promising is generally the only effective way of doing so. From this natural fact is allegedly derived the ethical fact that fidelity is a virtue, because it is an attribute that makes it possible for us to bind each other by promising.[12]

By contrast, one might hold instead that ethical facts can be ascertained only within an ethical outlook as a whole, and that such an outlook must include certain normative views about what it means to be human (call this "second nature"). On this view, whether fidelity is a virtue depends on whether there are good reasons to go in for the practices for which fidelity is necessary, that is, whether we have good reasons to be people to whom fidelity is important. Those reasons must be assessed within an overall ethical outlook, including our considered views about what it means to be human and to live a good human life. Importantly, those views about human nature are not value-neutral; indeed, the impetus for thinking about second as opposed to first nature is the conviction that nothing value-neutral could also be reason-giving. On this view, in

---

[11] Cf. Seneca, *Ep.* 124.8–20 (= IG II-110), who says that other animals have a kind of good and even a kind of virtue, but not in an absolute sense, which only a rational animal can have.

[12] The example is from Anscombe 1981, chap. 2. Cf. Kekes 1988, chap. 2; 1995, chap. 1. Foot 2001 develops a version of this type of naturalism as well; see Tiberius 2008, 16, for comment.

order for any facts to be reason-giving they must themselves be part of a normative outlook. Here, McDowell argues, practical and theoretical thought are in the same boat: there is no stepping outside any framework of thought, practical or theoretical, to independent things-in-themselves that ground the framework. Instead, the project of determining what we have reason to do is the "Neurathian" project of bringing our ethical beliefs, including beliefs about our own nature, into equilibrium, without ever stepping outside them, just as (in Neurath's metaphor) the occupants of a ship may rebuild it even while it continues to keep them afloat.[13]

With this distinction in mind we can now ask in which of these two ways we ought to think about human nature when thinking about eudaimonia or happiness. My own view is that we need a conception of human happiness in terms of *second* as opposed to first nature (even if some eudaimonists have thought in terms of first nature). For one thing, I believe that happiness requires fulfillment as a human being (more on this below), but of course on some conceptions of human nature, human fulfillment and happiness pull apart, and that disagreement, I believe, is a fundamentally normative one. For instance, Nietzsche holds that human nature is such that those with a capacity for greatness ought to strive for the fulfillment of their nature as extraordinary humans, whether doing so leads to their happiness or not. In that case, living according to nature involves living in a way that may have nothing to do with happiness.[14] Now, I do not accept this conception of human nature, but the main point at present is that I can see no way to adjudicate between (say) Aristotelian and Nietzschean conceptions of human nature *except* by situating them within a larger perspective on what matters in human life—and I can see no way that such a perspective could be value-neutral.[15] If that is the case, then discussions of human happiness should be framed in terms of second rather than first nature.[16]

A further reason to employ a normative conception of human nature also emerges from considering Nietzsche. In the previous chapter I argued not only that there is such a thing as a final end for practical reasoning, but also that there is *only one* final end, since otherwise ends would clash and leave deliberation powerless to harmonize our ends. Notice, however, that even this idea rests on a view about human nature: happiness as a human requires harmonizing our ends through practical reasoning. However, it is just

---

[13] See McDowell 1995a, 1995b, and 1996. See also Nussbaum 1995; Hursthouse 1999, chap. 8. I find persuasive McDowell's argument (1995a; 1995b, 149-51) that Aristotle's is a conception of second rather than first nature; see also Nussbaum 1986, chap. 8; Broadie 1991, 35; Nussbaum 1995. See also Annas (1988), who argues that ancient ethical thought in general was a form of reflection on (what we have called) second nature, a point she makes about the Stoics in particular in her 2004, 114-17, and 2007a.

[14] See Hursthouse 1999, 253-6, and Swanton 2003, chap. 4, for excellent discussions.

[15] Indeed, in *The Anti-Christ* Nietzsche identifies three different sorts of happiness, one for each of the three ranks of persons, who differ, not only in their natures, but also in the *quality* of their natures, as well as their happiness: the spiritual, being the highest; the mediocre, being the lowest; and in between, the temperamental. See Bett 2005, 50-1, for discussion.

[16] Importantly, this also means that a eudaimonist conception of human nature and the human *telos* need not, and indeed should not, be viewed as ethically neutral (*pace* Williams 1985).

such a view that Nietzsche rejects (see N. White 2006, 27–30, for discussion). On Nietzsche's view, the clash of our ends is in fact part of the human good, filling one's life with the excitement and passion of conflict and even frustration. Again, this disagreement is between two very different views about what matters for the kinds of creatures that we are, and that is an opposition between normative outlooks.

Finally, I agree with McDowell and others that the very fact that humans can engage in practical reasoning means that reflection on our nature can be reason-giving only if we think of that nature as second rather than first nature (see also LeBar 2004). To see this, suppose that, as a "bald" (first-natural) fact about me, I have the desire to eat rocky road ice cream. This desire, being a bald fact, is not all by itself a reason to eat the ice cream: being a creature who can reflect on his impulses, I can stand back and ask, "So I want the ice cream; but do I have a good reason to eat it?"[17] If I find that all told I have no such reason, then I may just give in to my desire anyway, but what I cannot do then is think that eating it is the thing I have *reason* to do. Now, suppose that it is also a bald fact about me that, as a human, my nature is such and such (for simplicity, call this fact φ). Consider, for instance, the bald fact that, by nature, humans have teeth well suited to eating other animals. The same is true of lions and polar bears, but of course what lions and polar bears *might* do cannot be different from what they *do* do. The same is not true of us, who can instead reflect on what we might have reason to do. So now this first-natural fact φ is in exactly the same boat as the bald fact of my desire to eat the ice cream: is living in a φ way something I have reason to do? That is the question I must now ask, and that is to engage in normative, evaluative reflection on φ. If I decide through such reflection that I do have a reason to live in a φ way, then φ will have ceased to be a *bald* fact about me, and instead will have become a part of my total normative perspective (a second-natural fact).[18]

Therefore, given the nature of practical rationality, humans cannot discover what they have reasons to do by examining what they "naturally" do, since what humans naturally do just is *to act for reasons*.[19] And as I have just argued, reasons, in order to be

---

[17] See Korsgaard 1996, 93; see also Plato, *Rep.* IV, 439e–440a.

[18] See also McDowell 1995b, 151–3, who argues that a creature that reasons about actions must be able to conceptualize its own behavior as really its own. In that case, such a creature must also be able to contemplate alternative actions, and so when presented with a "natural" fact, he must be able to ask what bearing that fact has on his actions. Consequently, it is never the sheer "naturalness" of such facts that carries the practical and normative weight.

[19] See Hursthouse 1999, chap. 10. See also Jacobs 2004, 106. Epictetus seems clearly to have been aware of this fact:

It is sufficient, therefore, for [the other animals] to eat and drink and rest and breed, and perform other such functions as belong to each of them; but for us, to whom god has granted in addition the faculty of understanding, these functions are no longer sufficient. For if we do not act in a proper and orderly manner, and each of us in accordance with his nature and constitution, we shall no longer attain our end. (*Diss.* I.6.14–15; see also Cicero, *Off.* I.11)

This, I think, is the source of Epictetus' frequent use of animal images to characterize vice (e.g. *Diss.* I.3.7–9, II.10.2, IV.5.20).

normatively binding as reasons are, must be part of a normative outlook.[20] That is why eudaimonist thought about happiness is an *evaluative* inquiry, one that, as Martha Nussbaum puts it, involves determining what things are such important human goods that a life without them is one we can no longer count as really worth living for a human.[21] Therefore, the conception of human nature at work in that inquiry is best understood in the second-natural sense and not in the first.

3 Perfection[22]

Happiness as we are trying to understand it here is the kind of thing I have described as a good life. More precisely, I have described it as a life that is good for the person living it, and I have done so because "good life" is ambiguous: in addition to the way I have used it, one could also use it to characterize lives that are "good" in other ways, such as a life that is lived well in the sense of "appropriately," or "with proper human functioning."[23] I shall characterize this as the difference between thinking of the good life either as a good for the one living it or as a good like being a good human. For brevity, I shall stipulate that this is what I mean in calling these goods "agent-relative" versus "agent-neutral," respectively. The difference is significant, because whatever else we say about happiness, it is clearly an agent-relative good—the kind of good that gives the person living that life a reason to value it that no other person could have. However, the objection is sometimes made that eudaimonia is an agent-neutral good, and if that is correct, then it is the wrong place to start if what we are trying to understand is happiness. This objection stems from a couple of things: one, the fact that eudaimonia has traditionally been taken to involve fulfillment as a human, and two, the assumption that that fulfillment is a sort of "perfection" of proper human functioning. So where does that leave us?

I shall explain in the next section why I strongly believe that happiness, like eudaimonia, involves one's fulfillment, not just as an individual but also as a member of humanity. First, however, in this section I argue that the sort of "perfectionism" in question here is indeed a non-starter as a way of thinking about happiness, but that my account does not involve "perfectionism" in this sense.

---

[20] See McDowell 1995a, 1996; see also Russell 2009, chap. 3.

[21] Nussbaum 1995. See also 1988, 175, 177; 1990, 217–19, 224; 1992, 208.

[22] Most of the remainder of this chapter I have adapted from a paper co-authored with Mark LeBar, called "Well-Being and Eudaimonia: A Reply to Haybron." I thank Mark for permission to adapt this material here, although I hasten to note that he can take no blame for any shortcomings in the way in which I have done so. Lastly, in order to maintain consistent style throughout the chapter, this material is presented in the first-person singular instead of its original first-person plural; I thank Mark for his permission to make this purely stylistic change.

[23] This is the sense in which e.g. John Kekes (1988, 1995, 2002) speaks of "good lives." See Feldman 2004, 8–12, for a useful separation of several senses of "good life."

3.1 Problems for Perfectionism

Daniel Haybron has recently offered an especially useful characterization of the treatment of happiness as involving human perfection:

Perfection is commonly regarded as the perfection of one's nature: being a good specimen of one's kind, for instance, or fulfilling one's capacities well. But I will understand perfectionism broadly enough to include any theory that takes happiness ultimately to consist at least partly in some kind of perfection, excellence, or virtue (or the exercise thereof).[24]

Now, in Haybron's discussion this class of theories gets conflated with "Aristotelian theories"—including theories like mine—at the outset because, Haybron says, Aristotelianism is the "best-known example of a perfectionist theory" of happiness.[25] But I want to begin by setting aside (for the moment) questions about the subscription of Aristotle (or Aristotelians) to the view Haybron is targeting.[26] So I'll simply use the term 'Perfectionism' (with a capital P) to designate the family of views that he targets, whoever may have held such views, and explain why I am not a Perfectionist.

There are two main problems for Perfectionism that I want to discuss, and which I think Haybron is correct to point out. The first is this: to say that happiness consists in "perfection" grossly under-specifies the nature of happiness. (Call this the *under-specification* problem.) Haybron makes this objection with a thought experiment about the imaginary Frank, who assumes care of an orphaned autistic child; Frank thereby perfects himself in one way, by showing "greater virtue" and making his life "more admirable" (2008, 164). However, Frank now has to spend more time caring for the child than developing his own capacities, interests, and talents, so that now his life "involves a lesser exercise of his human capacities: his functioning is sharply constrained and inhibited." Frank's situation, of course, is a perfectly typical case: perfection in one respect always costs opportunities for perfection in other respects. Indiscriminate perfection, therefore, is zero-sum.[27]

---

[24] Haybron 2008, 156. It is worth pointing out that while Thomas Hurka has developed a well-known account of Perfection and its goodness, he says explicitly that he does not think of Perfection as the sort of good that happiness is (Hurka 1993, 17). I should also note that the sort of good that I am calling "happiness"—namely a life that is good for the person living it—Haybron prefers to call "well-being." Furthermore, Haybron reserves the term 'happiness' for a specific sort of emotional fulfillment, which is an important part of, but not the same as, well-being.

[25] Haybron 2008, 155; cf. Griffin 1986, 56–8; Feldman 2004, 18–19; Crisp 2006, 102; 2008, § 5.2. See also Kekes 1988, chap. 2, for discussion of several historical versions of perfectionism. Some may think it confused to suppose that well-being could ever be construed as a matter of agent-neutral perfection. But even if it is, Haybron's arguments can be taken as arguments that an agent-neutral perfectionism *cannot count* as an account of well-being. Either way, I agree with Haybron for the reasons given in the text that it is a view that deserves to be rebutted. I thank Brad Hooker for raising this concern.

[26] As Haybron notes (2008, 156, 158), surely what really matters is whether some account is a viable theory of happiness, not whether or not it is Aristotle's. Nor do I mean to suggest that my view is the only possible interpretation of Aristotle's practical work, or that it captures every theme in that work. Instead, my aim is to extract a plausible "third way" from recognizably central Aristotelian ethical doctrines.

[27] This problem is also noted by Sumner 1996, 212; for discussion, see LeBar 2004. See also Griffin 1986, 58–60.

The second problem for Perfectionism arises on account of its taking happiness to consist in things like being a good specimen of one's kind. The problem is that Perfectionism, understood in this way, locates happiness in a sort of perfection that has agent-neutral rather than agent-relative value. In other words, the kind of perfection involved in Perfectionism is, we might say, *good simpliciter*, but not *good for the person* whose perfection it is. (Call this the *agent-neutrality* problem.) Agent-relative reasons include in their content an ineliminable reference to the agent whose reasons they are.[28] Reasons for perfection need not necessarily be agent-neutral, but the sort of contrast Haybron has in mind is built on the thought that well-being gives reasons of a special kind for the person whose well-being it is, in a way that perfection does not.[29] There is thus a mismatch between the kinds of reasons perfection and well-being generate.[30]

Put in terms of value, the kind of perfection involved in Perfectionism is, we might say, *good simpliciter*, not *good for the person* whose perfection it is. Agent-relative goods necessarily are good-for, while agent-neutral goods need not be. As Haybron notes, such perfection "bears no necessary connection to anything that can plausibly be viewed as an organism's goals" (2008, 169).[31] It is this agent-neutrality of the good of perfection that is essential to Perfectionism, and it is this that leads to a second objection: even if being a good specimen is some sort of good, it has little if anything to do with one's well-being. Well-being must be a good *for the agent* in question, and being a good specimen (say) just is not that kind of good.

Haybron underscores this point with the case of Angela, an aging diplomat choosing between retiring a few years early to a relaxing life in Tuscany, on the one hand, and staying on in her career long enough to take on one more important assignment, on the other. It seems clear, Haybron says, that there would be a higher degree of human functioning, and thus greater perfection, involved in taking the assignment, but retiring to Tuscany would make Angela better off (2008, 161–3). The example illustrates that perfection of this sort has little to do with happiness. Increases in perfectionist value improve the world insofar as one of its members has become more perfect, so this sort of value gives any agent whatsoever reason to sustain, promote, or increase it. By contrast, increases in happiness make life richer and more satisfying for the person living

---

[28] For a more careful formulation of the distinction, see Ridge 2011.

[29] It is certainly conceivable that one might think there are agent-relative reasons to seek one's own perfection. But it is difficult to imagine the motivations for a version of Perfectionism that held this; the combination of commitments is especially unstable for just the reasons Haybron gives.

[30] Richard Kraut (2007, chap. 3) has argued that well-being is best understood in terms of "flourishing," such that something is good for one in virtue of its being productive or part of flourishing; for a human agent, this consists in the maturation and exercise of human cognitive, social, affective, and physical skills. Although Kraut finds the label 'developmentalism' more felicitous than 'perfectionism,' his view shares the basic structure of the families of views we are here calling Perfectionist. It is worth noting that "good for" in Kraut's usage is in fact agent-neutral (as in, e.g. "Vegetables are good for people" or "Rich soil is good for plants").

[31] For a similar critique of Kraut's 2007 view, see LeBar 2008.

that life. This sort of value gives special reason for action to the agent whose life it is: it is because *this* agent has *this* connection with *this* life that this life is valuable *to her* in this way. Perhaps Angela's being a better specimen of humankind is *some* sort of good, but happiness in life is a good *for the one living that life*.[32]

I agree with Haybron both that Perfectionism as he describes it has these two problems and that they are devastating. Whatever perfection may have to do with happiness, any account of happiness so indiscriminate as to assign just *any* form of perfection this kind of value must simply be mistaken. Likewise, we must neither conflate goods for agents and perfectionist goods nor assume that one achieves the former by pursuing the latter (Haybron 2008, 168–70). Since Perfectionism is a non-starter as a theory of happiness, we might do just as well to ignore it—*except* for the fact that many philosophers (including Haybron) take Aristotelian approaches to happiness, including mine, to be forms of Perfectionism.[33] This, I argue now, is a mistake. Aristotelian approaches can offer an *alternative* to Perfectionism, and by treating Aristotelian approaches as forms of Perfectionism we risk overlooking such alternatives. To make the point, I want to consider Aristotelian eudaimonism with respect to these two problems just identified for Perfectionism.

3.2 The under-specification problem

Haybron argues that the under-specification problem especially plagues those theories that make virtue important for happiness. It was no accident that Haybron set up his thought experiment about Frank so that it was greater perfection *in virtuousness* that came at the expense of greater perfection in other areas of his life. Indeed, Haybron (2008, 168) concludes from such considerations that "perfection, excellence, or virtue probably forms no fundamental part of well-being. . . . Or, alternatively, if perfection is fundamental to well-being, then it plays a smaller and very different role from that posited by Aristotelian accounts."

But there is a further lesson to be learned from Frank's case, which Haybron does not mark: *any* view that takes some kind of self-development to matter for happiness must explain why *that* kind of self-development counts for happiness, since *all* kinds of self-development have opportunity costs. The under-specification problem is no *special* problem for anyone. It is a perfectly general problem for any theory that makes some kind of self-development important for happiness, and it must be addressed by saying

---

[32] A case that Haybron borrows from Sumner (1996, 24) makes this intuitive point vividly, by inviting us to consider a "talented but miserable philosopher": it seems that his misery gives the philosopher compelling reason to give up his profession, even though his competence in it represents a significant form of perfection. See Haybron 2008, 160ff.

[33] Cf. Tiberius and Plakias 2010, who pose the following dilemma for eudaimonism: either the goods necessary for eudaimonia are good in virtue of being pleasant or satisfying desires, in which case eudaimonism collapses into some other, very different account of happiness; or those goods are important in ways that lack practical significance for the agent. That is, to the extent that eudaimonism really has anything distinctive to say about happiness, it has far less to say about how one might have a reason to pursue happiness.

why that kind of self-development is important enough for happiness to warrant its opportunity costs. Perfectionism's problem in particular is that it fails to do just that.

Consequently, if Haybron's objection is to Aristotelian accounts, then it really must be on the grounds that such accounts similarly fail to explain why virtue should have that kind of importance. Of course, the case that virtue forms an important part of happiness must depend (inter alia) on what we take virtue to be. How does Haybron think of virtue? Importantly, Haybron does not articulate, much less defend, the assumption that Frank's decision to care for the orphan *is* more virtuous than the alternative decision. Nonetheless, the idea seems to be that we can understand "virtue" as "admirability," and admirability as a function of stereotypical "good deeds." This is hardly an exotic way of thinking about virtuous activity,[34] and if one thinks of virtue in such a way then (just as Haybron says) it is difficult to see why it should always warrant the sacrifice of opportunities for other kinds of self-development.

But that is not at all the sort of claim that Aristotle makes, because he does not think of virtue as Haybron does. For Haybron, virtuous activity is a special *type or class* of activity—the doing of "good deeds," perhaps, as opposed to doing other, more everyday sorts of things. By contrast, Aristotle thinks of virtuous activity as *any* kind of activity, insofar as it is done with practical wisdom and emotions that harmonize with practical wisdom—this is the activity, he says, that characterizes the virtuous person (*NE* I.13). A virtue is a state of character (II.5) concerned with one's actions and emotions (II.3), and thus with the making of good choices (II.6). Accordingly, Aristotle says that the virtuous person both cares about the right sorts of things and is intelligent in the decisions he makes about those things (II.4, VI.12). As such, virtue concerns a wide range of everyday affairs: how a person handles things like money (IV.1–2) and recognition (IV.3–4), how a person copes with desires (III.10–12) and emotions like anger (IV.5) and fear (III.6-9), how a person is with friends and acquaintances (VIII–IX), even how a person behaves in conversation (IV.8). Clearly, virtue involves a person's handling of both worldly circumstances and features of his own inner life that constantly come into play, in every area of life throughout even the most ordinary day. This is a long way from virtue as a matter of "admirable good deeds."

Again, my point is not mainly a historical one about Aristotle; it is that Haybron assumes a conception of virtue on which the under-specification becomes pernicious, but which we might do just as well to reject anyway. (In fact, in the next chapter I argue that we *should* reject such a view.) Activities involved in developing a talent (say) and virtuous activity do not form two sets of activities. Rather, activities involved in developing a talent *are* virtuous activities when they are done with appropriate forms of practical reasoning and emotion. So understood, virtue does have opportunity costs

---

[34] For instance, Driver 2001 defines the virtues as dispositions to promote good consequences; Thomson 1997 defines them as dispositions to do actions antecedently identified as virtuous; Slote 2001 defines virtuous acts in terms of how intuitively admirable they are. Even so, I reject all such approaches to the virtues in Russell 2009.

for other kinds of self-development—as a burglar, say, or a tyrant—but it is the kind of self-development that makes it possible for any other kind of self-development to be part of a good human life. An approach like mine can have much more to say about the special importance of virtue for happiness than Haybron allows.

3.3 The agent-neutrality problem

The second objection to Perfectionism is that, whereas happiness is of agent-relative value, Perfectionism identifies it with something of agent-neutral value. Haybron also directs this objection specifically against "Aristotelian" theories: because of the con-nection Aristotle makes between eudaimonia and virtue, Haybron says, Aristotle's notion of eudaimonia most naturally is an account of the "good life" as something distinct from happiness (2008, 173).[35] However, I argue that Aristotle understands eudaimonia as an agent-relative good, and understands the virtues as benefiting their possessor in an agent-relative way. There are no pretensions to merely agent-neutral value on the Aristotelian account, and it remains an account of happiness.

To take the second point first: if Aristotle did not think that the virtues benefit their possessors in an agent-relative way, much of his argumentation would make no sense whatsoever. Indeed, much of the argument offered not only by Aristotle but also by Platonists and Stoics is intended to show that virtue is *good for* the virtuous agent, and that the good life understood as a life of virtuous activity is *good for* the person whose life it is.[36] There would be little need to *defend* the place of virtue in eudaimonia if those two goods were seen as agent-neutral goods.[37] The burden these arguments try to discharge is one of removing the intuitive power of the thought that virtue comes at a *cost* to happiness, and that the life of virtue is *not* the best life one can live for one's own sake. It is because the conception of eudaimonia at stake is thought to be of great agent-relative value that these arguments are needed in the first place.

The larger point, that Aristotle takes eudaimonia to be an agent-relative good, is clear from his broader account of practical reasoning. As we saw in the previous chapter, Aristotle thinks that deliberation requires a final end—an end we seek for its own sake and for the sake of nothing further, and for the sake of which we seek all other ends—and that the good life or eudaimonia is what people already agree is that final end (NE I.4, 1095a14–22). Aristotle takes himself to be entering a conversation that thoughtful people have already been having about eudaimonia, and it is already a conversation about what makes a life good for the one living it. Aristotle observes that eudaimonia figures prominently in how people think about their goals, and so begins by considering the popular views that it lies in pleasure, or wealth, or fame, or being a good person (I.5, 1095b14–1096a4). To be sure, Aristotle goes on to reject all of these

---

[35] Cf. Griffin 1986, 69.

[36] E.g. think about the central arguments of Plato's *Rep.* or *Gorg.*

[37] See also Hursthouse 1987, 222, who also observes that in this context the "good life" is not to be thought of as the "good moral life."

views about eudaimonia, but the important thing to note is that they are all most naturally taken to be various views (better or worse) about what is a good life *for the person living it*. *That* is the conversation about the "good life" that Aristotle takes himself to join.

This becomes even clearer if we recall Aristotle's account of practical reasoning and in particular the need for a final end. Aristotle starts by observing that we cannot desire everything we desire for the sake of something else, since desire would then regress and thus be empty, so there must be at least one thing we desire that is such that we could desire everything for its sake and desire it for the sake of nothing further, so that it can finally bring deliberation to a halt (*NE* I.2, 1094a18–22). Aristotle thinks that there is exactly one such final end, namely eudaimonia, which he thinks is what everyone already agrees is the final end, even though there is widespread disagreement about exactly what it amounts to (I.4, 1095a14–22).

Aristotle then addresses that disagreement by discussing several *formal constraints* on anything that could properly serve as the final end.[38] One of these is that such an end must be something *active*: however noble one may be, a life in which one was inactive (in Aristotle's example, asleep the whole time) would not be the sort of life that we want (*NE* I.5, 1095b31–1096a2). Another is that it must be something reasonably within one's control: it cannot be a function of what other people are doing, or of how chance things happen to turn out, since a person's ultimate end would then have too little to do with that person and his own actions (I.5, 1095b23–6). Moreover, the ultimate end must of course be something for the sake of which we could adopt all of our other ends, and not itself adopted for the sake of any other end (I.7, 1097a15–b6). It also must not leave one missing anything important where one's central ends in life are concerned (I.7, 1097b6–21). And it must be a life that is a distinctly human form of life, and thus must exercise our practical rationality (I.7, 1097b22–1098a20).

Notice what all of the formal constraints on the ultimate end have in common: if any of them is unmet in a life, then that life is without some important good *for the person living it*. For instance, notice the requirement that the good life must be desirable to such a degree that it may be said to be lacking in nothing with respect to one's central ends. A life that is good in the sense of meeting this condition is Aristotle's proposal for the good life that can serve as our ultimate end in deliberation, answering to the demands we place on such an end from our own first-personal perspectives as livers of such lives.[39] As such, its value is deeply agent-relative.[40]

---

[38] We shall take a much closer look at these formal constraints in the next chapter.

[39] My point is not that it is *impossible* to read Aristotle as Haybron suggests, but that there is better reason not to, and forcing that reading on Aristotle obscures the possibility of just the alternative conception of eudaimonia I advance here.

[40] Aristotle's puzzling about whether or not we can be harmed after death (*NE* I.10) may induce the thought that his quarry is a life that is in some agent-neutral sense "choiceworthy" rather than *good for* the person whose life it is, in an agent-relative way. But it is worth noticing that he does not decide the issue; a more natural reading is that he is moved by the thought that we do see our well-being caught up in projects

This explains the centrality to Aristotle's outlook of practical wisdom and more generally the exercise of the virtues. For Aristotle, virtuous activity is an important good for a human, but not because without it one is an inferior specimen. It is important because anyone who thinks about his ultimate end without taking seriously his nature as an intelligent, emotional, and deliberating agent will live a life that is poorer for him, whether he realizes it or not.

This is an important point, but one that is often overlooked.[41] Aristotle's eudaimonism is not merely a theory about what happiness is, as if that question arose in a vacuum. Rather, it is a theory about what happiness is *given the centrality that Aristotle thinks happiness actually has in practical reasoning*. There really is a chasm between Perfectionism and an agent's own ends—but it is for precisely that reason that I think Perfectionism points us in the wrong direction for understanding what the good life consists in.

Return to the case of Angela, the diplomat considering the end of her career. Perhaps continuing her diplomatic work constitutes some sort of perfection that is of agent-neutral value, but in my view, as in Aristotle's, that certainly does not settle the question of what Angela has reason to do for the sake of living a good life. Perfection of that sort therefore cannot bring deliberation to a halt, so it cannot be what happiness is. Instead, the standard for wisdom here is: which option is congruent with the best life for Angela—that is, best agent-relatively?[42] Perhaps, arguably, *her* life will be better off for retirement. But it may also be the case that retirement would be less wise, because less good *for her*, if for instance it would involve a compromise on ends and commitments that Angela sees as giving her life meaning.[43] If so, then serving these ends and commitments contributes to her happiness. And that is the point: in order for eudaimonia to play its role in practical reasoning, it has to have *everything* to do with the agent's goals and the meaning she gives her life.[44]

---

that may survive us, and not sure just what to make of that thought. I thank Jason Raibley for pressing this point. I return to Aristotle's discussion of this puzzle in the next chapter.

[41] Sometimes this is overlooked because of interpretations that focus on Aristotle's conception of the good life as the life of contemplation (*theōria*), in *NE* X.6–8 (on which see notes to Chapter 3). I agree that the views expressed there are more amenable to being read as agent-neutral. My own view is that this is not the best reading of Aristotle's settled view, in part because of the vulnerability of such a reading to just the objections Haybron is pressing. But, obviously, I cannot argue for that here, and in the end the point is not what Aristotle intended but the agent-relative conception of the good life which certainly can be found in his work, as well as the work of Plato and the Stoics.

Furthermore, it is very likely that Perfectionist readings of eudaimonism and of Aristotle in particular are fueled by the supposition that Aristotle thinks of human nature as what nature has intended us to be (see e.g. MacIntyre 1981). On such an interpretation, the idea that virtue is necessary for happiness is easily taken for the idea that the virtues move us towards our natural *telos*, a kind of Perfection. I thank Laura Lenhart for this suggestion.

[42] See *NE* VI.5. It is important to note that this standard is not meant to provide the terms in which Angela is to deliberate.

[43] Recall the discussion of Tarzan in Chapter 1.

[44] Haybron (2008, 163) claims that "there is no credible sense, non-moral or otherwise, in which Angela, or her activities, would exhibit more excellence on the whole if she retired." This is too hasty: on my view, it

If the arguments of this section are sound, Haybron is right that Perfectionism cannot explain why one should seek Perfectionist "virtue" as opposed to other forms of self-development, and it cannot explain what such a good might have to do with one's happiness. However, it does not follow that there is no sense to be made of the idea that virtue is important for happiness. In particular, Aristotelian eudaimonism conceives of virtue, not as one kind of self-development among others, but the kind that makes it possible for any other kind of self-development to be part of a good life for creatures like us—creatures that live by practical reasoning and have emotions that can accord with practical rationality. Furthermore, Aristotelian eudaimonism holds that virtue is crucial for human life, not for the sake of our being good specimens, but for the sake of our happiness of a distinctively human sort.

4 Eudaimonia and *human* happiness

Understanding happiness as eudaimonia does not mean treating it as an agent-neutral good, like human perfection. Nonetheless, it does mean treating happiness as something distinctly *human*—but why think of happiness that way? Think again about the case of Angela. Clearly, what will be a good life for Angela depends crucially on what *Angela* is like—her unique make-up, we might say, and what she is such as to find fulfilling. But once we observe the importance of her unique make-up for her happiness, it may be difficult to see what else could matter. We might then make a bold generalization: happiness is "determined wholly by the particulars of the individual's make-up qua individual," and not at all by the attributes one shares with others qua human being.[45] We may agree that happiness involves fulfillment, but since happiness is a good life for the one living it, shouldn't such fulfillment be only the fulfillment of "the arbitrarily idiosyncratic make-up of the individual" (Haybron 2008, 193)?

The view that it should is what Haybron calls "welfare internalism," on which "the constituents of an agent's happiness are ultimately determined wholly by the particulars of the individual's make-up qua individual (vs. qua group or class member)" (2008, 157). The opposing view he calls "welfare externalism," on which an individual's happiness does not depend wholly on that individual's make-up. I trust it is obvious that my own view is what Haybron would call a kind of welfare externalism, and so his distinction raises a question that I ought to consider carefully: *why not* think that happiness depends *wholly* on individual make-up? Why think that happiness involves fulfillment and flourishing not only as a unique individual but *also* as a human being? Actually, I can think of several reasons—at least half a dozen.

is perfectly possible that Angela's decision to retire could exhibit precisely the sort of excellence in deliberation that counts as practical wisdom.

[45] Haybron 2008, 156–7. This is not to say, please note, that the question is whether Angela *thinks* that something would or would not make her happy as the individual she is. It is possible, after all, to be quite mistaken about such things. Haybron (chap. 9) does an excellent job of separating these two issues.

4.1 Happiness for humans

Consider an example from the documentary film *Crumb*, about underground cartoonist Robert Crumb. At one very memorable point in the film Crumb confesses to a former girlfriend that he never loved her, and indeed that he has never loved anyone; in fact, he says, he doesn't grasp the very idea of love. Likewise, his adult son says that although sometimes he would like to embrace his father—even just to shake his hand—his father "just can't do that." Suppose that all of this is true about Crumb, and his make-up is such that he is not capable of love. We can ask whether Crumb would be better off with love in his life. This is not to ask about Crumb's *judgment* on whether he would be better off; there is no reason to think that he must have the last word on his happiness, even if one is a welfare internalist. Rather, we can set aside what Crumb *thinks* and focus on what Crumb *is like*: would love make *that man* better off?

This question is importantly different from the question of whether, say, a new car would make Crumb better off: Crumb could still be the same unique individual if we gave him a new car, but to have love in his life he would have to change deeply in his make-up. So we can ask whether a new car would be fulfilling for *Crumb, given his unique make-up*, but the question whether love would be fulfilling for Crumb is precisely unlike that. After all, part of what makes Crumb the unique individual he is *just is* his incapacity to have love in his life. (Indeed, that is why his confession to his former girlfriend and his son's testimony are such important episodes in the documentary of his life.) Of course, a person's make-up changes over time, and perhaps Crumb could undergo such a massive change in his make-up as to become capable of love; call Crumb so transformed Crumb* to mark the difference. Furthermore, perhaps Crumb* would be better off than Crumb for having a capacity for love that Crumb lacks. But that is neither here nor there: our question is whether love would make *Crumb* better off, not Crumb*.

How does the welfare internalist answer this question? Well, if happiness is a function of a person's individual make-up and only that, then the question is ill-formed: we cannot ask whether Crumb would be happier with love in his life, because if he had love in his life then he would not have *Crumb's* individual make-up. Surprisingly, that is not even a question Crumb can ask himself. Crumb's happiness, on the internalist view, is his fulfillment given the make-up he has. And given the make-up he has, love is not part of *his* happiness.

But perhaps this is too quick: perhaps the internalist will say that if Crumb is really capable of becoming Crumb* by acquiring a capability for love, then that just *is* part of Crumb's "individual make-up."[46] That is true, but it does not help; in fact, the problem afflicting the internalist's strategy here is, ironically, similar to the under-specification problem facing Perfectionism. The very plasticity of the nature that the internalist draws our attention to here allows for an indefinite number of ways in which

---

[46] Haybron (2008, 185) makes a similar suggestion in another case.

we might retune our "emotional natures," without having the resources to tell better from worse ways of retuning where happiness is concerned. That is, some ways of making ourselves over allow for increases in happiness, but some do not, and internalism does not appear to have the resources to provide criteria to determine which is which. Externalism does, however. It can appeal to our shared nature as human beings, and to the process of shared reflection on those natures, and what makes us better off in light of our shared natures, to identify the lines of development that we find make us better off.

This is a serious problem for welfare internalism. When we ask whether Crumb is worse off for the absence of love from his life, one of the things we want to know is whether Crumb is worse off for *having* a make-up that is incapable of love. This question is not what counts as happiness-for-Crumb, but whether Crumb is capable of all the happiness there is reason for him to want for his own sake—perhaps whether he is capable of something that really counts as happiness at all. To think about *that* sort of question, we think about what matters in human life—what things are such important goods for human beings that life without them is a much poorer thing. In this sense, to say that a good like love is important for human happiness is to say something about what *we humans* are like. From this perspective, it is obvious that Crumb is significantly hampered in his potential for being well off. Of course, that likely gives us no license to interfere with his life. Moreover, Crumb himself may think we are crazy for thinking that there is anything he is missing. But that would not show that his potential for happiness has not been hampered. On the contrary, it would only show how deeply hampered it is.

The grain of truth in welfare internalism is this: if Crumb is not the sort of fellow to be capable of love, then perhaps those who care for him should not force the issue. Crumb is a subject with a welfare—he can be better or worse off—and we can do better or worse in trying to improve his welfare. There is such a thing as happiness-for-Crumb, after all, and that can matter. For those who interact with Crumb—including Crumb himself—it is important to know what sort of welfare he is capable of and what sort he is not. If he is the sort of fellow whose welfare just does not involve love, then it does not and that's that. After all, Crumb is just Crumb: make him comfortable, and leave him alone.

But notice that this is no more than what we say about the happiness of non-human animals. Like Crumb, a dog has a make-up and can be better or worse off. Many dogs enjoy living outdoors, but if Max is not like that, then that's that and it is no good making Max stay outside anyway. Furthermore, while many dogs are very affectionate, they are not capable of anything that counts as love; and that makes a dog's life no poorer. After all, a dog is just a dog; make it comfortable, and leave it alone.

So internalism does capture one way of thinking about happiness—happiness as a guide to "proper care and feeding," so to speak. But the problem is that that way of thinking about it falls too far short of capturing what happiness is *for us*. To live a flourishing human life is not merely to be better off—dogs, and for that matter ferns, can be better or worse off too. Surely those who care for Crumb would wish more for him than that he could be made comfortable and left alone—that would be a tragic conclusion. The optimistic possibility is that he could become the sort of person who could know what fully being a human is like. While this possibility may give them no reason to interfere with him, it is clearly a wish that he could experience real human happiness, to have the distinctive kind of happiness of which *humans* are capable.[47] To make sense of this further thought, we must attend to any potential Crumb might have for a better, more fulfilling make-up. This is a thought, not only about Crumb's individuality, but also about the *kind* of being he is: his humanity. And that is the point of welfare externalism.

4.2 Reasons to change

There is an analogy in Crumb's case to someone who is deaf. There is no point in urging the beauty of listening to Bach on someone who cannot hear. But if there is some possibility that a deaf person might acquire the ability to hear, and he is wondering whether he should do so, then the matter is different, and the urging is in order. As in the case of impaired hearing, it matters what the story is for Crumb's impaired capacity for love.

   If Crumb is not capable of becoming Crumb*, then his case is not relevant to those who *can* think about what will make them well off, given the normal range and panoply of capacities for human emotions and attachments. But suppose that he is capable of having Crumb*'s very different individual make-up. Is there a reason for him to pursue that possibility (by seeking the relevant therapy, say)? For some choices, deliberation cannot decide things one way or the other, and one might as well flip a coin. But this is not one of those cases. Crumb not only has a reason to choose, he also has a reason to choose on the basis of reasons, whatever choice he makes.

   Unfortunately, for reasons we have seen, welfare internalism can countenance no such reasons relevant to Crumb's happiness. For the internalist, Crumb's happiness *just is* his happiness with respect to his actual make-up—the make-up of Crumb, not Crumb*. On that view, therefore, there are no reasons for the sake of his happiness for Crumb to try to change, or indeed even to make a choice about whether to change or not. If Crumb can become Crumb*, it is only because Crumb shares the human panoply of capacities for emotions and attachments—it is his *humanity*, not his individuality, that opens this possibility. If Crumb has reasons for the sake of his happiness to change his individual make-up, this is not because of his individual make-up, but only because of features he shares with other human beings, such as the capacity to love. And if Crumb needs to choose for these reasons, again it can be only because he shares the capacity for rational agency that makes it possible for humans to do something about their make-up—in his case, becoming, in effect, Crumb*.

---

[47] See Darwall 2002, chap. 1, for a useful discussion of the distinction between caring about a person's happiness and respecting his dignity by not interfering with him.

This point about Crumb's reasons generalizes, since often what we deliberate about just is what sort of make-up to have and what sorts of things to find our happiness in. Rationality does not, as Haybron (2008, 193) suggests, contribute just by instructing us how to fulfill our commitments.[48] It contributes by directing choices and actions that make substantive changes to our natures, and our happiness. It is crucial to determining what commitments we ought to have. Curiously, the original impetus for internalism was the thought that one's individuality is reason-giving whereas one's humanity is not. But if there is such a thing as a reason to change one's individual make-up, then one's individuality is precisely what cannot give reasons of such a kind. So one's humanity must be reason-giving, too.

Now, before going any further, two brief points of clarification are in order here. One is that, as many readers will have noticed, in some cases the idea of *human* fulfillment will be too narrow. For instance, given what I have said here it makes sense for someone who is reckless in his choices to have reasons to change in that respect; but presumably this is because he is a *rational* agent, not specifically a rational *human* agent. This example reveals that speaking of "humanity" in this context is only a convenient simplification; that should be kept in mind.

However, it is also a harmless simplification: the important point for current purposes—the point that separates welfare externalists from internalists—is that one's belonging to certain kinds or classes, and not only one's individuality, must be reason-giving. Simply put, the issue is one's "kindedness," so to speak, not necessarily one's specifically *human* kindedness.[49] Furthermore, in many important cases any kind broader than humanity will be too broad. For instance, suppose that a race of non-human rational creatures were found to possess perceptual organs that enable them to have aesthetic experiences that make their lives richer, but which we humans lack. Further, suppose we learned that such organs could be implanted in humans. The relevant consideration for a human pondering such an implant is not that such capacities improve the lives of some rational creatures, but whether they would improve *human* life. Enhanced perceptual capacities may enrich the aliens' aesthetic experiences without doing the same for us; they may involve awareness of things in an expanded perceptual field that we would find distracting, disorienting, or over-stimulating.[50] So for this reason, as well as for the sake of simplicity, I shall generally speak of human kindedness in particular.

The other point of clarification is that welfare externalism does not assume that one necessarily has reasons to change in some way simply because it would involve becoming more statistically "normal" as a human being. For instance, externalism is

---

[48] I discuss this point at length in Chapter 1.

[49] E.g. Benjamin Yelle has suggested to me that the relevant group is not so much humans per se as creatures with the sort of cognitive, volitional, and psychological apparatus characteristic of what we might call "selfhood."

[50] Here I have benefited from discussion with Julia Annas and Guido Pincione.

neutral as to whether a deaf adult has a reason to have his hearing restored when the price of doing so is becoming cut off from a culture of deaf persons that has become an important part of his individuality.[51] After all, the need that each of us has to develop as a unique individual is itself a crucial part of our shared humanity. When individuality and statistical normality pull one in opposite directions, externalism does not prejudge which direction one ought to take. That is the role of practical wisdom, which—I say again—involves a normative conception of human nature; facts of human biology don't settle anything on questions like these. Even so, this gives nothing to the welfare internalist. What externalism urges is that persons pondering these sorts of changes be guided by the relevant normative considerations that are apt for creatures of their kind. By contrast, internalism seems to have nothing to offer by way of normative guidance.

4.3 Happiness and humane concern (or, Nussbaum's Paradox)

Happiness is best understood as human happiness for the following reason as well: externalism can make sense of certain genuine sentiments of concern for others, but internalism cannot. Martha Nussbaum has made an analogous point in connection with a paradoxical phenomenon among social scientists. On the one hand, many social scientists are moved by humane and democratic sentiments to make cultures sovereign where happiness is concerned. What counts as happiness is not a *human* question, the idea goes, but a *cultural* one; and only by taking this idea seriously can we have properly humane respect, regard, and concern for persons outside our culture. Unfortunately, the resulting view ends up undercutting the very sentiments that motivated it, by making happiness for such persons something foreign and in which we cannot share. Without such sharing, humane sentiments must then give way to "the sentiments of the tourist: wonder, curiosity, and amused interest" (Nussbaum 1992, 240). Without appeal to the humanity that we share, in many cases we cannot make sense of the idea that other humans *are* worse off as humans, since we must leave any "shared humanity" out of it and see them simply as *different* where their happiness is concerned. This phenomenon I shall call "Nussbaum's Paradox": those who make culture sovereign with respect to happiness start from and "trade tacitly on beliefs and related sentiments that their official view does not allow them."

An analogue of Nussbaum's Paradox is a problem for welfare internalism as well, in making, not cultures, but individuals sovereign where happiness is concerned. By making happiness wholly dependent on an individual's make-up to the exclusion of his humanity, welfare internalism can allow others only the sentiments of a tourist where that individual's happiness is concerned. As we have seen, the welfare internalist cannot make sense of the idea that Crumb would be better off if he were capable of loving others, and therefore cannot countenance any reasons Crumb might have for the sake of his happiness to try to develop such a capability. For the internalist, we

---

[51] I thank Elizabeth Philips for the example, and Mark LeBar for useful correspondence on it.

could not recommend the change as helping Crumb (or rather, Crumb*) to experi- ence "human happiness"—it is Crumb's individuality that is authoritative here, not his humanity. So instead of recommending therapy to Crumb, say, we look at him in wonder and curiosity and hope that he is well off, whatever that means in this case— just as we might with Max the dog, or even the fern in the pot. We lack any rational basis even for asking what might make him any better off than that. And that is to say that we must regard Crumb with nothing more than the sentiments of a tourist.

This point is important, because the world is absolutely *full* of people in just this predicament of living with a make-up that keeps them from having goods that otherwise really would benefit them. After all, that is precisely what gives many goods their particular importance, as in the case of education: to consume that good is to seize opportunities to discover what one might gain by growing into a sort of person that one is not already. To be sure, sometimes we discover what we were already such as to find happiness in, but often there just is no answer to the question what a person would be suited to prior to his beginning to make choices from among available options. In these cases what we find is the new person we become through choosing and living with our choices, and what things that new person is such as to find happiness in. Yet if a person's happiness were exhausted by his individual make-up, then there would be no reasons for the sake of his happiness to care about his access to those goods whose very point is to *change* that make-up.[52]

4.4 Happiness and autonomy

We saw earlier in this chapter (section 1.2) that autonomy is important for happiness. About this Haybron and I agree. When the judgment that one is happy is based on manipulation or brainwashing, say, "it isn't really *us* responding to our lives: our happiness is not autonomous."[53] More specifically, Haybron says that self-fulfillment requires that "happiness not be based on values that are manipulated," or on activities that one is forced to do (as in the case of slavery, for instance), or on pathological functioning (as in the case of someone perpetually high on feel-good drugs; 2008, 186, 191).

---

[52] I think the same issue separates Jeremy Bentham and John Stuart Mill. Bentham is famously described as holding that "push-pin is as good as poetry" (see Bentham 1830, 206; for the phrase, see Mill 1859, 389); for Bentham, happiness depends entirely on one's individual make-up, and this seems very democratic and broad-minded. By contrast, Mill thinks our humanity makes us capable of deeper and more rewarding happiness—in appreciating things like art, literature, and philosophy—so that each of us has a reason to become capable of such happiness (see esp. Mill 1863, 8–17). Now, because of this difference, it seems to me that on Bentham's view, there turn out to be no reasons for the sake of happiness to increase people's exposure to things like art, literature, or philosophy, as long as they are already comfortable. By contrast, on Mill's view we would generally make people happier by creating opportunities to become capable of enjoying more sophisticated pursuits. Consequently, Bentham's interest in the public's happiness, I think, devolves into the mere sentiment of a tourist, whereas Mill's remains genuinely humane. The difference matters: Mill can explain, I think, why communities have reasons to increase access to things like education and the arts much more readily than Bentham can.

[53] Haybron 2008, 185, italics in original.

But while Haybron's endorsement of autonomy is sound, his welfare internalism does not entitle him to make it. To see this, we should ask why autonomy in even the thin sense Haybron has in mind would ever be necessary for happiness in the first place. The answer is simply that it *isn't* always necessary for happiness full stop, but only for *human* happiness. Consider dogs again. Max has an individual make-up—some things will make him happy and others will not—and one can make Max better off by looking to that individual make-up. But it makes no sense to think that Max should perhaps be autonomous in his happiness: a dog is just not that kind of thing. (What would it mean to say that Max's happiness should be based on values that are not the result of manipulation?) So when autonomy is important for a human's happiness, this cannot be for the mere fact that humans each have an individual make-up and can be better or worse off with respect to that make-up. Rather, autonomy is important for a human's happiness because a human is a creature *of such a nature* that autonomy is necessary for the happiness of creatures of that type. Only human beings are capable of determining what they do on the basis of reasons in the first place; that feature of us is what opens up the possibility of "inauthenticity" or "heteronomy" in action, and that possibility is what gives autonomy its significance. The capacity for autonomy is therefore a property we share in virtue of the kind of being we are. So autonomy is important for a human, not qua being with an individual make-up but qua *human*. So welfare internalism cannot explain the importance of autonomy for happiness any more than welfare subjectivism can.

However, perhaps we could extend internalism the courtesy of an even thinner conception of autonomy that applies to all individuals with a make-up, dogs as well as humans. Perhaps all the "autonomy" that well-being requires is enough freedom from interference so that one can live in accordance with one's individual make-up—a freedom to be oneself, if you like—whatever the provenance of that make-up, and even dogs may need to be free in that sense. A being that is just a brain in a vat "is liable to strike us as pathetic," Haybron says, "failing badly to fulfill its nature" because it is responding not to its life but to a "mirage" (2008, 190). Even though Max is not capable of autonomy in any very robust sense, he is surely capable of living his own life, and a dog-brain-in-a-vat would indeed seem a pathetic thing for not living so. Since even Max does seem to be better off with the freedom to be himself, perhaps that freedom is important for a creature's well-being simply qua having an individual make-up.

But while this thinner form of "autonomy" suffices for dogs, it will not do for humans. Dogs and humans both need freedom to be themselves, but humans need the freedom to be themselves *by* exercising practical reasoning, by experiencing complex emotions, by making choices and living with their implications. Put another way, the kind of freedom that humans need to be themselves just *is* autonomy in Haybron's more robust sense, and it is important for a human, not just as a creature with a make-up, but as a creature with a distinctly *human* make-up. Insofar as autonomy is normative—insofar as it gives one reason to live or choose one way or another—it is so only for creatures that can respond to norms and act on reasons. It is because individuals are of a kind that has that capacity—that is, it is because they are human—that not being brainwashed or manipulated matters for their well-being.

Moreover, just as autonomy of this sort is crucial to well-being, it is crucial as well to human selfhood. To have a self in the way that humans do is to choose and act and live through the exercise of practical reasoning; in other words, autonomy is inseparable from human selfhood. Because dogs are not autonomous, there is no "self" that a dog has, even though a dog can have an individual make-up and be better or worse off. For a human, however, well-being requires the fulfillment not merely of whatever individual make-up one happens to have, but the fulfillment of a make-up that genuinely counts as a *self* of the sort that is characteristic of human beings. Indeed, Haybron takes the self in self-fulfillment to be a self by which one has an understanding of one's identity and life (2008, 184). But to say that well-being requires the fulfillment of such a self is to say that human well-being requires the fulfillment *of a distinctly human self.* Other welfare subjects simply do not have a self in anything like that sense.

So in order to make autonomy and selfhood important for human well-being, welfare internalism needs to smuggle in the centrality of one's humanity to one's well-being—the very idea that internalism rules out and that welfare externalism consists in.

4.5 The value of a richer life

There is a similar point to be made with respect to Haybron's claim that happiness depends in part on the "richness" of one's life. Haybron says plausibly that happiness is a greater good for one the "richer" it is (ceteris paribus), that is, the more one's happiness "is grounded in richer, more complex ways of living. For such ways of living more fully express one's nature" (2008, 186). Given his welfare internalism, by "expressing one's nature" Haybron must have in mind ways of living that more fully express one's individual make-up, not one's humanity. So, for example, if Fred is the sort of person who can find happiness in playing push-pin and in reading poetry, then on this criterion Fred would be better off devoting himself more to poetry than to push-pin (ceteris paribus), since (let's suppose) devoting more time to poetry would yield a richer and more complex way of living for Fred.

But whatever the merits of the richness criterion, it is clearly a poor fit with welfare internalism, because it is not clear what greater complexity has to do with more fully expressing Fred's nature as an individual. If Fred's individual make-up is such that he finds no more happiness in poetry than in push-pin, *and* if Fred's happiness depends entirely on his individual make-up, then it is very difficult to see what difference the greater complexity of reading poetry could make with respect to Fred's happiness. Surely it is because Fred shares the *human* property of being able to develop in complex and challenging ways that it makes sense to count richness as important for his happiness. Of course, one is always free to simply *stipulate* the richness criterion, but the point is that there is nothing in the internalist account to explain *why* there should be such a criterion in the first place, for any such explanation would have to advert to an aspect of our shared humanity.

Furthermore, observe that the welfare internalist must understand a "richer" activity as more complex than other activities *that also express one's individual nature*, not as more fully expressive of one's *human* nature. Thus, the richness condition requires that one not be a stunted version of oneself, but it still allows that one might be a stunted human being. This is the very problem with Crumb that we saw above: on the internalist view, as long as Crumb finds happiness in the things that his make-up is such as to find happiness in, he should be as well off—and as richly well off—as he could be. But he is a stunted human, and his life is poorer for it even though—indeed, precisely because—he is incapable of understanding what makes it poorer. Only welfare externalism can make sense of that kind of poverty.

4.6 Happiness and emotional fulfillment

My final argument concerns the importance for happiness of being emotionally fulfilled. There can be no question, I think, but that happiness involves emotional fulfillment, and I think Haybron offers an especially subtle and compelling account of such fulfillment. He argues that this fulfillment is best understood as a long-term, broadly positive emotional condition, a "stance of psychic affirmation," which is "not merely a state of one's consciousness" but "more like a state of one's being—not just a pleasant experience, or a good mood, but *psychic affirmation* or, in more pronounced forms, *psychic flourishing*" (2008, 182, italics in original). This is the fulfillment of one's "emotional nature," that is, fulfillment as a unique individual who is "disposed characteristically to be happy in certain circumstances and not others" (2008, 184). Furthermore, Haybron argues that such fulfillment is crucial to one's happiness (or what he calls well-being; see esp. 2008, 179–82). On Haybron's view, there is a deep connection between happiness and the "self" insofar as the things that (would) make one happy are central to the self. For that reason, emotional fulfillment is a central aspect of a person's happiness.

Surely that is true, but I think we can make much *better* sense of that point by recognizing the importance our humanity has for our happiness. When we talk about psychic affirmation or flourishing, we mean at least that a person views his life with joy rather than sorrow or regret, and feels a sense of satisfaction with his life and a sense of engagement in his central activities.[54] This way of thinking about psychic affirmation has two important implications: one, happiness is diminished if certain forms of emotional experience are missing from one's life; and two, happiness is diminished if one's emotional experience is of the wrong kind. The first point is one we have seen already in the case of Robert Crumb: because Crumb cannot love others, he cannot experience the emotions associated with love, either. That way of psychically affirming

---

[54] This is the idea behind Aristotle's thesis that pleasure, which for Aristotle is a genus of certain human emotions (*Rhetoric* II.1), is what "completes" activity (*NE* X.4).

the relationships in one's life is one that Crumb cannot have, and that lack makes Crumb worse off, whether he thinks so or not. Of course, dogs are not capable of those emotions, either, but they are no worse off for it. So the importance of such emotions to human happiness stems not from the fact that a human has an individual make-up but from the fact that one is a human rather than some other kind of creature. That is a point the externalist, not the internalist, is in position to make.

The second point is this. If an adult were to have an emotional nature that was roughly that of a child, say, this would be a serious hindrance to his capacity for human happiness, even if that childish emotional nature were as "fulfilled" as it could be. Consider Chance the gardener (a.k.a. Chauncey Gardiner), portrayed by Peter Sellers in the film *Being There*. Chance is a sunny but simple-minded middle-aged man who, for instance, would still rather watch cartoons on TV than make love to a beautiful woman (or even notice her in the room). Chance seems to be about as emotionally fulfilled as he can be, and that is not trivial—which of us, after all, can say the same? But even so, the emotional fulfillment of which Chance is capable is a poor thing; he is a curiosity for us, not an object of envy. And the reason for this is that Chance is incapable of a normal emotional life for *the kind of creature he is*, namely an adult human being. Chance has an individual make-up and can be better or worse off, but to be capable of real human happiness Chance's emotional nature would need to be, well, more human.

We can further appreciate these points by noticing something significant about the kind of life we wish for our children.[55] We do not wish for them a life of pleasant sensations, or of constant bliss. That would be unrealistic and unnatural for beings of our kind; they would not be human lives.[56] Moreover, we would not wish for them the life of Genghis Khan, however successful or delighted a tyrant he might have been. Now, Haybron takes this point, but dismisses its significance as not relevant to, and in fact more important than, our concerns for our children's happiness (2008, 160). But I do not think so. It is because we care for our children as we do—that is, for their own sakes—that we want them to have lives that *they* experience as choice-worthy and good, as lives that it is *good for them* to live. If it isn't their happiness that is at stake, I don't know what it is. And we see the contours of such lives as fixed by the kinds of being they are. We do not wish for them happiness as appropriate for a dog, or for Crumb, or for Chance, or for Genghis Khan. To be sure, there will be many reasons that we do not want the life of Genghis Khan for our children: such a life would be morally horrific, disgustingly violent and bloody, and so on. However, those are reasons not to wish that life for *anyone*, whereas by focusing on what we would or would not wish for *our own* children, we occupy the perspective of someone whose primary interest is in their welfare. From that perspective, it becomes clear that we

---

[55] Cf. Kraut 1979; Hursthouse 1999, 174–7.

[56] For the same reason, Aristotle rejects the suggestion that we could wish for our friends that they were gods (*NE* VIII.7, 1159a3–8), and thus non-human.

want for them well-being and fulfillment of the sort of life possible for human beings, given the kinds of capacities adult human beings are normally capable of, and we want it for them for *their* own sake. So if emotional fulfillment has anything to do with human well-being, it must be understood along externalist lines.

◇ ◇ ◇

In a scene from the movie *As Good as it Gets*, a man suffering from obsessive-compulsive disorder reaches a point of utter despair during a visit to his therapist. As he storms out of the office, he shouts to the other downcast patients in the waiting-room, "What if this is as good as it gets?" The point can be seen in his and everyone else's face: there is a world of difference between a *happy* life and a life that is *as good as it's going to get*. What welfare internalism captures is what makes a life as good as it's going to get: *given* the individual make-up one has, being fulfilled with respect to that make-up is the best one can hope for. And that is, to be sure, a valuable thing to know. But it is another question what happiness is, and only thinking about our humanity can give us the resources to bridge the gap.

And so Aristotle said famously that any adequate conception of human happiness must always keep in view the mode of living that is distinctive of human beings (what he calls their *ergon* or "function"; *NE* I.7, 1097b22–1098a20). This is not because Aristotle thought that happiness is the perfection of human capabilities. It is because we can never hope to give an adequate account of human happiness unless we first say what is *human* about human happiness. And about that I think he was exactly right.

So far, then, I have located the basic concept I want to deploy in thinking about happiness: eudaimonia, or a good life for the person living it that is also the final end for practical reasoning. Now I can begin to say just what I think happiness is—my "conception" of that concept.

3

Happiness and Virtuous Activity

So far I have clarified the basic *concept* of happiness that I am using—eudaimonia—but I have not yet given my own *conception* of it. However, even philosophers who agree that happiness is both the final end for deliberation (Chapter 1) and a life of both individual and human fulfillment (Chapter 2) might still disagree with the claim I now want to put forward in the rest of this book, namely that happiness is a life of virtuous activity. Actually, that is much too stark a way of putting my thesis, which involves some very crucial qualifications that will occupy me in the next chapter and, in fact, the rest of the book. But regardless of how that thesis is qualified, surely the elephant in the room is *the very idea* that virtue could have so much to do with happiness in the first place. This chapter is about that very idea.

The problem is perfectly easy to see, as Aristotle's critics will be quick to point out. On any garden-variety view of virtuous activity—roughly, some range of stereotypical "good deeds"—the question whether virtuous activity is somehow central to happiness has such an obvious answer that we should by mystified that anyone ever thought they had to ask. And yet, the objection goes, Aristotle says that virtuous activity is of major importance for eudaimonia, so either he just cannot mean by "eudaimonia" what we mean by "happiness," or else he must be confused about what kind of good happiness is. From this perspective on virtuous activity, Aristotle's critics make exactly the right objection.[1] The trouble, though, is that such a perspective could not be farther from Aristotle's actual view of the virtues. On the contrary, by beginning with the concept of happiness that I outlined in the previous chapter, we can arrive at a much more sophisticated way of thinking about virtuous activity—and about what virtuous activity has to do with happiness. That is some of the gold that is still in Aristotle's hill.

1 Being happy and being human

Even before tackling the very idea that happiness is a life of virtuous activity, with or without further qualifications, we must first address the more basic idea that happiness

---

[1] Philosophers sometimes suppose that ancient eudaimonists made this rather desperate move of introducing the virtues into their account of well-being because, having developed an agent-centered account of the good, they then realized that they had to figure out what to say about morality, with its other-regarding focus (e.g. Crisp 2008, § 5.2).

should be understood mainly in terms of *activity* at all. Why not think of happiness by beginning instead with some kind of *state*, say, whether a mental state like pleasure, or a state of having (certain of) one's desires satisfied?

Now, we might have thought that as soon as we began to think of happiness as eudaimonia, we had already left behind the idea that happiness could be a good like pleasure or desire-satisfaction. In fact, though, eudaimonism about happiness is formally neutral on that issue. To be sure, what eudaimonism says is that human happiness is just that: the happiness *of a human*. But eudaimonism as such does not say what human nature *is*, and so the view of human nature that we take will make an enormous difference in our conception of human happiness, even understood as eudaimonia.

Consequently, the way to begin developing a conception of happiness in general, and the idea that happiness is something active in particular, is by reflecting on what we humans are. As we do so it will be important to remember the point made in the previous chapter, namely that this is not to begin outside of normative inquiry. Our aim here is not to try to reveal some value-neutral "nature," but to determine what things are so important to our humanity that we cannot understand a good human life without them.[2]

1.1 Human nature

Human life is active: we have ends, we make plans, we put plans into action, and the upshot is that our lives are full of day-to-day activities, but also activities in the broader sense of the major relationships and projects we get involved in, and which are the point of most of the day-to-day activities in the narrower sense. So, a fortiori, a happy human life is also an active life, in both the narrower and the broader sense. But here we come to a crucial question: even if a happy *life* is active, does that mean that the *happiness* of that life is something active? Suppose we could watch the course of a person's life, and we wanted to focus on the happiness (or unhappiness) of that life. What should we look for—what should we be "tracking" as this life unfolds? This person's life is one of activity; is the *activity* what we should track in order to tell whether it is a happy life? Perhaps so: perhaps, that is, there is something to be said for focusing on what this person does with his life when we think about whether his life is a happy one. But perhaps we should focus on something else instead, such as how things go for this person in his life: whether it is pleasant, whether (certain of) his desires are satisfied, whether he has good fortune, or what have you. Of course, this is not to ask which focus should be our *exclusive* focus. Humans are both agents and patients, so even when we focus on activity and agency, this must be understood as the agency of someone *who is also* a patient; and likewise, *mutatis mutandis*, for a focus on "patiency," so to speak. So what should be our focus? Agency? Patiency? Both equally?

---

[2] For this way of framing the task, see Nussbaum 1995.

Aristotle raises this question at the beginning of *Nicomachean Ethics* I.10, when he considers the advice of the Athenian law-giver Solon that we should never judge another person's life to be happy while that person is alive: after all, until a person has died, there is always time for his fortunes to change (1100a10–13). Aristotle takes the point, since it seems obvious that misfortunes not only can be terrible in their own right, but also can get in the way of what one is doing with one's life (I.8). However, Solon's advice suggests that we should "track" (*synakolouthoiēmen*, I.10, 1100b4) a person's fortunes in order to assess his happiness (or otherwise),[3] and Aristotle finds this to lead to a couple of puzzles. For one thing, not only can a person's fortunes change while he is still alive, but it seems that there is time for them to change even *after* he has died (1100a13–30). After all, among people's desires are desires for all kinds of states of affairs in the more distant future, and many of these desires—for instance, that things go a certain way for one's children—extend well past one's own lifetime. But in that case, tracking a person's fortunes means allowing that certain events can actually reverse the happiness of a life already finished.[4]

Another puzzle is that even if we look at only those changes of fortune that occur within a person's lifetime, it seems that we must either sometimes rewrite history, as if a person for whom things went well for fifty years cannot be considered to have been happy even during that time, because of the misfortunes that occurred later; or else we must say that happiness lasts only as long as the good fortunes do, in which case it seems to come and go, and there is really no more answer to the question whether a person's *life* is happy than there is to the question what color a chameleon is (I.10, 1100a32–b7).

So Aristotle finds Solon's advice paradoxical, and he seems to be unsure just what to say about it in the end.[5] What does seem clear, though, is that while Aristotle agrees that fortunes matter for happiness, he nonetheless finds these puzzles to be definitive strikes against making fortunes our main *focus* when we think about happiness. Rather, Aristotle says, we should focus on agency, that is, not on how things go within an active life but on the activities themselves (I.10, 1100b7–11).

However, that does not follow, for a couple of reasons. For one thing, even if Aristotle can show that we should not focus on patiency, it does not follow that we should focus on agency, either; it may be that happiness depends on both, neither any more than the other. And for another, Aristotle has not even shown that we should not focus on patiency, since there are other ways of focusing on patiency besides tracking a person's fortunes. For instance, as Epicurus would later make clear, we might focus instead on a person's pleasures, which both last only as long as his life does and can be extremely stable, at least if pleasure is understood to be a sort of tranquility or peaceful

---

[3] Cp. the view discussed in Plato's dialogue *Euthydemus*, put forward by Socrates' young interlocutor, Cleinias, that happiness is something brought about simply by amassing good things like health and wealth and social position. I discuss this dialogue in Chapter 6.

[4] See also Griffin 1986, 17.

[5] Not surprisingly, this question remains controversial. See e.g. Griffin 1986, 23, 317–18; Sumner 2000, 7–9.

calm, and if people can acquire a high degree of control over such tranquility. Somewhat more precisely, Epicurus took human happiness to consist entirely in the absence of all physical pain and mental anxiety.[6] This state of perfect tranquility or *ataraxia*—literally, the absence of all distress (*tarachē*)—he identified as the pleasure upon which no improvement is either possible or desirable. In fact, Epicurus went so far as to say that the gods' lives are the perfect ideals of happiness insofar as the gods are completely inactive and troubled neither by any desire to act nor by the business of acting itself.[7] Happiness, on Epicurus' view, isn't anything *active* at all. And of course, if happiness does not consist in activity then (a fortiori) it does not consist in virtuous activity, either. Now, Epicurus did believe that for humans the virtues are both necessary and even sufficient for happiness, since they aid us in avoiding painful excesses, worries, and anxieties, thereby making possible the tranquil state that happiness is.[8] But of course, he vigorously denied that virtuous activity is any *part* of happiness whatsoever.[9] Eudaimonism just as such doesn't do anything to rule out this sort of possibility, and neither do Aristotle's paradoxes.

However, eudaimonism does take happiness to be a life, not just of individual, but of *human* fulfillment, so to accept a view like Epicurus', or Solon's, is to agree that by nature humans are above all else *patients*. And this, I think, reveals what is really at the bottom of Aristotle's focus on agency, namely his view of human nature: if we are to identify happiness—that is, if we are to identify genuine human fulfillment—then we should focus on what defines us as humans, and that is our agency, not our patiency. That this view is Aristotle's is clear, I think, from a couple of things. One is of course his well-known view that practical rationality is our characteristic human "function" (*ergon*). A human life, by nature, is "a practical sort of life of what possesses reason," and to be human is to be active in accordance with practical reason. From this Aristotle concludes that human happiness is a life of activity in accordance with practical reason (*NE* I.7, 1098a3–18). Likewise, Aristotle holds that loving oneself is primarily loving that element in one that thinks and is intelligent about practical things (IX.4, 1166a17–19). This is the role of practical wisdom (*phronēsis*), by which one deliberates well about what is beneficial for people, including the good life itself (VI.5, 1140a26–28). And it is also our nature to construct our lives as organized systems of ends, and in so doing to create ourselves—so that "in a way, the work *is* the maker in actuality" (IX.7, 1168a7).

Aristotle's belief that our agency defines us and our capacity for happiness is also clear from his view that even though having and enjoying good things is necessary for happiness, something will count as a *good* thing for someone only insofar as practical

---

[6] DL X.128–32, 136; *Principal Doctrines* III, XVIII–XX; *Vatican Sayings* 42; Cicero, *Fin.* I.37–8; Lucretius, *On the Nature of the Universe* II.1–61 (= LS 21W); Porphyry, *On Abstinence* 1.51 (= IG I-139).

[7] DL X.76–7, 97; Cicero, *On the Nature of the Gods* I.51–6.

[8] See esp. DL X.132–3 (*Letter to Menoeceus*), 138; *Principal Doctrines* V, XVII; *Vatican Sayings* 7, 54, 70–1.

[9] See DL X.138; *Principal Doctrines* X, XXXI–XXXIX; Cicero, *TD* III.41–2, V.87–8; *Fin.* I.25, 42–3, 54, II.19–20, 35, IV.49–50; *Acad.* II.131; Athenaeus, *Deipnosophists* (*Logic-Choppers*) 12, 547a (= IG I-151); Lucretius, *On the Nature of the Universe* V.1105–57.

reasoning enables it to occupy the right sort of place in his life.[10] For other sorts of animals, all it takes for them to be better off is to be *recipients* of good things; that is to say, what defines them, their mode of living, and their well-being is just their patiency. On Aristotle's view, though, things are different with us: there is no fact of the matter whether some windfall counts as good fortune except in relation to eudaimonia, a good human life—and things are beneficial for us in that way only insofar as we *make* them beneficial through the successful exercise of practical rationality.

But is that really how it is with us? We might have thought instead that some goods make our lives better just on their own strength—for instance, isn't love exactly that kind of good? Actually, I don't think so. Suppose for instance that two people fall deeply in love with each other. Are their lives better for it? Well, we surely must say, it depends. Perhaps one of them is pathologically dependent on the other; perhaps they are so consumed with one another that they lose their other close relationships; or perhaps their circumstances make it impossible for them to be together but they go on torturing themselves with their unrequited passion.[11] The fact that "it depends" on considerations like these is very important: it shows that before even such a wonderful thing as a loving connection between two people can be part of the good life of either of them, there must be the exercise of wisdom to give that relationship the right place in their lives in the first place.

Now, on this view of human nature, it becomes clear why agency is what we should track when we think about the happiness of a human life. In particular, such a view of human nature makes it difficult to take seriously the idea that agency might be no more important, not to mention less important, than patiency where happiness is concerned (the two possibilities, we saw above, that Aristotle brushes past). For once we appreciate the difference that our agency makes for the sorts of patients we are, we must appreciate that in fact it makes *all* the difference in the world. To be a patient who is also an agent is not to be two things instead of just one—both a patient (in a way that a dog might be) and also an agent (which a dog is not). It is instead to be a radically different *kind* of patient. For instance, the need for autonomy and self-direction in a happy human life is a need that we have as agents and not merely as patients, and that need makes a radical difference with respect to what can count as genuine happiness *for a human*. Simply put, once we realize that our agency makes *some* difference for our happiness, we cannot stop there—we have to go on to see that what it actually makes is a *radical* and *defining* difference for our happiness.

Furthermore, the very arguments for thinking that our happiness requires our fulfillment as humans (Chapter 2) are also arguments that our agency defines the

[10] See *NE* I.10, 1100a24–9; III.4, 1113a22–33; IV.1, 1120a4–8; V.9, 1137a26–30; VII.13, 1153b21–5; X.6, 1176b23–7; *EE* VII.15, 1248b31–2; *Pol.* VII.13, 1332a22–7. I discuss these texts in Chapter 5. This is an important point, one that is entirely missed by construals of eudaimonism as beginning with some independent notion of good or worthwhile things, and then identifying happiness with a life that has those things (e.g. Telfer 1980, chap. 2).

[11] This is the unfortunate story of Werther's love for Lotte in Goethe's *The Sorrows of Young Werther*.

kinds of patients we are, and the distinctive way in which our patiency matters for our happiness. It makes sense to say of humans that they can lack the right kind of patiency for happiness—by having an emotional life that is seriously incomplete, say, or immature[12]—and therefore that humans have *reasons* to be certain kinds of patients rather than other kinds. For the sake of happiness, we can have reasons to change our patiency, if we are able, as well as reasons to wish for improved patiency for others. For the sake of happiness, human patiency must be autonomous, rather than manipulated or duped, and amenable to right reason rather than controlling or alienating. For the sake of happiness, human patiency needs to be in touch with a world rich with things we have reasons to value—beauty, other people, ourselves. For the sake of happiness, human patiency needs the satisfaction, not just of desires per se, but of those desires that enter our lives by way of the things we most dearly care about.[13] For the sake of happiness, we must think, not only about getting the things we want (e.g. to take up a prestigious title), but also, and importantly, about the choices we make to get them (e.g. to take up that title at what cost).[14] In sum, where happiness is concerned we are, to be sure, patients and not just agents. Nonetheless, it is in virtue of our being agents that even our fulfillment as patients must be understood as the fulfillment of *patients who are also agents.*

Consequently, on this view our agency defines our happiness in at least two ways: it defines what kind of thing our happiness is (mamely a life of activity), and it defines what role our patiency might have with respect to our happiness. I shall call the broad view that our happiness is defined by our status as agents the *rational self-construction* view.

It is no great surprise that this broad view of human nature has predominated in the eudaimonist tradition. For instance, it is apparent in many of Plato's dialogues, perhaps nowhere more clearly than the *Euthydemus*. To his young interlocutor's claim that happiness comes from having things like health, wealth, and social position, Socrates quickly replies that none of those things does us any good unless we use it (280c–e), and indeed that using such things does us no good either unless we use them well (280e–281a). Socrates concludes from this that human happiness is something that is active and defined by our capacity for practical intelligence—indeed, he takes practical intelligence to be our greatest good, perhaps even our only good (281c–282a). Clearly, then, Socrates takes our status as agents to be what defines our happiness and even our status as patients.[15]

Likewise, the Stoics too hold that human nature is rational self-construction. For instance, Seneca represents the Stoic position as understanding human nature to be essentially a rational nature, in the sense that the fulfillment of our nature is the

---

[12] These were the problems with Crumb and Chance, respectively (Chapter 2).

[13] See Griffin 1986, chaps. 1–2.

[14] I discuss such an example in Chapter 1, section 3.

[15] On Plato's Socrates, see Chapter 6.

fulfillment of practical rationality. All animals, Seneca argues, have an overriding drive to preserve themselves, and humans are no exception, but as humans develop they find that the self they are driven to preserve is above all a rational self (*Ep.* 121, see also 124; Cicero, *Fin.* III.16–23). "When reason has been given to rational animals as a more perfect governor of life," the Stoics say, "then for them the life according to reason becomes what is natural for them" (DL VII.86). This is the sense in which the Stoics said, famously, that happiness is living "according to nature," that is, according to our nature as rational beings.[16] The drive to preserve oneself is therefore transformed into a need to act and choose rationally—which just is to preserve what we really are.[17] This means that it is our nature to be practically rational, and so happiness—the fulfillment of our nature—must consist in our living our lives with practical wisdom.[18]

The rational self-construction view has been predominant among modern eudaimonists as well. For instance, Martha Nussbaum has argued that what benefits us as patients benefits us only insofar as our patiency is transformed by our agency. As Nussbaum observes, among all the various aspects of human nature there are some that are "architectonic," insofar as they shape, construct, and "interpenetrate" the rest of our nature. These architectonic functions are our planning and structuring our lives, and our doing so with each other. By contrast, the other features of our nature—such as our capacity for pleasure—only become part of a good life insofar as they are directed by practical wisdom.[19]

Likewise, Rosalind Hursthouse argues that enjoyment is necessary for human happiness, but that this must be understood as the kind of enjoyment that is characteristic of our kind, namely, creatures who can respond to reasons. What is distinctive of human nature given our practical rationality, Hursthouse argues, is the deep fact that we can genuinely transform our lives and even what we take human nature to be:

Our way of going on is just one, which remains the same across all areas of our life. Our characteristic way of going on, which distinguishes us from all the other species of animals, is a rational way. A "rational way" is any way that we can rightly see as good, as something we have reason to do. Correspondingly, our characteristic enjoyments are any enjoyments we can rightly see as good, as something we in fact enjoy *and* that reason can rightly endorse. (1999, 222, italics in original)

Finally, notice that while being a patient gives a dog something to live for, just like that, living for something benefits us only if it amounts to living as rational creatures do, as Mark LeBar has argued:

Your good lies in the realization of ends that are fashioned according to practical wisdom—including, first and foremost, the development and nurture of yourself as a creature who is

---

[16] DL VII.87–9; see Frede 1999, 79–84.

[17] Cf. Hursthouse 1999, chap. 10.

[18] The Stoics referred to this transformative process as *oikeiōsis*, "familiarization" or "appropriation." I shall say more about it in Chapter 7.

[19] See Nussbaum 1990, 219–26; see also 1988, 1992, and 1993.

capable of assimilating the tumult of your impulses into a coherent schedule of ends and plans for realizing them. (2004, 206)

On this view, one's happiness as a unique patient is something that one constantly defines by adopting and pursuing ends in accordance with practical reason (LeBar 2004, 204–6).

1.2 Two corollaries

A corollary of the conception of human nature as rational self-construction is the thesis that human happiness is a life of activity. This is because humans are by nature active creatures who live by practical reason. Human action and practical reason are inseparable: humans do not merely *behave*, but rather they *act* because they are capable of reflecting on their impulses and feelings and can—indeed *must*—find reasons for the things they do and the ways they feel.[20] It is our status as agents of this kind that defines human nature and happiness. Now, I have argued that happiness is a life in which one is fully human, and since our nature is above all else an active nature, happiness must therefore be, above all else, a life of *activity*. So we can summarize this corollary: since human nature is rational self-construction, human happiness is first and foremost a life of *activity*, whatever else it may turn out to be.

Now, what *kind* of activity must human happiness be a life of? This brings us to a second corollary of the rational self-construction view. Begin again with the idea that we are *rational and emotional* creatures, creatures in whom action and emotion are both shaped by practical rationality. To be fulfilled as that kind of creature is to be active in accordance with practical wisdom and emotional soundness, since that is how practical rationality functions in a distinctively human way. So the second corollary is this: the activity that human happiness is, is activity in accordance with practical wisdom and emotional soundness, whatever else that activity may be. This corollary means that our status as agents with practical rationality is what defines our happiness, above any other fact about us. It also means that acting with wisdom and sound emotions is a *constituent* of happiness, and not merely a means to it.

Now, it is important to observe that nothing I have said entails that such activity is the *only* constituent of happiness, or that it has no need of other goods that are outside our control. In other words, nothing I have said takes either one side or the other on the heated ancient debate over whether virtuous activity is sufficient for happiness.[21] Even so, this way of thinking about human nature has already moved us a little closer to saying more precisely what human happiness is. It has done so by telling us some things that happiness must be, whatever else it might be. Not surprisingly, Aristotle himself approached a conception of happiness by this method as well—that is, by formulating

---

[20] The human need for reasons to act is what Korsgaard calls "the problem of the normative" (1996, 93).

[21] The rest of this book will be about that very debate, beginning in the next chapter.

what we can call "formal constraints" on any such conception. So there should be a lot to gain by thinking through the formal constraints he proposed.[22]

2 Formal constraints on happiness

The method that Aristotle devises for arriving at formal constraints on happiness is just the one we should by now expect. We arrive at them by working from two directions: we determine what sort of good happiness must be by, one, focusing on its role as the final end for practical reasoning, and two, reflecting on the fact that it is a good human life for the one living it.[23] Doing so allows us to come up with a principled way of adjudicating between competing conceptions of happiness. For instance, if a formal constraint on happiness is that we must want it for its own sake and strictly for its own sake, then it is hard to see how happiness could consist in having a lot of money, for instance. This is not because some barefoot philosopher has a prejudice against money-making, but because money just cannot be all that happiness has to be in order to be a final end in the first place—it does not relate to our goals in the right way. By thinking through such formal constraints on the concept of happiness as these, we can sharpen our conception of it.[24]

2.1 Happiness is active, dependent on the agent, and non-derivative

One of the central constraints on happiness that Aristotle considers is one that we have already discovered: happiness must be something *active*, not passive. For Aristotle, living a good human life means actually *living*, being active, and so it is not enough that one merely be in some state of mind, say, or asleep one's whole life.[25] As Aristotle says, happiness is something that attaches to a person's life because of what he or she *does*, and not just as a gift or good luck.[26] This rules out the idea that happiness could consist in just *being* virtuous—"being a good person," in our idiom—as opposed to being engaged in virtuous activity.[27] It is also clear that this constraint stems directly from

---

[22] Valerie Tiberius (2008) suggests that there are two ways to construct philosophical advice about how to live a good life: one, by beginning with a top-down view about what the good life is (the "target"), or two, by characterizing the process of deliberating well about how to live. As we shall see in the rest of this chapter, thinking about living a good life by beginning with the formal constraints on doing so offers a third alternative.

[23] I discuss these two sides of happiness in Chapters 1 and 2, respectively. It is important to see that the job here is not one of mere conceptual analysis. It grows from what we discover about happiness: for instance, that happiness is "final" not in the sense that everything else is a means to it, but in a sense that allows other ends to be valued for their own sakes. See Richardson 1994, 211–18, for an excellent discussion of this point.

[24] It will be especially relevant for our purposes that although the Stoics disagreed with Aristotle over the nature of happiness, they did not disagree over Aristotle's formal constraints on the notion of happiness. See Rist 1969, chap. 1; Irwin 1986, 208, and 1996, 72–3; Lesses 1989, 98. Aristotle's constraints build on earlier discussions in some of Plato's dialogues, such as *Euthydemus* and *Philebus*; see Annas 2002, 4–7; Cooper 2003.

[25] *NE* I.5, 1095b31–1096a2; X.6, 1176a33–1176b2; *Pol.* VII.3, 1325a32–34, 1325b12–16.

[26] Cf. *EE* I.3, 1215a7–19; see McDowell 1995a, 210–11; see also Broadie 1991, 36.

[27] Cf. *EE* I.4, 1215a20–25; *MM* I.3, 1184b14–17; I.4, 1185a9–13. Telfer (1980, 46) finds this idea puzzling: "there seems no reason," she says, "why a man's eudaimonia should not consist, or partly consist, in

Aristotle's conception of human beings as active, practically rational creatures—which, I have argued, is the right thing to say about humans and human happiness. It is this that explains why Aristotle will go on to say that it is activity of a certain sort that "controls" happiness (NE I.10, 1100b8–11).[28]

Another constraint, clearly related to the first, is that happiness is not something to be bestowed or taken away by others (NE I.5, 1095b22–6). Simply put, the activity on which the happiness of your life depends must be *your* activity. Your happiness cannot consist in what I am doing in my life, as if I could live your life for you, but only in what you are doing in yours. This constraint rules out the idea that happiness is a life of fame and prestige, for example, since to say that someone is famous is really to say something about what *other* people are doing.

The fact that happiness is our final end also means that happiness cannot be a dependent or derivative good, that is, a good the value of which is derived from something more basic. For instance, living for the sake of prestige is again the wrong kind of end, because prestige is valuable only as an acknowledgement of things like excellence and intelligence (NE I.5, 1095b26–31). Again, this is not to say that that end is the wrong kind because it is shabby or shallow or what have you—this constraint is, after all, *formal*—but because it is not the kind of good that could be the final end for deliberation, since a good like honor is ultimately valuable on account of something else. Likewise, as I hinted above, pursuing wealth cannot be the final end either, because wealth is valuable only as a means to something else (1096a5–10). Whatever happiness is, it cannot be a derivative good.

2.2 Happiness is final

Another formal constraint on happiness, again clearly arising from the very fact that it must be able to halt deliberation, is that happiness must be *final*. In this respect too, the money-seeking life is an obvious failure: because money is not good for its own sake, having reached one's end of amassing money would still leave one with the need for further ends for the sake of which to use the money (NE I.5, 1096a5–10; EE I.7, 1217a29–40).

But Aristotle has more in mind than that happiness cannot be identified with an instrumental good. Something pursued for its own sake, he says, is more final than something pursued only for the sake of something else; and something pursued strictly for its own sake, and never for the sake of anything else, is absolutely final (NE I.7, 1097a15–1097b6). Happiness, for Aristotle, is the most final thing of all, on two grounds: one, happiness is not for the sake of anything else, and two, because there

---

what he *is*." However, I suspect her surprise is due to the facts (a) that she (mistakenly) takes eudaimonia to be understood in terms of things that are good independent of eudaimonia, and (b) that she takes eudaimonism, like her own account of happiness, to be primarily an exercise in conceptual analysis rather than beginning with the significance of happiness in deliberation.

[28] Here I follow Irwin's (1985) translation. More on this notion of "control" below, and in Chapters 4 and 5.

is only one final end and it is happiness, everything else must be for the sake of happiness. This is unsurprising, since these are the two features of the final end that (one) keep practical deliberation from regressing and (two) give a framework for practical deliberation that encompasses and unifies all the various areas of one's life.[29] To say what our final end is, we must specify what happiness consists in, and this constraint tells us that whatever we consider as providing that specification must be final in both of these ways.

Now, here an important question arises, as we saw in Chapter 1: in what sense are other things "for the sake of" happiness? In particular, is happiness some separate good that I *aim at* through things that I do, or does it *consist in* things that I do? The fact that happiness is an "end" does not settle the question either way, since for Aristotle some ends are fulfilled in activity, while some are distinct from the activities that attain them. Nor does Aristotle speak directly to the question here, and indeed many of his examples of ends are taken from various productive skills, where the for-the-sake-of relation is perhaps easiest to grasp, but where too the ends one seeks are all products that are separate from the pursuits that produce them.

However, recall that for Aristotle happiness consists above all in *activity*, on account of his conception of human nature. In that case, there must be some activity or activities that are "for the sake of" happiness in the sense that happiness is fulfilled in them, not by means of them. So happiness is the final end in life, and it is not distinct from the activity in virtue of which a life is happy.[30] What is this activity in which happiness consists? Because the finality constraint is formal, it cannot answer that question all by itself. Nor do we know yet, for instance, whether there is only one good in which happiness consists, or whether it consists in some plurality of goods. So far, we know only that *whatever* it is that happiness consists in above all, it will be active, and it will not be distinct from happiness itself.[31] But again, the formality of the constraint is one of its strengths, because however vehemently two parties—say, the Aristotelians and the Stoics—may disagree over the nature of this good, they can agree nonetheless that to identify this good is not to identify something distinct from happiness but to give a specification of the content of happiness.[32]

2.3 Happiness is self-sufficient

A further formal constraint is that happiness must be *self-sufficient* (*NE* I.7, 1097b6–21; X.6, 1176a35–1176b9; cf. *MM* I.2, 1184a7–14). The main idea here is that if such-and-such is what happiness comes to, then that such-and-such must make life desirable and lacking in nothing. At a common-sense level, the idea seems fairly clear: what we say that happiness is must not be something that makes us *nearly* live well, but

---

[29] I discuss these two features in Chapter 1.
[30] Cp. *MM* I.2, 1184a28–29.
[31] See Ackrill 1999; Van Cleemput 2006, 135–6; see also Heinaman 2007.
[32] Cf. Irwin 1996, 73.

something that makes us live well without qualification. Not surprisingly, Aristotle thinks that this constraint follows from the finality constraint: because happiness is final, Aristotle says, it must also be self-sufficient (I.7, 1097b7–8).[33] After all, if happiness were just *nearly* living well, it could not be the point at which deliberation ceases, and therefore it could not serve as a suitable specification of the final end.

'Self-sufficiency' in Greek (*autarkeia*) must have had many of the connotations of the equivalent English term, because Aristotle is quick to point out that he does not mean that a self-sufficient person must be able to get on without others (*NE* I.7, 1097b8–11), and elsewhere he says that self-sufficiency is not the same thing as being very wealthy or powerful (X.8, 1179a3–9). The idea is rather that whatever happiness consists in, it must be the best thing there is, otherwise we could always go on deliberating about how to go for something even better.

At a more fine-grained level, though, this constraint is very difficult to specify precisely and has been surrounded by enormous controversy. For one thing, what does Aristotle mean by saying that happiness is the "best" good—best compared to what? Aristotle's Greek is frustratingly ambiguous on this point (*NE* I.7, 1097b16–20):[34] he may be saying (a) that happiness must be the greatest good when compared to *each* other good, taken one by one; or (b) that happiness must be the greatest good when compared to any *set* of goods.[35] If Aristotle means the distributive comparison (a), then happiness is the greatest *single* good (i.e. what scholars call a "dominant" good), which may be consistent with the thought that happiness is improvable by the addition of other goods. But if he means the collective comparison (b), then the requirement is just that happiness must be a totality of goods that is not improvable (i.e. an "inclusive" good).[36] That is a significant ambiguity! Does this constraint envision happiness as consisting in one super-good—some single good superior to every other single good—or as consisting in a totality of goods that is greater than any other totality?

Some readers have preferred the first option on the grounds that if happiness is a totality of goods that is not improvable, as on the second option, then it must include every good anyone might desire—thus making happiness clearly unattainable even in

---

[33] Cf. Irwin 1986, 206-7.

[34] See also *EE* I.1, 1214a7–8.

[35] See Heinaman 1988, 42–3, and Van Cleemput 2006, 137–43, for discussion. The author of the *MM*, on the other hand, is explicit in his rejection of option (a): because goods are defined in terms of their role in happiness, and happiness is the best of all; we cannot count happiness as a good among them, or else it will be better than itself, which is absurd (I.2, 1184a14–29). In fact, he directly targets the view that happiness might be the best in the sense of comparing it to other goods one by one, and says that this is not the sense in which "the best," being the most complete, is to be understood (1184a29–38).

[36] This controversy is further complicated by the fact that there is no consensus on what the dominant/inclusive distinction distinguishes. Sometimes it is a matter of whether happiness consists in more than one kind of good (i.e. excellent activity as well as other goods?), as I am using it here; and at other times it is a matter of whether happiness consists in more than one kind of activity (i.e. excellent contemplative activity as well as excellent practical activity?).

principle.[37] But I do not think that that follows: happiness could be a totality not of every good thing there is, but of those goods that become desirable within one's attachments and projects. In fact, Aristotle says that self-sufficiency is a feature of the happiness of a person considered as, say, a parent, a spouse, a friend, a member of a community, and so on (NE I.7, 1097b8–11). Again, this constraint is about making happiness the sort of thing that can stop deliberation, and happiness would not need to include everything desirable in order to stop deliberation.[38] More than that, because happiness is a good life for the one living it, the focus should not be on merely amassing goods but having those goods one needs for the sake of the relationships and projects that one has chosen to live for.[39] Likewise, even if happiness consists in multiple goods, it could be the case that among those goods is one that transforms the person—such as virtue—so as to alter that person's perspective on what other things are desirable in the first place.[40]

Adding further fuel to this controversy is the sharp disagreement among Aristotle's readers over whether he thinks that happiness really consists in the activity of pure contemplation (theōria)[41]—and therefore in a single, dominant, super-good—and whether the self-sufficiency constraint in NE I.7 should be understood as anticipating such a view. This makes sorting out these two issues—how happiness is the "best" good, and whether it consists in contemplation—all the more difficult, because they have to be sorted out in tandem. So it may come as little surprise that there is no scholarly consensus on this point, and probably none on the horizon.[42]

---

[37] See Reeve 1992, 120–2, and Kraut 1999, for whom this argument is a *modus tollens*; by contrast, Engberg-Pederson (1983, 11–12, 27) accepts it as a *modus ponens*.

[38] See Annas 1993a, 40–1; see also Broadie 1991, 32–3; McDowell 1995a, 210–11.

[39] Alternatively, Richardson (1994, 216) suggests that the necessary goods are limited to those that are valuable for their own sake "for all men by nature."

[40] Cp. Annas 2002, 9.

[41] NE X.7–8; cp. Pol. VII.3, 1325b16–23.

[42] For an excellent review of these two related debates, see Bostock 2000, 21–5 and chap. 9. See also Purinton 1998, whose argument I find particularly persuasive. Even more complexity is added by the fact that in the EE, Aristotle appears to make contemplation just one part of the good life (but for a dissenting view, see Roopen 2005).

As I see it, the main question here is a philosophical rather than a textual one, and one that is rarely raised: how can happiness fulfill its role as the final end for deliberation about one's life as a whole, if happiness is not inclusive of one's life as a whole? In those few cases in which proponents of the dominant end view have considered the question, some have bitten the bullet and said that virtuous deliberation must therefore aim always at increasing one's opportunities for speculative contemplation (Reeve 1992, 154–5), or at action that approximates contemplative activity (Richardson Lear 2004; Kraut 1989 combines these approaches), while others have perceived Aristotle to be simply silent on the matter (Cooper 2003, 143). N. White (2002, 250–2) suggests that Aristotle's recommendation to pursue contemplation as the highest end is "imperfect" in Kant's sense, so that not all other ends are subordinated to that end. There is also the problem that we can still ask of a life of contemplation whether it is a good life and lived well, with its singularity of focus. Indeed, the Stoics raise exactly this question: Plutarch, Contrad. 1033c–d (= LS 67X), cited by Annas 1997, 36n. The same question cannot be asked about virtuous activity, which encompasses all of life.

Lastly, I think it is also important to note that even if Aristotle set out to define happiness as some single activity (like contemplation), surely the place to make that argument is precisely *not* in his discussion of *formal* constraints on happiness. Surely that argument would have to depend on substantive rather than formal

Fortunately, we do not need to sort out these issues at present, because insofar as we have any purely scholarly aim in looking at Aristotle's formal constraints, it is only to get a better sense of where exactly the ancient eudaimonists disagreed over the precise relation between virtuous activity and happiness. And as it happens, that debate—mainly between Stoics and Aristotelians—was not one of disagreement over any formal constraints on happiness but over different substantive conceptions of it.[43] Furthermore, it will become clear as we proceed through Part 2 that these debates never turned on *how many* goods happiness can be said to consist in, but rather over *what* thing or things really are good and are parts of happiness. Whereas the Aristotelians hold that happiness requires goods of the soul (the virtues) as well as bodily and external goods, the Stoics hold that virtue is the only good there is, so that a virtuous person thereby has all the goods that happiness needs.[44] Furthermore, leaving the self-sufficiency constraint open-ended on this point also explains how later members of Aristotle's own school could have characterized happiness as consisting in mental, bodily, and external goods and still thought that it was an Aristotelian conception of happiness they were working with. And lastly, the ancient debates never centered about the relation between happiness and pure contemplation anyway, but only about the relation between happiness and the virtues of character (courage, generosity, and so on).[45]

2.4 Happiness is distinctly human

A further constraint follows from the fact that, as we saw in the previous chapter, anything that genuinely counts as our happiness must be a distinctly *human* form of happiness. This constraint comes in Aristotle's so-called "function argument" (*NE* I.7, 1098a3–18). I discussed this argument above and shall return to it in Chapter 5, so my remarks on it here will be brief. The key idea in this argument is one we mentioned in connection with the activity constraint: a deep fact of our humanity is the fact that we guide our actions and put our life together through the use of practical reasoning. For that reason, Aristotle holds that human happiness, which is something active, must lie in activity that represents the intelligent use of practical reasoning. Now, as Aristotle will make clear (in I.13), activity in accordance with practical reasoning is not some distinct *kind* of activity, some way of spending one's time that takes time away from things like pursuing a professional career, say, or following one's artistic passions, or living a mystic's life on a mountain in Tibet. To speak of "acting in accordance with

---

claims about the good. And by the same token, this would not be the place for Aristotle to rule out that happiness consists in some single activity, either. I strongly suspect, then, that the formal constraints on happiness per se deliberately leave the question open, as indeed they should.

[43] To be sure, Cicero (*Fin.* V.81) rejects Antiochus' reading of the Aristotelian position on the formal grounds that happiness cannot be improved (clearly taking self-sufficiency in sense (b) above), but even then the problem with that position can be restated in substantive rather than formal terms anyway, as we shall see in Chapter 5.

[44] E.g. Cicero, *TD* V.40.

[45] So although I myself think that Aristotle's self-sufficiency constraint envisions happiness as an "inclusive" rather than a "dominant" good, nothing in this book will depend on this.

practical reasoning" is not a way of describing some *species* of activity, but a way of describing *any* activities insofar as one incorporates them into one's life in an intelligent way, as opposed to pursuing them at all costs, say.[46] (I shall say more about this in section 3, below.) This is because humans are creatures that do not just behave but act for reasons, as I said above. Nothing less than a life of practically wise activity, Aristotle argues, could count as a life that is fully human, and nothing less could count as happiness that is fully human happiness.

2.5 Happiness is stable

Lastly, Aristotle argues that happiness has a certain stability over time, and thus that any good that properly counts as a specification of happiness must have a similar stability (*NE* I.10, 1100a32–b30). (This point we noted above as well, in Aristotle's discussion of Solon.) As Aristotle observes, if we track a person's fortunes over time, we will notice that they constantly shift—as he puts the point, they change like a chameleon's colors. But happiness does not have that kind of arc: it is not episodic in the way that luck is, but tends to be lasting over time despite (modest) episodic changes in luck. Of course, Aristotle is quick to point out that he does not think that happiness is invulnerable, and indeed he thinks it is vulnerable to turns of fortune when these are extraordinary and significant (1100b22–30; I.5, 1095b31–1096a2). Even so, good fortune could not be the final end—not only because good fortune has too little to do with what we do, but also because it is too episodic and shifting to be the good that happiness is. We want our lives to go well *and* to go well in a stable and lasting way; that is the kind of good that we take happiness to be. Whatever happiness consists in, then, it must be something that is stable and lasting in the way that happiness seems to be.

We should now have a better understanding of what it means to say that something is the right kind of thing to be central to human happiness. Because humans are fundamentally active creatures, any adequate conception of human happiness must make activity central, and must be such that happiness depends primarily on the agent himself and what he does. Because the final end must be such as to stop deliberation, happiness as our final end must be good for its own sake and not for the sake of anything further, as well as desirable enough to stop deliberation once one has it. Furthermore, human happiness must be something that is, after all, *human* happiness, and it must have the sort of stability we think our well-being has.

3 How virtuous activity satisfies the constraints

We can now approach the main question I posed at the outset: why think that virtuous activity is central to happiness? Aristotle evidently thinks that his conception of human nature and the formal constraints on happiness lead in this direction. Do they? One

---

[46] Here I have benefited from discussion with Guido Pincione.

might have looked at Aristotle's formal constraints on happiness and arrived at the idea that happiness must consist in activities like doing satisfying work, say, or engaging in certain close relationships, or perhaps some set of such activities in balance. So why *virtuous* activity specifically? On many ways of thinking about the virtues, there would be no obvious connection at all between virtue on the one hand and happiness on the other. At best they seem to be different goods, and at worst downright rival goods. And yet, I have argued, Aristotle does seem to have our concept of happiness. So if there is any sense to be made of the alleged importance of virtuous activity for happiness, it must lie in how we are to think about the virtues.

Think about a couple of ideas that have come up several times now. One is that happiness is the final end in the sense that it is a life in which one finds things to live for and lives for them in a way that counts as a good life for the one living it. Another is that a life that is good in that way must be fulfilling for one, both as a human and as a unique individual. Something important follows from these ideas when taken as a pair. In order for my life to be fulfilling for me, *what* it makes sense for me to live for must depend on what *I* am like, and what sorts of things *I* am such as to find fulfilling in my life.[47] To be sure, I may not be the final authority on what those things are, but outside of some very general advice, being told what to live for is really not what I need from a philosophical theory. Philosophers can give me good reasons not to choose a career as a con-man, but whether I should devote my life to medicine, or to engineering, or to music, or to volunteering, or to something else entirely—to just taking opportunities as they come, maybe—is not really something I go to them to find out. However, in order for my life to be a fulfilling *human* life, I would need to find out *in what way* to live for those things, and here philosophy should try to offer all the help it can. If I decide to focus on medicine, for instance, I still need to think about what it would mean to do so wisely, responsibly, in balance with my other commitments, and in general in a way that will count as a good life for someone with that focus. What I really need normative reflection to tell me, in other words, is *how* to live for things that make my life my own and *personally* fulfilling, as well as a good *human* life. In short, when I ask philosophers for normative guidance about happiness, I am not really asking for nouns. I am asking for adverbs.[48]

This is exactly how I intend the idea that happiness is, above all, a life of virtuous activity: that idea tells us more about adverbs than about nouns. A life in which one pursues a career as a physician is obviously a different life from one spent as a concert cellist, but *neither of them is necessarily something different from a life of virtuous activity*. Rather, a life of virtuous activity is just an *active life*, but one that is lived with the virtues. What do I mean by acting "with the virtues"? I mean what I said above when I talked about human fulfillment: acting with practical wisdom and emotional soundness.

---

[47] On this important point, see Haybron 2008.

[48] Cf. Rist 1969, 2, on this point in Aristotle. For a similar point in the Stoics, see Inwood 1985, 213.

This is also what Aristotle means when he says that happiness or the human good is activity in accordance with virtue (*NE* I.7, 1098a16–18; I.13, 1102a5–6). As Aristotle notes, this account of happiness is incomplete without an account of virtue (I.13, 1102a6–7), and so he goes on to say more precisely what he thinks virtue is. Virtue, he says, is the excellence of the practical rationality that makes our lives distinctly human, and this practical rationality is twofold: on the one hand, we are practically rational in the sense that such rationality is a directing capacity that we possess; and on the other, we are also practically rational insofar as our emotional life is capable of being shaped by that directing capacity (1102a26–1103a3). Success or excellence of a practically rational creature, taken in the first sense, is practical wisdom, an excellence of practical intellect, and the success or excellence of rationality in the second sense is virtue of character, such as generosity and temperance (1103a3–10).

Aristotle says the same thing about virtue in the *Eudemian Ethics* as well (II.1, 1218b37–1219a39). There Aristotle considers what our humanity comes to—what is the mode of life that is fully human. That mode, he says, is active: not just organic life, but living one's life through the exercise of practical reasoning, including bringing harmony to our inner lives through the agreement of practical reason and emotion. But of course, he says, that kind of harmony is just what we mean by virtue, so it must be the virtues that make us fully human. Likewise, the Aristotelian author of the *Magna Moralia* (I.4–5, 1184b22–1185b13) argues that it is through the exercise of practical reasoning that we are active in a way that can be our good, and the virtues just are our success as practically rational creatures. In sum, on the Aristotelian view, an active life of virtue is a life in which one is fulfilled, excellent, and thriving as a human being—a life in which one is "fully human," in Christine Korsgaard's phrase.[49]

Furthermore, it seems clear that in saying that happiness is virtuous activity, so understood, Aristotle means to tell the reader not *which* life to live but *in what manner* to live a life of the reader's own so that it can be a good, fulfilling life. For notice that telling someone to be wise, generous, and temperate does nothing to give him a final end, insofar as it gives him no end to live for. What *does* give someone advice about a final end is to tell him to find ends that he finds meaningful and fulfilling, and then to live for them in a wise way, a generous way, a temperate way—that is, in an intelligent and harmonious way. This, I think, is how we should understand Aristotle's thesis that happiness is a life of virtuous activity. It is certainly how *I* intend that thesis.

Notice, then, just how far off the criticism is that Aristotle—and eudaimonism in general—starts with some garden-variety view of virtuous activity and then goes to great lengths (for what reason?) to prove that it is also part of happiness. This gets things entirely backwards: Aristotle in fact starts with the notion of human happiness and moves from there to a clearer picture of what could count as a human virtue in the first

---

[49] Korsgaard 1986. See also Broadie 1991, 35; McDowell 1995a. Cf. *EE* I.5, 1215a30–1216a10.

place. Indeed, Aristotle is clearly thinking of "virtue" (*aretē*) here in its very broadest sense of "excellence," since he has to go to the trouble of explaining that by "human excellence" in this context he does not mean having a strong body or sound digestive tract (*NE* I.13, 1102a32–b12). What he has in mind is that, in a living thing, its excellence is whatever enables it to live in its distinctive, characteristic mode in a flourishing way. In a human, this flourishing is not just health or vigor, but happiness, and we live best in a distinctly human way when we live with practical wisdom and emotional soundness—and *that* is how we know that such things are our excellences, that is, our "virtues."

Now, how in particular is virtuous activity supposed to meet the various formal constraints on happiness? Of central interest to Aristotle is the fact that virtuous activity—the activity of a creature with practical rationality—is activity of a distinctly human sort; it is, in fact, the very activity that makes human existence human (*NE* I.7, 1097b22–1098a18). This point is not focused exclusively on the practical intellect, however, as Aristotle also draws attention to the fact that such activity is enjoyable, since virtue involves emotional harmony, and this is important because it is obvious that human happiness is an enjoyable life (I.8, 1099a7–21). It is also clear, as Aristotle points out, that such a life is of course an active one (1098b18–1099a7), and furthermore, because it lies in activity it is especially a life of one's own, not something easily given or taken away by others (I.9, 1099b9–28). Likewise, a life of virtuous activity is especially stable, because practical rationality is useful in negotiating many changes in our fortunes (I.10, 1100b11–22). The other constraints Aristotle does not belabor, although it is not difficult to see that a life of virtuous activity is good in a way that is not derived from or dependent on something else, and that it can unify our other various ends without itself being for the sake of any further end.

However, the remaining constraint is the one that draws Aristotle's attention more than any of the others, and that is the self-sufficiency constraint (*NE* I.8, 1099a31–b6; I.9, 1099b25–8, 1100a4–9; I.10–11). In particular, it is this constraint that leads to a crucial qualification of his account of happiness: because happiness must be self-sufficient, it cannot consist in virtuous activity alone, since this would leave out other important goods for human life, namely certain goods of the body (like beauty or strength) and external goods (like social position). Aristotle therefore summarizes his conception of happiness in this way: "What then stops us from calling happy the one who is active in accordance with complete excellence, sufficiently equipped with external goods, not for some random period of time but over a complete life?" (I.10, 1101a14–16).

In effect, then, Aristotle denies that virtuous activity is sufficient for happiness. This is one of the best known features of Aristotle's account of happiness—and surprisingly, at the time it was by far the most controversial. In fact, Aristotle himself seems perplexed over this point; he does not *simply* deny the sufficiency of virtue for happiness, but belabors that denial and agonizes for long chapters over it, arriving not at a bold statement but at a hesitating query. This is extraordinary: why should Aristotle find such an apparently simple claim such a difficult one to make? Come to that, why should he have thought such an intuitively obvious point should need to be made in the first place? And most puzzling of all, why should *this* point have been the one that drew the heaviest fire from other ancient philosophers? As we shall see in the next chapter, and even more in the ones that follow, this point was in fact the greatest difficulty for Aristotle's conception of happiness. And it is every bit as difficult for my own.

4

New Directions from Old Debates

I have argued that happiness is a life of virtuous activity. Even so, I do not believe that virtuous activity is sufficient for happiness. I shall not argue for that claim; to do so amongst modern readers would seem like the ultimate case of pushing against an open door. However, we know that ancient Greek philosophers argued for several centuries over precisely that claim—mainly, Stoics arguing that virtue is sufficient for happiness and Aristotelians that it is not—and we need to understand why. Where intelligent people are having lasting disagreements over what looks to us to be obvious, there must surely be more than meets the eye. What were they seeing that we don't see?

That debate—call it the "sufficiency debate" for short—did not stem from conceptual disagreement over eudaimonia. (I really meant it in Chapter 1 when I described Aristotle's account of eudaimonism as seminal.) Likewise, Aristotelians and Stoics seem to have agreed about the formal constraints on happiness, and that those constraints favor the idea that virtuous activity is central to happiness. And while there were important differences between Aristotelian and Stoic theories of the virtues, even so they both thought of virtuous activity as activity done with practical wisdom and emotional soundness.[1] Rather, I argue in this chapter that the key issue in this debate—and a crucial issue for developing my own thinking about happiness in the rest of this book—is the question of how activity might, or might not, connect us to the volatile world in which we act. It is here, in clarifying this central issue, that I shall first introduce my conception of activity as *embodied*, that is, as so connecting us to particular parts of our world that our happiness is inseparable from them, precisely because our activity is inseparable from them. This is the issue I had in mind when I said in the previous chapter that I take happiness to be a life of virtuous activity, subject to an important qualification. On my view, happiness is a life of what I shall call *embodied* virtuous activity, and in this chapter I begin to explain what I mean by that.

---

[1] I discuss this aspect of Stoicism in Chapter 8, where I also explain the characterization of Stoic virtues as involving emotional soundness rather than the *absence* of emotion.

1 Why was there ever a sufficiency debate?

1.1 *The stories we tell*

Why would anyone ever have thought that virtuous activity might be sufficient for happiness? We may resent having to believe that that is false, but it is hard to see what else to believe. If the triumph of the good over evil is a common theme in the stories we tell, so too is the triumph of evil over the good.

Harper Lee's *To Kill a Mockingbird* is a story of both kinds. At the center of Lee's story is the battle of small-town lawyer Atticus Finch to defend Tom Robinson, a black man falsely, even maliciously, accused of raping a white woman. This is an almost certainly fatal accusation in the deep American South in the decades following the abolition of slavery; Atticus knows it but throws himself completely into Tom's defense nonetheless. The story of Atticus and Tom shows us some of the darkest evil of human life—stupid cruelty, senseless hatred, blatant injustice—but it also shows some of the greatest good in the triumph of genuine human decency in the very act of confronting that evil. That confrontation becomes quite literal in a memorable scene in which Atticus stays up all night on the sidewalk in front of the jailhouse, waiting for the lynch mob that will inevitably come for Tom. The men in this mob, like so many of Atticus' neighbors, accuse him of betraying them, not just by agreeing to defend someone like Tom, but by—how unthinkable!—taking the defense seriously. As an angry mob they come upon Atticus alone and unarmed, and he tells them simply to go back home. Meanwhile, Atticus' young children had sneaked down to the town square to see what Atticus could be doing there in the middle of the night. His daughter Scout, not knowing a lynch mob when she sees one, starts talking to some of the men she happens to recognize, greeting them cordially and sending her greetings home to their families. The spirit is now gone from the mob, and they all go back to their homes. Courage and innocence stared down evil, and it was evil that blinked. That night, the good triumphed.

Had the story ended there we might have called Atticus a happy man. He found something to live for—even to die for—and he lived for it. He could find his life personally fulfilling, a life he could regard with satisfaction and pride, saying "That was *my* life—*that's* what I made it about." His life was fulfilling for him as a human as well, a life characterized by practical wisdom and sound emotions. In addition to the gift that Atticus gave Tom and his own children, there was the gift of a good life that Atticus gave himself.

But as we all know, the story does not end there. For his troubles, Atticus is hated by his neighbors, and his children only narrowly escape being murdered. And in spite of all of his effort, not to mention the mountain of circumstantial evidence in Tom's favor, Atticus loses the case anyway; even worse, Tom gives up all hope of justice, tries to escape custody, and is fatally shot running away. Now, even here Atticus is no failure—on the contrary, he shows us something to aspire to, since his goodness triumphs in the very act of standing against evil, of finding something good to live for and then living and perhaps even dying for it. Even so, evil also triumphs over the good in this story, as the good and the innocent turn out to be powerless against the tragedies that ultimately unfold. (Come to that, even Atticus' triumph on the night that he faced down the mob had been out of his power as well: mostly, he was lucky that his children turned up when they did.) If things turned out well for Atticus one day, they went very badly the next. We have no trouble calling Atticus good, but we cannot call him happy.

This is the story that Lee tells, and it has become one of our stories. It says that happiness does not belong to everyone who deserves it, and in that respect, the story is true. Not surprisingly, the story is also very old. The Psalmist writes,

> Surely in vain I have kept my heart pure
> and have washed my hands in innocence.
> All day long I have been afflicted, and every morning brings new punishments.[2]

That our existence should be like this is tragic, but it is not surprising. After all, we are agents, but we are also patients.

And yet we find several ancient Greek philosophers telling us that evil *cannot* triumph over the good. At his trial, Plato's Socrates says that no good man can ever be harmed (*Ap.* 41d), and he says it to the very jury that has already convicted and sentenced him to death. Likewise, from their earliest origins the Stoics stood upon the belief that virtuous activity is sufficient for happiness (DL VII.127–8). (Call this the "sufficiency thesis.") Furthermore, while many Greek philosophers—most notably Aristotle and his successors—firmly rejected the sufficiency thesis, even they found the business of rejecting it to require surprisingly concentrated philosophical effort.[3] Nor was the debate over the sufficiency thesis a mere side-debate in ancient Greek and Roman ethics—on the contrary, Cicero tells us that ultimately it was the *whole* debate. In his account of the major movements within Greek ethics, Cicero says that the lines between them ultimately came down to differing views about "the highest good" for the sake of happiness, and in particular whether virtuous activity is sufficient for happiness or happiness requires goods beyond our control (*Fin.* V.12–15).[4] Why would so many skilled philosophers give so much serious attention to an idea as outrageous as that virtue might be sufficient for happiness?

We cannot explain this away by saying that they just hadn't imagined stories like Harper Lee's—quite the contrary. There are, after all, Plato's very stories of Socrates, the virtuous sage who is executed for his service to the city, in the *Apology* and *Phaedo* as well. What's more, Plato devoted no less a work than the *Republic* to confronting a story about a magic ring that enabled its wearer to get away with doing anything he

---

[2] Psalm 73:13–14, New International Version.

[3] I discuss these efforts in Chapter 5. See also Russell 2008.

[4] I discuss Cicero's reconstruction of the history of Greek ethics in Chapter 6.

wanted to do and live quite literally like a king. Plato's point is that such stories force questions upon us about whether it is virtue or vice that makes us better off, and indeed what virtue could have to do with happiness in the first place. Likewise, in a seminal discussion of the sufficiency thesis Aristotle carefully pondered the story of Priam, the Trojan king who, though renowned for virtue, came to the end of his life amidst utter catastrophe (*NE* I.9–10). Far more spectacularly than Atticus Finch, Priam is the good man over whom evils triumph.

So, Greek philosophical discussion of the relation between virtue and happiness was framed by *exactly* the sorts of stories that we still tell each other. Furthermore, it is important to note that Plato's and Aristotle's stories were both drawn from the surrounding Greek culture. Aristotle's worries about Priam were prompted by a popular aphorism—attributed to the Athenian lawgiver Solon, no less—that we should "count no man happy while he is alive" (*NE* I.10, 1100a10–11), since we can never know whether a person is happy until he has lived out his whole life and escaped any very serious misfortunes. In fact, the Greeks told stories not only about Priam but also about his upright widow Hecuba, who following the destruction of Troy went on to endure the sacrifice of her daughter, and even the treachery of her son's murder at the hands of a trusted friend.[5] Moreover, as I have already argued in Chapter 2, we cannot dismiss the Greeks' interest in the sufficiency thesis by saying that they just thought about human happiness in a way that we do not and perhaps cannot. On the contrary, Aristotle reports that many people in his time simply took happiness and good luck to be the same (*EE* I.1, 1214a21–5). There is no getting around it: the ancient Greeks told each other the same sorts of stories about virtue and happiness that we do, and they had the same sorts of worries about them that we have—and wouldn't it be shocking if they hadn't! So if they saw the problems as clearly as we do, then why did their best philosophical minds still take the sufficiency thesis so seriously?

1.2 Kinds of goods: a crucial asymmetry

Stories like the one about Atticus Finch, or Socrates, or Priam, seem to teach a very simple lesson: if virtuous activity is necessary for happiness, then so too are all sorts of other goods that depend on circumstances outside our control ("goods of fortune" for short). This is the point that Aristotle makes when he says that happiness requires several kinds of goods: it requires the right kinds of activities and *also* the right kinds of bodily and worldly circumstances (*NE* I.8, 1099a31–b8; I.10, 1100b8–11, 1101a14–16). If this is correct, then since happiness is that in relation to which all goods are to be understood (I.12; *EE* II.8, 1219b10, 1219b11–16), there are therefore two broad kinds of goods—practical wisdom and the goods of fortune—and they are each necessary for happiness, and jointly they are sufficient.

---

[5] For discussion of Euripides' *Hecuba* and other Greek stories of human vulnerability to fortune, see Nussbaum 1986.

However, to say that these two kinds of goods are necessary for happiness tells us very little about the actual role that each kind plays in happiness, as well as how they are related to each other. Perhaps they are necessary in the way that oxygen, fuel, and ignition are all necessary for fire: without any one of them there is no fire, but all that it takes for fire is to bring these three together. Yet if this is what Atticus' story first prompts us to say, then a moment's further reflection on that story will reveal why saying that is not quite adequate. After all, having been put into the position of having to defend Tom Robinson in the first place was a bit of very bad luck for Atticus—come to that, so was the fact that the world into which he was born was one in which people like Tom should have to be defended against such accusations in the first place. Yet *that* is not why we don't call Atticus happy, as if circumstances had simply condemned him from the start. On the contrary, we recognize that Atticus is an *agent*, someone who can make a difference within his circumstances, and who can give himself the gift of a good life by how he lives his life and the difference that he makes. It would be closer to the truth, I think, to say that wisdom and the other goods are necessary for happiness in the way that it takes both a potter and clay for there to be a pot. Each of them is necessary for the pot, but there only comes to be a pot when one of them *does* something with the other that it cannot do for itself.[6]

It is a cliché that we are like leaves in the wind, and there is some truth in that cliché. Humans are patients: needy creatures, full of desires, and vulnerable to circumstances that we ultimately cannot control. However, if we were *really* like leaves in the wind, we would have to be like highly extraordinary leaves, the sort that could make a study of air currents and deliberate about how to float on them. That is because we are agents as well, and our agency is responsible for a crucial *asymmetry* between wisdom and everything else: our bodily and worldly circumstances do us good insofar as we give them a direction through the exercise of practical rationality that they cannot give themselves. That is why, as in Atticus' case, agents can direct even regrettable circumstances so that they are nonetheless part of a good life. Consider another example. Christine Swanton (2003, 36–7) tells of a world-class yachting team that handled themselves so excellently in both competition and defeat that the winning team invited them to join in the victory parade anyway. Thinking about that sort of reaction to loss, we can see that even a defeat can become a high point in an athlete's life, depending on what he or she makes of the defeat.

How shall we characterize the distinction between these two kinds of goods, so as to capture this important asymmetry between them? Philosophers have always been careful to distinguish between "final" and "instrumental" goods, goods that are valuable for their own sake versus those that are valuable for the sake of other goods. However, this is clearly not the distinction we are after here. To be sure, the sorts of

---

[6] The example suggests that there is a similar asymmetry in the case of producers and their products; in fact, I think that that asymmetry is what underlies John Locke's discussion of the definitive role of labor in the production of useful goods in *Second Treatise of Government* V. See Russell 2004 for discussion.

exercises of practical rationality we are discussing are final goods—they are part of the goodness of a good human life—but many of the other goods, such as loving relationships, are final goods as well.

The distinction we need must therefore be an even deeper distinction than that. I shall call it a distinction between "fashioning" and "fashioned" goods. We can think of a fashioning good as a good that makes other things good by giving them the direction they need in order to belong to a good life, but does not require that sort of direction itself. Simply put, a fashioning good is a *source* of goodness for other things. And a fashioned good, very simply, is one that depends for its goodness on a fashioning good.[7]

Although I did not draw attention to it at the time, we have encountered fashioning goods before, in our discussion of the formal constraints on happiness (Chapter 3). The connection is, after all, a natural one, since the formal constraints are heavily shaped by our picture of human nature, and the idea that practical rationality is a fashioning good is a major element in that picture. Consider the formal constraint that happiness must be active. The human mode of living is an active one, because we live by exercising practical rationality as a skill upon the otherwise inchoate "materials" of our lives.[8] Another constraint is that happiness is not something to be bestowed or taken away by others, because a good life is something for one to make through the exercise of practical rationality. And perhaps most important, happiness is *human* happiness, and consists in our being fully human; this means not just having good things, and not just acting with them, but acting with them in a practically rational way. So, as the author of the *Magna Moralia* writes, there is a crucial distinction between things that are good in an absolute way and things that are not, which is separate from a distinction between things valuable for their own sake or for the sake of other things (*MM* I.2, 1183b37–1184a7).

Not surprisingly, the distinction between fashioning and fashioned goods was a central idea in other ancient discussions of happiness as well. For instance, in Plato's *Euthydemus* Socrates begins with the commonsense notion that happiness consists in a laundry list of various goods, only to note that one good on the list—wisdom—is importantly different from the others: it is, he says, the only one that is good without needing something else to make it good, whereas all other goods depend on it for their goodness.[9] In fact, here Aristotle understood himself as looking into

---

[7] In that case, note that the final/instrumental distinction is a distinction within the class of fashioned goods. It is clear, I trust, that the distinction between "fashioning" and "fashioned" goods corresponds to Korsgaard's (1983) distinction between unconditional and conditional goods, respectively. See also Russell 2005, chap. 1. Significantly, Korsgaard's distinction stems ultimately from the opening of Kant's *Groundwork*, which in turn draws upon the Stoics' much earlier version of the distinction (for which see Chapter 8), which in turn systematizes a distinction that first appears in some of Plato's dialogues, especially the *Euthydemus* (see Chapter 6).

[8] I return to the idea of practical wisdom as a skill in Chapter 8. See also Russell 2009, chap. 1, and Annas 2011.

[9] For discussion of this fundamental division between goods in Socrates and Plato, see Annas 1993b and 1997.

the very same question as Plato—namely what is the greatest good and the "original good and the cause by its presence in other things of their being good"—although he thinks that Plato is mistaken to seek it in the so-called "Form of the Good" (*EE* I.8, 1217b1–16).

Likewise, the Stoics held that the only thing with its own life-improving power is practical wisdom (what they call "knowledge" and "expertise," *epistēmē* and *technē*). Just as coldness is a power that does not need something else to make it cold, they argued, so too the goodness of wisdom does not require something else to make it good, since it is impossible to make bad use of it; rather, it is what is responsible for making good use of other things (DL VII.103). Furthermore, the Stoics held that our capacity for emotion and feeling is not life-improving itself, but can become a life-improving good only insofar as it can come to "participate in" virtue (AD II.5a–5b).[10]

1.3 Control and dependency

So although happiness requires both practical wisdom (since we are agents) and bodily and worldly goods (since we are patients), these two broad types of goods are radically different from one another with respect to happiness. From these observations we can draw an important conclusion as to which of these goods is central to and definitive of happiness, the good life for a human being. In fact, it is a conclusion that Aristotle himself draws. Although happiness requires bodily and worldly goods that we cannot control, Aristotle also insists that it is a mistake simply to track a person's fortunes in assessing the happiness of his life. This, he says, is because a person's fortunes

are not where living well or badly is located, but rather human life needs them in addition, as we have said, and *it is activities in accordance with virtue that control our happiness*, and the opposite sort of activities that control the opposite state.[11]

This is extremely significant. Notice that although goods of circumstance are necessary for happiness, we should not take this to mean that happiness either comes *or goes* depending on how we fare with respect to such goods. Of course, Aristotle says, there is a limit to this insulation against fortune, and at some point things beyond one's control can go so badly that it no longer makes sense to describe one as happy—as, for instance, no one would call King Priam happy at the fall of Troy (*NE* I.9–10). Nonetheless, it is the exercise of practical wisdom—in a word, virtuous activity— that *makes* a human life such as to be a good human life, and it is on this power that happiness depends above all else. This is because, although humans are both agents and patients, it is primarily their nature *as agents* that defines what it is for a human to live,

---

[10] The Stoic view of the emotions and their value is very controversial. I discuss it in greater detail in Chapters 8 and 11.

[11] *NE* I.10, 1100b8–11, italics added to Rowe's translation. I have also modified Rowe's translation by substituting Irwin's rendering of *kuriai* as "control" for Rowe's rendering as "are responsible for" (see Irwin 1985, ad loc.).

and to be happy, in a distinctly human way. And this is what we *should* say about human happiness, since (as we saw in the previous chapter) it is our agency that gives our entire existence its humanity—even our very "patiency," so to speak, itself. So, to borrow a term from Aristotle, I introduce what I shall call the *control thesis*: it is upon virtuous activity above all else that human happiness depends (see I.10, 1100b8–11). Of course, humans are not only agents but also patients—and this is an important fact about human happiness as well. This fact is captured by what I shall call the *dependency thesis*: there are bodily and external goods that are necessary for and parts of happiness (see I.10, 1100b9, 1101a14–16).

There are several important points to note about these two theses. For one thing, it is important to see that the control thesis is a *comparative* thesis: it is a thesis about the role and importance of virtuous activity relative to the role and importance of other goods where happiness is concerned. While our patiency has an important role to play in our happiness, the control thesis can be seen as setting a limit on the magnitude of its importance: whatever bearing virtuous activity has on our happiness, that bearing must always be commensurate with the centrality of our agency to our nature. (That will seem like an open-ended characterization of the control thesis, because it is. Making it more precise is the point of everything that follows.)[12]

Furthermore, the control thesis also reflects the difference *in kind* between virtuous activity and other goods with respect to happiness: in a word, it is not simply one final good among others. This rules out a simplistic "laundry list" approach to happiness, as if it just consisted in a plurality of goods all of a piece (as Socrates shows in the *Euthydemus*). For creatures of our kind, virtuous activity is a part of happiness in a way that nothing else can be, much as the potter is part of the pot-making process in a way that nothing else can be.[13]

However, lastly, it is not enough merely to offer the control and dependency theses as a pair of claims about human happiness. We must also understand how these two claims are to be *unified*. Is there any viable way of thinking about human happiness that makes happiness depend on practical wisdom, *and* takes seriously the importance of our patiency for our happiness? There is no guarantee that there will be. On the contrary, there is every chance that taking our agency seriously and taking our patiency seriously will be zero-sum, frustrating any attempt to unify those two dimensions of ourselves within a single conception of human happiness. And it is this difficulty of such a unification that is really at the center of the ancient sufficiency debate. Or so I argue now, in a preliminary way; the full argument for this historical claim is the task of Part 2 of this book.

---

[12] It is therefore very difficult to make the control thesis precise, as we shall see in Chapter 5. I offer my own version of the control thesis in the final section of that chapter.

[13] Cf. Irwin 2007, 337, who argues that for Aristotle and the Stoics, virtue cannot be one part of happiness among others since virtue is not among the things to be weighed as relevant to our happiness, but the thing that does the weighing, since it is essential to the self for whom other things might count as good.

2 The center of the debate

The obvious reply to the sufficiency thesis is to point out that humans are both agents and patients, so that their happiness requires virtuous activity as well as bodily and worldly goods, just as Aristotle says. In other words, the obvious reply is that the control thesis and the dependency thesis are both true. How hard could it be?

Actually, it turns out to be surprisingly hard. In fact, although Aristotle today is generally taken to have settled this issue definitively, in the ancient world this was not the verdict at all.[14] Why not? The difficulty is not in *saying* that the control and dependency theses are both true, but in saying that both are true *while* taking each as seriously as it demands to be taken.

Begin with the dependency thesis. Suppose we say that happiness is the fulfillment of good things, both goods of rational agency and goods of dependent patiency. Happiness, we say, consists in good activity as well as goods of fortune. Such an account of happiness clearly preserves the dependency thesis that there are goods of fortune—such as careers, loving relationships, bodily health, and so on—that are necessary for and indeed parts of our happiness. On this view, good activity is a good that matters for happiness, but it is only one among many such goods. However, in that case when we say that a life of virtuous activity will count as a happy life when goods of fortune are also present, we may just as well say that having the goods of fortune will count as a happy life when virtue is also present. But that is to deny our practical rationality and activity the *special* and *central* role that we assigned to them when we thought about human nature. Consequently, while this account of happiness clearly takes the dependency thesis seriously, to that extent it also seriously jeopardizes the control thesis.

So suppose instead that we begin with the control thesis and say that while happiness consists in the fulfillment of all kinds of goods, still it is primarily in virtuous activity that happiness is to be found. We might mean by this that goods of fortune are parts of human happiness only in some fairly small way—it is really our activity that defines our happiness, other goods playing some other sort of ancillary role. However, it is difficult to see how any good could be simultaneously so important that happiness is threatened without it *and* so unimportant that it is vastly overshadowed by some other good. How could such goods really be parts of our happiness if losing them makes so little difference to our happiness? Yet how *could* they make more of a difference to happiness than this without making as much of a difference as virtuous activity does? In that case, we have taken the control thesis seriously only at the cost of the dependency thesis.

Alternatively, we might mean that although happiness consists entirely in virtuous activity, still we need the goods of fortune in order to facilitate that activity. That is, such goods are important for happiness because they are important for the sake of virtuous activity, for instance by providing a rich and interesting sphere for virtuous activity. In that case, goods of fortune are important for happiness without being

---

[14] The details of this come in the next chapter.

important in at all the way that virtuous activity is. However, while such a view seems to take the control thesis seriously, it too does so only by not taking the dependency thesis seriously enough. For on this view bodily and external goods now seem, for happiness, to matter in the wrong way: surely my involvement in *this* career and *these* relationships should be *parts* of my happiness, and not just necessary for the sake of my acting virtuously. Perhaps my relationships with my children, say, do make for a rich sphere of opportunities for me to exercise the virtues, but if I think that these relationships are necessary for my happiness, presumably I think so because I also regard them as among the things in which my happiness *consists*. And of course, it is just that sort of thought that motivates the dependency thesis in the first place. Therefore, if this approach preserves the control thesis, it does so only by making too great a compromise on the dependency thesis.

What is more, it is not clear that this view really does preserve the control thesis anyway. While it is certainly true that virtuous activity always takes place within *circumstances*, it does not follow that it can take place only within *favorable* or *desirable* circumstances. So the idea that special, favorable circumstances are necessary for happiness stems not from the necessity of virtuous activity for happiness—after all, even Priam's virtue continues to "shine through" (*NE* I.10, 1100b30–3)—but presumably from the idea that such circumstances are themselves among the goods we need in order for a life of virtuous activity to be a happy life. But that is just to say that favorable circumstances are important for happiness for their own sake, and *not* just for the sake of virtuous activity. In other words, it is difficult to see why happiness should require special, favorable circumstances in which to act *unless* goods of fortune are important for their own sake—after all, having favorable circumstances in which to do things is *itself* a good of fortune. So this possibility gains no ground, either.

Now, this discussion has been quick, but it sketches many of the difficulties that plagued Aristotle and indeed several generations of his successors, as we shall see in the next chapter. The discussion has also been far from exhaustive, as ancient Aristotelians offered many subtle variations on these very basic themes that I have outlined. So I do not want to overstate what I have shown so far, which is simply that these are the general sorts of problems that arise as soon as one tries to pair the control and dependency theses. We have to find a way to unify those two theses, and clearly it will take real work to find it. There is also a lot riding on it, for if we cannot unify these two basic ideas about happiness, then we shall be left with an uncomfortable pair of options. On the one hand, we could think of happiness mainly in terms of our patiency, giving pride of place to the dependency thesis. However, to do so is nothing less than to alter our entire picture of human nature and human fulfillment. On the other hand, we might hold on to that picture and say instead that happiness ultimately depends on acting with practical wisdom and emotional balance after all. But of course, that would be to embrace the idea that virtuous activity is indeed sufficient for happiness after all.

To summarize, what we want to say is that happiness involves fulfillment both as an agent and as a patient, but our efforts to do justice to those two sides of our nature run the risk of being zero-sum. *That* is why it is so difficult to reject the sufficiency thesis *and* give a unified account of human nature and happiness. It is also why a debate over the sufficiency thesis could generate so much controversy, as in fact it did in ancient Greek ethics. No wonder Cicero found fulfillment in both our agency and our patiency to be, as he called it, an "unlikely combination" (*Fin.* II.42). And no wonder he thought that the whole debate boiled down to just one issue: whether or not there are goods besides virtuous activity (V.83).

Therefore, *whatever* we may say in the end about the sufficiency thesis, *what we absolutely* cannot *do is ignore it*. To ignore that issue would be to ignore a host of deep and important questions about what it means to be human and what it means to live a happy human life. That is, it would be to ignore the very questions about the meaning of our lives that we set out to address in the first place. For us, a counter-intuitive thesis that looked like something to be written off is now something that demands to be reckoned with.

Reckoning with this issue is my task in the rest of this book, and my hope is that by doing so I might learn enough from this important ancient debate to deepen and enrich my own account of happiness. Taking on this task means doing two things. One, it means carefully reviewing the main sides of the sufficiency debate—primarily the Aristotelians and the Stoics—in order to identify the main point or points of contention. This I do in Part 2. And two, I shall try to develop my own account of happiness in hopes of making some progress on that main point, in Part 3. Right now, in the final section of this chapter, I offer a preview of what I take that main point of contention to be and how I intend to approach it.

3 Moving past the debate: two conceptions of the self

Aristotle's account of happiness is more intuitively appealing than the Stoics' alternative. Of course, the Stoics knew that, but they rightly replied that the issue was not as simple as that: what Aristotle gains in intuitive appeal, he loses by having no unified account of human nature and happiness. However, the Stoics make their own trade-off as well: they can present a unified view of happiness, but the cost of doing so is excising our patiency from their account of human fulfillment. Perhaps this is as far as we can go. Cicero seems to have thought so, taking the lesson of the sufficiency debate to be that we must choose between intuitive plausibility and theoretical unity (Cicero, *Fin.* V.83; cp. Annas 1993a, 424–5). In a word, pick your favorite virtue in a theory of happiness and go from there.

But surely the issue is not *theories* of happiness but *happiness*. Human happiness is a life shaped by practical wisdom, *and* it also involves goods outside our control. If available theoretical options cannot deliver both of these ideas, the next thing to do is not to repair to meta-theoretical reflection on the virtues of theories. The next thing to do is to keep looking, for even if a better theory cannot be found we still shall have learned something important: perhaps no theory of our happiness is a unity because our existence, our *nature* is not a unity. Failure is always an option; perhaps we are just a mess. That would be a disappointing lesson, but there is never a guarantee against having to face that kind of disappointment.

However, I do think that there is another option to explore. This option does not involve going back on anything we have said so far about human nature, or human fulfillment, or virtuous activity. Instead, I want to think more carefully about the nature of activity itself, distinguishing two ways of thinking about how activity might, or might not, connect us to the world in which we act. In the end, where I disagree with Socrates and the Stoics is not over what kind of *good* virtuous activity it is, but over what kind of *activity* it is.

3.1 The formalized and the embodied conception

To take a simple example, suppose that Fred is a parent, so that among Fred's activities is his activity as a parent. By "activity" here, I do not mean some clockable errand but an active area of his life. This is in keeping with my focus on happiness as a matter of finding things to live for and then living for them; if we were to individuate the things Fred is living for, the result would be a list of the central "activities" of his life in the sense that interests me. So, if parenting is among the things that Fred's life is about, then parenting is one of his life's activities in my sense.

Now, there are two broad ways in which Fred might characterize his parenting activity. First, Fred's parenting activity can be characterized as Fred's exercise of his will or faculty of choice with respect to his child. That activity has his child as its object, and of course without a child for its object that activity would not count as a *parenting* activity in the first place. However, Fred regards himself, understood as a unique individual, as the will that engages in activity, and his parenting activity is part of his life in the very thin sense that some of the exercises of his will have a child as their object. It is really in his very patterns of exercising his will that Fred experiences his life as his own. Alternatively, second, we might say that Fred's parenting activity just is his relationship with this particular child. Fred as a unique individual is (among other things) this child's parent, that is, the person who is in this unique relationship with this unique child. Likewise, Fred's parenting activity is a part of his life in the sense that the things he does within this relationship with this child are among the things in virtue of which Fred experiences his life as his own. They are part of who he takes himself to be. Whereas on the first characterization Fred's activity is something that he does in relation to the world, on the second it is one of the very modes by which he embeds himself within the world.

For Fred, these two characterizations of his activity are in fact two different ways in which he might understand what individual he is. He might think of himself as separable, or inseparable, from his various relationships and projects. In other words, they are two ways of thinking about what *self* he is, and where that self ends and everything else begins—we might say, where the boundaries of the self lie. On the former conception of the self, one is a will or power of choice, and every activity has the same form as every other: it is the exercise of the power of choice in relation to objects in the world. The actions of this self are performed *in relation to* the world around one, and to act is to direct one's will in a certain way in relation to the world around one; but the self and its actions remain always *distinct from* that world, strictly speaking. This view I shall call the *formalized conception of the self*, and such a self a formalized self. This label reflects the fact that all activities have the same form—the exercise of the power of choice—regardless of their objects and circumstances.

On the other conception of the self, by contrast, the self includes one's sense of practical and physical possibilities—possibilities for engaging the world—insofar as these are essential to the sense of what person one is. Here, the self is not merely *located* in a physical, social world, but inextricably *fused* with certain parts of that world. This view I shall call the *embodied conception of the self*.

The remainder of this chapter is devoted to clarifying this basic distinction. Now, since "self" is said in many ways, it makes sense to begin there. By "self," I do not mean a metaphysical entity—a bearer of thoughts, say, or a thinking thing that may or may not be a physical thing, or the bearer of identity (metaphysical or personal) over time or through change, or what have you.[15] Nor do I have in mind moral personhood or the like. Rather, I have in mind the self as a person's own sense of what person he or she is. To have a sense of self, so understood, is to have a sense of the totality of those central relationships, commitments, attachments, and projects that give one's life its unique shape as being one's own. As such, it makes sense to think of the self in this sense as a kind of *identity*, by which I mean all of those features of a person without which he could no longer recognize his life as his.[16] As Marya Schechtman has put the point, identity of this sort concerns how a person should be characterized—"which beliefs, values, desires, and other psychological features make someone the person she is"—and it is in this sense of identity that one may have what Erik Erikson calls an "identity crisis" (Schechtman 1996, 2, 74). This identity, as Schechtman characterizes it, is the totality of characteristics making one the person one is, and as we move to the center of one's identity these characteristics are those that "are more truly expressive of who [one] is" (pp. 75–7). We can call this a person's "psychological identity."[17]

---

[15] Most of the recent literature on ancient conceptions of self has focused on the metaphysical self, in particular whether the self is better understood in intentional terms or as a locus of certain processes and functions. See Gill 1991, 1996, 2006, 2008a, 2008b, 2008c; see also Kahn 1988; Engberg-Pedersen 1990a; Long 1991, 1996, chaps. 12, 17; Reydams-Schils 2005, chap. 1; Bartsch 2006, chaps. 1, 4–5; Sorabji 2006, 2008.

[16] I do not assume that one's sense of self is necessarily something of which one is consciously aware. On the contrary, it seems to me that a person can be surprised by discoveries of what things lie within the boundaries of the self. In particular, loss is often an occasion for just such discoveries (I discuss loss in Chapters 9 and 10).

[17] The term "psychological identity" I borrow from McKenzie 2009, whose paper I have found very helpful; I thank her for sharing an early typescript of it with me. See also Sorabji 2006, chap. 9.

I think that a focus on the self as psychological identity is particularly appropriate when thinking about happiness in terms of eudaimonia. Human happiness is something I have described as a life of rational self-construction. Part of that idea is that it takes practical wisdom to shape the pursuit of one's ends into a good human life. But the self under construction here is the self that must choose who to be and what pursuits to find fulfillment in as an individual. So for the purposes of thinking about happiness, the self is best understood as what makes an individual who he is, what makes his life *his*, and what makes a happy life *his* happiness.[18] After all, this is why Aristotle and other ancient eudaimonists took eudaimonia to be *self-sufficient* (*autarkēs*): eudaimonia requires having enough of what one needs with respect to the central activities and attachments in one's life.[19] Eudaimonia, in other words, is something that belongs to the whole self, whatever the "whole self" turns out to be.

3.2 Honing the two conceptions

I want to sharpen these two conceptions of the self first by distinguishing them along four main dimensions, which will also make it clearer how these two conceptions can be brought to bear on the sufficiency thesis. But before I do so, I should first try to avoid misunderstanding by pointing out some things that are *not* at issue in this distinction. Four points are in order here. First, the distinction between these two conceptions has nothing to do with the relation of mind and body. Questions about the conception of the self concern whether one takes anything outside the power of choice to be essential to one's psychological identity; those questions have nothing to do with the metaphysical status of any of those things. Second, we should not suppose that the formalized view puts any less weight on social roles in the account of virtuous activity than the embodied view does. For instance, even if activity is identical with the exercise of the power of choice, it could still be the case that the virtuousness of activity depends on committing to certain social roles in one's choices.[20] Third, there is no reason to suppose that formalized activity involves diminished care or affection for others. It is one thing to think of oneself as identical to one's power of choice, and quite another to think that that power of choice is the only thing worth loving. And lastly, on the formalized conception there is no reason to suppose that friends, lovers, relations, or children are fungible—that any object for one's activity is the same as any other. Even if the particular others in one's life are not taken to be part of one's own identity, this is not to say that one's care, concern, or affection for those others is insensible of their particularity. For a formalized self, friendship can involve love for another as the unique person that he or she is. For instance, it is true on both the formalized and the embodied conceptions that as one's friend changes, what counts as

---

[18] It is, I think, life in this sense that Nozick (1974) thought we would give up if we were to plug into his imaginary "experience machine." See also Sanders 2002, 41–4.

[19] See esp. Aristotle, *NE* I.7, 1097b6–16.

[20] We shall see this point in connection with Epictetus in Chapter 7.

acting wisely with respect to one's friend will change too. This is because acting wisely in such contexts may require certain forms of appreciation of the very uniqueness of the other person.[21] The difference is that on the formalized view, virtuous activity is the exercise of wisdom in the various areas of one's life, such as in one's friendships. On the embodied view, virtuous activity is one's involvement in *that* friendship itself, insofar as the involvement is wise.

This brings us to the more precise contrasts we can draw between the formalized and the embodied conceptions—from what the distinction is not to what it *is*. The first contrast concerns the connection between activity and the particularity of the activity's objects. On the embodied conception of the self, "activity" in the abstract is really a fictitious shorthand, since activity in a real life is always a multitude of *activities*, in the plural—*this* relationship with *this* child, *this* relationship with *this* partner, *this* career in *this* field, *this* participation in *this* community, and so on. The same is true, a fortiori, of virtuous activities. What makes each of these activities virtuous is that it is adopted and pursued within one's life with practical wisdom and emotional balance; but such activities are always identical to one's particular pursuits within particular relationships and projects. For this reason, *the continuity of embodied activity is precarious*, since activity so understood can always be interrupted or terminated altogether by circumstantial changes. To lose some central attachment—a spouse, say, or a career—on this view, is to lose for ever a particular way of being in the world, leaving one to find a new self to be. By contrast, on the formalized view ongoing activities and projects are seen as patterns of selection and response with respect to the world around one, and such patterns can continue unabated even when one's worldly circumstances change. To be sure, the loss of a particular other may be the loss of something significant, but what it cannot be is the loss of the ability to continue the virtuous activity in which one's happiness consists. That activity just is the practically wise and emotionally sound exercise of will, and it takes no *particular* object in order to do that. Put another way, it always takes some object, but there is no object that it always takes.

Second, it follows that these two conceptions of the self involve correspondingly different views about the continuity of *happiness* and its vulnerability to circumstantial changes. On the embodied view of the self, activity is vulnerable to fortune in exactly the way that formalized activity is not: one's activity always has as its very substance one's particular attachments and relationships, and of course these are vulnerable to fortune. Therefore, if happiness consists in virtuous activity, then for that very reason happiness consists in something that is vulnerable to fortune, and so of course happiness itself must be vulnerable to fortune. *Reversals of fortune, that is, touch on happiness because they touch on the very activities in which happiness consists.*

---

[21] E.g. consider how in *East of Eden* Adam Trask is surprised when he first notices the individuality of his twin baby boys—and how Adam ultimately fails to take their individuality seriously as young men, with tragic results.

By contrast, a formalized self is clearly less vulnerable to serious interruption or upheaval brought about by external or even bodily changes: I may lose my career or my spouse, say, but while this may be a serious and distressing loss, its impact is mainly on what projects are available to me, not on who I am. It does not even impact what I can do, on a formalized understanding of doing: if what I do, really, is to direct my will in a certain way—so as to act and react well, say—in relation to the world around me, then I can continue to do the same in my new circumstances, too. In that case, the activities of the virtuous are far less vulnerable to circumstantial changes, and so the happiness of the virtuous person, which consists in such activities, can therefore be put beyond the reach of bad luck.

Third, it also follows that these two conceptions of the self yield very different views of how it is appropriate to respond to significant losses in our lives. On the embodied view, it is appropriate to respond to such losses as *threats to our activity, our happiness, and our very selves*, because that is precisely what they are. On the formalized view, by contrast, such losses may indeed be significant, but their significance is not that of a threat to happiness or the self.

Lastly, the formalized and embodied conceptions of the self differ radically over the necessity of the goods of fortune. On the formalized view, goods of fortune are not necessary for the sake of virtuous activity. Virtuous activity, on this view of the self, is of course the "use" of other things, as the Stoics would say, but even so there are no *particular* sorts of things—such as goods of fortune—that virtue needs in order to make good use. On an embodied view, by contrast, a person's happiness and well-being are more vulnerable to circumstantial changes, since the person's selfhood and activities depend so crucially on the particular ways in which one inhabits the world. This means that *particular bodily and external goods are necessary for and even parts of happiness*, insofar as such goods constitute the possibility of continuing in embodied virtuous activities— that is, in activities that are embodied within one's particular attachments and ends. On this view, the self and its activities depend on particular goods of fortune, and this is why happiness is vulnerable to fortune, since it is in these vulnerable activities that happiness consists.

3.3 The boundaries of the self

Notice that several of these contrasts concern the nature of loss and its impacts. This is no accident, since it is in the context of loss that the notion of the boundaries of the self becomes especially clear. In fact, I owe the phrase "boundaries of the self" to grief and bereavement psychologist Colin Murray Parkes, who observes that the loss of a close attachment—whether a beloved person, or a career, or a home—is very often experienced as a loss of part of oneself, a loss that forces one to construct a new self. This is a striking feature of human experience: "Why should the loss of someone 'out there,'" Parkes asks, "give rise to an experience of the loss of something 'in here'?" (Parkes 1987, 108) His answer, very simply put, is that the person, activity, or thing lost had become such a part of one's life and identity that one now struggles to recognize oneself and one's life without it. In other words, what one has lost is something within the boundaries of the self.

Not only does thinking about the experience of loss make the notion of the self as a thing with boundaries a little clearer, but it also provides a context for thinking about what can be at stake depending on where one places those boundaries. It is, first of all, appropriate to talk of persons *placing* these boundaries in one place or another (whether consciously or not). As is obvious, not everything is within those boundaries, and people differ considerably and importantly in where their boundaries are placed: for some, living in a particular geographical location (say) is crucial to their psychological identity, but for others it is not.[22] Moreover, we seem to have a considerable degree of control over where we place (or re-place) our own boundaries. For instance, Epictetus banks on this fact when he repeatedly urges his hearers to remember that the people they love are as fragile as jugs (e.g. *Handbook* 3). His point is not that we should love them no more than jugs, but that we ought to prepare ourselves so that we do not experience the loss of them as a loss *of self* (see Reydams-Schils 2005, 68).

Apparently, Epictetus would advise against expanding the boundaries of the self to include one's children, and we may disagree. What sorts of reasons are there, then, for placing those boundaries in one place or another? Well, clearly there are things that it would be ridiculous to include within the boundaries of the self, simply because they don't have that kind of importance for us—a mobile phone, say, or a shoelace, or a shrub. However, there are reasons for caution in the placement of the boundaries, even in the case of clearly important things. The loss of things within the boundaries of the self threatens one's happiness by interrupting a life that one can recognize as one's own—that is, after all, how we have defined these boundaries. Of course, such losses are devastating, but there are reasons not only to be resilient in recovery from devastation, but also to be less susceptible to devastation in the first place. For instance, imagine a doctor who specializes in palliative end-of-life care, and who regularly loses patients to horrible diseases that strike too young. How susceptible to devastation does it make sense for such a doctor to allow herself to be? She really should remind herself of how fragile—how like jugs—her patients are. Perhaps she should do so to manage the pain of loss; but there are other reasons too. She owes it to her patients (present and future), their families, her co-workers, and her employer not to be susceptible to devastation, which would take her "out of the action," so to speak, and make it difficult for her to do the good that we depend on her to do.[23] And she owes it to herself: the tragic loss of a human life is a terrible thing, and there is value in mourning that loss; but there is also value in living without constant emotional upset, and she has reason to let herself live a happy life without constant interruptions. Of course, we will probably feel that too great a detachment from the suffering and loss of her patients

---

[22] Recall this contrast between Samuel and Liza Hamilton, from the Introduction.
[23] This is a central theme in Cicero, *TD* III, a text we shall examine in Chapter 11.

is dangerous as well, perhaps numbing her feeling for others and threatening her happiness in that way too.

This example illustrates that the boundaries of the self cannot be placed *anywhere* without a cost. The question, then, is not where we humans might place the boundaries for free, but what placement of those boundaries is one we can best afford. In the coming chapters I argue that it is precisely that question—where to place the boundaries of the self—that divided the two sides of the ancient sufficiency debate.

3.4 Control, dependence, and self

By now we should have a fairly good sense of the respective implications of these two conceptions of the self for the sufficiency debate. Consider first the formalized conception of the self. On that view, bodily and external goods are always separate from virtuous activity, and so treating the goods of fortune as necessary for happiness means making them necessary right alongside virtuous activity, as if happiness consists in these two goods. In that case, reconciling the control and dependency theses is the task of explaining how happiness could lie in two distinct things that vie for significance where happiness is concerned—and this of course generates exactly the tension between the control and dependency theses that we explored above. On the formalized view of the self, therefore, it is difficult to see how one might retain the dependency thesis, given a commitment to the control thesis. In other words, the control and dependency theses are zero-sum *provided that the self is a formalized self*. In that case, the obvious thing to conclude is that virtue is sufficient for happiness, just as the Stoics did.

In fact, in Part 2 I argue that the Stoics drew that conclusion for exactly that reason. For now, it will suffice simply to point out their formalized conception of the self. The self, on this view, is one's will, or what the Stoics call one's power of choice (Greek *prohairesis*, Latin *voluntas*) and "assent." Consider what Epictetus says in this spirit, in an especially revealing passage in which he imagines someone trying to force him to act against his will:

What, then, should we have at hand upon such occasions [i.e. when people try to force us to do things]? Why, what else than to know what is mine, and what is not mine, what is within my power, and what is not? I must die: and must I die groaning too? – Be fettered. Must it be lamenting too? – Exiled. Can anyone prevent me, then, from going with a smile and good cheer and serenity? – "Betray the secret." – I will not betray it; for this is in my own power. – "Then I will fetter you." – What are you saying, man? Fetter *me*? You will fetter my leg; but not even Zeus himself can get the better of my choice. "I will cast you into prison." My wretched body, rather. "I will behead you." Did I ever tell you, that I alone had a head that cannot be cut off? – These are the things that philosophers ought to study; it is these that they should write about each day; and it is in these that they should exercise themselves.[24]

---

[24] Epictetus, *Diss.* I.1.21–5, italics in trans.; cf. I.1.10–13, I.18.17, I.29.5–8, III.18.3; Cicero, *Fin.* III.75. See Sorabji 2006, 44, 47, 181–2; 2007, 87–8.

Notice that Epictetus does not reply merely, "Go ahead, fetter me—I can take it; I will still conduct myself well; you won't break my will." His reply is more radical—that *he cannot* be fettered, because as far as he is concerned, he *is* only his will. Such a conception of the self was also crucial to the Stoics' conception of virtuous activity. Virtuous activity, on the formalized Stoic view, is the activity of selecting and reacting well with respect to one's circumstances, whatever they may be.

However, the embodied conception of the self offers an alternative. This view makes bodily and external goods parts of happiness, not as further goods besides virtuous activity, and not merely for the sake of virtuous activity, but as the very pursuits in which one's embodied activity consists. For instance, on such a view my loving relationship with my spouse is part of my happiness because my participation in that particular relationship is one of the central activities that my life consists in. To lose that spouse is to lose *that life*, and thus *that happiness*.

Importantly, given an embodied conception of the self, the control and dependency theses cease to be in tension. On the contrary, if the control thesis is true and it is upon virtuous activity above all that happiness depends, *and if* such activity is embodied activity, then the dependency thesis *must also* be true: one's particular attachments and relationships must be goods that are parts of one's happiness (the dependency thesis), inasmuch as they are the very stuff of the virtuous activity in which one's happiness consists (the control thesis). In other words, the dependency thesis is not true in spite of the control thesis but *precisely because of it*.

Clearly, the embodied conception makes happiness vulnerable to fortune, just because the activities, projects, and relationships of which virtuous lives are made are vulnerable to fortune. And to say that happiness is vulnerable to fortune just is to deny the sufficiency thesis. Now, this is not to say that happiness must be permanently ruined by reversals of fortune. Often one can (in time) take up new activities and a new life, and one's life can once again begin to make sense and be recognizable as one's own. Even so, once attachments central to the self have been severed, *that* happiness— the happiness of *that* self—is forever gone, even if some new happiness may still be possible. If one's life becomes once again recognizable as one's own, it is because it is recognizable as belonging to this newly reconstructed self.

Several questions now remain. One is whether the conception of the self was in fact as major a factor within the ancient sufficiency debate as my brief discussion here would suggest. I argue in Part 2 that it was, and this suggests that the conception of the self is a deep and important issue for anyone thinking about happiness to confront. Another is to what extent the participants in that debate recognized for themselves that this issue was the line along which their sides were drawn. Here, I argue, the answer is mixed. As we shall see in the next chapter, there is good reason to suspect that Aristotle may have thought of the self as embodied, since he suggests at times that the self may be embodied in certain close relations with others, such as friendship. However, this idea was not much developed in the Aristotelian tradition, and more important, such an idea never seems to have been brought explicitly to bear on the sufficiency debate anyway. Consequently, in the ancient sufficiency debate the formalized view seems to have dominated, largely by default, and that left the Aristotelians—with their dependency thesis—at a serious argumentative disadvantage. Indeed, it seems to have left them with an inconsistent triad: the control thesis, the dependency thesis, and a default view of the self that makes the control and dependency theses conflict.

Things are very different on the Socratic and especially the Stoic side, though, where the importance of the formalized conception of the self for the sufficiency thesis actually was made explicit, particularly by Epictetus. However, this raises a further, very important question: *why* would the Stoics have chosen the conception of the self as the line along which to draw up sides? Was there some problem that they perceived in the embodied conception that made it an unacceptable option? In Part 3 I argue that indeed there was. In fact, I argue not only that the problem they perceived was real but that as far as I can see, the problem has no solution. But perhaps, at best, it may allow a compromise we can live with.

PART 2

Happiness then: the sufficiency debate

5

Aristotle's Case Against the Sufficiency Thesis

Ask a philosopher today about the thesis that virtue is sufficient for happiness, and you will hear not only that it is obviously false, but also that if you are in any doubt about it you need only brush up your Aristotle. Specifically, you will probably be directed to the tenth chapter of the first book of Aristotle's *Nicomachean Ethics*, where he observes that a person cannot be happy if he is terribly unlucky, however virtuous he may be. That question, you will hear, is one that Aristotle put to rest long ago.[1]

However, while I agree that the sufficiency thesis is false, I cannot share this sanguine assessment of Aristotle. For one thing, his most memorable point on the issue was to remind us of Priam, the virtuous Trojan king who met a tragic end. But Socrates' life ended badly too, and the point hardly could have been lost on such proponents of the sufficiency thesis as Plato and the Stoics, for whom Socrates was a paragon, not only of virtue, but of happiness. Something more had to have been going on here.

For another, the sanguine assessment of Aristotle's legacy conflicts sharply with its actual history. Writing about three centuries after Aristotle, Cicero tells us that the sufficiency thesis had been the watershed issue in ethics the whole time. "Whoever disagrees about the highest good," says Cicero, disagrees not just about ethics but "about the entire philosophical system" (*Fin.* V.14, my translation; cf. IV.14). This is the crucial issue in ancient ethics, Cicero says, because it concerns the nature of the greatest good in life and the key to happiness, and in particular how virtue is related to happiness. Once we determine the highest good, "we shall have found out how to live and how we ought to act, and therefore the standard to which we should refer. From that point, we can do what everyone wants to do—discover and construct a plan for living happy lives" (V.15). And when we think about happiness, Cicero says, the fundamental question is still whether virtue is sufficient for happiness or whether happiness requires good fortune as well (V.12).[2] So things stood in the middle of the first century BC; somehow, the sufficiency thesis had become the main issue, and disagreements surrounding it could even be seen as the fault-lines between one school

---

[1] See e.g. Hursthouse 1999, 75 n. 11, cf. 172; Foot 2001, 96–7; Swanton 2003, 60 n. 7.
[2] See also *Fin.* II.34–35, III.30, and *TD* V.84–5, where Cicero offers much quicker sketches.

and another. Evidently, neither Aristotle nor his successors appeared as having put anything to rest on this score.

I argue that, on philosophical grounds, it is Cicero's assessment that is more accurate. So far from settling the debate over the sufficiency of virtue for happiness, what Aristotle actually did was to reveal just why that debate should be so difficult to resolve. Likewise, I think Cicero is also correct in his assessment that none of Aristotle's philosophical heirs had resolved that debate, either. In other words, it is still unfinished business for philosophy.

My specific aims in this chapter are threefold. One, I want to examine several forms of the Aristotelian case against the sufficiency thesis, first in Aristotle himself (section 1) and then in the subsequent Peripatetic tradition (sections 2–5). Two, I argue throughout that these attacks on the sufficiency thesis were unsuccessful because ultimately they were all in tension with a picture of human nature that the Aristotelians were rightly unwilling to give up. And three, I argue in a programmatic way that rejecting the sufficiency thesis while avoiding that tension requires developing an alternative conception of the self and applying it to the sufficiency debate, as the ancient Aristotelians themselves did not (section 6). This is the view of the self that I called the "embodied conception" in the previous chapter.

1 Aristotle's rejection of the sufficiency thesis

1.1 The Priam problem

Aristotle's denial of the sufficiency thesis comes on the heels of his general discussion of happiness and the good in the first book of the *Nicomachean Ethics*. The seeds of his denial appear in I.8–9 with Aristotle's discussion of the role of good things in the happy life. These goods are of three types: mental goods, bodily goods, and external goods (*NE* I.8, 1098b12–16; cp. *Pol.* VII.1, 1323a24–7).[3] The things he identifies as bodily and external goods are those that would seem so to anyone: friends, wealth, influence, being well-born, having good children, being attractive, and so on.[4] He then identifies two roles that such goods play in happiness: one, they are useful as "instruments" that support and facilitate activity, and two, they are desirable for their own sake, adding as he says to the "luster of happiness"[5] (*NE* I.8, 1099a31–1099b6; I.9, 1099b27–28; I.10, 1100b9, 28–30; cf. *EE* I.2). Aristotle then draws the natural conclusion: bad luck, such as losing good things or lacking them altogether, keeps one from being happy, at least if the loss or lack is very serious (*NE* I.8, 1099b3–6; I.9, 1100a5–9; I.10, 1100b22–30, 1101a6–13). Here Aristotle points to King Priam, a prime literary example of a good,

---

[3] The thesis that there are three types of goods, all necessary for happiness, remained a staple of the Aristotelian position; see e.g. *MM* I.3, 1184b1–4 and DL VII.30.

[4] Aristotle also talks about the role of friendship in happiness in *NE* IX.9, 12. See Sherman 1987, 589–613, for discussion.

[5] This phrase is from Ross's 1980 translation.

upright man who also lost everything—his kingdom, his family, and then his own life in an impious murder, at the fall of Troy. As good a man as Priam may have been, Aristotle says, no one could take seriously the suggestion that Priam's life was a happy one. Indeed, no one could deny the vulnerability of happiness to fortune unless he was just defending a thesis for its own sake (I.5, 1095b31–1096a2).

However, these common-sense points about bad luck need to be reconciled with Aristotle's claim that virtuous activities are what "control happiness" (NE I.10, 1100b8–11).[6] How exactly is power over happiness to be divided between virtue and luck? The example of Priam gives this issue a shape that Aristotle can inspect from all sides. On one side, Aristotle insists that no virtuous person could ever become "wretched," as if conducting one's life with wisdom and emotional soundness—living one's life virtuously, that is—just made no difference in the face of luck (1100b33–5, 1101a6–8). Yet on another side, Aristotle cannot bring himself to say that a person who suffers the kinds of things Priam suffered could seriously be called happy. This means, then, that Priam cannot be happy, *and* that he cannot be unhappy, either (1100b33–5). Aristotle offers no third way, and so he remains perplexed about cases of virtue faced with serious bad luck. He then ends his discussion, somewhat feebly, with a question: "What then stops us from calling happy the one who is active in accordance with complete virtue, sufficiently equipped with external goods, not for some random period of time but over a complete life?" (1101a14–16). In truth, the question acknowledges the Priam problem without settling it: if happiness consists in virtuous activity as well as other goods, then somehow Priam is neither happy nor unhappy nor some third thing. In the end, it is just not clear what to say about someone like Priam on Aristotle's view.

Now, there is far more at stake for Aristotle here than merely finding some third category into which Priam might fit. (If the problem were just that, it would be a fairly simple one to solve.) The real problem, I argue, is that Aristotle's discussion of Priam reveals a triad of theses that turn out to be in tension with each other:

1) Happiness is controlled by virtuous activity;
2) There are bodily and external goods that are parts of happiness; and
3) These bodily and external goods are not themselves activity or parts of activity.

Of course, the first two are the theses which in the previous chapter I labeled the "control thesis" and the "dependency thesis," respectively. Thesis (3) is a corollary of what I there called the formalized conception of the self—the self as will acting in relation to other things—and for simplicity I shall call it the "formalized thesis." Let's examine these theses more closely to see how they create a tension for Aristotle's account of happiness.

---

[6] So Irwin 1985 translates the relevant phrase.

1.2 Aristotle and the control thesis

Aristotle believes that happiness is controlled by virtuous activity: "it is activities in accordance with virtue that control our happiness, and the opposite sort of activities control the opposite state" (*NE* I.10, 1100b9–11). What does Aristotle mean in saying that virtuous activities "control" happiness? To answer this question, we should begin by recalling that for Aristotle, human nature is complex. On the one hand, we are *patients* whose happiness depends to some extent on bodily and worldly resources that are not entirely up to us. As we have seen, for Aristotle our happiness depends in part on such things as the fertility and attractiveness of our bodies, our social position, our material resources, and so on. On the other hand, we are also *agents* whose happiness depends not just on how things turn out for us but, crucially, on how we act and lead our lives. Happiness is something *active*: it involves actively pursuing ends, not standing by as things unfold.[7] For Aristotle, happiness just *is* a kind of activity (*energeia*, I.10, 1101a14–15; X.7, 1177a12).

For Aristotle, this idea stems directly from his conception of human nature. Aristotle reveals this conception in his identification of our rationality with our characteristic human "function" (*ergon*): by nature, a human life is

a practical sort of life of what possesses reason; and of this, one element "possesses reason" in so far as it is obedient to reason, while the other possesses it in so far as it actually has it, and itself thinks. Since this life, too, is spoken of in two ways, we must posit the *active* life; for this seems to be called a practical life in the more proper sense. If the function of a human being is activity of soul in accordance with reason, or not apart from reason, and the function, we say, of a given sort of practitioner and a good practitioner of that sort is generically the same . . . if all this is so, and a human being's function we posit as being a kind of life, and this life as being activity of soul and actions accompanied by reason, and it belongs to a good man to perform these well and finely, and each thing is completed well when it possesses its proper virtue: if all this is so, the human good turns out to be activity of soul in accordance with virtue (and if there are more virtues than one, in accordance with the best and the most complete). (*NE* I.7, 1098a3–18; italics in Rowe's translation)

Likewise, Aristotle holds that loving oneself is primarily loving that element in one that thinks and is intelligent about practical things (*NE* IX.4, 1166a17–19); in fact, he says that each of us just is his practical intellect, or at any rate each of us is this most of all (IX.9, 1168b34–1169a3). Thinking intelligently about practical things is the role of practical wisdom (*phronēsis*), the intellectual virtue by which one deliberates well about the good life (VI.5, 1140a26–8). Aristotle's insistence that happiness is active and not merely passive therefore has deep roots in his very understanding of human nature.[8]

---

[7] *NE* I.5, 1095b31–1096a2; X.6, 1176a33–1176b2; *EE* I.3, 1215a7–19; I.4, 1215a20–5; *MM* I.3, 1184b14–17; I.4, 1185a9–13; *Pol.* VII.3, 1325a32–4, 1325b12–16. This is one of the formal constraints on eudaimonia that we discussed in Chapter 3.

[8] Of course, Aristotle also maintains in *NE* X.7–8 that a human is really his *theoretical* rather than practical intellect; I shall return to this point in a later note (see also the note in Chapter 3).

It is important to see that for Aristotle, it is by practical reasoning that we guide our lives, *including* our lives as patients. This is why Aristotle denies that conventional goods apart from virtue have a power to benefit us just as such.[9] For instance, he says repeatedly that things that are genuinely or properly good are those that are so for the virtuous and wise person (*NE* III.4, 1113a22–33; X.6, 1176b23–7; *Pol.* VII.13, 1332a22–7), whose use of them is always good (*NE* I.10, 1100a24–29; IV.1, 1120a4–8). As the author of the *Magna Moralia* makes clear, Aristotelians generally understood these to be things like public office, wealth, strength, and beauty, which the good person uses well and the bad person badly (*MM* I.2, 1183b27–35, 1183b39–1184a4; II.9). Furthermore, Aristotle says that such goods do not benefit fools who use them (*EE* VII.15, 1248b31–2), and even harm bad persons who use them (*NE* V.9, 1137a26–30). In fact, Aristotle says provocatively that even if fools or bad persons should be very lucky in an everyday sense where these things are concerned, we should not really consider it *good* luck for them, since good luck has to be understood in relation to happiness (VII.13, 1153b21–5). Here Aristotle seems to have been greatly influenced by Plato's argument in the *Euthydemus* (278e–282a) that even if we were to start defining happiness by simply listing all sorts of conventionally good things, we would soon realize that it would take practical wisdom for any of those things to benefit us in the first place; in that case, good things are so only for those who use them well. As for Plato, then, goodness for Aristotle is, in the first instance, a creative, fashioning power belonging to rational agents who act with practical wisdom and emotional soundness.

It is clear, therefore, that for Aristotle our status as rational agents is not one part of our nature among many, but is what defines us—it even defines what sorts of patients we are. Since Aristotle believes that happiness is activity, and in particular our activity as practically wise agents, it is clear that our success in living as rational agents must play a unique and defining role in our happiness. "Let us state that wisdom and intellectual accomplishment," Aristotle says, "must necessarily be desirable in themselves, if virtues they are, each of one of the two soul-parts in question, even if neither of them produces anything at all" (*NE* VI.12, 1144a1–3). As Christine Korsgaard (1986, 278) puts Aristotle's point, the virtues "are just those qualities that actualize our potential for rationality: they make us human beings."

How should we characterize the role of virtuous activity in happiness more precisely? It is tempting to answer this question by pointing to the fact that, for Aristotle, conventional goods can be parts of happiness only if one is virtuous. However, it is equally true for Aristotle that virtuous activity can be part of happiness only if one also has conventional goods, since happiness requires both. A somewhat deeper answer would be that other goods can count as good in the first place only when one makes use of them in a virtuous way. However, this answer is consistent with the thought that

---

[9] Here I have benefited greatly from Roche 2008.

once such things count as good, our happiness depends primarily or even entirely on them, and thus that it is they that play the defining role in happiness. In other words, this answer tells us that the happiness of people *in general* does not depend just on their fortunes with respect to conventional goods (since vicious people are not happy even with such goods), but for all that it might still be the case that the happiness of *virtuous* people just lies in their being conventionally well off.

Rather, Aristotle says that while it is true that happiness does require some measure of conventional goods, still it is not this that we should consider in judging whether a life is happy but the sorts of activities that characterize that life. Conventional goods, he says, "are not where living well or badly is located, but rather human life needs them in addition, as we have said, and it is activities in accordance with virtue that control our happiness, and the opposite sort of activities control the opposite state" (*NE* I.10, 1100b8–11). This is also why happiness is something relatively stable: happiness does not just follow one's fortunes, in which case happiness would be like a chameleon's colors, but follows rather the goodness of one's activities (1100a32–b30). This, then, is what Aristotle means by virtue's "controlling" happiness: whatever else we may need, it is primarily virtuous activity that defines the tenor of a life where happiness is concerned.

As instructive as this is, however, Aristotle still does not make the notion of virtue's "control" over happiness nearly as precise as it should be. This is because virtue's "controlling" role is defined in contrast to the role of other goods in happiness, and of course it is just that contrast that Aristotle struggles to articulate in *NE* I.10. And as we shall see, Aristotle's successors characterized that contrast in different ways, so that as happiness depended more on virtuous activity the role of other goods diminished, and vice versa. But what is clear enough is that any account of the relative roles of virtue and other goods must take as seriously as possible the crucial fact that it is our rational agency that is distinctive of our nature and thus central to our happiness as creatures with that nature.

1.3 Aristotle and the dependency thesis

Aristotle also holds that there are bodily and external goods that are parts of happiness. This we have already seen, inasmuch as Aristotle holds that some such goods add to the "luster" of happiness, and are such that, as in the case of Priam, their loss is incompatible with happiness. If the idea that virtuous activity controls happiness reflects our nature as rational agents, then the idea that bodily and external goods are parts of happiness reflects the fact that by nature we are also patients. By saying that such goods are "parts" of happiness I mean that they are more than things that facilitate our acting or things in relation to which we act. Rather, they are such that (for the virtuous, anyway) life is better with them than without them, for their own sake. As we saw above, Aristotle says that there are bodily and external goods that are bad to lack, just for their own sake (*NE* I.8, 1099b2–8), and which are thus necessary for happiness for their own sake (I.9, 1099b27–8). Of course, we know already that Aristotle insists that it is our rational agency and not such goods that controls happiness (I.10, 1100b8–11), but at the same time it is undeniable that we are also patients, and it is this thought which keeps Aristotle from thinking of Priam as a happy man.

Now, it might seem at first that the dependency thesis must already conflict with Aristotle's belief in the control thesis: if a life of virtuous activity cannot count as happiness unless these other goods are also present, then why should we think that it is virtuous activity that controls happiness? Aren't virtuous activity and external goods equally powerful with respect to happiness, since neither can count as happiness without the other? To be sure, Aristotle denies that virtue and the other goods are equally powerful with respect to *unhappiness*, saying that as long as a person is virtuous he cannot become unhappy or wretched. But ultimately this does not do nearly enough to re-establish virtuous activity as the controlling part of happiness. The more that we take seriously the idea that we are patients for whom bodily and external goods are important parts of happiness, the less convincing is the thought that unhappiness should depend *only* on viciousness anyway. And the less convincing that thought is, the more it seems that when virtue and serious misfortune are both present, one is unhappy. Wouldn't that mean that serious misfortune has *at least* as much control over happiness as virtue has, after all? Wouldn't it compete with the thought that our agency is what is central to our nature?

It would, *provided that* we understood virtuous activity and the other goods as distinct from each other and contributing to happiness in distinct ways. But we need not think of them in that way. Suppose that the boundaries of the self are broad enough to include, not only the mind or will that engages in projects and relationships, but also those projects and relationships *themselves*. For instance, on such a view my "being a good husband" is not a matter of acting well where matrimony is concerned, but is my acting well in *this* matrimonial relationship, an activity that has *this* partner as its unique target and without whom *that* activity must cease to be. This is what I called the embodied conception of the self in the previous chapter. On this view, we are not forced to decide whether it is my virtuous activity or these other goods that controls my happiness, because my happiness consists in this relationship (inter alia) as inextricable from the very activity in which my happiness consists. So the control and dependency theses do not conflict per se; that depends on whether the self is embodied or formalized.

1.4 Aristotle and the formalized thesis

However, it is clear that Aristotle never brought an embodied view of the self and its activity to bear on the relation between virtuous activity and happiness. This is not to say, please note, that he did not *have* such a view. On the contrary, it seems undeniable that in his discussion of friendship Aristotle thinks of a beloved person, not merely as an object or recipient of love, but as a "part of love itself," in Martha Nussbaum's phrase (1986, 344). Indeed, Aristotle says famously that "the friend is another self" (*NE* IX.9, 1170b6–7), and that such a friend seems to be the greatest external good of all

(1169b8–10). In that case, we might say that activities of friendship go on not merely *in relation to* particular close relationships, but *as embodied in* those particular relationships, as Nussbaum suggests (ibid.). Likewise, Nancy Sherman interprets Aristotle as holding that friendships and other loving relationships provide "the very form and mode of life within which an agent can best realize her virtue and achieve happiness," and "are the form virtuous activity takes when it is especially fine and praiseworthy (1155a9, 1159a28–31)."[10] Here friendship is not a good in addition to, or as a context for, virtuous activity, but is itself a kind of virtuous activity from which one's friend is inseparable. On this view, the loss of a loved one does not, of course, necessarily prevent one from ever exercising friendship again, but it does mean that one of the particular constitutive activities of one's life is forever lost, closing off the possibility of living *that* life any more. And notice that on such a view we would not be forced to choose between virtuous activity and friendship as having the greater control over happiness: the friendship of the virtuous, on this view, just is "the very form and mode" of virtuous activity. Thus on this view, happiness consists not in virtuous activity *plus* friendship, but in that virtuous activity that *is* friendship.

Aristotle may also suggest a similar view of the self and activity when he explains why craftsmen have so much affection for their creations:

The explanation of this is that existence is an object of desire and love for everyone; that we exist by being in actuality (since we do so by living and acting); and that in a way, the work *is* the maker in actuality; so he loves his work, because he loves his existence too. And this is a fact of nature; for what he is in potentiality, the work shows in actuality. (*NE* IX.7, 1167b31–1168a9, italics in Rowe's translation)

Aristotle's point seems to be that the maker's work is not merely the object of his productive activity but is part of the very form of that activity and internal to it. It is therefore cherished as part of the maker's existence, which is something active. Aristotle suggests a similar phenomenon between parents and their children (1168a2–3).

If this view were generalized to other sorts of goods and activities, it would follow that virtue is not sufficient for happiness, not *despite* the fact that happiness is controlled by virtuous activity, but precisely *because* it is. Nevertheless, and unfortunately, Aristotle never brings any such view to bear on his discussion of goods and happiness. On the contrary, what seems noteworthy about Priam in Aristotle's discussion is not the life of particular, embodied activities he has lost, but just the plain fact that he is so spectacularly unlucky. In a word, embracing such a view of the self would shed much new light on Aristotle's problem, but neither Aristotle nor (as we shall see) any of his followers ever brought such ideas to bear on the sufficiency debate, however far they had or had

---

[10]   Sherman 1989, 127. See Sherman 1987 and 1989, chap. 4; see also Nussbaum 1994, 395. I do not go as far as Sherman, however, in finding an embodied conception of the self in *NE* I.

not developed such ideas.[11] (Towards the end of this chapter I speculate as to why Aristotle did not avail himself of that view of the self in *NE* I.)

Without such a view of the self and activity, however, the control thesis *does* compete with the dependency thesis. To see this, suppose that virtuous activity and the goods in relation to which we act are distinct from each other and matter in distinct ways for happiness (the formalized thesis). On the one hand, the more we take seriously the thought that it is our rational agency that defines our nature (the control thesis), the more we are led to think of virtuous activity as supremely stable and the sort of thing to endure reversals of fortune. Indeed, since it is our rational agency that must shape even our nature as patients, the more it seems on this line of thought that our status as patients is yet another worldly circumstance that serves as material for virtuous activity to use (as the Stoics and perhaps even Socrates believed). However, in that case, goods besides virtue would seem to have rather little to do with happiness after all (*contra* the dependency thesis). What we needed was a way to unify our nature as agents and our nature as patients; instead, one part of our nature has now eclipsed the other. On the other hand, the more we take seriously the importance of our nature as patients (the dependency thesis), the greater power conventional goods acquire over our happiness, and the more one's happiness comes to depend on what is happening to one (*contra* the control thesis). In that case, our nature as agents is now in danger of being eclipsed by our nature as patients.

Simply put, if misfortune with respect to bodily and external goods, considered as distinct from virtuous activity, has a significant detrimental effect on the happiness of the virtuous, then it is unclear how it is virtuous activity that controls happiness. And of course, if they do not have such an effect, then it is unclear why they are so important for happiness in the first place. That is the tension between the triad of theses that I noted above.

1.5 The Priam problem again

What is more, it is clear from Aristotle's discussion that he feels just such a tension rather acutely.[12] We can see this clearly in his discussion of Priam, as Aristotle shifts restlessly between the idea that virtuous activity controls happiness and the idea that special goods are also necessary for happiness. Aristotle begins with the idea that happiness must be something that is stable and up to the happy person, since happiness must not change like the chameleon's colors, and he finds this idea to reinforce his claim that virtuous activity is what controls happiness (*NE* I.10, 1100b4–11). This is because "in no aspect of what human beings do is there such stability as there is in

---

[11] Indeed, as Nussbaum 1986, 365, notes, while Aristotle insists *that* friendship is important in the good life for its own sake, he has far less to say about *the way in which* it has that importance.

[12] It is difficult to tell whether the conflict is one between Aristotle's own considered views, or only one that he perceives between views he finds to be commonly accepted (I thank an anonymous reader for pointing this out). However, nothing in the following discussion rests on taking either of these possibilities over the other.

activities in accordance with virtue," so that the happy virtuous person should "always, or most of all,[13] do and reflect on what is in accordance with virtue, . . . and as for what fortune brings, 'the man who is truly good and four-square beyond reproach' will bear it in the finest way, without any note of discord of any kind" (1100b12–13, 19–22). So, on the one side, virtuous activity can keep on even through adversity, since it does not need any special sorts of goods, and so it is the sort of thing to control happiness and make it stable. This suggests one way out of the inconsistent triad, namely accepting that virtuous activity controls happiness and that virtuous activity is not tied to any bodily or external goods (i.e. accepting the control and formalized theses) and then marginalizing the role of bodily and external goods in happiness (i.e. rejecting the dependency thesis).

But Aristotle is no Stoic, and he abruptly pulls away from such a view and re-emphasizes the importance of bodily and external goods for happiness. While small fortunes and setbacks do not change happiness, he says, nonetheless

turns of fortune that are great and repeated will if good make one's life more blessed (since they themselves are such as to add luster to life, and the use of them is fine and worthwhile), and if they turn out in the opposite way, they crush and maim one's blessedness; for they bring on pains, and obstruct many sorts of activities. (*NE* I.10, 1100b22–30)

Here he insists on the dependency thesis by arguing that serious bad luck is obviously incompatible with happiness.

But now there are at least three related problems. One, this line of thought seems to bring with it a new way of thinking about virtuous activity as now requiring special goods after all, since virtuous activity is "obstructed" without them—a very different idea from the idea that virtuous activity is what does well despite circumstances of fortune. Clearly, Aristotle is working with two very different ways of thinking of such activity, and he makes no suggestion as to how they might go together. Two, it also seems that the tragic loss of a loved one, say, "crushes and maims" happiness either by obstructing activities or by being painful in its own right. However, neither option seems adequate: surely what is tragic about such a loss is not the mere fact that one now has one fewer person on whom to bestow generosity, for instance; and although it is more plausible to describe such a loss as "bringing on pains," Aristotle has just finished saying that such pains are the sorts of things which virtue "will bear in the finest way" nonetheless. And this brings us to the third problem, namely that it is still unclear how to square the importance of bodily and external goods for happiness with the idea that virtuous activity controls happiness. The more he emphasizes our nature as patients, the more he struggles to maintain the centrality of our nature as agents.

Aristotle apparently takes the point to heart, as he now makes yet another abrupt shift, saying again that "even in these circumstances the quality of fineness shines

---

[13] I have changed Rowe's translation so that "most of all" (*malista*) qualifies, not the attribution of this activity to the virtuous person, but rather the claim that this activity is what he "always" does.

through" (*NE* I.10, 1100b30–1).[14] Here we are back to the idea that acting virtuously is living your life well, and thus is what really controls happiness: "If one's activities are what controls the quality of one's life, as we have said, no one who is blessed will become miserable; for he will never do what is hateful and vile" (1100b33–5). And then a volley back the other way: although such a person will not be wretched, "neither will he be blessed if he meets with fortunes like Priam's" (1101a6–8). And so he goes between these two lines of thought, now that happiness consists in virtuous activity, and now that happiness consists also in good things besides, apparently seeing no way to unify these two ideas. The result is that Aristotle's discussion of Priam is not the *solution* of a problem about happiness, but the *articulation* of one.

I have already suggested one way to avoid Aristotle's inconsistent triad, namely by rejecting thesis (3)—the formalized thesis—and making bodily and external goods parts of happiness insofar as they are internal to virtuous activity. But there are other options as well, and these are attested among Aristotle's various followers. One of these is to reject thesis (1)—the control thesis—and hold that happiness consists in a plurality of goods, with virtuous activity as but one good among many. Less extremely, one might try again to strike a balance between these three theses, accepting all three as they stand and showing that although happiness consists in a plurality of goods, nonetheless virtuous activity is somehow still the dominant or controlling part of happiness. Alternatively, one might reject or perhaps revise thesis (2)—the dependency thesis— and say that while happiness does require certain bodily and external goods, it does not require them as parts but only as somehow facilitating or expanding virtuous activity. Lastly, one might distinguish between levels of happiness so that the control thesis concerns one level of happiness for which virtue is sufficient, and the dependency thesis another level of happiness that also requires certain further goods as well.

Each of these strategies has a long history reaching from Aristotle's ancient followers and commentators right down to our own time. So we should look at each strategy and its history more closely to see how each fares, on philosophical grounds, as a way of dealing with Aristotle's problem. This I shall do in the rest of this chapter (sections 2–5), arguing that in the end none of these strategies is satisfactory. Instead, I advocate the alternative strategy I have already suggested, namely to reject the formalized thesis and understand the bodily and external goods that are parts of one's happiness as parts of the self that acts, and thus as parts of the virtuous activity in which happiness consists (section 6).

2 Happiness as a plurality of goods: Theophrastus and Lyco

Surely the most straightforward view of the parts of happiness is the view often attributed to Aristotle's successor as head of the Lyceum, Theophrastus (381–*c.* 287 BC).

---

[14] See also *Pol.* VI.13, 1332a19–25, cited by Heinaman 1993, 40.

Cicero portrays Theophrastus' view as stark but internally consistent: since he held that there are three kinds of goods—the standard Aristotelian trio of mental, bodily, and external goods—and that their opposites are bad things, it was only natural for him to conclude that happiness requires these various goods and that their opposites bring unhappiness (*TD* V.24–5; see also *Fin.* V.77, 84–6; *TD* V.85). Interestingly, Cicero says that for Theophrastus, such bad things actually have a certain "great power" over one's life—they have the power to make a life go poorly and wretchedly (*magnam vim habere ad male misereque vivendum*).

In a similar vein Lyco (*c.* 300–*c.* 225 BC), the third head of the Lyceum after Aristotle, also made happiness consist in virtue and other goods. According to Lyco, happiness consists in pleasure and virtue. More precisely, Lyco held that our final end is "true joy of the soul . . . based upon what is honorable," or more simply upon what is "fine" (*epi tois kalois*; Clement, *Misc.* 2.21.129.9). Evidently, Lyco held that happiness consists in virtue and the joy of virtue (see S. White 2004, 392). Or rather, Lyco made a point of locating happiness *in joy*, and then qualified it as joy of a specific kind (the kind that is "in what is fine"). Perhaps, then, Lyco's view was not that the good is virtue and therefore also joy, but rather that the good is joy, in particular the sort of joy that requires virtue.

It seems undeniable that Theophrastus and Lyco take very seriously the idea that there are goods besides virtuous activity that play a crucial role in the happiness of the virtuous person (i.e. the dependency thesis). And after all, it is just that idea that makes it so difficult to suppose that Priam could be happy. However, our evidence about these two views is rather thin, and in particular it is difficult to determine exactly where they stood with respect to the first thesis of Aristotle's triad, that is, that happiness is controlled by virtuous activity. They either rejected or accepted that thesis, and we should consider each possibility.

The first possibility is that Theophrastus and/or Lyco rejected the thesis that happiness is controlled by virtuous activity, and held instead that happiness depends simply on a plurality of goods. Now, on such a view, virtuous activity would be but one good among many where happiness is concerned. We can see this as follows. On the view in question, bad things are said to have a life-ruining power, and these are not limited to bad activities but include all three kinds of evils, such as grief (mental), beatings (bodily), and banishment (external). Presumably, then, good things are those with a life-improving power, and this power will belong to all three types of goods as well. In that case, if virtue is a good, then it is one good among many, all of which have a life-improving power, and all of which are parts of happiness.[15] And even if it takes virtuous activity for these other goods to make

---

[15] See also Annas 1993a, 387–8. Cicero seems to attribute this sort of view to Theophrastus, yet Cicero also suggests that he is responding to a picture of Theophrastus built up over time, and he finds it difficult to pin specific theses to specific texts (e.g. *TD* V.24–5; see Annas 1993a, 386, for discussion).

one happy, it is also true that it takes these other goods for virtuous activity to make one happy.[16]

If this was indeed Theophrastus' or Lyco's view, then it was considerably starker than Aristotle's in three important ways. One, such a view comes down with a clear, decisive verdict about cases like Priam's: bad things make life go badly, so Priam is unhappy. Two, notice that virtue therefore would have even *less* power over happiness than serious bad luck would, since when both are present, as in Priam's case, one is unhappy. Three, and most important, such a view rejects the Aristotelian view of human nature as fundamentally active, in favor of human nature as recipient and patient of good things. On Aristotle's picture, it is this part of our nature that accounts for our need to construct a hierarchy of ends so that good reasons can be given for our activities (see *NE* I.1–2). And as Aristotle argues in the "function" argument of *NE* I.7, it is the exercise of our practical rationality that is the fundamental and defining activity of creatures with our nature. This is why, for Aristotle, virtuous activity is what controls human happiness. Therefore, we cannot reject the control thesis without also rejecting Aristotle's very conception of human nature.

In the end, therefore, this first type of strategy gives up too much in terms of its picture of human nature and happiness. However, perhaps Theophrastus and/or Lyco did not take such a stark strategy, but sought instead to conjoin somehow the thought that bodily and external goods are parts of happiness with the thought that virtuous activity controls happiness.[17] In fact, this was the very strategy of Critolaus and at least a few other Aristotelians, so let's turn to that strategy now.

3 Virtue as the dominant good: Critolaus et al.

Critolaus (*c.* 200–*c.* 118 BC), a later head of the Lyceum, held that the final end is "perfection of life flowing well according to nature, indicating the tripartite perfection jointly completed from the three classes" (Clement, *Misc.* 2.21.129.10).[18] In other words, happiness consists in "fulfillment" with respect to the three families of goods that Aristotle had identified. However, and importantly, Critolaus explicitly tried to balance his position that happiness consists in all the goods (virtue among them), on the

---

[16] I leave aside the even starker view of Hieronymus, an Aristotelian contemporary with Lyco, who is said to have held that happiness consists in living without mental anguish, and (as Cicero insists) not in virtuous activity at all. See Cicero, *Fin.* V.14, and S. White 2004. Such a view would have been marginal to the Hellenistic sufficiency debate, which (as *Fin.* V makes clear) concerned parties who agreed that virtuous activity is part of happiness.

[17] Indeed, some of our other sources suggest that Theophrastus may have thought that virtue was a thing apart from all other goods after all (e.g. Ambrose, *On the Duties of Ministers* 2.2; *Depository of Wisdom Literature*, #6), and some tell us that Theophrastus gave good and bad fortune less credit than Cicero says he did (e.g. John of Lydia, *De Mensibus* 4.7; Vitruvius, *De Architectura* 6, Introduction, 2).

[18] Trans. S. White 2002, 85–6. See also Stobaeus, *Anthology* II.46, 10–13; Clement, *Misc.* 2.21.128.5. For discussion, see Annas 1993a, 413–15, and S. White 2002, 85–90.

one hand, with the idea that happiness is controlled by virtuous activity, on the other.[19] Cicero tells us that Critolaus

claims that if in one scale he puts the good that belongs to the soul, and in the other the good that belongs to the body and good things which come from outside the man, the first scale sinks so far as to outweigh the second with land and seas thrown in as well. (*TD* V.51)

The likely motivation behind Critolaus' metaphor of the scale is clear, since without it he would be committed to the hard-line view that happiness just consists in a collection of goods. With the metaphor, however, Critolaus seems fairly clearly to mean that while happiness does consist in many goods, nonetheless virtue is far from being one among many goods, but can even be what controls happiness. To press on a pan of the scale, in Critolaus' metaphor, is to be important for happiness, and since virtue exerts more pressure on the pan than anything else can, and more than even everything else taken together, it must matter for happiness in a way that nothing else does.[20]

In a similar fashion Callipho, an otherwise unknown Aristotelian philosopher of the second century BC, is said to have held that the greatest good in life is to do what one can to attain and enjoy pleasure, together with virtue,[21] a view also attributed to the likewise unknown Dinomachus (see S. White 2002, 90–1). Callipho makes happiness consist in virtue and another good, but he says that everything besides virtue must be ranked "a long way behind it" (Cicero, *TD* V.87). Callipho was joined in this strategy, Cicero tells us, by his student Diodorus (fl. *c.* 118 BC), who in turn held that the good is "living untroubled and honorably," or in other words that happiness consists in virtue and freedom from pain.[22] Critolaus' strategy has had its modern advocates as well. For instance, Terence Irwin has argued that for Aristotle, happiness can be seen as consisting in every type of good, including virtue, and that virtue is still the "dominant" (or controlling) part of happiness, so that the loss of such goods never renders one *unhappy* provided that one is virtuous.[23]

The idea behind the general approach of Critolaus and the others is to retain the deep Aristotelian thesis that virtue controls happiness and fit it with the thought that happiness also consists in other sorts of goods. And since the contributions of virtue and other goods to happiness appear to be treated as more or less distinct contributions (as per the formalized thesis), the strategy here is not so much to reject some part of

---

[19] It is not unlikely that Critolaus held something like the view of Reeve 1992, 166, who argues that if "activity expressing virtue is present in a life, some *eudaimonia* is present in it, although not necessarily enough to make the life itself *eudaimōn*."

[20] Evidently, Critolaus understands the self-sufficiency constraint in *NE* I.7 to be that happiness must be a greater good than all other goods together, and not merely greater than each other good on its own. (I discuss this issue in Chapter 3, and briefly below.)

[21] Cicero, *TD* V.85; *Acad.* II.131; *Fin.* II.19, 34–5, V.21, 73, cp. IV.49–50; *Off.* III.119.

[22] Clement, *Misc.* 2.21.127.3; Cicero, *Fin.* II.19, 34–5, IV.49–50, V.14; *Acad.* II.131; *TD* V.85, 87.

[23] Irwin 1999, 8–10. Irwin's proposal also gives us a way to sort Priam, who is not happy (because his life lacks many types of goodness) but is also not *unhappy* (because he is virtuous and thus always possesses the dominant part of happiness). This means that there is an intermediate state between happiness and unhappiness where someone like Priam belongs.

Aristotle's triad as to deny any serious tension in the first place. However, that tension in fact reappears for this strategy in the form of the following dilemma: either the commitment to the dependency thesis will attenuate the commitment to the control thesis, or the latter will attenuate the former.

We can see the first horn of this dilemma, I think, in the very metaphor offered by Critolaus: it is just the same kind of thing that a scale measures on either side, so prima facie the scale metaphor seems a particularly poor choice to demonstrate a difference in *kind* between virtue and other goods where happiness is concerned. Moreover, the more we take seriously the thought that goods besides virtue are important for our happiness, the less plausible it is to think that unhappiness depends strictly on vice. Since this strategy relies on the latter thought in order to maintain the "dominance" of virtue with respect to happiness, that dominance is correspondingly unstable.[24]

Alternatively, perhaps Critolaus intended by his metaphor, not merely a quantitative difference between virtue and other goods, but indeed a qualitative one—a difference by an order of magnitude, so to speak. So read, the metaphor is to convey the idea that while both virtue and other goods have a life-improving power, nonetheless virtue has such a power to such a great degree that it is in fact a different and wholly superior kind of good after all.[25] In that case, Critolaus' metaphor is consistent with a fully robust commitment to the control thesis. However, now we come upon the second horn of the dilemma, which is apparent in Critolaus' metaphor as well: the point about "earth and seas" tipped into the pan, or other things being "a long way behind," is clearly that no matter what we set alongside virtue, it never makes all that much difference where happiness is concerned. But if these things make so little difference, then why do we say that happiness consists in them too and is "crushed and maimed" without them? Surely no one who is moved by the considerations that led Aristotle to refuse to call Priam happy will be satisfied with the idea that everything else in one's life matters only very, very little where one's happiness is concerned.

Critolaus' strategy therefore reveals a crucial, deep, and instructive philosophical problem. As long as we persist in maintaining the distinctness of our status as agents and our status as patients where happiness is concerned, efforts to maintain the control thesis and efforts to maintain the dependency thesis will be zero-sum, and therefore our attempts to unify those two pictures of our nature will be continually frustrated.

---

[24] It is worth noting that Critolaus described happiness as the "joint fullness" (*sumplērousthai*) of the three species of goods (Clement, *Misc.* 2.21.128.5, 2.21.129.10; Stobaeus, *Anthology* II.46, 10–13). Stephen White (2002) argues that "joint fullness" should be understood as indicating those goods that are parts of happiness (which fulfill happiness by bringing together all of its parts), and not merely necessary tools. However, Brad Inwood has suggested to me that that description could also suggest a view of persons as receptacles to be filled up by the various goods. Either way, it would follow that "Critolaus thus asserts both the sovereignty of moral virtue and the commensurability of its component ends" (S. White 2002, 89), leaving it mysterious how these two views are to be reconciled.

[25] I thank Brad Inwood for this suggestion, which is inspired by Seneca's argument in *Ep.* 118.14–16 that some things take on a different quality when they are increased quantitatively, as when a child by becoming bigger also changes qualitatively, by becoming an adult. See Inwood 2007, 313–15, for discussion.

We can see this dilemma more clearly by considering Stephen White's version of Critolaus' strategy.[26] White argues that, although virtuous activity is not sufficient for happiness without bodily and external goods, virtue is nonetheless a "sovereign" good with respect to happiness because

> it determines or controls whether happiness is attained. This involves three claims: first, that happiness depends primarily on virtuous activity; second, that it has other needs as well; and third, that each need is in turn dependent on that activity. Hence, the way in which happiness depends on virtuous activity differs crucially from the way in which it depends on anything else: all other needs are "additional" because they are necessary either for virtuous activity in the first place or for that activity to suffice for happiness. (S. White 1992, 122–3)

Other goods, on White's view, serve as resources for virtuous activity, but they are also important for happiness in their own right: they are necessary in order for virtuous activity to suffice for happiness.[27] Fair enough, but couldn't we just as well say that virtue is also necessary for those other goods to suffice for happiness? If so, then virtue and other goods would be equally poised with respect to happiness after all. Here White faces Critolaus' dilemma, and the other goods will matter either too much or too little. The first horn of the dilemma is this: if virtue and other goods are equally poised with respect to happiness, then virtue could hardly warrant the description "sovereign," and we would be back once again with something like the stark view we discussed in connection with Theophrastus. In that case, goods besides virtue would matter too much since they would then matter in just the same way that virtue does. In other words, the commitment to the dependency thesis would jeopardize the commitment to the control thesis.

To avoid this horn of the dilemma, White must insist that, although both virtue and other goods are constituents of happiness, nonetheless virtue is a constituent of some special sort. And this is just what he does say: "any who are happy find their happiness in their virtuous activities."[28] This is what it means for happiness to "depend primarily" on virtuous activity. However, White now faces the second horn of the dilemma: since on this view virtuous activity is distinct from these other goods, White must diminish considerably the extent to which the virtuous find happiness in such things as, say, their intimate relationships with others, as opposed to their virtuous activities. But to the extent that that move succeeds, those other goods come to matter far too little—surely

---

[26] S. White 1992, esp. part 2, chap. 5.

[27] Cp. Heinaman 2007, 245: "some of the goods other than virtuous activity which Aristotle counts as necessary for eudaimonia are neither constituents of eudaimonia nor of merely instrumental value. Rather, the presence of such goods is required if the fortunate circumstances of life are to exist in which virtuous activity can be considered eudaimonia."

[28] S. White 1992, 122. See also Cooper 2003, 132–5, who identifies eudaimonia with that part of life that makes it choice-worthy or worth living at all, and holds that this part can be improved by the addition of other goods (though this does not make for a higher form of happiness, see pp. 127–30). On this view, virtue is a dominant good because it is the only good that, on its own, can make life choice-worthy at all.

those who wish to deny the sufficiency thesis and hold on to the dependency thesis will be motivated by the thought that it is in precisely those sorts of goods that our happiness is found to a very important extent. Indeed, if happiness is found in them to such a small extent, then why do they have the enormous power of crushing and maiming happiness when they are missing?

The root problem for all versions of Critolaus' strategy is that it merely conjoins two competing views of human nature without unifying them, maintaining both that human nature is such as to live rationally and, somehow, also such as to be a recipient of good things.[29] And without unifying those two views, it is difficult to see how Critolaus' strategy is to avoid amounting either to the hard-line claim that happiness consists in a bunch of goods, virtue merely among them (giving up the control thesis), or to the sufficiency thesis after all (by giving up the dependency thesis). One way to unify them would be to understand bodily and external goods as important for happiness insofar as they provide (in Sherman's phrase) the very form and mode of virtuous activity, but we do not find any such move in Critolaus' strategy. As long as virtuous activity is understood not to include those other goods, this dilemma is inescapable. In that case, no version of Critolaus' "dominance" approach can give a really satisfactory account of why virtue is not sufficient for happiness.

4 Goods as necessary for virtuous activity: Arius and Aspasius

The next strategy maintains that virtue controls happiness, but holds that bodily and external goods are not *parts* of happiness, while allowing that they are necessary for happiness in some other way: that is, it either rejects or at least significantly modifies the dependency thesis. In particular, this strategy holds that other goods besides virtue are necessary for happiness, not for their own sake, but for the sake of somehow facilitating virtuous activity; this strategy thus accepts the formalized thesis, as well, by making virtue and other goods distinct from each other. This view is found in some of Aristotle's ancient as well as modern commentators.[30]

Writings on Peripatetic ethics, the doxographer Arius Didymus (fl. *c.* 30 BC) defined happiness as the exercise of virtue "in certain kinds of circumstances"—that is, *en prohēgoumenois*, literally "in the leading circumstances."[31] His strategy was to show that, although virtuous activity can be done in a wide range of circumstances, still the virtuous activity in which happiness consists is of a specific sort, and that sort requires certain other goods. However, these goods are not themselves parts of happiness (see Huby 1983, 127).

---

[29] See also Cicero, *Acad.* II.139 and *Off.* III.119 for similar concerns in different contexts.
[30] Recall that it was also suggested as an option by S. White 2002 in the passage quoted above.
[31] For texts and discussion, see Huby 1983.

There are two likely options for reconstructing what Arius may have meant by these "leading circumstances."[32] One, he may have meant that although the virtuous can act well even in adverse circumstances, nonetheless the virtuous require *favorable* circumstances in order to act virtuously in a "complete" way. Here we might compare the virtuous person to a cobbler, for instance, who can make shoes even out of poor leather, even though cobbling is done in a complete way only with leather of good quality. Similarly, we might say that while a person can be generous even with little, still one can be generous in a complete way only if one controls enough resources to make a more significant impact. Or two, he may have meant that even though a generous person, say, must know how to deal even with poverty, nonetheless the *proper* circumstances for generosity are those concerned with wealth. Here we might think of a physician who must understand the nature of sickness, but whose proper concern is nonetheless how to bring about health. In fact, this is how the 2nd century AD commentator Aspasius characterized the Aristotelian view, namely as holding that happiness consists in virtuous activities within their proper circumstances (Aspasius, *In NE* 22.35, 26.15).[33] Aspasius evidently picks up on a view that Aristotle himself suggests: virtue needs other goods as instruments, Aristotle says, since virtuous activities require certain kinds of goods to use as well as access to certain parts of society in which to use them (*In NE* 23.30–24.23, 26.20–4).[34] Either way, the general point seems to be that virtuous activity is not sufficient for happiness because other goods are also needed—not for their own sake, but to facilitate virtuous activity in some way or other so that that activity can count as happiness.[35]

This is an ingenious strategy. If the problem facing Theophrastus and Critolaus is that the Aristotelian cannot make happiness consist in virtue plus other goods without compromising either the dominance of virtue or the necessity of other goods, then one clear solution would be to make those other goods necessary for happiness by making them necessary for virtuous activity itself. And not surprisingly, this clever strategy has had its modern advocates as well, most notably John Cooper and Richard Kraut. As Cooper is correct to point out, a "central conviction" of Aristotle's is "that what determines the character of a person's life is what *he does*" (Cooper 1999, 308–9). However, Cooper notes that even if the value of goods besides virtue "is not independent of the value of virtuous activity, that does not mean that the good that virtue does is available without them" (1999, 306). The role of such goods for Aristotle, Cooper

---

[32] Huby 1983, 126–9; see also Annas 1993a, 415–18.

[33] See Huby 1983, 126–7, citing *In NE* 3.7, 52.34, 96.14, 35, 97.16, 29–30, 98.8; see also Sharples 1999.

[34] The commentator Alexander also says that virtuous activity requires special circumstances; see Irwin 1990, 75–6, for discussion.

[35] The third possible philosophical use of *en prohēgoumenois*, as Huby notes, would restrict happiness to virtuous activity done at the full level; consider the difference between merely doing things that doctors do, like cutting or stitching, and really practicing medicine. However, it is unlikely that this is what Arius intended, since he takes this point to be distinctively Aristotelian, whereas all ancient virtue theorists agreed that really acting from generosity (say) is different from merely going through the motions of generosity.

says, is to make virtuous activity free of impediments,[36] both by serving as instruments for virtuous activity (e.g. money, connections) and by expanding one's sphere for virtuous activity (1999, 298–300). For instance, one's children are a good insofar as they afford a context for virtuous activity, and without that context "one's virtuous activities are diminished and restricted" (1999, 300). In fact, it is in this way that Cooper understands even those goods that Aristotle says add luster to happiness:

It is true that . . . [Aristotle] distinguishes between those [goods], like money, that are used only as instruments in the virtuous man's projects, and others like health and good looks, but even these latter . . . are needed as antecedently existing conditions that make possible the full exercise of the happy man's virtuous qualities of mind and character. In each case the value to the happy man consists in what the external goods make it possible for him, as a result of having them, to do. (1999, 304)

Likewise, Richard Kraut treats goods besides virtuous activity as necessary resources for virtuous activity, without which "virtuous activity would be diminished to some extent" (Kraut 1999, 83, 85). However, these goods do not add any value to life in addition to the value added by virtuous activity but are only means (1999, 85–6, 89).

Nonetheless, as ingenious as this strategy is in both its ancient and modern incarnations, it suffers from at least two very serious problems. The first is that while this strategy initially appears to avoid making happiness consist in any goods besides virtuous activity, in fact this appearance is deceiving. To see this, note that the view at hand insists on much more than that our virtuous interactions with the world require objects in the world with which to interact. Sickness and poverty, after all, are objects with which one might interact virtuously, just as much as health and wealth are, as the Stoics were fond of pointing out. Rather, this strategy requires more than *some* worldly sphere of activity or other, but a *specific sort* of worldly sphere. So far from restricting happiness to virtuous activity, this strategy only concocts another good in which happiness consists: in addition to virtuous activity, happiness also consists in a sufficiently *broad and interesting sphere* for virtuous activity. Consequently, on this view, happiness still consists in two things: virtuous activity *plus* certain desirable states of affairs within which to act. And we are thus pushed back to one of the previous two strategies after all: either we deny that virtue controls happiness, or we show that virtue's control over happiness can somehow be reconciled with the importance of the other parts of happiness. No ground has been gained.

We can see this problem also in a possible variation on Arius' general strategy, on which certain goods are necessary in order for action to be virtuous at all. Indeed, on Aristotle's view, in order for an action to be virtuous, not only must it be done from the right internal states of the agent, but it must also succeed in hitting its external target (see Irwin 1990). In that case, perhaps a virtue like generosity (say) requires special resources because it has a special target, so that one will not have engaged in bona fide

---

[36] Cooper 1999, 298, citing *NE* VII.13, 1153b17–19.

generous activity without hitting that target, and thus without using those special resources. Such a thought might be at least part of what motivates Aristotle's account of things necessary for happiness (e.g. in *NE* I.8–9), but the question at present is whether it does anything to help him out of his problem, and it is clear that it does not. To say that activities will count as virtuous in a way that matters for happiness only if they are externally successful, is to say that happiness consists in virtuous activity understood as including, not only how one acts, but also certain external states of affairs that result from how one acts. But in that case, those states of affairs must also be valuable for their own sake, and not only for the sake of facilitating virtuous activity (on pain of circularity). And once we have gone that far, we have conceded that worldly states of affairs can be good for their own sake, so that it is no longer clear why there should not be good worldly states of affairs that are even parts of happiness. Happiness has now gone from consisting in what one *does* to consisting (also) in states of affairs one *brings about* (see Irwin 1998, 169–72). But of course, this is simply to reaffirm the original dependency thesis, the very thesis that Arius' general strategy had intended to modify.

The second main problem for Arius' general strategy is that it gives many goods the wrong place in happiness anyway. We can see this by thinking about the difference between never having had some good and losing a good one previously had—that is, the difference between lack and loss. For instance, remaining childless need not be a tragedy at all, but losing one's child is tragic; and in any case, even though having no children and losing a child may each be a bad thing, they surely are not the *same* bad thing. Now, on the view of happiness we are considering at present, the impact of goods on happiness is to increase the area or appeal of the circle of one's opportunities for virtuous activity. But, in that case, losses and lacks would have to impact happiness in exactly the same way: in each case, the circle of opportunities is just smaller or less appealing than otherwise. That is not only deeply implausible but also at odds with our reaction to Priam: it is a strike against his happiness to lose his kingdom, even though it is no strike against another's happiness never to have had a kingdom at all.[37] The sorrow experienced by the one who suffers a loss will be very different from the sorrow of the one who suffers a lack,[38] but the view in question will struggle greatly to account for that difference, since loss and lack appear to impact happiness in just the same way on that view, namely by affecting the breadth and appeal of the sphere of activity.

A proponent of Arius' strategy might respond that the "holes," as it were, in one's sphere of activity resulting from losses affect happiness not just because they reduce the overall area or appeal of that sphere, but because those holes also have the peculiar *shape* of the thing lost. Less metaphorically, the loss of a particular loved one renders impossible not just another activity but *that* activity that was possible only with *that* person in one's life.[39] I find this thought very plausible—it is, in fact, more or less my

---

[37] I thank Mark LeBar for this point.

[38] Here I have benefited from comments from an anonymous reader.

[39] I thank another anonymous reader for suggesting this response.

own view. However, notice that this is to say that goods like one's loved ones are parts of happiness that are not distinct from one's virtuous activity itself; in other words, it is to accept the dependency thesis but not the formalized thesis. By contrast, the entire thrust of Arius' general strategy is to *distinguish* such goods from virtuous activity—they are rather its context or its means—and deny that they are parts of happiness. In that case, to the extent that we succeed in plausibly separating lacks from losses where happiness is concerned, we must to that extent give up Arius' strategy. This Aristotelian view, therefore, cannot do justice to the distinction between losses and lacks, and that seems to me to be a most serious strike against it.

We can generalize from these two problems. By making bodily and external goods important for happiness on the grounds of their subservience to virtuous activity, we merely create yet another new good in which happiness consists (the breadth and appeal of the sphere for virtuous activity) and give short shrift to the other goods that led us away from the sufficiency thesis in the first place. In a way, then, this strategy finds itself impaled on both horns of Critolaus' dilemma at once.[40]

5 Levels of happiness: Antiochus

The final ancient strategy to consider is that of the Academic philosopher Antiochus (born *c.* 130 BC). Antiochus opposed the skepticism of the so-called "New" Academy and championed a return to the "Old" Academy of Plato and his pupils, which Antiochus considered to be an Academy of developed, systematic doctrines.[41] But Antiochus held, not only that the Academy stood for a positive view of the nature of happiness and the good, but indeed that that position was in fact shared by Aristotelians and Stoics as well, and that the alleged disagreement over the definition of happiness between the latter two schools was merely verbal rather than substantial.[42] For Antiochus, this "Ur" position was that even though virtue is sufficient for a happy life, it is not sufficient for the *happiest* life, which needs other goods as well (Cicero, *Fin.* V.81). In other words, there are actually two sorts of happiness, one for which virtuous activity is sufficient (the "happy life," *vita beata*) and another, greater sort that requires bodily and external goods in addition to virtuous activity (the "happiest life," *vita beatissima*).[43] According to Antiochus, the Stoics should be understood as focusing on the sufficiency of virtue for the former sort of happiness, and the Aristotelians as

---

[40] I therefore do not share Annas' assessment that Arius' strategy is the most promising of the lot (1993a, 424–5).

[41] It is therefore appropriate that Cicero should place the dramatic setting of his discussion of Antiochus in *Fin.* V—a discussion of what it means to be in the Academy—on the very grounds of Plato's Academy, where the discussants are met at once with visions of Plato and his pupils, on the one hand, and of Carneades on the other (V.2, 4).

[42] For Antiochus' insistence on the agreement of Academics and Aristotelians, see Cicero, *Fin.* V.7, 14, 21; on the agreement of Aristotelians and Stoics, see V.22, 74, 78, 90, 93.

[43] See Cicero, *Fin.* V.21, 77–86, for discussion; see also *Acad.* II.22, 134; *Laws* I.55. For discussion, see Barnes 1989, esp. 79, and Annas 1993a, 419–23.

focusing on its insufficiency for the latter sort. Rather than disagreeing, he maintained, the two schools are simply talking past each other. In support of this philosophical merger, Antiochus argued on the Stoic side that their so-called "preferred indifferent" things were really just goods under a different name, and that these were necessary for the highest happiness, just as they were on his reading of the Aristotelian view.[44] And on the Aristotelian side, Antiochus perhaps drew on Aristotle's remarks that no one could be "blessed" (makarios) if he was as unlucky as Priam, which Antiochus perhaps contrasted with being "happy" (eudaimōn) (NE I.10, 1101a6–8).[45] On this view, a virtuous person is "happy" come what may, but if he is very unlucky he will not also be "blessed."

Antiochus was not alone in reading Aristotle this way. There was a controversy among Aristotle's ancient readers, one that continues today, as to whether Aristotle (at NE I.7, 1097b17–19) had claimed (a) that happiness is the most choice-worthy good, even if we do not count other goods alongside it, although it can be improved by the addition of other goods; or (b) that happiness is the most choice-worthy good, there being no other good that can be counted alongside it, so that happiness cannot be improved by the addition of other goods (recall this ambiguity from Chapter 3).[46] The latter reading holds that happiness just is the fulfillment of all goods, and therefore not improvable, so that to add more goods to happiness would be, absurdly, to create an excess of happiness (see Cicero, Fin. V.81). Happiness, on this reading, is not a good, not even the greatest among goods, but that in terms of which all goods are understood. But the former reading, by contrast, holds that happiness can be improved by the addition of other goods, even though it is already more choice-worthy than any other good.

Moreover, in his view that happiness can be improved by adding other goods to it, Antiochus has been followed by some modern readers as well. For instance, David Ross's (1980) translation of the Nicomachean Ethics italicizes 'blessedness' at 1101a7, reflecting Ross's view that Aristotle intends such a contrast as this.[47] Robert Heinaman argues that happiness is self-sufficient in the sense that it is the most desirable of all goods, when it is compared with them one by one, but is nonetheless improvable by the addition of other goods.[48] John Cooper has argued recently that happiness is self-sufficient in the sense that happiness is sufficient for a life's being choice-worthy, that is,

---

[44] Fin. V.81, 88–91; Acad. II.22, 134; Laws I.55. Although I find Antiochus' interpretation of the Stoics on this point utterly unacceptable, I shall leave it aside at present. Cicero begins his own critique of it at Fin. V.77. I discuss Stoic "indifferent" things in the next chapter.

[45] See also Annas 1993a, 420, for discussion.

[46] See Sharples 1999, 88–90.

[47] See Nussbaum 1986, 329–30, for discussion. See also Broadie and Rowe 2002, 287–8, who interpret "blessedness" at NE I.10, 1101a16–21, as not just happiness, but happiness that lasts until the end of one's life.

[48] Heinaman 1988, esp. 42–3; Heinaman 2002. Heinaman (1988, 42–4; 2002, 103, 109, 117–18, 120–1) has been an especially vociferous defender of the view that eudaimonia is a good among others and can be improved by the addition of other goods, primarily on the basis of NE I.7, 1097b16–20 and X.2, 1172b27–35.

preferable to no life at all, but that a happy life can also be improved with the addition of other goods.[49] And Terence Irwin argues that happiness is complete and self-sufficient in including all determinable *types* of goods, but improvable by adding further *tokens* of these types.[50]

Now, it seems unlikely (*pace* Ross) that such a view can be extracted from Aristotle's very use of the words for "happiness" and "blessedness," which in fact he uses interchangeably (see esp. *NE* I.10, 1100a10–1100b11).[51] Moreover, what really seems to vex Aristotle about Priam is not that he was not as happy as he might have been, but that there seems to be no sort of happiness worth the name that a life like Priam's could be said to have. But more important for our purposes is the fact that Antiochus' strategy would not even address the real problem for the Aristotelian position anyway, which (once again) is not just to find a third category for someone such as Priam. The problem lies in showing how happiness can *both* be controlled by virtuous activity *and* consist in bodily and external goods as well, a problem which by now is quite familiar.[52] That problem remains, regardless of whether we say that such goods are necessary for the happy life or for the "most happy" life. Therefore, the Antiochean strategy turns out to be a variant of Critolaus' general strategy after all, namely that virtue is far greater than any other good but happiness consists in them all. Antiochus says that there is some form of happiness for which virtue suffices, even if one needs other goods in addition in order to reach an even greater happiness. But of course, Antiochus still holds that happiness—or, in his own terms, the greatest happiness—consists in virtue and all the other goods, and thus it too conjoins two very different dimensions of human nature and happiness without doing anything to unify them.

Notice, then, that Antiochus' strategy ends in a now familiar place. If goods besides virtuous activity are unnecessary for something that is genuinely *happiness*, then those goods matter far less than Aristotle would allow. And if there is some other sort of happiness that consists in both those goods and virtuous activity, then we must determine how to conjoin this thought with the thought that it is virtuous activity that controls that sort of happiness. So yet again we face Critolaus' dilemma. It is therefore instructive that Antiochus' spokesman in *On Goals* V should repeatedly insist that while bodily and external goods are necessary for the happiest life, nonetheless they have far less weight for our well-being than virtue does, even with earth and sea thrown into the scales (V.91–2; see also V.68–72, 88–91). Antiochus' spokesman

---

[49] Cooper 2003, esp. 130–1.

[50] Irwin 1999, esp. 8–9. See also Sharples 1999, 89 n. 12, for other modern proponents of broadly Antiochean views.

[51] Barnes (1989, 87) thus refers to this strategy as one of Antiochus' "novelties." See also Nussbaum 1986, 330–3.

[52] It is therefore instructive that Antiochus takes it that things can count as goods not only in relation to virtue (Cicero, *Fin.* V.90–1). See Karamanolis 2004, 85–6.

apparently perceives the tension between the control and dependency theses, and it is on the dependency thesis that he (like Critolaus) chooses to compromise. But the compromise is again unstable: surely it was the idea that bodily and external goods carry rather considerable weight that motivated their necessity for the highest level of happiness, and indeed the very distinction between levels of happiness, in the first place.

This doggedly persistent dilemma should tell us something about the structure of the Priam problem—and not just as a historical curiosity but as a deep issue for eudaimonism, ancient and modern alike. That problem arises because we are simultaneously attracted to two different ideas: that we are rational self-constructors whose happiness depends fundamentally on what we do, and that our happiness is nonetheless vulnerable to fortune where bodily and external goods are concerned. We have found that if we treat virtuous activity and these other goods as distinct from each other, then no matter what we do, those other goods will turn out to matter in the wrong way for happiness, in one way or another. But if that is so, then surely we should ask whether virtuous activity and those other goods really should be regarded as distinct from each other. There is no evidence that the ancient Aristotelians raised that question, at least where the sufficiency debate was concerned. But I want to raise it now in a suggestive and programmatic way (I make it my focus in Part 3).

6 Reconsidering the self

Tinkering with the control thesis jeopardizes the deep Aristotelian view that virtuous activity—acting with practical intelligence and emotional balance—is the fulfillment of our human nature and thus what controls happiness (sections 2–3). Tinkering with the dependency thesis jeopardizes the deep Aristotelian view that bodily and external goods are important parts of a person's happiness (sections 3–4). And by making these two theses refer to different levels of happiness, we simply swap the difficulty in the case of one sort of happiness for the same difficulty in the case of some other sort of happiness (section 5).

It would seem, therefore, that the only remaining option would be to reject the formalized thesis and its narrow view of the self. On that view, virtuous activity is a matter of directing one's will in relation to the world around one, in which case the virtuous activity that controls happiness should continue unabated despite changes in one's worldly circumstances. Such a view leaves it unclear at best how those circumstances are nonetheless as important to our happiness as Aristotle thinks they are. That problem, of course, is the Priam problem. However, if we reject that view in favor of the embodied conception of the self, then virtuous activity is vulnerable to fortune insofar as it always has particular attachments and relationships as its "very form and mode," and these are vulnerable to fortune. Therefore, if happiness is controlled by virtuous activity, then happiness is controlled by something that is vulnerable to fortune, and so of course happiness itself must be vulnerable to fortune. Fortune touches on happiness because it touches on the activity in which happiness consists.

The Priam problem is that, *given the separateness of virtuous activity and other goods*, if virtue controls happiness then those other goods matter too little, and if virtue does not control happiness then they matter too much. Do we gain anything by thinking of bodily and external goods as important for happiness insofar as virtuous activity is embodied in them? I think that we do. On this view, such goods can be important for happiness insofar as they can be within the boundaries of the self, so it should be clear already that such goods will not matter too little for happiness, consistent with the dependency thesis.

The bigger question is whether those goods will matter too much, that is, whether their importance will be compatible with the control thesis. That thesis is important, after all, because it reflects a deep conviction that it is our rational agency that defines our nature and thus must play a unique and defining role in our happiness. Now, the strategies we have considered have struggled to unify this idea with the competing idea that other goods are also important parts of happiness. However, recall that concerns about such a conflict between virtue and other goods arose for the other strategies only because they depicted virtue and other goods as being important for happiness in *distinct* ways. By contrast, the present view makes no distinction between one's virtuous activity and one's particular engagements with particular worldly goods in a virtuous way. On this view, there is no distinction between a virtuous person's activity as a parent, say, and his active relationship with *this child* of his. That relationship—that worldly good—therefore does not matter for his happiness *alongside* his virtuous activity somehow, or for the sake of that activity, but just *is* his virtuous activity in the life he is leading. Here at last, I think, bodily and external goods can be characterized as mattering for happiness in just the right way: they are inextricable from the virtuous person, his virtuous activity, and the happiness of his life of virtuous activity.

On this view, it is still true that good things (such as a career or a family) can be parts of happiness only for those who act with virtue, that is, practical wisdom and emotional soundness. As we have seen, if we think of virtuous activity as distinct from these other goods, then the claim that good things can be parts of happiness only for the virtuous is just the bland claim that virtue and these other goods are all necessary for happiness, and thus fails to establish any "controlling" role for virtue. But once we reject the formalized conception of the self, we can see a much more intimate relation between virtuous activity and such goods. For instance, a career that one pursues with practical wisdom and emotional soundness is itself an on-going pattern of virtuous activity—it is one of the very "forms and modes" of the life of a virtuous person with a career—and therefore is the sort of good that is available only to virtuous persons. And this gives virtuous activity a defining, controlling role in happiness after all: *it is only insofar as things like careers can be transformed into on-going patterns of virtuous activity that we should think of them as potential parts of happiness in the first place.* That, on the embodied view, is the control thesis.

Likewise, we have also seen that, given a separation between virtuous activity and other things conventionally regarded as goods, the claim that such things can be genuinely good only for the virtuous is consistent with the idea that such goods are even more important as parts of happiness than virtue is. By contrast, on the view of the self that I propose, things like careers, intimate relationships, the use of wealth, and so on, count as goods for virtuous persons insofar as they are transformed into ongoing patterns of virtuous activity. The question therefore does not arise whether such goods might be important for happiness in a way that is distinct from and greater than the way in which virtue is. Rather, on this view virtue controls happiness because virtuous activity transforms other goods into itself. And this gives a firmer basis for the deep conviction that it is a person's activities and not just his circumstances that determine the tenor of his life.

The remaining question concerning virtue and its control over happiness is whether we can understand how virtue, on the view I propose, makes happiness stable. To sharpen this question, we would do well to return to Priam. I have said several times that the Priam problem is not Aristotle's failure to classify Priam one way or another; that failure is at most the symptom of a far deeper struggle. Nonetheless, I would like to indicate briefly how the view I have proposed here would characterize Priam, and virtuous but tragically unfortunate persons generally. On the present view, Priam will not of course count as happy; the bigger question is whether he will count as unhappy. Here we have two options. First, we might agree with Aristotle that it takes vice to become *un*happy, and say that Priam is merely "not happy," or what have you. The advantage of doing so would be that we could thereby mark an important difference between those who lack happiness because they do not act well and those who lack happiness because they are unlucky. However, this way of marking that distinction seems artificial and strained, especially (as I have said) for one who thinks that bodily and external goods really are crucial parts of human happiness; surely for such a one it is more natural to say that Priam is unhappy. And that, of course, is the second option. To be sure, this involves denying Aristotle's claim that unhappiness requires vice, but again I think that we (and indeed Aristotle himself) should deny that anyway, given the seriousness of the dependency thesis.

However, if we concede that Priam can be made unhappy by serious reversals of fortune, can we still make sense of the idea that virtue controls happiness and makes it stable? If bad luck can render Priam unhappy even though he is virtuous, has virtue made no difference to the tenor of his life after all? To answer this question, we should distinguish two sorts of virtuous activity, each of which contributes to the stability of happiness on the view that I propose. First, there is virtuous activity that is identical with an ongoing pattern of engagement in a particular relationship or endeavor; this is the sort of activity on which I have focused in this section. Second, there is also virtuous activity that "shines through" despite the interruption of activities of the former sort, the activity of enduring life's uncertainty and rebuilding one's future. These two sorts of activity are not entirely separate on my view, since the way that one endures uncertainty and rebuilds one's future is inseparable from how one's unique character and personality have shaped and been shaped by one's ongoing relationships and endeavors. However, since I agree with Aristotle that happiness is an attribute of the life of a person within his particular worldly attachments (NE I.7, 1097b6–11), on my view it is in activity of the first rather than the second sort that happiness consists. Even so, this activity will be stable in just the way that Aristotle thinks that virtuous activity should be. First, because the events that bear significantly on one's ongoing patterns of virtuous activity are only those that bear significantly on one's central, defining attachments to the world, happiness will be affected, not by just any changes of fortune, but only by those that are great and compounded (I.10, 1100b25). Second, because virtuous activity is also capable of "shining through" and rebuilding one's life, the loss of the happiness that was inseparable from a worldly attachment now lost can in time be followed by the happiness of new ways of engaging the world.[53]

And this brings us again to Priam, and to a way of marking an important distinction that virtue and vice make between unhappy persons. Whereas some are unhappy because they fail to give their life the right direction, others who are unhappy nonetheless have the resources of character to give their life the right direction, but need instead to put their life back together. The difference between them is that some will live well once life is rebuilt, whereas some will not live well even with all the help that fortune can give. The difference between them, in other words, is *hope*: virtue is no guarantee of happiness, but it makes all the difference in what happiness one can really hope for.[54] The present view not only captures the difference between someone unhappy although virtuous, and someone unhappy because vicious, but also seems to capture it in just the right way.

But a further question remains about the stability of happiness. Whatever else we say about the formalized view that virtuous activity is distinct from the goods with which the virtuous interact, at least that view keeps misfortune and vulnerability outside the boundaries of the self. On that view, what is truly ours is virtuous activity, and because it is separate from the world beyond us it is always secure. On my embodied view, by contrast, what is truly ours is inextricable from the world beyond us. Perhaps happiness is no more vulnerable to misfortune on this view than on Aristotle's, but it certainly seems that the *self* is more vulnerable.[55] What are we to say about this?

This question, I believe, presents the greatest challenge for my theory of happiness. (Consequently, it is also the central question of Part 3.) In the end, it is a question about how to understand one's selfhood in relation to one's loved ones and other worldly attachments. It is, in other words, a question about the meaning of life. To be sure,

---

[53] Here I have benefited greatly from Lewis 1976.
[54] See also Hursthouse 1999, 264–5.
[55] I thank Brad Inwood for raising this insightful query.

there are ways of thinking of the self that make it far less vulnerable to misfortunes. We might identify the true self with a pure power of choice and practical reasoning, as the Stoics did, or with pure theoretical intellect, as Aristotle himself does in *NE* X.7–8. Either way, we would reject the idea that one's status as a patient is part of one's happiness, that is, we would reject the dependency thesis. But for those of us who, like the Aristotle of *NE* I.10 and IX.9, are not prepared to make that move, there remains the messy task of confronting our resulting vulnerability.[56]

The question I have addressed in this chapter is how we can understand the idea that virtue controls and stabilizes happiness, given that other goods are parts of happiness too. The question that now faces us is this: even if we can find a way in which virtue might control and stabilize happiness, does virtue give us all the stability that we need? To answer the second question is, of course, to decide how much stability we need, and at what cost of closeness of attachment to things outside our control. For the moment, I hope to have made it clearer that this *is* the main question for anyone who thinks that virtue should control happiness. If I am very lucky, I may also have made that question a little clearer for us to consider. The role of bodily and external goods in happiness is one that Aristotle left unresolved, but I believe the way forward lies in reconsidering the nature of the self—and then asking whether we can live with the complications that follow.

---

[56] I must remain agnostic as to whether and to what extent this approach to the Priam problem is an "Aristotelian" one. Indeed, it could be that Aristotle was ultimately unwilling to accept the highly vulnerable view of human nature that would have resulted from adopting a more expansive view of the self, and chose to locate true happiness instead in highly invulnerable activity, such as pure contemplation (as in *NE* X.7–8).

6

Socrates' Case for the Sufficiency Thesis

Towards the end of John Steinbeck's wartime novel *The Moon is Down*, the mayor of an occupied town is facing execution by the occupying forces as part of an attempt to quell local resistance. Just before his execution, the mayor confides in a life-long friend that he is afraid to die and, to his shame, has considered running away. But now he is resolved to stay and be killed, he says, believing it is better to die resisting than to live fleeing. It is at this point that he recalls a passage of Plato's *Apology* that he had memorized at school:

Do you remember in school, in the *Apology*? Do you remember Socrates says, "Someone will say, 'And are you not ashamed, Socrates, of a course of life which is likely to bring you to an untimely end?' To him I may fairly answer, 'There you are mistaken: a man who is good for anything ought not to calculate the chance of living or dying; he ought only to consider whether he is doing right or wrong.'"

This is more than sentimental reminiscence on the mayor's part. For him, this idea is the essence of a truly free people: if we are willing to die resisting oppression and injustice, then any one of us can step forward as a new leader, however many others have been killed before. As his old friend says, their invaders

think that just because they have only one leader and one head, we are all like that. They know that ten heads lopped off will destroy them, but we are a free people; we have as many heads as we have people, and in a time of need leaders pop up among us like mushrooms.

The mayor gives voice to such freedom when he says at last to the colonel in charge, "I have no choice of living or dying, you see, sir, but—I do have a choice of how I do it." I agree with Steinbeck that what Socrates said in the *Apology* was something absolutely crucial for the world to have heard, not only for the sake of philosophy but also for the sake of freedom: it is not really what you do but what *I* do that is ultimately harmful or beneficial to me.

The mayor draws confidence from the Socrates of Plato's *Apology*, but from where did Socrates draw *his* confidence? An answer is not hard to find: Socrates' confidence came from his conviction that virtuous activity is sufficient for happiness, so that nothing but how he conducted himself could do him either any good or any harm.

Of course, this raises another question: *why* did Socrates believe *that*? That is a more important—and harder—question to answer, and in this chapter I want to work towards an answer by looking back at Socrates through the eyes of some who also drew confidence from his example. In particular, I want to look at the Socrates who in his philosophical afterlife became the forebear of the Stoics.

It is well known that the Stoics took themselves to have appropriated a Socratic view about the nature of the good and happiness. For instance, Epictetus combines Socrates and the Stoics into one philosophical tradition, on which virtuous activity is sufficient for, and indeed the same, as happiness (e.g. *Diss.* III.24.38, 40; III.26.23). Likewise, an ancient tradition (in various forms) had it that Zeno of Citium, the founder of the Stoic school, was first drawn to philosophy by the influence of Socrates (see Long 1988, 161). Moreover, the ancient doxographer Diogenes Laertius (3rd century AD) tells us that Socrates was perceived as the originator of a continuous line of philosophical succession through the Cynics and from there to the Stoics (DL I.14–15), with the result that the early Stoics actually wished to be known as "Socratics."[1]

Of course, modern readers might easily suppose that *most* ancient philosophers viewed Socrates as their philosophical forebear. Not so. For instance, Aristotle was notoriously critical of Socrates, but later Aristotelians actually smeared Socrates, even portraying him as a bigamist. The Epicureans were at least as hostile: to them Socrates was a fraud with disastrous ethical views, and they even wrote treatises against several of Plato's Socratic dialogues.[2] Such polemic not only shows that Aristotelians and Epicureans saw themselves as no heirs of Socrates. It also strongly suggests that in attacking Socrates these schools were targeting their main shared philosophical rivals, the Stoics, who had embraced Socrates as a chief moral exemplar and forebear. As far as the major Hellenistic schools were concerned, then, it was really the Stoa that was the school of the Socratics.[3]

Not surprisingly, the Stoic reception of Socrates in general and Socratic eudaimonism in particular is generally recognized as an important datum in our understanding of Stoic ethics. However, that datum has had far less impact on modern scholarship on *Socratic* ethics.[4] I think that there is much we can learn about Socratic ethics by looking at it from the perspective of Hellenistic moral philosophy, and especially from the Stoics' assimilation of Socrates. Doing so will allow us to imagine Socrates in the context of Hellenistic ethics where, as Cicero reports (*Fin.* V.12–15), the question of

---

[1]   Philodemus, *On the Stoics*, cols. 12–13, cited in Long 1988, 151n.

[2]   Long 1988, 155–6; see also Long 1999, 619–20. The Platonic dialogues attacked by the Epicureans include the *Euthd.* and *Gorg.*, discussed below.

[3]   To be sure, some Academic skeptics also portrayed Socrates as their forebear, but Long (1988, 157–8) argues convincingly that this portrayal post-dated the rise of Stoicism and was never taken seriously outside the Academy anyway. And in any case the skeptical Academy, being *skeptical*, was not a major source of positive ethical doctrines. Likewise, the Cynics and Cyrenaics were also self-styled Socratics, but these schools were relatively short lived in their influence; indeed, the chief influence of the Cynics was their inspiration of the early Stoics, who like the Cynics focused on the Socratic thesis that virtue is sufficient for happiness.

[4]   But see Long 1988; Annas 1993b; Gill 2000; McCabe 2002.

whether virtue is sufficient for happiness was the central point of debate. Now, as it happens, ancient historians of philosophy such as Cicero were already interested in classifying major philosophical positions in ethics with respect to the relation between virtue and happiness. One way to explore Socrates' belief in the sufficiency thesis, then, is to read his arguments again while asking where in such a classification he would have fit most plausibly. That is, which of the major Hellenistic options would have offered the most natural avenue for developing a distinctly Socratic moral philosophy?

My answer is: the Stoa. The central theme in my argument is that the conception of the self that we find among the Stoics makes the best sense, on independent grounds, of Socrates' arguments in the *Apology*, *Euthydemus*, and *Gorgias*, dialogues that were especially important in the Stoic reception of Socrates. Furthermore, as we shall see in the chapters to follow, an additional benefit of this approach is the light it casts on several Stoic theses as ways of addressing issues that Plato's Socrates had left uncertain.

I begin in section 1 with an overview of the Hellenistic classification of major positions in ethics and a thumbnail sketch of the view of the self that is distinctive of the Stoic position. Then in section 2 I discuss independent grounds for attributing a similar view to Socrates, before considering and rejecting some rival interpretations of Socrates in section 3.

1 How Hellenistic philosophers classified each other

As far as Hellenistic philosophers were concerned, the central question in ethics was, and always had been, what happiness consists in, or anyway so Cicero says in *On Goals* V.[5] Accordingly, it is with respect to this question that Cicero classifies the basic positions in ethics, using a schema that had been in use since the time of the Academic skeptic Carneades (214–129 BC; see *Fin.* V.16). What emerges from that schema is a division that Cicero takes to be fundamental: it is a division between those who hold that virtue is sufficient for happiness and those who do not.

According to this schema, every school of Hellenistic ethics identifies the highest good (*summum bonum*) as one's standing in a particular relation to something to which humans are "naturally attached." Cicero identifies six main candidates for these "basic natural attachments": pleasure, freedom from pain, or the "primary natural things" (health, strength, soundness of mind, etc.), and then each of these three also paired with virtue. Likewise, Cicero also identifies two main relations in which we might stand to these things, namely either attaining them or merely pursuing them. Consequently, some philosophers think that the highest good in life is attaining some natural attachment or other, disagreeing over what that attachment is; and other philosophers differ much more radically in thinking that the highest good is how we act—and in

---

[5] See also *Fin.* II.34–5; III.30; *TD* V.84–5.

particular the choices or selections we make—in relation to such things, but not in the attainment of the things themselves (*Fin.* V.17–20).[6]

It will be useful to represent Cicero's classification with the following diagram:

	Chief good is attaining:	Chief good is selecting:
Pleasure	*Aristippus*	*(No proponent)*
. . . and virtue	*Callipho, Dinomachus*	---
Absence of pain	*Hieronymus*	*(No proponent)*
. . . and virtue	*Diodorus*	---
Primary natural things	*[Carneades]*	*Stoics*
. . . and virtue	*Academics, Aristotelians*[7]	---

For the Stoics, the "chief good" of selecting other things is the same as virtuous activity, that is, acting with practical intelligence and emotional soundness where other things are concerned. That, we can presume, is why there are no positions in the right-hand column for identifying the chief good with the selecting of virtuous activity (hence the "---" in those positions).

There are a few things to note about this classificatory schema, chiefly the fact that it makes the debate ultimately one between Stoics and Aristotelians. The only non-Aristotelians on the left-hand side are Aristippus of Cyrene, who was not a eudaimonist anyway;[8] Carneades, who took the position attributed to him only for the sake of argument (hence the brackets around his name);[9] and the Academics, who in the Hellenistic period were skeptics.[10] Furthermore, the sans-virtue views on the left-hand side are all marginal: Aristippus and Carneades again, and the minor Aristotelian Hieronymus, who Cicero says hardly merits the label "Aristotelian" anyway since he makes virtuous activity no part of happiness (*Fin.* V.14). What remain for Cicero as "serious" options, then, are all mainstream Aristotelian views (cf. II.38).[11] Perhaps it is significant that the discussions of Stoic ethics between Cicero and Cato in *Fin.* III–IV

---

[6] Strikingly, Cicero presents this as a classification, not just of what views were extant but of what views are possible (*Fin.* V.21, 23).

[7] As examples of these, Cicero mentions Polemo (*Fin.* II.34–5; V.14), the third head of the Academy after Plato, and of course Aristotle himself (II.34, V.14).

[8] Aristippus of Cyrene (*c.* 435–*c.* 356 BC), the founder and main figure of the so-called Cyrenaic movement, held that our good is the pleasure of the moment. Apparently, then, the Cyrenaics did not think of happiness in terms of a final end for deliberation; however, their reasons for this are uncertain. See Irwin 1991 and N. White 2006, 26–7.

[9] Cicero, *Fin.* V.20. Cicero does not tell us why this view had no proper proponent, but surely the view that the good is having the goods of the soul, but yet not the virtues, would be a pretty odd view to hold (cf. II.41–2).

[10] Furthermore, the placement of the Academics on this side of the schema, and not on the Stoic side, is actually somewhat surprising: once the main lines of ethical debate in the ancient world had been drawn as between Stoics and Aristotelians, among ancient thinkers it was a very controversial question where to put Plato and his followers. See Annas 1997.

[11] I discuss Callipho, Dinomachus, and Diodorus in Chapter 5.

begin with the two of them bumping into each other at the private library of a mutual friend, the one to borrow books on Aristotle and the other to borrow books on the Stoics (III.7, 10).

The conspicuous absence of the Epicureans from the schema is odd as well, both because the Epicurean school is the subject of the first two books of *On Goals* (see also V.80), and because ethical theory flourished more among the Epicureans than among the Hellenistic Aristotelians (see also Long 1988, 617). But this is no oversight: by distinguishing pleasure from the absence of pain, the schema squeezes the Epicureans out from the beginning (as Cicero points out: *Fin.* II.35; see also Annas 2007b, 202–3). Perhaps this is because the Epicureans held virtue to be only instrumentally valuable, which made them marginal with respect to the sufficiency debate (even though they accepted the sufficiency thesis, DL X.132). But it is surely significant that omitting the Epicureans from the schema also makes it much easier to portray the sufficiency debate as just a two-way debate.

Lastly, notice that the Stoics are all alone on the right-hand side of the schema; they are truly in a class by themselves, in at least two ways. One, only the Stoics make the good consist entirely in how we act and not in anything we might attain by acting.[12] If our final end is to find something to live for and to live for it wisely, then for the Stoics that "something" just is the very exercise of wisdom itself. And two, within the schema only the Stoics hold that virtue is sufficient for happiness.

The schema, then, makes the sufficiency debate really a two-way debate between Stoics and Aristotelians, and this is no accident. Although the schema originated with Carneades, the version known to Cicero was that of the Academic philosopher Antiochus, who maintained (as we saw in the previous chapter) that the entire sufficiency debate came down to the Stoics and Aristotelians talking past each other. Their apparent disagreement, he argued, could be settled by simply distinguishing two levels of happiness: one for which virtue is sufficient and one for which it is not (see Cicero, *Fin.* V.81).

However, Antiochus' proposal was not just simple but grossly simplistic: the difference between the right- and left-hand columns of this schema—that is, the difference between the Stoics and everyone else—is a *radical* difference with respect to very basic questions about the nature of goodness. The right-hand, Stoic side maintains that somehow persons are such that the only thing that could matter for their happiness is how they exercise their faculty of choice; by contrast, the left-hand, Aristotelian side holds that persons are such that things in the world beyond their faculty of choice can matter for their happiness as well. This is a real problem for Antiochus' version of the schema, which opposes the left- and right-hand sides as if both meant the same thing in

---

[12] Cicero does not tell us explicitly why no one had defended the view that the good is pursuing pleasure or trying to avoid pain, rather than actually being pleased or free from pain, but what he does say must surely be the key: no one has found either such thing to be "worth pursuing in its own right independently of whether one actually did" attain it (*Fin.* V.20).

saying that virtue is good, and disagreed only as to whether anything else might be good too.[13] In fact, the interpretation of the Stoics in this passage flips between these two different views, as if there were no difference: Antiochus' spokesman in *On Goals* tells us first that the Stoics believe that the only good is acting well with respect to other things (V.20), and then that the Stoics just agreed with the Academics and Aristotelians that the good is "the conjunction" of goods of all types (V.22). Indeed, the Stoic view, he says, is just the Aristotelian view expressed in novel words. However, Cicero says, it is anything but that:

> Consider now the dispute between the Stoics and the Aristotelians. The Stoics argue that there is nothing good except what is moral, the Aristotelians claim that there are certain bodily and external goods as well, even while attributing by far and away the greatest value to morality. Here we have a truly honourable contest, a tremendous clash. *The whole dispute centers on virtue and its value.* (*Fin.* II.68, italics added)

In fact, for this reason some scholars speculate that perhaps as early as Carneades himself the whole schema had been only what we now have as the left-hand side of, with the Stoics portrayed as a distinct group completely *outside* the schema.[14]

The radical difference between the right- and left-hand sides of the schema, I believe, ultimately comes down to a difference in views about the nature of the self: on the right-hand side, the self is such that the only thing that could matter for happiness is how one exercises the faculty of selection, whereas the left-hand side holds that the self is such that things in the world beyond the faculty of selection can matter for one's happiness as well. In particular, on the Stoics' view, a person is fundamentally a power of choice, and virtuous activity is the wise exercise of this power.[15] So understood, a person's ongoing activities and projects are really patterns of selection and response with respect to the world around one. In that case, virtuous activity is not vulnerable to external circumstances: such activity just is the practically wise and emotionally sound exercise of the power of selection, and one requires no special resources in order to exercise that power. Virtuous activity, on this view of the self, is of course the "use" of other things, as the Stoics would say, but even so there are no particular sorts of things—such as favorable rather than dismal circumstances—that virtue needs in order to make good use.

As we saw in Chapter 4, this way of thinking about the self is particularly clear in Epictetus, where it is always at the core of his ethical advice. In fact, both the *Discourses* and the *Handbook* begin with a discussion of what a person really is. Epictetus maintains, first, that there is only one thing that is ever within our control (*Diss.* I.1.7–14), namely "the power to deal rightly with our impressions" (I.1.7), which he identifies with the capacity for choice (II.23.9) or, more simply, "assent" (e.g. IV.1.72). For

---

[13] See also Annas 2007b, 194.

[14] See Annas 2007b, 193–5 and references.

[15] We shall examine this feature of Stoicism very closely in the next two chapters.

Epictetus, the idea that choice alone is ours is a central ethical principle, because regarding anything else as ours makes us encumbered, burdened, and dragged down (see I.1.14–16; I.19.7–15; I.25.4; IV.10.19). Indeed, Epictetus says, not only that choice is all that is *mine*, but also that choice is all that is *me*: imagining a tyrant threatening to fetter him, Epictetus replies, "What are you saying, man? Fetter *me*? You will fetter my leg; but not even Zeus himself can get the better of my choice" (I.1.23, italics in original translation).

Epictetus clearly means that that aspect of a person that cannot be chained—the power of choice—is also who that person really is. And that is why, as Epictetus says, "virtue promises happiness" (*Diss.* I.4.3), and no virtuous person is ever left disappointed (I.4.11; I.9.34; II.23.42). That is Stoic invincibility: "Who, then, is the invincible man? He whom nothing outside the sphere of choice can disconcert" (I.18.21). This view of the self is the one that I have called in previous chapters the formalized conception of the self.[16]

If it is the Stoics' view of the nature of the self that accounts for their thesis that virtue is sufficient for happiness, then this gives us a way of focusing our question about Socratic ethics: is Socrates plausibly read as having thought about the nature of the self in that way as well? I argue that he is, and in particular that such a view would fill a number of otherwise confusing gaps in Socrates' discussions of virtue and happiness in *Apology*, *Euthydemus*, and *Gorgias*.

2 Socratic eudaimonism

2.1 Socratic eudaimonism in the Apology

Plato's *Apology* uses the dramatic setting of Socrates' trial, conviction, and sentencing to explore the question, What is it that harms a person: his own wrongdoing or his being wronged by others? Socrates claims repeatedly in the *Apology* that because of how he has already lived his life, no one can do him any harm. He tells the jury that as far as he is concerned, a person should make sure to do what is right, rather than merely to extend his own life (*Ap.* 28b), and that "Neither I nor any other man should, on trial or in war, contrive to avoid death at any cost.... It is not difficult to avoid death, gentlemen of the jury, it is much more difficult to avoid wickedness, for it runs faster than death" (38e–39b). Even more provocatively, Socrates insists that although he can be banished or even killed, nonetheless this is no harm to him (30c–d). Specifically, he says that it is one's goodness that so insulates one from harm: "A good man," Socrates says, "cannot be harmed either in life or in death" (41d).

Socrates' thesis could hardly be starker: if you do well in how you lead your life, then you *cannot be harmed*. The thesis here is not that you can be harmed but not very much, or that even if you are harmed you will be compensated, but that you are *beyond* harm

---

[16] Epictetus' account of the self is the subject of the next chapter.

in the first place. It is tempting to water down such a stark thesis,[17] but surely the place to start anyway is with taking Socrates at his word. All the more so, since it is exactly this striking thesis that Socrates, once imprisoned and facing execution, would repeat to his friend Crito: the most important thing is not to live but to live a good life (*to eu zēn*), and a good life and a just life are the same, whatever others may do (*Crito* 48a–d). It is for this reason that Epictetus continually exhorts his pupils to remember Socrates and his claim that "Anytus and Meletus can kill me, but they cannot harm me."[18] Indeed, Epictetus takes Socrates' claim as affirming the Stoic thesis that the good lies in how we choose and in nothing beyond how we choose (see esp. *Diss*. I.29; II.2).

Consequently, what Epictetus takes away from Socrates' *Apology* is the idea that real goodness and real freedom lie in how one bears oneself in the face of circumstance (see esp. *Diss*. IV.1; frag. 35; cf. Cicero, *Fin*. III.75). This, Epictetus says, is what distinguishes a virtuous person as extraordinary—this makes him the purple hem in the robe, setting him apart from all the other threads (*Diss*. I.2.12–18; III.1.23). Likewise, Epictetus says that this stark Socratic thesis is what makes a real man—to bear oneself well, he says, is to show the "bulging muscles" of the philosopher (II.8.29; cp. I.6.32–37, I.24.1–2), and someone who "trains" in this fashion will come to know the might of his will against onslaughts, as the bull knows its power against the attacking lion (I.2.30–32). For Epictetus, Socrates in the *Apology* is the exemplar of such a bull against the lions and such a purple thread in the robe (III.1.19–23, citing *Ap*. 28e).

But does Epictetus go too far here? To determine that, we need to see how Socrates defends his striking claim that even if he should be killed he still cannot be harmed. One thing Socrates says is that, as we see in cases of military valor,[19] some things are worth dying for, and that the search for wisdom is one of those things (*Ap*. 28c–30b). But while this shows that some harms are worth suffering, it does not show that a good man is beyond the very reach of harm. Socrates also says that being dead is one of two things—either nothingness or an afterlife—and either way a good man has nothing to fear (40c–41b). However, it is far from clear that there is nothing to be lost in ceasing to exist, and the promise of an afterlife shows at most that even if a good man should be harmed, there is a chance that he will be compensated.[20] And in any case, the real spirit of Socrates' thesis is that the very goodness of the good man is what puts him beyond harm—that his immunity from harm stems, not from some next life, but from *this* one.

---

[17] E.g. Vlastos 1991, 219 on 30c5–d5. Vlastos notes that Socrates goes on to say that whereas his accusers think they are doing him some great harm, he disagrees, and Vlastos concludes from this that Socrates' thesis is merely that the virtuous person can be harmed but not in any *great* way. However, that conclusion does not follow: after all, if Socrates believes that his accusers can do him no harm at all, then a fortiori he must also believe they can do him no great harm.

[18] *Diss*. I.29.18; II.2.15; III.23.21; *Handbook* 53. Cp. *Diss*. IV.1.123. See Plato, *Ap*. 30c.

[19] Here Socrates cites the *Iliad*, as well as his own service record (on which see also Epictetus, *Diss*. IV.1.159–60).

[20] See also Brickhouse and Smith 1994, 120–1.

It is only Socrates' third line of defense, I think, that really speaks directly to his stark thesis: a life of virtue puts one beyond harm because such a life *already* is a happy life:

I go around doing nothing but persuading both young and old among you not to care for your body or your wealth in preference to or as strongly as for the best possible state of your soul, as I say to you: "Wealth does not bring about virtue, but virtue makes wealth and everything else good for men, both individually and collectively." (*Ap.* 30a–b)[21]

Likewise, Socrates says that the very doing of wickedness, even if you get to do what you (think you) want, makes you worse off. Socrates says that his accuser Anytus "might kill me, or perhaps banish or disfranchise me . . . [but] I think he is doing himself much greater harm doing what he is doing now, attempting to have a man executed unjustly" (30d). And once he is sentenced Socrates says to the jury, "I leave you now, condemned to death by you, but [my accusers] are condemned by truth to wickedness and injustice" (39b). Wickedness, it seems, is its own punishment, and indeed worse than death. In this same spirit Socrates makes his parting remark: "Now the hour to part has come. I go to die, you go to live. Which of us goes to the better lot is known to no one, except the god" (42a).

It is this line of thought that goes to the heart of the idea that a virtuous life is already a happy one and thus beyond harm. And therefore it is no surprise that the Stoics— who held that virtue and its attributes are the only goods, and vice and its attributes the only evils (AD II.5a)—would have found Socrates' defense in the *Apology* such a close kin to their own view. Indeed, the proto-Cynic philosopher Antisthenes would later appeal to the fortitude of Socrates to support his own claim that virtue is sufficient for happiness (DL VI.11),[22] a portrayal of Socrates that Zeno presumably inherited from his Cynic forebears (see Long 1988, 161). This point is also picked up by Epictetus, who takes Socrates in the *Apology* to hold that the things that matter to the virtuous person are all entirely beyond the reach of others.[23]

Socrates' belief that happiness depends on virtue alone explains his thesis that virtue puts one beyond harm, but of course it raises a question of its own: *why* does Socrates believe that happiness depends on virtue alone? Furthermore, when Socrates says that it is virtue that makes wealth and all other things good, this seems to suggest that wealth is after all a *good*, at least for a virtuous person, and thus perhaps important for happiness after all.[24] The argument of the *Apology* therefore leaves Socratic eudaimonism with some important gaps, and it will make all the difference how these gaps are to be filled in: some things he says are suggestive of the right-hand side of Cicero's schema, but without sufficient argument; and some other things actually suggest the left-hand side.

---

[21] Cf. Irwin 1995, 58–9. The translation and interpretation of this passage are controversial; an alternative rendering would say that virtue brings about wealth and all other good things.

[22] Cf. Epictetus, *Diss.* IV.1.159–70.

[23] Epictetus, *Diss.* I.9.21–4, citing *Ap.* 28e, 29c; *Diss.* IV.1.159–69, citing *Ap.* 32b–c and several other Platonic texts. See also *Diss.* IV.7.30, citing *Ap.* 32c–d.

[24] See also Brennan 2005a, 120.

To see how we might fill in Socratic eudaimonism, there are two further passages I want to explore: one in Plato's *Euthydemus* and one in the *Gorgias*.

2.2 Eudaimonism in the Euthydemus

The well-known protreptic passage in Plato's *Euthydemus* (278e–282a) offers the most concise and focused statement of Socratic eudaimonism we have.[25] It begins with everyday thoughts about happiness but soon advances to a radical view about the role of virtue in the happy life: namely that virtue is the use of other things and is the only good. For the sake of clarity I shall divide Socrates' argument for his radical view about the good into five main stages.

In the first stage Socrates begins by noting, simply enough, that everyone wants to "do well" or "fare well" (*eu prattein*; *Euthd.* 278e), which is generally taken as interchangeable with "happiness" (e.g. *Gorg.* 507c; Aristotle, *NE* I.4). Socrates and his interlocutor find it obvious that this is what we want for our lives. In the second stage, they also find it obvious that happiness or doing well comes about from good things (*Euthd.* 278e–279c). Socrates begins with a simple laundry list of things he thinks everyone would say were good: bodily goods like health, external goods like wealth, and goods of the soul like "being self-controlled and just and brave," as well as wisdom.[26] Lastly, Socrates hastens to add that good luck is the greatest good of all.[27]

The mention of good luck brings Socrates abruptly to the argument's third stage and one of the argument's main points of controversy, namely his surprising claim that he has blundered by adding good luck to his list, since wisdom actually makes good luck redundant (*Euthd.* 279c–280b). It is a general feature of our experience, he says, that to be wise about something is always to have the best luck at it: it is flautists who have the best luck at flute playing, expert sailors who have the best luck at sailing, and so on. Socrates concludes, surprisingly, that wisdom makes its own success, with no further need of good luck.

How must Socrates think of "success" and "good luck" here, if wisdom is sufficient for success and makes good luck redundant? It is clear, after all, that however skilled the flautists or sailors may be, there are all sorts of things outside their control that can interfere. Of course, Socrates' claim is obviously true if all he means is that wisdom makes what we might call "dumb luck" redundant, where dumb luck is the sort of thing one needs to make up for a lack of wisdom.[28] However, I do not think that this is all that Socrates can mean, for a couple of reasons.[29] One, when Socrates introduces

---

[25] I discuss the passage at greater length in Russell 2005, chap. 1.

[26] Socrates apparently thinks of self-control, justice, and bravery as mental attributes that are not proper virtues since he goes on to say that they can be used either well or badly. Cf. Aristotle's so-called "natural virtues" in *NE* VI.13.

[27] This addition to the list is significant, since the Greek word *eudaimonia* derives originally from the idea of having a favorable (*eu-*) guardian spirit (*daimōn*), which suggests being lucky in conventional ways, and an idea Aristotle cites as common even in his time (*EE* I.1, 1214a21–25).

[28] See Brickhouse and Smith 2000b.

[29] See also Russell 2005, 32–5.

good luck as one of the goods—indeed, *the* greatest good—that happiness needs, he intends this as a very common-sense point about happiness. But surely common sense would think of good luck in that context as the sort of luck that lets things go well, full stop—and not merely the sort of luck that blocks just one of the many ways in which things might go badly. And two, Plato clearly expects the claim that wisdom replaces luck to be *surprising*, not obvious.[30] Socrates' interlocutor finds the whole idea very surprising, and Plato noticeably takes pains to have Socrates say that while he and his interlocutor eventually agreed that wisdom makes good luck redundant, still he is not sure "quite how" they managed it (280b). And to drive the point home even harder, Socrates responds tongue-in-cheek to his interlocutor's surprise by saying that the idea is one that even a child would grasp. In order for the surprise, perplexity, and irony to make any sense, Socrates and his interlocutor would have to be assuming that "good luck" is just all the luck one needs for success, full stop.

If wisdom is meant to make redundant the sort of good luck *that seals one's success*, then Socrates must be radically rethinking what it means for someone to *succeed*. The most natural reading, in that case, is that by "success" he means *how one does* what one does, rather than *what one accomplishes* by what one does. And notice how well this jibes with Socrates' claim at his trial that it is *he* who is going away from the trial a success because it is he who has acted well, despite what he may or may not have accomplished thereby. It also jibes with the right-hand side of Cicero's schema—a point not lost on Epictetus, who would later draw on precisely this part of the *Euthydemus* in making the point that it is the "knowledge of how to live" that makes a person completely free and beyond the reach of either circumstances or other people (*Diss.* IV.1.62–77).

Yet another controversial claim comes in the fourth stage of the argument, namely that things besides wisdom are good depending on how we use them (*Euthd.* 280c–281c). The "good things" on the laundry list, he says, do not do us any good unless we *use* them, and in particular unless we use them *well* (280c–281a). Here Socrates invokes the point just made that it was wisdom[31] "that ruled and directed our conduct in relation to the right use of all such things as these," and thus that wisdom "seems to provide men not only with good fortune but also with well-doing, in every case of possession or action" (281b). Consequently, without wisdom, nothing is of any advantage to us and will no more be part of a good life than a bad one.

In the fifth and final stage, Socrates draws several conclusions about the nature of the good (*Euthd.* 281c–282a). First, he asserts the surprising thesis that things we ordinarily consider "good" may actually make us worse off if we lack wisdom, since they can encourage and facilitate the bad behavior in which failure consists (281c–e). And this, he then says, shows that nothing but wisdom has any goodness of its own or by its very nature:

---

[30] See also Resthotko 2006, 143–4.

[31] Or, more precisely, knowledge; he uses these interchangeably here. By them Socrates seems to mean either virtue considered as a whole or that aspect of virtue that it makes it excellent in action.

So, to sum up...it seems likely that with respect to all the things we called good at the beginning, the correct account is not that in themselves they are good by nature, but rather as follows: if ignorance controls them, they are greater evils than their opposites, to the extent that they are more capable of complying with a bad master; but if good sense and wisdom are in control, they are greater goods. In themselves, however, neither sort is of any value. (281d–e)

Socrates immediately takes a crucial step further: the result of this whole discussion, he says, is "that, of the other things, no one of them is either good or bad, but of these two, wisdom is good and ignorance bad" (281e).

Clearly, this further step requires explanation, since Socrates just said in the previous breath that wisdom makes "greater goods" of the things he now says are not good at all.[32] This tension parallels one that we encountered in the *Apology*, where Socrates suggested both that virtue is the only good and that it makes other things good too. Some scholars have addressed this tension in the *Euthydemus* by softening the claim that virtue or wisdom is the only good: for instance, things like health and wealth really are "good" in the sense that they facilitate virtuous activity in some way; wisdom, then, is the only good *of its kind*.[33] Such an approach, please note, would land Socrates on the left-hand side of Cicero's schema after all—indeed, just such an approach was developed by two of Aristotle's ancient commentators, Arius Didymus and Aspasius (see Chapter 5).

However, this approach does not resolve the tension after all, for the simple reason that Socrates cannot suppose here that wisdom requires any *special* resources for its exercise. To be sure, special resources would be needed in order for wisdom to yield certain kinds of products or outcomes, or to engage in certain kinds of projects. But recall that Socrates' claims about wisdom making luck redundant are difficult to understand *unless* he locates the success of wise action in the very *exercise* of wisdom, whatever the circumstances. In that case, special resources would be needed to facilitate, not the exercise of wisdom per se, but rather its exercise in a particular, desirable way. Happiness would therefore depend on two goods after all: wisdom, plus the further good of exercising wisdom in a certain favorable way. Such a reading of Socrates' view would therefore leave the tension exactly where it was: wisdom is the only good that matters for happiness for its own sake, *and* something else is good in that way too.

Furthermore, such softening of Socrates' claim is hard to square with the text: later in the *Euthydemus* (288d–292e) Socrates returns to the conclusion of the present argument, and there he clearly takes that conclusion to be his claim at 281e that virtue is the only good, and that nothing else is either good or bad at all.[34] According to Socrates,

---

[32] On this point, see also Long 1988, 168; Brickhouse and Smith 1994, 107; 2000a, 138; Irwin 1992; Irwin 1995, 57–8.

[33] See e.g. Vlastos 1991, 228–31; Brickhouse and Smith 1994, chap. 4; Dimas 2002.

[34] This tells against Vlastos' reading of that conclusion as the much weaker claim that virtue is the only thing that is good "just by itself" (Vlastos 1991, 228–31); see Annas 1993b and Gill 2000, 136–7.

where he and his interlocutor ended up was agreeing "that nothing is good except some sort of knowledge," and that as for all other sorts of things, "all these appeared to be neither good nor bad" (292a–c, d).

The better way to resolve the tension, therefore, is to treat wisdom in the *Euthydemus* as a skill that does well with whatever is at hand, where those things themselves are neither good nor bad.[35] When Socrates says at 281d that things like health and wealth can be made "greater goods," it seems, he is still speaking about them in everyday terms, whereas at 281e he finally breaks with everyday talk and denies that such things really should be counted as goods at all. In fact, even the Stoics would sometimes call some "indifferent" (neither good nor bad) things "goods" in debate, just because 'good' is such a familiar term.[36]

This is also how the Stoics read this passage. Zeno interpreted the *Euthydemus* as requiring a distinction between good things that are crucial for happiness—namely, virtue—and other things conventionally regarded as goods, which are natural for us to prefer, but do not bear on our happiness. They are, that is, "preferred indifferent" things: indifferent with respect to happiness, but preferred with respect to selection.[37] And not only Zeno but the Stoics in general regarded the *Euthydemus* as the clearest and most authoritative statement of Socrates' ethics, and they seem both to have taken its conclusion to be a statement about indifferent things, and to have adopted its premises in their own account of good, bad, and indifferent:

The virtues . . . are good; and their opposites . . . are bad; neither good nor bad are those things which neither benefit nor harm, such as life, health, pleasure, beauty, strength, wealth, good reputation, noble birth, and their opposites . . . For just as heating, not cooling, is a property of the hot, so benefitting, not harming, is a property of the good; but wealth and health do not benefit any more than they harm; therefore, neither wealth nor health is good. Again, [the Stoics] say that what can be used [both] well and badly is not good; but it is possible to use wealth and health [both] well and badly; therefore, wealth and health are not good.[38]

In fact, this way of reading the *Euthydemus* became so ingrained during the Hellenistic period that Diogenes Laertius could later summarize Socrates as believing that

---

[35] See Ferejohn 1984 and Santas 1993.

[36] See Plutarch, *Contrad.* 1048a (= LS 58H), cited by Annas 1997, 27n; see also Bonhöffer 1894/1996, 20; Irwin 2007, 341; Lesses 1989, 116; Rist 1969, 12.

[37] See Long 1988, 164–71, for discussion. McCabe 2002, 386–97, offers a very different account of Zeno's reconstruction of Socrates' point.

As Long and McCabe both point out, Zeno and his pupil Aristo seem to have disagreed sharply over this passage, Zeno saying that things like health and wealth are naturally preferable but not good (i.e. not important for happiness), and Aristo that things like health and wealth have no value whatsoever (and so not even naturally preferable). I think that Zeno's reading makes better sense of the passage, but what is more important for our purposes is that both readings take the passage to clearly deny that things like health and wealth are important for happiness.

[38] DL VII.102, 103 (= IG II–94.102, 103). See also AD II.5a–b. For discussion, see Annas 1993b; Barney 2003, 309; Long 1988, 164–9; McCabe 2002, 386.

knowledge is the only good and ignorance the only bad.[39] And of course, such a reading makes it plausible to regard Socratic eudaimonism as clearly belonging on the right-hand side of Cicero's schema.

It is worth noting that the idea that wisdom makes good luck redundant explains why it is, as Socrates holds in the *Apology*, that happiness depends entirely on virtue, namely because when one is wise or virtuous there is no need for good luck where other resources are concerned. But of course, Plato seems well aware that his argument now opens a new gap at just this point, since he makes Socrates confess his uncertainty as to how he arrived at the conclusion that wisdom makes good luck redundant. So the *Euthydemus* fills in some gaps in Socratic eudaimonism only to open up a further one: *why* does virtue make good luck redundant?[40] Socrates considers this all-important idea in a passage of the *Gorgias*, so let's turn to that now.[41]

2.3 Eudaimonism in the Gorgias

In the *Gorgias*, Socrates thinks of virtue as a kind of organization or orderliness of the soul, as health is of the body and structural soundness is of a building (*Gorg.* 506d–507d), and argues that to live with such soundness is our good. Socrates begins his discussion by saying that, in general, a thing is good "when some excellence has come to be present" in it, and such excellence "is due to whatever organization, correctness, and craftsmanship is bestowed on each of them" (506d). In the case of the soul, we call its proper order *sōphrosunē* or self-discipline (506e–507a), so self-discipline is the good of the soul, and the opposite is its bad (507a).[42]

Socrates then goes on to examine what this good of the soul does, or what power it has. It is, he says, that by which the soul acts well, without qualification (*Gorg.* 507a–b): with respect to other humans (justice), with respect to the gods (piety), and with respect to what is appropriate in the face of pleasures and pains (courage or fortitude). In that case, acting well without qualification is just the same thing as acting with all the virtues, or virtue taken as a whole (507b–c). Moreover, he says that acting or doing well (*eu prattein*) without qualification is also just the same thing as living well, that is, happiness or eudaimonia (507c–d).

It is on the basis of this line of reasoning that Socrates then turns repeatedly in the *Gorgias* to a central theme of the *Apology*, namely that one's well-being depends on what one does rather than on what others do (*Gorg.* 508d–e, 509c) or what otherwise happens (512a), and thus that one should be attached to goodness rather than to merely

---

[39] DL II.31. See Long 1988, 158.

[40] See also Irwin 1995, 58.

[41] Socrates himself goes on to make heavy weather of another gap later in the dialogue (*Euthd.* 288d–293a) concerning his own comparison of virtue to skill: while wisdom may be like a productive skill, productive skills are valuable, not for their own sake, but only for the sake of the things they produce; so how, Socrates asks, can we hold that the relation between wisdom and the things it fashions is just the reverse? See Annas 1993b, 58–66; McCabe 2002, 372–5. As we shall see in Chapter 8, the Stoics took this to be an important question for themselves too.

[42] *Sōphrosunē* is often translated "temperance."

staying alive (512d–e). Such an argument would, at last, provide a rationale for Socrates' stark thesis that the virtuous person cannot be harmed. If the virtuous person acts well in all respects (507a–c), and if to act well in all respects just is to have a happy life (507c–d), then the virtuous person always possesses within himself the power to have a happy life, whatever others may do to him. Perhaps it is not surprising, then, that Epictetus in the *Discourses* should cite the *Gorgias* more than any other dialogue, and that Cicero should note the special importance of the *Gorgias* to Stoic ethics.[43]

However, many scholars have objected to Socrates' argument at precisely this point. When Socrates says that virtue suffices for "doing well" (*eu prattein*), the objection goes, this means that virtue suffices for acting appropriately; but then Socrates shifts to "doing well" in the sense of faring well, and this is something very different. That is, Socrates identifies "doing well" with a person's *goodness*, and then shifts to "doing well" in the sense of a person's *good*.[44]

Now, this objection relies on an implicit assumption that is very easy to overlook, and in fact I think that it is by making this assumption explicit that we come to the central issue for assessing how "Stoic" Socrates' eudaimonism might be. The assumption is simply that for the purpose of predicating eudaimonia of a person's life, a person is something more than the power of choice and self-direction. After all, if a person were identical with such a power, then the goodness of that power—acting appropriately in all respects—just would be the good of the person, and thus would be eudaimonia. Given such a view of the self, that is, the fulfillment of that power would be the same as the fulfillment of the person.

But as it happens, there is good reason to think that that is precisely the view of the self that Socrates has in mind in the *Gorgias*. In setting up his argument for the happiness of the virtuous person, Socrates notes that a thing possesses its good when it has its proper order (*Gorg.* 506d–e), and moves immediately to the idea that a human being's good lies in the order of the soul, which he considers primarily to be a power of self-direction (506e–507a); hence the focus on the virtue of self-discipline as a sort of Ur-virtue (507a–c). To be sure, Socrates advertises no theory of the self here at all, but the most natural reading of the remarks that he does make would strongly suggest that the self *is* the soul, understood as a self-directing power, in which case the fulfillment of that power is the same as the fulfillment of the person.

Of course, this is just the view of the self that we find among the Stoics. Such a view is especially prominent in the thought of Epictetus, who taught that a person is his power of choice, that nothing lying outside of choice can be an evil, and that choosing well is every good thing:

---

[43] *TD* V.34–6. Long (2002) conjectures that Epictetus may have known *Gorgias* by heart. Besides *Gorgias*, Cicero also notes the importance of Plato's *Menexenus*, which Cicero takes to express the sufficiency thesis (although this is dubious); see Annas 1999, 41, for discussion.

[44] The *locus classicus* of this objection is Dodds 1959, 335–6. See also Russell 2005, 68–71 and references, for discussion.

"So-and-so's son is dead. What do you think of that?" It lies outside the sphere of choice, it is not an evil. "So-and-so has been disinherited by his father. What do you think of that?" It lies outside the sphere of choice, it is not an evil. "Caesar has condemned him." This lies outside the sphere of choice, it is not an evil. "He has been distressed by all this." This is within the sphere of choice, it is an evil. "He has borne it nobly." This is within the sphere of choice, it is a good. (*Diss.* III.8. 2–3)

Likewise, he says elsewhere, "what is essentially of good lies in things up to us" (*Handbook* 19).

Moreover, this view of the self is also prominent in Epictetus' reception of Socrates:

If any of you, withdrawing himself from externals,[45] turns to his own faculty of choice, working at it and perfecting it, so as to bring it fully into harmony with nature . . . this is the man who is truly making progress, this is the man who has not travelled in vain. . . . No, what matters is . . . to learn what death, what exile, what prison, what hemlock is, so that he may be able to say in prison, like Socrates, "My dear Crito, if that is what pleases the gods, so be it," and not "Wretched old man that I am, is it for this that I have kept my grey hairs!" (*Diss.* I.4.18, 21, 23–4)

Likewise, in his long disquisition on disentangling oneself from everything beyond one's faculty of choice, Epictetus says that such disentanglement explains why it was not Socrates who was harmed but only his jurors and accusers (IV.1.123).

Epictetus therefore notes correctly that if Socrates identifies the fulfillment of the soul with the fulfillment of the person, then there is no gap in his argument for the stark thesis of the *Apology* that the virtuous person cannot be harmed and that happiness depends entirely on virtue: *if* the person is identical to the soul, understood as a self-directing power, then happiness depends entirely on the power of conducting oneself well whatever the circumstances. Furthermore, such a view of the self would also fill an important gap that we noticed in the *Euthydemus*: *if* a person just *is* his soul, then as the soul fares well so too does the person, in which case wisdom or virtue as a whole is all the "luck" a person needs for happiness. So it is very perceptive of Epictetus to notice that if Socrates identifies the virtuous person with his power of self-direction, a power that is the same as virtue and the same as the good, then Socrates can assert confidently that the virtuous person cannot be harmed, since the good on which his happiness depends is something always within his own power.

However, Epictetus' Socrates is clearly tidier than Plato's, and for our purposes at least three questions still remain. One, the question whether the things that virtue uses might be "good," and thus parts of happiness, resurfaces even in the *Gorgias*. For instance, Socrates still speaks of things like illness as making one's life "wretched" and "miserable," in common-sense fashion (*Gorg.* 505a, 512a–b; cp. *Crito* 47d–48a). Likewise, elsewhere in the *Gorgias* Socrates places things like health and wealth among

---

[45] By "externals" Epictetus means everything that is not up to us, which he takes to be everything outside the faculty of choice; see esp. *Diss.* I.1 and *Handbook* 1.

good things *as opposed to* things whose value depends on use (467e–468a), and this is completely different from what Socrates says about those things in the *Euthydemus*.[46] It is possible that Socrates means merely that such things as health are natural for us to prefer for their own sake, in the fashion of Zeno, but we cannot suppose this for certain.

Two, in light of all this, we might doubt whether Socrates really does identify the fulfillment of the person with the fulfillment of his power of choice and self-direction. Now, we have seen that if Socrates does indeed have such a view of persons, then some otherwise very serious gaps in his argument for the immunity of the virtuous from harm can be closed, as that identification would explain why happiness depends entirely on virtue and why virtue brings all the success that happiness needs. But as it stands, Socrates' own position is extremely difficult to make out. Likewise, three, there would be the further question *why* Socrates had adopted the sort of view of the self that we find in Epictetus, if indeed he had.

Where does this leave us? One thing is all too clear: Socrates' position needs sorting out; and although the Stoics' way of sorting out Socratic eudaimonism is plausible, it does not prevail by default. But my claim is not merely that the Stoic reception of Socrates is plausible but that it is the *most* plausible way to develop Socrates' view in the context of subsequent Greek ethical debates. So in the final section, I consider several modern alternatives to the Stoic development of Socratic eudaimonism.

3 Socratic eudaimonism: left, right, or center?

3.1 Socratic eudaimonism in the center

We have seen that Socrates says some things that suggest that he belongs on the left-hand side of Cicero's schema, and other things that suggest he belongs on the right-hand side. I have argued for resolving this tension in the direction of the right-hand side, but perhaps we should *dissolve* the tension instead. In other words, perhaps Socrates holds both that virtue is sufficient for happiness, so that the virtuous person cannot be harmed in any way that counts against his happiness, and *also* that other goods can make the virtuous person even happier.

Gregory Vlastos famously defended this reading of Socrates by arguing that Socrates could not otherwise explain our everyday choices. For instance, if Socrates thought that only virtue mattered for happiness, then he could not explain why it makes sense to prefer a clean bed over a filthy one (Vlastos 1991, 214–16). Since all choices are ultimately between things that matter for happiness (1991, 203), virtue must not be the only thing that matters for happiness—clean beds must matter for happiness too, albeit in a far smaller way than virtue does.

---

[46] See also *Meno* 87e–88d and Long 1988, 170.

Interestingly, this is also how Antiochus tried to collapse the left- and right-hand sides of the schema: the Stoics, he argued, held that virtue suffices for happiness (*vita beata*), whereas the Aristotelians held that other goods made one even happier (*vita beatissima*; Cicero, *Fin.* V.21, 77–86). Now, Cicero makes it clear that Antiochus' view was a novelty, a controversial one at that, and not a major contender in ancient eudaimonism; so it would be extraordinary if Socrates' view had prefigured it. But even setting that point aside, I think that for Vlastos and Antiochus alike, there are at least three serious problems with this approach.

One, this view makes conventional goods matter in the wrong way. On the one hand, some goods turn out to matter too much: surely it makes a difference which bed one chooses, but it is far-fetched to make the difference bear on one's well-being across one's whole life. On the other, some goods turn out to matter too little: if I go far enough to think that something in my life really is important to my happiness, then surely I will not agree that without it I am still perfectly happy, just not *as* happy as before.

Two, Vlastos' reading assigns goods besides virtue a confusing role in our lives. The more powerful those goods are to make the virtuous person's life a happier one, the less sense it makes for Socrates to think that wisdom makes good luck redundant (as in the *Euthydemus*), and that doing well with respect to choice is just the same thing as happiness (as in the *Gorgias*). Yet the less powerful such goods are for happiness, the less interesting the difference is between happiness and "greater" happiness anyway. Moreover, Socrates' view, on this reading, would be strangely convoluted: our conventional ideas about goods and their relation to happiness are deeply mistaken, since such things have no value of their own, as Socrates argues in the *Euthydemus*— and yet those same conventional ideas are exactly right when we think about virtuous persons.[47]

Finally, and most importantly, Vlastos' approach must paper over the chasm between the very different views of the nature of the self that it seeks to conjoin. As we have seen, it takes one view of the nature of the self to say that virtue makes one happy, and a different view to say that conventional goods make the virtuous even happier. Consequently, a development of Socratic eudaimonism along Antiochean lines would be fundamentally unstable. And that is not surprising, since Antiochus' own efforts to split the difference between the left- and right-hand sides of Carneades' schema must also paper over exactly such a chasm, as Cicero himself complains (see esp. *Fin.* V.81–96). Simply put, the sufficiency thesis belongs with the idea that persons are to be disentangled from the world in which they are situated, and its denial says they are not. These two lines on happiness belong to two completely different world-views.

Nevertheless, Vlastos has a point: if happiness is not improvable by the addition of conventional goods, then how *are* conventional goods related to choice?[48] Not

---

[47] See Annas 1999, 42–4.   [48] See also Irwin 1995, 58.

surprisingly, this is an issue that the Stoics were to take head-on, arguing that things like clean beds do not have to have a life-improving power in order for us to have a reason to prefer them. Very roughly, they argued that if it is more natural to prefer clean beds to dirty ones, then going for the clean bed is the more intelligent thing to do, and it is acting intelligently and in accordance with our nature that has life-improving power, not the conventional goods in relation to which we act.[49] Of course, the Stoic view of practical reasoning was controversial, but if there is a preferable alternative it is clearly not the Antiochean view.

3.2 Socratic eudaimonism on the left-hand side

Among the main options in Hellenistic ethics, the remaining alternative would be to put Socrates on the left-hand side of Cicero's schema, reading him as making happiness consist in both virtuous activity and conventional goods. There are two broad ways in which we might develop such an interpretation of Socrates. First, we might argue that for Socrates, virtue and other goods are all parts of happiness, a view shared by the ancient Aristotelians. Of course, Socrates insists in the *Euthydemus* that virtue or wisdom is the only good, but we could perhaps take this to mean simply that virtue is the only good of its kind, namely one that directs and uses other goods.[50] However, such a view must still take the self to be more than the power of self-direction, and is therefore difficult to square with Socrates' arguments in the *Gorgias* that directing oneself well just is the same kind of "doing well" (*eu prattein*) that eudaimonia is.

The other way to put Socrates on the left-hand side of the schema would be to make happiness consist in something besides virtue, maintain that virtue is good for the sake of that in which happiness consists, *and* maintain that virtue is the "only good" in the sense that it is somehow uniquely related to that in which happiness consists. In other words, the idea is that happiness is to be identified with the attainment of some good *G*; virtue is good for the sake of the attainment of *G*; and virtue is somehow specially related to the attainment of *G* so that it can plausibly be called the only good of its kind. Indeed, on this approach Socrates could even hold that virtue is sufficient for happiness, as long as it is sufficient for that good *G* in which happiness really consists. In this respect Socrates could be classed, in a broad way, with the Epicureans, who are conspicuously absent from Cicero's schema, but who held that virtue is sufficient for happiness (DL X.132) even though virtue is not what happiness consists in.

Several scholars have taken such an approach to Socratic eudaimonism. For instance, Terence Irwin reads Socrates as holding that virtue is instrumentally valuable for the sake of happiness, understood as pleasure or desire-satisfaction,[51] although he rightly worries that virtue may turn out not to be a unique good in this regard. However,

---

[49] See e.g. Seneca, *Ep.* 92; Epictetus, *Diss.* II.5.6–7, cp. II.6.1, IV.2; see also Frede 2007, 165–6. I discuss this issue in Chapter 8.

[50] Cf. the view of Critolaus, discussed in Chapter 5.

[51] Irwin 1992; 1995, 44–5, 67–8, 89–90, 118–20; cf. 1998, 155.

Naomi Reshotko (2001, 2006) argues that for Socrates virtue is a unique good with respect to happiness, being the only good that is always, in all circumstances, the best way to obtain that in which happiness consists (again, a certain kind of pleasure), although not itself a part of happiness.[52] Lastly, George Rudebusch (1999) argues that for Socrates virtue and virtue alone has as one of its inseparable attributes the very thing in which happiness consists—a certain kind of pleasure—so that virtue is not only a unique good but indeed the same thing as happiness, that is, that type of pleasure.[53]

Now, as one scholar has pointed out, there is something rather awkward about approaches of these sorts. Socrates says in the *Euthydemus* (278e) that it would be absurd for anyone to dispute whether happiness is all he wants. However, such a claim is much more plausible if he understands happiness in formal terms—as a "good life," whatever that proves to be—than if he identifies it with some particular good (McCabe 2002, 378–9).

But I want to press a different point here. It is important to note where all of these views agree, namely that it is not virtuous activity *qua virtuous activity*—a kind of rational self-direction, say—that is part of happiness. On the views of Irwin and Reshotko, virtue is not part of happiness at all but only an instrumental good; on Rudebusch's view, virtuous activity is the same as happiness, but only qua a special type of pleasant activity.[54] What these three anti-Stoic readings of Socrates all have in common, then, is the idea that whatever happiness is, it does not have as one of its constituent parts virtuous activity qua virtuous activity.

However, I take this idea to be incompatible with what Socrates says about happiness. For instance, Socrates argues in the *Apology* that conducting oneself virtuously is *already* to be well off and indeed beyond harm, and the most natural reading of this is that the virtuous person is fulfilled strictly *qua living virtuously*. And surely this is exactly the impression that Socrates means to leave in the minds of his accusers and jurors.

Furthermore, this point of convergence between these views is also incompatible with how Socrates thinks of human nature. To see this, note first that for Socrates (and for eudaimonists in general), to live a happy human life is to be fulfilled in ways that are specific to our nature.[55] Consequently, if some good is part of the fulfillment that is specific to our nature, then that good, qua the good that it is, will be a part of happiness. Now suppose, with the reading of Socrates under consideration, that virtuous activity

---

[52] See also McCabe 2002, 370–2, 375–6, who proposes such a view in regards to *Meno* 87e–88d.

[53] Three modern interpretations, three hedonistic Socrateses. For historians of philosophy, times have changed since Cicero could say that Socrates held pleasure to be "of no account" (*Fin.* II.90; see Long 1988, 162, for discussion).

[54] I discuss this aspect of Rudebusch's view in Russell 2000 and 2005, 71–5.
The Aristotelian Lyco may have held a similar view in identifying happiness as the attainment of a kind of pleasure that was peculiar to virtue (see Chapter 5). However, a Socratic version of this view must part ways with Lyco over the sufficiency of virtue for happiness, since Lyco seems to have denied that virtue is sufficient for the attainment of this pleasure.

[55] This is the thesis labeled "welfare externalism" in Chapter 2.

is either not a part of happiness at all, or is a part of happiness but not *qua* virtuous activity. In either case, it follows that virtuous activity, qua virtuous activity, is not part of the fulfillment that is specific to our nature.

Now Socrates, on any reading of him, believes that virtuous activity just is the leading of one's life in a rational and intelligent way. It also seems clear that *if* our nature is that of rational, self-directing creatures, then leading one's life rationally and intelligently must be part of the fulfillment that is specific to our nature. It follows, then, that if our nature is that of rational, self-directing creatures, then virtuous activity qua virtuous activity is part of the fulfillment specific to our nature. Therefore, on the reading of Socrates we are now considering, Socrates would have to believe that our nature is not one of rational self-direction.

But surely Socrates believes no such thing. Recall that in the *Gorgias* (506d–507d) Socrates identifies a person's good as the good of his or her soul, where the good of that soul just *is* to be complete in all the virtues. That is why Socrates concludes that such a soul is already a happy one: it "does well" and acts rationally and intelligently in all areas of life, because in so acting one is fulfilled as a human, that is, as a well-ordered constructor of a life. A necessary condition of identifying "doing well" as virtuous activity with "doing well" as happiness is that human nature consists in rational self-direction. So if Socrates believes that fulfillment is tied to our nature, and if he thinks that virtuous activity as such is a kind of fulfillment, then he must think that our nature is to be rational self-directors. In that case, not only must virtuous activity be part of our happiness, but it must be so qua virtuous activity. Therefore, the attempts to move Socrates to the left-hand side of the schema that we are presently considering cannot be sustained, given Socrates' apparent view of our nature and what it is for beings with that nature to be fulfilled.

Cicero tells us that the debate over whether virtue suffices for happiness was the central debate in Hellenistic ethics, but it was also a debate that post-dated Socrates. Even so, one Hellenistic school—the Stoics—insisted that their view was essentially a Socratic one. *Any* way of positioning Socrates within this framework of debate, I have argued, would require developing, clarifying, and articulating the views of Plato's Socrates in ways that go well beyond what we find in Plato's Socratic dialogues. And I have argued that positioning Socrates on the Stoic side of this debate would have been the most plausible option. The case for the sufficiency thesis in ancient Greek ethics, therefore, would seem to begin with Socrates. Furthermore, if my conjectures about the basis of Socrates' case are correct, then the fundamental point of disagreement in the ancient sufficiency debate, right from the very beginning, would seem to have been over the nature of the self and its relation to the world around it.[56]

[56] I thank the participants at the 2011 Arizona Colloquium in Ancient Philosophy for their comments on an earlier version of this chapter, and especially Robbie Wagoner for his very thoughtful written comments.

7

Epictetus and the Stoic Self

Socrates of Plato's *Apology* believed that a good man cannot be harmed, and that conviction gave him the courage to live his life in the way he believed was best even when it led to a death sentence. A couple of millennia later John Steinbeck (*The Moon is Down*) took Socrates' point—freedom means being ready to die for what you believe in—and made it a case for joining the fight against the Nazis. But already in antiquity the Stoics had declared themselves the heirs of Socrates' legacy, arguing that nothing can harm a good person because conducting oneself virtuously is the same thing as happiness, even in the face of certain death.

Why did the Stoics believe that? Cicero gives one answer: it comes down to their belief that virtuous activity is the only good. Virtue is sufficient for happiness, he says, if and only if the Stoics' thesis about the good is true:

Concede there is nothing good except what is virtuous (*honestum*), and you must concede that the happy life consists in virtue. Or look at it the other way round: concede the latter, and you have conceded the former. (*Fin.* V.83)

I argue that Cicero was only half right. The idea that virtuous activity is the only good is *necessary* for the Stoic view of happiness,[1] but it is not *sufficient* for it. What *is* sufficient for their view of happiness is that idea about the good *plus* their doctrine that virtuous activity is the virtuous exercise of the will, an exercise that is in relation to the world around one but not embodied in it. In other words, the Stoics' thesis that virtue is sufficient for happiness follows from their joint belief in the unique goodness of virtue and what I have called the formalized conception of the self. That argument will be completed in the next chapter. In this one, we must first take a more careful look at just what the Stoics thought about the self.

To do so, I focus on the articulation of the Stoic view of the self that we find in the work of Epictetus. Since Epictetus has not been a part of the modern philosophical curriculum in anything like the way that, say, Plato and Aristotle are, I begin with a discursive outline of Epictetus' view of the boundaries of the self and the role of that view in his ethics (section 1). Then in section 2 I clarify Epictetus' view of the self in some of its key details and make explicit the ways in which it is a formalized conception of the self. Finally, I argue that although Epictetus' presentation of his formalized

---

[1] Cf. *Fin.* III.11.

conception of the self is in many ways unique to him, there is no reason to suppose that that conception is anything but an orthodox Stoic position.[2]

1 Epictetus on the self

1.1 Epictetus: some background

Epictetus (c. AD 55–c. 135) was born a slave in southwestern Asia Minor but later came to be acquired by a wealthy owner in Rome, where he would eventually study Stoic philosophy under Musonius Rufus. At some point during his life as a slave, a serious injury left him partially crippled. Even so, once freed, he became a teacher of Stoic philosophy in Rome. However, in the 90s the emperor Domitian banished all philosophers from Italy, and Epictetus went in exile to Nicopolis, a town on the west coast of Greece, where he then started his own school. But despite his life as a handicapped slave and then an exile, Epictetus did not really consider his story atypical—on the contrary, his philosophy starts from the premise that every one of us is in a constant battle against attacks on his freedom. Epictetus' lessons are therefore filled with discussions of enslavement, imprisonment, banishment, extortion, political powerlessness, coercion by bureaucrats and patrons, and even homesickness and allergies and everyday headaches and hassles—all of the ways in which we experience daily our utter lack of control over our circumstances.[3]

Like his teacher, Epictetus left no writings. However, one of Epictetus' students, Arrian, compiled collections of Epictetus' teachings—not what he taught in his areas of specialization (Stoic logic and philosophy of language), but what are presented as his "off-the-record" lessons and responses to students' queries about the significance of Stoic philosophy in everyday life. These records have come down to us as the four books of Epictetus' *Discourses* as well as the much shorter *Handbook* (or *Enchiridion*),[4] and they capture not only the words of Epictetus' short sermons but also his direct and sometimes downright confrontational delivery.

The work of Epictetus is the best place for us to look for the Stoic view of the self, for a couple of reasons. For one thing, no one else is as vociferous about the Stoics' Socratic legacy as Epictetus is. One might even say that Socrates was to Epictetus what Aristotle was to Aquinas. A. A. Long has put the point well: "The reader who knew the history of Greek philosophy only from Epictetus would form the impression that Stoicism was the philosophy of Socrates" (Long 1988, 150). In fact, Long goes so far as to call Socrates the "patron saint" of the Stoics and of Epictetus especially (1988,

---

[2] On Epictetus' complex relation to Stoicism over all, see Gill 1995, xix–xxiii.

[3] It is for this reason that, as is well known, Admiral James Stockdale found inspiration in the philosophy of Epictetus while a prisoner of war in Vietnam. See Sherman 2005 for an excellent discussion of Stockdale's case and of Stoicism in military contexts more generally.

[4] *Enchiridion*, incidentally, means "little hand-held one" in Greek—it was "the portable Epictetus."

150–1, 160). So it is natural to begin with Epictetus following our discussion of a Socratic-cum-proto-Stoic view of the self in the previous chapter.[5]

But the more important reason to begin with Epictetus is how central his view of the self is to his entire philosophy. Both of the main collections of Epictetus' teachings begin in the same way: with a discussion of what each of us really is. Although Epictetus compiled neither book, it is surely no accident that they begin as they do:

> Some things are up to us and others are not. Up to us are opinion, impulse, desire, aversion, and, in a word, whatever is our own action. Not up to us are body, property, reputation, office, and, in a word, whatever is not our own action. . . . [I]f you suppose only what is your own to be your own, and what is not your own not to be your own (as is indeed the case), no one will ever coerce you, no one will hinder you, you will find fault with no one, you will accuse no one, you will not do a single thing against your will, you will have no enemy, and no one will harm you because no harm can affect you. (*Handbook* 1)

Some things are ours, he constantly reminds us, and some things are not—and the difference between them is whether they are ours to control. It is only by grasping which things are which that we can act wisely, have appropriate emotions, and above all retain our basic human freedom in everything we do. This lesson is quickly sketched in *Handbook* 1 but presented much more carefully in the first chapter of *Discourses* I. In fact, so foundational is that first chapter that I want to build my discussion around it in its entirety.

1.2 The self in Discourses I.1

Epictetus opens his lesson in *Discourses* I.1 by observing that there is only one faculty or skill that concerns, not merely how to make use of things, but indeed whether, when, and what use to make of things:[6]

> 1. Of the arts and faculties in general, you will find none that contemplates, and consequently approves or disapproves, itself. 2. How far does the contemplative power of grammar extend? As far as the judging of language. Of music? As far as the judging of melody. 3. Does either of them contemplate itself, then? By no means. Thus, when you are writing to a friend, grammar will tell you that this is the way you should write: but whether or not you are to write to your friend at

---

[5] It is worth noting that Epictetus' other patron saint is Diogenes the Cynic (*c.* 400–*c.* 325 BC)—literally, "Diogenes the Dog-like"—himself another Socratic. The Cynics were philosophers who cast off all social conventions as unnatural, lived as beggars, and focused on public preaching of ethical diatribes, modeled on the Socratic "gadfly." One of the longest chapters of the *Discourses* (III.22) is an encomium to Cynicism, which Epictetus sees not as a separate school from Stoicism but rather as a "higher calling," so to speak, within Stoicism (see esp. III.22.67; cf. IV.8.30–3; Schofield 2007, 76–85)—not unlike, we might say, the higher calling of the missionary (cf. Schofield 2007, 81). Epictetus frequently puts Socrates alongside Diogenes; e.g. III.24.40, III.26.23. For discussion, see Rist 1969, chap. 4; Schofield 2007, 71–5.

On the Socratic legacy in Stoicism, see esp. Long 1988 and 1999; see also Annas 1993b and 1997; Brennan 2005a, 119–21; E. Brown 2006; Sellars 2009, 59, 62–3; Striker 1994. On Epictetus' relation to Socrates, see Brennan 2006; Long 2002, chap. 3. Tsouna McKirahan (1994) discusses Socrates' legacy in Cynicism.

[6] For the theme of a superordinate skill in Plato, see *Laches* 195c, *Charmides* 164ff, and *Euthd.* 291d–e; see Dobbin 1998, 70.

all, grammar will not tell you. The same is true of music, with regard to melodies; but whether it be proper or improper at any particular time to sing or play the lyre, music will not tell you. 4. What will tell you, then? The faculty which contemplates both itself—what it is, what it is capable of, and with what valuable powers it has come to us—and all the other faculties likewise. 5. For what else is it that tells us gold is beautiful? For the gold itself does not tell us. 6. What else distinguishes grammar, and the other arts or faculties, and inspects the use that is made of them, and points to the proper occasions for their use? Nothing but this.

This faculty he goes on immediately (I.1.7) to describe as "the power to deal rightly with our impressions," and he identifies it with the human capacity for choice (*prohairesis*, II.23.9), which he sometimes calls simply our "assent" (e.g. IV.1.72).[7] In one place Epictetus illustrates the process of dealing with impressions by imagining a man looking at another man's wife: he sees her and (we imagine) finds her appealing, but it is not the task of the power of eyesight to judge how he should look at her or even whether he should look at her at all (II.23.12). The same point holds for the things we hear, as well as our impulses to believe certain things, or to act, or to speak (II.23.5–15). In all of these cases, a person is presented with any number of ways in which he might go—in looking, hearing, speaking, acting, believing—but in a human being, it is through choice that one sets oneself in motion. Making such choices is what Epictetus means by "making use of our impressions," a phrase that is ubiquitous throughout the *Discourses*.

Having identified this very special human capacity, Epictetus goes on to say that it is the only thing that is ours to control:

7. It was fitting, then, that the gods have placed this alone in our own power, the most excellent faculty of all which rules all the others, the power to deal rightly with our impressions, whilst all the others they have not placed in our power. 8. Was it indeed because they did not want to? I rather think, that if they could, they would have entrusted us with those also: but there was no way in which they could. 9. For seeing that we are on earth, and confined to an earthly body, and amongst earthly companions, how was it possible that in these respects we should not be hindered by external things? 10. But what says Zeus? 'Oh Epictetus, if it were possible, I would have made this poor body and property of yours free, and not liable to hindrance. 11. But as things are, you must not forget that this body is not your own, but only cleverly moulded clay. 12. Since, then, I could not give you this, I have given you a certain portion of myself, this faculty of exerting the impulse to act and not to act, and desire and aversion, and, in a word, making proper use of impressions. If you attend to this, and place all that you have in its care, you will never be restrained, never be hindered; you will not groan, will not find fault, will not flatter any man. 13. Well then, do all these advantages seem small to you?' Heaven forbid! 'Are you then satisfied with them?' I pray so to the gods.

---

[7] As Long says, for Epictetus "choice" (*prohairesis*) is "the human mind . . . in just those respects that are dependent on nothing that we cannot immediately judge, decide, and will, entirely for and by ourselves" (Long 2002, 212). See also Rist 1969, 299, on the identification in Epictetus of *prohairesis* and the mind (*hēgemonikon*). For an excellent overview of Epictetus' account of *prohairesis*, see Dobbin 1991.

Epictetus holds that something is "in our power" (*eph' hēmin*, "up to us") just in case it is something that we can do and that nothing could keep us from doing.[8] And he says that there is exactly one thing that is in our power: our making use of our impressions, that is, our capacity of choice. In saying this, Epictetus makes two claims. One of these is that it *is* always up to us what use we will make of our impressions:

Of all the things that are, god has laid down that some are within our powers, and some are not. Within our power is the finest and most excellent of things, and that through which he himself is happy, the capacity to make use of impressions. (Fragment 4)

Epictetus does not take this point for granted; on the contrary, he discusses it frequently, often using vivid and deliberately shocking examples: it is not the tyrant and his thugs (with their sharp gleaming swords) that make us afraid, but only our own belief that the things they threaten to do would be bad for us (see *Diss.* I.19.7–8; IV.7.16, 25–32; cp. IV.1.69–71).

Epictetus' other claim is more directly relevant here: nothing *outside* the power of choice is up to us (see also *Diss.* II.19.32). As Epictetus—himself a freed slave, an exile, and lame in one leg—observes, bodies can be chained down or crippled; there is nothing that we might do with our bodies that cannot be hindered by something we cannot control, a point he makes at I.1.9–10, above. Notice, then, that when Epictetus says that choice is up to us, he does not mean that it is up to us to go for a walk (say) when we choose to, but only that it is up to us to assent to the impression that walking is the thing to do:

In the area of assent, then, you are unrestrained and unhindered. . . . 'Yes, but what if my impulse is to walk freely and another person hinders me?' What part of you can he hinder? Not your assent, surely?—'No, but my poor body.' Yes, as he could a stone.—'So be it; but I can no longer go for my walk.' And who told you that walking was an action of your own that cannot be hindered? For I said only that your impulse[9] to do so was not subject to hindrance; but when it comes to the use of our body, and cooperation from it, you have heard long ago that nothing is your own. (IV.1.69, 72–3)

---

[8] Epictetus' account of choice (*prohairesis*) as concerning what is "up to us" is therefore very different from Aristotle's (*NE* III.2–3), who thinks that things are "up to us" when they are things we can deliberate about, such as what kind of diet to have, as opposed to things that people cannot do anything about. See Bobzien 1998, 331–8; Sorabji 2000, 215, 331–2; 2006, 188–91; Stephens 2007, chap. 1. Sorabji (2000, 332) argues that Epictetus was the first Stoic to make this idea explicit. Bobzien, however, argues that here Epictetus differed from the earlier Stoic Chrysippus, who had a broader conception of "up to us" as what has its causal origins within us (e.g. walking when unhindered). Nonetheless, she argues, this difference is mainly one of focus: whereas Chrysippus focused on backward-looking ascriptions of responsibility for action already done, arguing that there is such a thing as something up to us, Epictetus focused on the forward-looking perspective of someone planning, taking as given that things can be up to us and asking exactly what those things are from that perspective.

[9] In Stoic psychology, "impulse" sometimes refers to one of our impressions—an impression of something we might do—and sometimes to a determination to act in accordance with such an impression (see Annas 1992 for discussion). It is clear that Epictetus means the latter here.

Put another way, what is up to us is not our engagement of the world in certain ways, but how we determine our will—including how we react to impediments: "A physician may hinder you from drinking," Epictetus says, "but he cannot hinder you from bearing thirst aright" (III.10.9).

Notice the crucial move that Epictetus makes at *Diss.* I.1.11–12 above: because the body can be hindered by others, it is not really *ours*. In the mythical terms of the passage, the body is something that Zeus has not given us—not out of stinginess, but because no such thing could ever be given to us, no such thing could ever be ours. Rather, the only thing Zeus gave us was the only thing that ever *could* belong to us, namely our power to make use of our impressions (see also I.6.40), that is, choice (*prohairesis*).[10] Here, then, we begin to approach the core of Epictetus' ethics, namely what sort of being one is:

Examine who you are. In the first place, a man, that is, a being in whom there is nothing more sovereign than his power of choice, but in whom all else is subject to that, whilst choice itself is free from slavery and subjection. (II.10.1)

[C]hoice is by nature free and not subject to compulsion, whereas all else is subject to hindrance and compulsion, and in bondage to others and not our own. (II.15.1)

Whatever is subject to hindrance, compulsion or deprivation is not [one's] own; whatever is not subject to hindrance is [one's] own. . . . 'What is [one's] own, then?' The proper use of impressions. (III.24.3, 69)

And of course, recall the opening of the *Handbook*:

Up to us are opinion, impulse, desire, aversion, and, in a word, whatever is our own action. Not up to us are body, property, reputation, office, and, in a word, whatever is not our own action. The things that are up to us are by nature free, unhindered, and unimpeded; but those that are not up to us are weak, servile, subject to hindrance, and not our own.

For Epictetus, the claim that nothing outside choice is ours is not just a restatement of the idea that choice is the only thing we can control. Rather, it is an important ethical principle: if we regard things outside choice as our own, we become encumbered, burdened, and dragged down—we become, that is, unfree. This point he makes clear as he continues in *Discourses* I.1:

14. But as it is, although it is in our power to take care of one thing alone, and devote ourselves to that, we choose instead to take care of many, and to encumber ourselves with many; body, property, brother, friend, child, and slave; 15. and being thus bound to a multiplicity of things we are burdened by them and dragged down. 16. Thus, when the weather does not happen to be fair for sailing, we sit fussing ourselves, and perpetually looking out.—Which wind is

---

[10] We find the same idea in Marcus Aurelius, *Med.* II.2 and V.26; see Gill 2008b, 362, for discussion. Indeed, for Epictetus the soul is not only a gift of a god, but is itself a kind of god; see Dyson 2009 for discussion.

blowing?— The north wind.—What have we to do with that?—When will the west blow?—When itself, friend, or Aeolus pleases; for Zeus has not made you dispenser of the winds, but Aeolus.

Here Epictetus has in mind the boundaries of the self—that is, the boundaries around all that I take to be me and all that I take my happiness to consist in. It is no truism to say that only the power of choice is within the boundaries of the self—people bring all sorts of other things within those boundaries all the time: their bodies, their property, their friends, their loved ones (cf. I.22.9–11).[11] As Epictetus says in the opening of the *Handbook*, some things and not others are our own, but we nonetheless have a choice about what we will *take to be* our own: "But if you suppose only what is your own to be your own, and what is not your own not to be your own (as is indeed the case), no one will ever coerce you." When Epictetus talks about what is "our own," then, he means what it is appropriate, reasonable, and healthy to regard as our own—what it is appropriate, that is, to bring within the boundaries of the self.

Having come this far, however, Epictetus must address at least three things: the implications of his view of the self for thinking about our good; the more precise nature of the self as he understands it; and the ethical motivation for that view.

Epictetus addresses the first issue next, as he considers the nature of the good and says that a person's good lies entirely in his proper use of impressions, that is, in the proper exercise of the power of choice, which he describes in this way:

17. What, then, is to be done? To make the best of what is in our power, and take the rest as it naturally happens. And how is that? As god pleases.

In a chapter titled "What is the True Nature of the Good?," Epictetus says that the good lies in right reason, which he identifies at length with making the right use of our impressions (*Diss.* II.8; cp. I.20.5). This is a theme which Epictetus repeats constantly in his teachings:

[I]f you ask me what is the good of man, I can only reply to you that it consists in a certain disposition of our choice. (I.8.16; cf. II.13.10; III.10.18)

[W]e say that good or ill for man lies in choice, and that all else is nothing to us. (I.25.1; cf. I.29.24)

The essence of the good is a certain disposition of our choice, and the essence of evil likewise. What are externals, then? Materials for the faculty of choice, in the management of which it will attain its own good or evil. (I.29.1–2)[12]

[B]oth good and evil rest essentially in the proper use of impressions, and things that lie outside the sphere of choice are not by nature either good or evil. (II.1.4)[13]

[W]hat is essentially of good lies in things that are up to us. (*Handbook* 19)

---

11 Cf. Sorabji 2000, 245; 2006, 181–2; Stephens 1996, 200.
12 Cf. II.5.1, 7–8; II.6.1; III.8.1–3; III.22.20.
13 Cf. I.30.3–4; II.16.1; III.16.15–16; *Handbook* 6.

Given that the right use of impressions is the only good, it is also the same thing as virtue, since for Epictetus—and indeed for all Stoics—virtue alone is good (*Diss.* II.19.13), being that by which we act "in accordance with nature and perfectly" (III.1.25). Epictetus goes on to explain that making right use of impressions—that is, virtuous activity—consists in successfully distinguishing, among all the things I experience, what things are mine and what things are not:

18. What, am I to be beheaded now, and on my own? Why, would you have all the world, then, lose their heads for your consolation? 19. Are you not willing to stretch out your neck, like Lateranus[14] at Rome, when Nero ordered him to be beheaded? For he stretched out his neck and took the blow, but when that blow was too weak, after shrinking back for a moment, he stretched out his neck again. 20. And, before that, when Epaphroditus, the freedman of Nero, approached somebody and asked him why he was in conflict with the emperor, he said, 'If I have a mind to say anything, I will tell it to your master.' 21. What, then, should we have at hand upon such occasions? Why, what else than to know what is mine, and what is not mine, what is within my power, and what is not?

Here again we find Epictetus being shocking, but his point is fully serious: if it is true that a doctor who prevents me from drinking cannot stop me from facing my thirst well, then neither can a tyrant who demands my head keep me from bearing my execution well. And that, Epictetus means to tell us, is all the good one can ever do, namely to do one's best at handling what one is given, to bear what one is given to bear—taking this alone as one's own and in one's power—and to leave aside every-thing else as not one's own.

[W]hat is the divine law? To preserve what is one's own, not to claim what is another's; to use what is given us, and not desire what is not given us; and, when anything is taken away, to give it up readily, and to be thankful for the time you have been permitted the use of it, and not cry after it, like a child for its nurse and its mamma. (II.16.28)

Second, Epictetus comes now to consider more explicitly the nature of the self and its boundaries on his view, in a passage that we saw in Chapter 4:

22. I must die: and must I die groaning too?—Be fettered. Must it be lamenting too? – Exiled. Can anyone prevent me, then, from going with a smile and good cheer and serenity?—'Betray the secret.' 23.—I will not betray it; for this is in my own power.—'Then I will fetter you.'—What are you saying, man? Fetter *me*? You will fetter my leg; but not even Zeus himself can get the better of my choice. 24. 'I will cast you into prison.' My wretched body, rather. 'I will behead you.' Did I ever tell you, that I alone had a head that cannot be cut off? 25.—These are the things that philosophers ought to study; it is these that they should write about each day; and it is in these that they should exercise themselves. (Italics in original translation)

---

[14] As Dobbin (1998, 74, 78) points out, the historical figures discussed in *Diss.* I.1.18–32 were all members of a conspiracy, led by Gaius Calpernius Piso, against Nero in AD 65, and consequently suffered either exile or death.

Epictetus has already said that the use of impressions is all that is *mine*, and now he says that the power of using impressions is all that is *me*. As Richard Sorabji (2006, 47) has observed, Epictetus is not saying either that a tyrant cannot chain a person (of course he can) or that there is some aspect of a person that cannot be chained (of course there is). Rather, his point is that that aspect of a person that cannot be chained is also the self of that person—it is who that person really is. Moreover, it is not as if that aspect of the person is beyond chaining because it is an immaterial spirit—the Stoics all believe that the mind, like everything else in the world, is physical. Rather, it is beyond chaining because it is the power of choice, and "you yourself are not your flesh and hair, but your choice" (III.1.40): "But the tyrant will chain—what?—Your leg.—He will cut off—what?—Your head.—What is there, then, that can neither chain nor cut off?—Your choice." (I.18.17)[15]

Notice that if the self is identical to the power of choice, and if the chief goal in life is to preserve the power of choice by making the right use of impressions—that is, to live virtuously—then it follows that the chief goal in life is really the preservation of the self. In fact, the Stoics held that all animals have the same goal and function, namely to preserve themselves, but that in humans our goal is to preserve right reason—the proper use of impressions—since that is what our humanity consists in.[16] And this is just what Epictetus says:

This is not mere self-love; for every animal is so constituted as to do everything for its own sake.... [A]ll beings have one and the same original instinct, attachment to themselves. (I.19.11, 15)

Where, then, is the great good or evil of man? Where his difference lies; if that is preserved and remains well fortified, and neither his honour, nor his fidelity, nor his intelligence is destroyed, then he himself is preserved likewise; but when any of these is lost and taken by storm, he himself is lost also. (I.28.21)

This brings us, third, to the ethical motivation for Epictetus' view of the self as identical to the power of choice. Epictetus is explicit about his reasons for attaching so much importance to our distinguishing between what is our own and what is not: if once we think our well-being requires us to preserve something outside the power of choice, then we shall try to do so, even when this violates right reason.[17] To use one of Epictetus' own examples, if I am committed to my bodily integrity as something of my own—something that is necessary for me to be *me*—then someone with power over my body thereby has power as well to coerce me; I give him power over my very choice. And that is a power I cannot afford to give away:

---

[15] See also Stephens 2007, 23–5. For references to the theme of immunity to restraint or harm elsewhere in ancient literature (e.g. at Plato, *Ap.* 30c), see Dobbin 1998, 77.

[16] See DL VII.85–9. This is the process of *oikeiōsis* or "appropriation"; I discuss it in more detail below.

[17] This is Epictetus' argument against what I have called the embodied conception of the self. I examine it carefully in Chapter 11.

Guard by every means what is your own: what belongs to others do not covet. Your good faith is your own; your sense of shame is your own. Who, then, can deprive you of these? Who can restrain you from making use of them but yourself? And how do you do so? When you concern yourself with what is not your own, you lose what is your own. (I.25.4; cp. I.19.7–15)

But, if you wish for anything at all that is not your own, what really is your own is lost. That is the nature of the matter: nothing is to be had for nothing. (IV.10.19)

Virtuous activity therefore consists in making the right use of impressions, and never allowing anything to come within the boundaries of the self that could lead us to deviate from the right use of impressions.

This, I believe, is the ethical motivation for Epictetus' view of the self. And it is also why Epictetus finds it so important that our happiness be invulnerable to fortune, as he says at the end of *Discourses* I.1:

26. Thrasea used to say, 'I would rather be killed today than banished tomorrow.' 27. How, then, did Rufus answer him? 'If you prefer that as the heavier misfortune, how foolish a preference! If as the lighter, who has put it in your power? Why do you not study to be contented with what is allotted to you?' 28. And so, what was it that Agrippinus used to say? 'I will not become an obstacle to myself.' News was brought to him: 'Your case is being tried in the Senate.' 29.—'May good fortune attend it. But the fifth hour has arrived' (the hour when he used to exercise and have his cold bath): 'let us go off and take our exercise.' 30. When he had taken his exercise someone came and told him, 'You are condemned.' To exile, he asked, or death? 'To exile.'—What of my property?—'It is not confiscated.'—Well, then, let us go to Aricia, and eat our meal there. 31. This is what it means to have studied what one ought to study; to have rendered one's desires and aversions incapable of being restrained, or incurred. 32. I must die. If instantly, I will die instantly; if in a short time, I will dine first, since the hour for dining is here, and when the time comes, then I will die. How? As becomes a person who is giving back what is not his own.

Yet again Epictetus goes out of his way to be shocking: a virtuous person is beyond the reach of misfortune; even one's exile or death is regarded as no more than returning something that was only on loan, like taking a book back to the library. But in this one way one becomes invincible, knowing that no threat against one's freedom can ever be made good. "Who, then, is the invincible man? He whom nothing outside the sphere of choice can disconcert" (I.18.21).

Socrates was willing to face execution ultimately because he believed that the power of choice was all he was and thus all that his happiness depended on. The lesson that Epictetus takes from Socrates' example would seem to be the same one that gives Steinbeck's mayor confidence as he faces his own execution: if all that my happiness requires is that I conduct myself wisely, then there is no one who can threaten to take my happiness away—and therefore there is no such threat to induce me to give away my freedom.[18]

---

[18] Bonhöffer (1894/1996, 20) put the point this way: "Happiness consists exclusively...in the moral, rational operation of the will. He who wants to know what autarky means, strictly realized, can inform himself about it best in Epictetus."

2 The formalized self in Epictetus

I now want to return to the four dimensions along which we distinguished the formalized and embodied conceptions of the self in Chapter 4, in order to clarify Epictetus' view of the self. But before I do that, I should point out what I do *not* think is going on in Epictetus' discussion of the self, in order to table a number of issues that might otherwise needlessly complicate our assessment of it.

2.1 Misunderstanding Epictetus on the self

For one thing, it bears repeating that when Epictetus says (for instance) that one's body is not one's own, his point has nothing to do with the metaphysics of the mind and body. To be sure, Epictetus is fond of using dualistic language and imagery, as he contrasts the soul with the "corpse and a pint of paltry blood" that the soul carries about,[19] and even echoes Socrates in describing the body as like chains that imprison us in spite of our kinship with the gods (*Diss.* I.9.10–11).[20] But as we have seen, his aim in using such imagery is to make an ethical point, not a metaphysical one. Nor is Epictetus alone among the Stoics in his use of such imagery: Seneca, for instance, also describes the body as chains entrapping the soul and weighing it down (*To Marcia*, 24.5–25.1), or as a house or inn for the soul (*Ep.* 65.17; 70.16–17; 120.14).[21] Although Epictetus, Seneca, and indeed all Stoics are staunchly opposed to dualism in their metaphysics, it is not uncommon for them to adopt the language and imagery of dualism in order to make distinctly ethical points about how we should identify ourselves.

For another thing, there is no reason to conclude that, in identifying the self with the power of choice (*prohairesis*), Epictetus means to offer a theory of the nature of personhood as highly individualistic.[22] On the contrary, Epictetus thinks that persons are by nature deeply social, and that in acting according to our nature we must (among other things) act in accordance with the nature of those roles in which we have been stationed, whether as son, brother, father, public official, or what have you (see *Diss.* II.10; III.2.4). In fact, Epictetus says that "the rational animal" can preserve himself only by acting in a way that is appropriate to the kind of thing he is; and since that animal is by nature social, he can preserve his rational nature only through a deeply social and shared existence (I.19.11–15). Epictetus puts the point this way:

---

[19] See e.g. *Diss.* I.9.33–4, and frag. 26: "You are a little soul, carrying a corpse, as Epictetus used to say." See also Long 2002, 164; Sorabji 2006, chap. 6.

[20] See Long 2002, 156–9, for discussion. Cf. Plato, *Phaedo* 78b–84d; *Phaedrus* 250c; *Timaeus* 90a–b. Annas 2004, 105, discusses similarly dualistic language in Marcus Aurelius, again without any actual dualistic beliefs.

[21] See Bartsch 2006, 173, for discussion of these texts. See also Gill 2006, 96–100; Long 2006, 364; Reydams-Schils 2005, 35.

[22] See Gill 2006, chap. 6, esp. 385, 389; 2008a, 46–55; 2008b, 367–71; Long 2006, 367. See also Reydams-Schils 2005, 17 and chaps. 2–5.

"I am your father." But not my good. "I am your brother." But not my good. But, if we place the good in right choice, then the preservation of such relationships does in itself become a good. (III.3.7–8)

No other person, and no relationship with another person, is a good, but our good has everything to do with what we make of our relationships with others.

Nor does Epictetus mean to suggest that we should have less concern or affection for others. On the contrary, Epictetus argues that concern and affection are part of what is natural for us, so that preserving the self—choosing in accordance with nature—involves intimate regard for others. For this reason, Epictetus constantly invokes the social connectedness of persons, including their particular social roles, in offering advice as to what his listeners should do. In a particularly moving chapter of the *Discourses*, Epictetus speaks to a father who had run out of the house because he found it too difficult to cope with his young daughter's illness (*Diss.* I.11.1–4). The father defends himself by saying that his reaction was only natural; but Epictetus replies that to act naturally is to act rightly, so the question really is whether his behavior really *was* natural in the first place (I.11.4–8). Epictetus then engages in a gentle Socratic dialogue with this father, and shows him that since fathers naturally love and care for their children, and since loving and caring for them means looking after them and not abandoning them, the right and natural thing for a father to do is to stay with a daughter when she is ailing (I.11.8–40). The father's good depends only on the wise exercise of his will—but that wisdom *includes* proper care and affection for his daughter. Indeed, one scholar has argued that Epictetus' advice would have been particularly striking at the time, both because fathers typically delegated care of children to others, and because it was usually sons who were the main objects of a father's care. Epictetus, then, seems to be urging even more intimate care on the part of fathers than was conventionally expected, and so his discussion seems to have been crafted to put especially great emphasis on the importance of family ties.[23]

This is significant. In identifying the self with choice, Epictetus means to say that where our happiness is concerned, the only thing we can afford to preserve—the only thing we can afford to identify with the self—is the freedom and goodness of our choice. To be sure, Epictetus holds that we therefore cannot become so attached to others as to make our happiness depend on them, since this makes us susceptible to abandoning the use of right reason. But he also holds that loving and caring for others is one of the very things that right reason requires of us.[24]

---

[23] See Reydams-Schils 2005, 121–3, who also discusses similar themes in Musonius Rufus, emphasizing the intimacy of bonds between mothers and children (pp. 126–30) and between spouses (pp. 148–59).

[24] As Brad Inwood (1985, 119–24) has put the point, Epictetus does not recommend indifference to one's loved ones, but rather tempering one's attachment to them with "reservation," that is, desiring their presence *for as long as* their presence remains part of the actual course of events. Cf. Bonhöffer 1894/1996, 69–72, who says that for Epictetus the disposition not to mourn the loss of something should be paired with a disposition to be joyful and thankful while one has it.

Lastly, there is no reason to suppose that, for Epictetus, we should regard the persons we love as fungible or replaceable. Nowhere does Epictetus suggest that it is inappropriate for a parent (say) to love his or her child as a unique and uniquely lovable individual. What Epictetus does make clear is something very different, namely that the only sort of love that it is appropriate *to make part of one's happiness and one's self,* is love considered as a case of exercising the power of choice in accordance with right reason, insofar as one is a parent and this is one's child. In other words, for a parent, happiness depends on one's loving one's child in the sense of acting in accordance with right reason where one's child is concerned, but this is not to say that such love is indifferent to one's child as a unique individual.[25]

Even so, we may wonder exactly how these two thoughts are to be merged—namely to love others as unique individuals while not allowing them within the boundaries of the self. Epictetus perceives no such worry here when he asserts boldly that "there is no conflict between family affection and that which is reasonable" (*Diss.* I.11.18). But perhaps Epictetus is simply whistling past the graveyard: what exactly would one's love for another be like if it were not *that* love of *that* person that is part of one's *happiness*? Indeed, this is really *the* question for a view like Epictetus': it is obvious that that view will transform our relationships, but are the transformations ones we should really accept? We shall return to this issue in Part 3.

2.2 *The formalized self*

We are now in a position to clarify Epictetus' version of what I have called the formalized conception of the self. As I said when I outlined the formalized and embodied conceptions in Chapter 4, the fundamental difference between them concerns the connection between the activities in which happiness consists and the particular objects of those activities. As we have just seen in Epictetus' discussion of family affection, the activities of a loving parent, when in accordance with right reason, are part of the parent's happiness, but *only* considered as appropriate exercises of the power of choice in relation to an external object. Even though it is appropriate for a parent, as such, to love and care for a child, and even though this love and care may embrace the child in all its non-fungible particularity, *where happiness is concerned* that child is external to the parent's activities. And this, of course, is just the point for Epictetus of identifying the self with the power of choice: happiness consists in virtuous activity, and virtuous activity is identical with self-preservation; so if the self just is the power of choice, then nothing outside the power of choice can be internal to virtuous activity—that is why "no harm can affect you" and "no one will ever coerce you." For Epictetus, then, all virtuous activity has exactly the same form: the exercise of the power of choice in relation to items in the world. Therefore, on Epictetus' view happiness consists exclusively in *formalized* virtuous activity.

---

[25] See also Reydams-Schils 2005, 75–6, for a similar point in relation to Seneca, *Ep.* 9.

We can make this point even clearer by examining four more specific defining features of the formalized conception, all of which are apparent in Epictetus' view of the self. First, the virtuous activity in which happiness consists is, for Epictetus, *continuous and invulnerable to interruption* by misfortune. Indeed, that is precisely why Epictetus restricts the self to what is "up to us," in the sense of what we can completely control, and in particular the power of choice: since no person or thing can take control of that power away from us, and since happiness just is how we exercise that power, no person or thing can ever make a believable threat against our happiness and so move us to abandon right reason. Moreover, because Epictetus understands the virtuous activity in which happiness consists as distinct from its particular objects, he views such activity as a totality of patterns of selection and response with respect to the world around one. So understood, therefore, virtuous activity can continue unabated even when the details of one's worldly circumstances change.

Second, because Epictetus takes happiness to be the same thing as a life of such activity, he holds that *happiness is invulnerable to worldly circumstances* as well. To be sure, the loss of a particular other may be the loss of something significant, but since it involves no disruption of the continuity of the activity in which one's happiness consists, it does not disrupt happiness, either. Accordingly, third, there is *no reason to respond to loss or bereavement as if it were a threat to the self.* This is why Agrippinus, in Epictetus' example, perceives no threat to his well-being either when his case goes before the court or when he is sentenced to exile (*Diss.* I.1.28–30). It is also why Epictetus himself can say to a tyrant that he may threaten his body, but he can never threaten *him.* And so, lastly, Epictetus holds that *no goods of fortune are necessary for the sake of virtuous activity.* On his view of the self, virtuous activity is the "use" of other things, but there are no particular things that one needs in order to continue making good use of things. What matters for happiness is the virtuous use of circumstances—and appropriate circumstances for acting virtuously never run out, since *all* circumstances are appropriate for that.

3 How "Stoic" is Epictetus' view?

The Stoics hold that happiness consists entirely in virtuous activity, and we have seen that Epictetus understands virtuous activity as *formalized* activity. From these two ideas it follows that virtuous activity is sufficient for happiness, and I shall argue in the next chapter that these are in fact the two Stoic pillars upon which they make their case for the sufficiency thesis. But before we can turn to that, we must ask whether the formalized conception of the self we have found in Epictetus is really a *Stoic* view at all, rather than just his own idiosyncratic view.

3.1 Stoics selves

There are a couple of reasons to see this view of the self within Stoicism beyond Epictetus. For one thing, orthodox Stoicism seems to have understood the self—the one who acts—as identical to the mind, or what they call the "commanding-faculty" (*hēgemonikon*). Revealingly, we are told that two of the earliest Stoics, Cleanthes and Chrysippus, disagreed over how to define walking: the former said that walking is something the commanding-faculty does with respect to one's feet, the latter that walking is a state of the commanding-faculty itself (Seneca, *Ep.* 113.23). What concerns us at present is not where these two early Stoics disagree but rather where they *agree*, namely the striking view that even such a paradigmatically "external" action as walking is in fact something that the commanding-faculty does, however we should characterize the finer details of its doing it.[26] If it is the self who walks, and if what walks is the commanding-faculty, then the self just is the commanding faculty. Note that what the self does, on this view, is not characterized in the first instance as any kind of engagement of the world, but only the determination of the will and, as Epictetus might have put it, the use of impressions.

Furthermore, Cicero and Seneca also describe the Stoic final end as self-preservation, and equate this with acting according to right reason.[27] This idea occurs in their account of human development, and in particular a process the Stoics call "appropriation" (*oikeiōsis*), a process by which we "appropriate" ourselves. Each living creature, they tell us, has an instinctual awareness of its constitution and what it must do to preserve that constitution: for instance, what sort of posture is appropriate to the kind of thing it is, as well as what to eat, what to run away from, and so on.[28] In other words, all animals, humans included, have a fundamental natural drive to preserve themselves. Now, in most animals development is entirely along these lines, but because humans have a unique constitution—they are *rational* animals—an important shift eventually occurs as they develop: they become aware that they live by making choices and using reason to work out what to do, and it is *this* that they are then naturally moved to preserve. This shift is not a departure from the preservation of one's human constitution, since that constitution just *is* a rational one. When the process goes well, then, what humans learn is that they live by reasoning, and that to preserve their constitution is to reason well. For the Stoics, this process does not lead humans to ignore their physical needs, but it does lead them to put a radically different kind of value upon the reasoning power by which they provide for their needs. As Cicero puts the point, looking after our needs reveals, in time, the reasoning we use in doing so, and it is that reasoning itself that we really come to prize; it is as if one friend had introduced us to another, whom we come to love even more than the first. So in saying that the self we preserve is our reasoning—our power of choice—Epictetus is in line with this standard Stoic account of self-preservation.

---

[26] For discussion, see Annas 1992, 99–100.

[27] See Cicero, *Fin.* III.16–34; V.24–64; Seneca, *Ep.* 121; DL VII.85–9.

[28] For discussion, see Inwood 1984, 154–78; Ramelli 2009, 39–57; and esp. Engberg-Pedersen 1990b, chaps. 2–4.

However, coming to love our power of reasoning as the constitution we preserve is only half of the process of appropriation (*oikeiōsis*). The other half concerns how we "appropriate" other people, and here the Stoics say that good development will bring us into ever closer affiliation with others.[29] We shall examine a text below that will describe this sort of development in greater detail, but the basic idea is that by nature all animals look after, not only their own constitution, but also their offspring, and in humans this natural attachment to others is the source of our capacity for broader benevolence, friendship, and justice (see Cicero, *Fin.* III.62–3). This second stage of appropriation requires effort, reasoning, and practice, since the goal is to close the gaps between us until each of us cares for others as he does for himself. But it is at this point that we might wonder whether Epictetus might part ways with "mainstream" Stoicism after all, not because he is indifferent to our sociality—quite the contrary—but because he insists on keeping other people beyond the boundaries of the self. So I want to examine two key texts that some scholars have thought might suggest a more expansive Stoic view of the self: one from Seneca on the experience of loss and grief, and one from Hierocles on the importance of expanding the boundaries of our other-regard.

3.2 Seneca on friends and body parts

In the ninth of his *Letters to Lucilius*, Seneca compares the loss of a friend to the loss of a body part, that is, a part of oneself. The wise person, he says, is self-sufficient (*sibi ipse sufficiat*), but not in the sense of doing without others; on the contrary, the wise person wants to have friends and companions. Moreover, when the wise person loses a friend, he will still be contented with what he has left, but in the same way that he would be contented with what is left of his body if he should lose a hand or eye (*Ep.* 9.3–5). Epictetus would of course agree that the wise person will be contented with what he has left when he loses a friend, but Seneca's comparison of that loss to the loss of a body part—a part of *oneself*—suggests that the loss strikes the wise person much closer to home than Epictetus would allow. What should we make of this?

Margaret Graver says the following about Seneca's analogy:

[I]t illustrates not only the rationale for imperturbability but also the depth of the connection that existed. The relation of the wise person to friends is . . . as intimate as one's attachments to one's own body. The friend is to the self as part of the same organic whole, which only some violent invasion could break apart. The person of perfect understanding can survive such an invasion without loss of well-being, but only because he or she is able at need to redefine the boundaries of the self to encompass a smaller but still harmoniously integrated whole. (Graver 2007, 183–4)

One point that Graver seeks to make is that part of what Seneca's wise person perceives in the loss of a friend is the loss of someone particular and irreplaceable.[30] I suspect she is

---

[29] For a good recent discussion of the two stages, see Reydams-Schils 2005, 55–9. Somewhat surprisingly, Arius Didymus discusses this second, social form of *oikeiōsis* in his summary of Aristotelian (rather than Stoic) ethics; see Görgemanns 1983.

[30] See also Reydams-Schils 2005, 76.

right about this; in any case, I have argued that there is no indication that Epictetus would say otherwise. Seneca's analogy may also be intended to show the closeness with which wise friends care for each other: just as we look after our bodies in a natural way—and not as alien things that might as easily slip our minds, or seem someone else's business—so too the wise person looks after a friend. And Seneca's analogy also illustrates that loss of a friend, like loss of a body part, requires substantial adjustment: in both cases, a part of our familiar environment for action is now gone, and we shall need to adjust our behavior to take account of its absence.

But Graver's larger point goes beyond these. In effect, Graver is attributing to Seneca what I have called an embodied view of the self: other people are within the boundaries of the self of the wise person, so that their loss is a sort of "invasion" of the self; the advantage of virtue in the face of such loss is the hope of being able, in time, to redefine those boundaries and move on as a new self.

However, if that is the message that Seneca means to put across, then it is Seneca whose view of the self is out of sorts with Stoic ethics. Graver's interpretation takes its cue from the idea that one's care for a friend is to be "as intimate as one's attachments to one's own body," and in concluding that a friend is within the boundaries of the self she assumes first of all that Seneca means for *one's own body* to be within the boundaries of the self. But surely Seneca cannot think that we are to be attached to our bodies in *that* way, since that would mean that happiness could be threatened by bodily losses. If Seneca thought that, then he would hold that bodily integrity and functionality are part of pre-loss happiness. In that case, Seneca would have to reject a fundamental tenet of Stoic ethics in favor of something far more Aristotelian, denying that virtuous activity is sufficient for happiness on the grounds that bodily integrity and functionality are also goods, so that happiness is vulnerable at least to loss of goods of the body.[31]

Consequently, it is unlikely that Seneca departed significantly from Epictetus in thinking about how the wise person's body and friends stand with respect to the boundaries of the wise person's self. More important, it is now very clear that Epictetus places the boundaries of the wise person's self *exactly* where the Stoic account of the good and happiness *requires* them to be.

3.3 Hierocles on drawing others nearer

The remaining view for us to examine is that of the later Stoic Hierocles (117–138 AD), about whom we know little aside from a few passages on the nature of "appropriation." These passages bring out two main features of his view of human nature: one, an

---

[31] For the same reason, I cannot agree with Reydams-Schils (2005, chap. 2) when she moves from the closeness of human bonds in Stoicism to the claim that, in Stoicism, such bonds are goods. Her move is based on texts such as AD II.5e, where friends are described as external goods; however, it seems more likely that we should understand friends as "goods" in the sense in which Arius glosses "having good children" as being good *oneself* in relation to one's children (AD II.5m). I discuss this point of Stoic value theory in the next chapter.

emphasis on human physicality, and two, an emphasis on human sociality. It is the second point that concerns us at present.[32]

In one of our excerpts, Hierocles says, rather like Aristotle (*Pol.* I.2), that humans are gregarious animals who need one another and therefore live in political communities and form friendships with each other.[33] In another excerpt he goes even further, comparing each of us to a set of concentric circles representing increased personal attachment as they approach the center, and urging us to draw the "outer" circles ever closer to the center.[34] The "center" of this set of circles, he says, is the mind (*dianoia*), and the first circle around it is the body and the things we need for its sake; this circle, he says, is the smallest and almost touches the center. The second circle includes parents, siblings, wife, and children, the third includes more distant family relations (uncles and aunts, grandparents, nieces and nephews, and cousins), and the fourth more distant relations still. The fifth circle is for clan relations; the sixth for tribe relations; the seventh for fellow-members of one's *polis*; the eighth for members of bordering *poleis*; the ninth for members of the same people-group; and the tenth for the entire human race.

Our task in moral development through appropriation—or perhaps in this context, "familiarization"—is to transfer other people from the circle they occupy to the next circle nearer the center, and we do this through the regard, or more precisely, respect (*timēteon*) that we show them. Hierocles acknowledges that distance in blood-relation normally makes more distance in our regard (*eunoia*) for people, but he encourages us to do all we can to reduce that distance. To do so, he suggests that we modify how we address others, for instance calling aunts "mothers" and cousins "brothers," since this practice would both show others the profundity (*spoudēs*) of our regard for them and would help us reach out to draw the circles closer.[35]

It is significant for our purposes that the circle nearest the center, and almost touching it, is the person's body. As we have seen, the Stoics do not believe that the body is part of the agent's own good, so it is unlikely that Hierocles thinks that the body is part of the self (in this sense) or, consequently, that to bring other persons nearer the center is to bring them within the boundaries of the self. Rather, the passage concerns the respect and good will or humane regard we have for others, and urges us to think beyond conventional borders and adopt a cosmopolitan outlook. Simply put, Hierocles' basic idea seems to be that just as each of us finds it obvious that his own body is something for *him* to look after, and not some alien thing that could just as well be left for someone else to take care of, so we should all think of each other, regardless

---

[32] For complete text and commentary, see Ramelli 2009.

[33] *Hierocles, Elements of Ethics* 9.3–10, 11.14–18 (= LS 57D).

[34] Stobaeus, *Anthology* IV.671, 7–673, 11 (= LS 57G). See also Sorabji 2006, 44 for the most recent translation. For discussion, see Ramelli 2009, 61–2.

[35] One wonders what we are then to call actual mothers and brothers. See also Annas 1993a, 268–9, who worries that the more likely effect of Hierocles' suggestion would be to dilute the significance of the nearer relationships and their names.

of distances in kinship or political allegiance. This also makes better sense of his claim that the circle representing the body almost touches the center. He makes a special point of noting this proximity; if his point is that closeness to the center is closeness to being part of one's good, this is difficult to understand: what are we to make of the idea that something is *almost* part of one's good? Yet if his point is that closeness to the center tracks how naturally one looks after a thing as one's own, that point is a very easy one to understand.

However, Richard Sorabji has argued that in this regard, there is a tension between Hierocles' account of appropriation and Epicteus' view of the self, with its focus on invulnerability. Whereas Epictetus narrows what is "mine" to the power of choice (*prohairesis*; see *Diss.* I.1.10–12; cp. II.22.19), Sorabji argues, Hierocles expands it:

> If [Hierocles] were only making concern for other people a matter of deliberate choice, he would not so far be placing *mine* outside his *prohairesis*. But insofar as he is also extending his feeling of attachment to his own body, in the traditional Stoic way, to other people, there is at the very least a tension with Epictetus. Hierocles' extension of *mine* to include other people is designed for the different purpose of securing justice to others. It inevitably involves a tension with Epictetus' purpose of securing invulnerability. (Sorabji 2006, 194, italics in original)

Clearly, Sorabji has a point: in thinking of the body and even other people as "mine," Hierocles is not limiting "mine" to the power of choice. As Sorabji puts it, it is Epictetus but not Hierocles who makes "me" and "mine" identical.

If Sorabji is right about this, then Epictetus is in tension not just with Hierocles but with the oldest traditions of Stoic thought. Zeno himself (and apparently Chrysippus) seems to have defended a form of communism, a classless and moneyless ideal society with, importantly, things held in common as among friends.[36] The Stoics believe that the Earth was given to us all (Cicero, *Off.* I.22); accordingly, on one Stoic metaphor "private" ownership is really only a temporary leasehold, and on another, something is "yours" only in the sense that a seat in the public theater can be yours.[37] The race of

---

[36] This seems to have been the central thesis of Zeno's renowned and controversial *Republic*, of which only brief reports survive. See e.g. Plutarch, *On the Fortune of Alexander* 329a-b (= LS 67A); DL VII.32–3; Athenaeus *Deipnosophists* 561c (= LS 67D); see also Mitsis 2005, 241–2. There is general scholarly consensus that early Stoic communism reflected the more general leanings of the early Stoa towards Cynicism (Zeno, we should note, was the pupil of the Cynic philosopher Crates), which rejected civic for more "natural" communal ties (see Long and Sedley 1987, 435). It is a controversial question whether Stoic communism, like Cynicism, was also anarchical; see Schofield 1991, chap. 2, for discussion.

[37] On the tenant metaphor, see Plutarch, *On Exile* 600e (= LS 67H); Seneca, *Ep.* 88.11–12; Mitsis 2005, 242–3. On the theater metaphor, see Cicero, *Fin.* III.67; Seneca, *On Favors* VII.12.3–6; Epictetus, *Diss* II.4.9; Long 2006, 349–51 and references; Brennan 2005b, 252–3; Mitsis 2005, 234–5. Interestingly, Nussbaum (1997, 13) identifies this aspect of Stoicism as inspiring Kant's discussion of common world ownership in *Perpetual Peace*.

Surprisingly, Cicero uses the theater analogy to *support* the institution of private property (*Off.* II.73). While this is consistent with Cicero's own political agenda of opposing redistribution (see Long 2006, 328–9), nonetheless the metaphor seems to originate with Chrysippus, who probably intended it in support of the abolition of private property in favor of common ownership (but see Erskine 1990, 105–10). So Cicero seems

rational animals is one whole group, and the Stoics view each individual person as one continuous part or "limb" of this collective "body," without any distinctive claims as to the disposition of appropriable things, so that on such matters it is the collective that has say.[38] Closer to home, the Stoic Hecato said that the wealth of an individual is actually society's wealth (Cicero, *Off*. III.63). For the Stoics, then, "mine" includes every member of humanity, and "ours" includes one another and even the whole world.

Moreover, an anonymous commentary on Plato's *Theaetetus* (LS 57H) reveals both that what we have from Hierocles is a genuine Stoic account of the second, social stage of appropriation, and also how radical this account was taken to be in closing the gap between oneself and others. According to the commentator, the Stoics hold that appropriation is the basis of human justice, and that appropriation is meant to close the gap between one and even "the furthest Mysian."[39] But while the commentator applauds their concern for justice, he denies that appropriation could fully close the gap between persons, on two grounds: one, affinity to oneself is natural and automatic, whereas assimilating others takes effort and reasoning; and two, we do not become at odds with ourselves when we do wrong in the way that we become at odds with others when they do wrong. The commentator suggests that these points are not just academic: in zero-sum situations (e.g. "lifeboat" cases), even when there is philanthropic concern, the difference between *self* and *other* matters.[40] The details and fairness (or otherwise) of these objections are of less concern to us at present than is the very fact that they were made, since the objections make it clear that the standard Stoic view of social appropriation, as in Hierocles, was perceived as stating in the strongest terms how radically the distances between persons could, and should, be closed.

So is Epictetus' view of what is "mine" and within the boundaries of the self an idiosyncratic view, outside more mainstream Stoic ethics? It would be surprising if it were, since Epictetus himself seems to be as firm a Stoic advocate of cosmopolitanism as

to be reversing Chrysippus' metaphor to suit his own purposes, in a way that clearly strains the metaphor itself. See Mitsis 2005, 234–8, 242–3; see also Long 2006, 350–1; Brennan 2005b, 252.

It is worth noting, though, that by Cicero's time some Stoics had moved away from the more Cynic leanings of the early Stoa in general (cf. *Fin*. III.68; Clement, *Misc*. 5.9.58.2 [= LS 67E]; Long and Sedley 1987, 435), including Panaetius, who is Cicero's source for much of *Off*. As Sellars (2007, 20–4 and references) notes, Panaetius shifted Stoic moral thought in general from a focus on perfected sages to imperfectly virtuous persons, and his focus on the legislative measures inevitably required within communities of imperfect persons can be seen as part of that larger shift (see also Seneca, *Ep*. 90.5–7 [= LS 67Y] on Posidonius).

[38] See Marcus Aurelius, *Med*. VII.13; Nussbaum 1997, 10.

[39] The Mysians were an ancient people of northwest Asia Minor—very remote by ancient Greek standards. The reference to them here is meant to suggest people "on the other side of the world" as we might say.

[40] For shipwreck cases in this context, see Cicero, *Off*. II.90. Annas (1993a, 273) takes the commentator's point to be that each survivor will try to grab the remaining flotsam for himself, but it seems to me that his purpose in stipulating the presence of philanthropic concern is to raise a very different kind of objection. That objection, I think, is that *even when* each survivor yields philanthropically to the other, the sacrifice made is perceived as exactly that—a sacrifice, putting "yours" ahead of "mine," rather than trading one "mine" for another "mine." For general discussion, see Inwood 1984, 179–83; Ramelli 2009, xliii–iv.

any other. As we saw above, Epictetus insists that even though our final end is self-preservation, this is an end we achieve only through contributing to what we might call the common good (*Diss.* I.19.11–15). This common good extends to all humanity, since one should not think of oneself as a citizen of Athens or Corinth, but a citizen of the whole world and one of the children of the god (I.9.1, 6). Moreover, Epictetus argues that we can discover how it is appropriate for us to act by determining what it is that we are: in the first instance, we are human beings, and humans are citizens of the universe—and to be a citizen of the universe is never to do anything as though detached from the whole and for purely personal gain (II.10.1–4). This point he repeats elsewhere, and adds that in the same way that a foot is no longer a foot when detached from the body, so a human is no longer a human when detached from the whole of humanity in the pursuit of his own private interests (II.5.24–6). In this respect, Epictetus says, all human beings are friends by nature (III.24.11).

However, this does not fully address Sorabji's worry: he concedes that Epictetus might make "concern for other people a matter of deliberate choice," but argues that he does not expand the notion of "mine" to include other people. But here I think we would do well to revisit a passage we saw above:

'I am your father.' But not my good. 'I am your brother.' But not my good. But, if we place the good in right choice, then the preservation of such relationships does in itself become a good . . . (*Diss.* III.3.7–8)

Notice that Epictetus does not reply to the imagined relative, "No, you are not my father (or brother)," that is, "You are not mine"; what he says is that the relative is not "his" in the sense that that relative is not *part of his good*. Nor does Epictetus suggest that his father or brother would not be his to look after—on the contrary, in the very passage in which he urges us to remember that we are humans and citizens of the universe, he immediately goes on to remind us that we are also sons and brothers, and that these relationships are also relevant to what it is appropriate for us to do (II.10.7–9). The same idea, we may recall, is also the basis of his advice to the father who fled his ailing daughter: he is her father, and so by nature she is *his* to look after (I.11).

So here we must draw a distinction that Epictetus clearly intends. It is one thing to call someone or something "mine" in the sense of mine-to-look-after, and another to say "mine" in the sense of part-of-my-good. "Mine" in the former sense concerns our care, regard, and concern for others, and here Epictetus insists that we should close the distances between oneself and others: those gaps are unnatural, they are inappropriate, and they jeopardize one's very humanity. But it is clear that this is the very sense in which Hierocles also thinks that what is "mine" should be expanded to include others with ever diminishing regard for familial, geographical, and political distance. This is also the sense in which Seneca thinks that a friend is "mine," as we saw above. As for what is mine-to-look-after, then, Epictetus, Hierocles, and Seneca could not agree more. Of course, Epictetus does not allow anything but the power of choice to count as "mine" in the sense of part-of-my-good—that is, "mine" in the sense that is identical to "me"—but then there is also no suggestion whatever that Hierocles thought anything different.[41] Indeed, even if the social stage of *oikeiōsis* involves extending family-feeling to those more distant, it is important to remember that in Stoicism our loved ones—even our children—are still regarded as *others*, and not as "second selves" as in Aristotle's view.[42] On the contrary, to think anything different on this point just is to reject Stoic ethics, by making happiness vulnerable to fortunes outside our control.

I have articulated a conception of the self that we find in Epictetus, on which the self is the faculty of choice (*prohairesis*), and virtuous activity is the wise exercise of that faculty with respect to whatever the world presents to us. Now, it is often thought that the Stoics' case for the sufficiency thesis stands or falls depending entirely on their view that virtuous activity is the only good. Not so, I argue in the next chapter. It took these *two* ideas—one about the unique goodness of virtuous activity, *and* one about the kind of activity it is—to get the sufficiency thesis off the ground.

[41] Cf. Graver 2007, 177.
[42] See Reydams-Schils 2005, 57. I discuss Aristotle's "second self" in Chapter 5.

8

The Stoics' case for the sufficiency thesis

Diogenes Laertius tells us that according to the Stoics, virtue "is sufficient for happiness, as Zeno says, and Chrysippus . . . and Hecato . . . " referring to the two founders of the Stoic school and one figure of Middle Stoicism, respectively (DLVII.127). Likewise Cicero, here:

Wherefore as no wicked and foolish and idle man can have well-being, so the good and brave and wise man cannot be wretched. Nor yet can he whose virtue and whose character deserve praise fail to live a life that is praiseworthy, and further, a life that is praiseworthy is not a life to flee from; yet it would be a life to flee from if it were wretched. Therefore what is praiseworthy must also be deemed to be happy and prosperous and desirable. (*PS* 19)

And here:

How dignified, how noble, how constant is the character of the wise person drawn by the Stoics! Reason has shown that virtue (*honestum*) is the only good. This being so, the wise person must always be happy, and the true possessor of all those titles which the ignorant love to deride: more rightly "king" than Tarquinius . . . ; more rightly "master of the people" than Sulla . . . ; and richer than Crassus . . . (*Fin.* III.75)

So too Seneca:

What is proper to man? Reason. This, when upright and complete, has fulfilled the happiness of man. Therefore if each thing, when it has perfected its very own good, is praiseworthy and attains the goal of its own nature, and if reason is man's very own good, then if he has perfected this he is praiseworthy and has reached the goal of his own nature. This perfected reason is called virtue and this same thing is what is noble. (*Ep.* 76.10, trans. Inwood 2005, 251)

And of course Epictetus:

Now if virtue promises happiness, and untroubled mind and serenity, then progress towards virtue is certainly progress towards each of these. (*Diss.* I.4.3)

So the Stoics say that virtue is sufficient for happiness.[1] Hardly anyone says that these days, though, and neither do I. But this is not because I disagree with the Stoics about what kind of *good* virtuous activity is. I disagree about what kind of *activity* virtuous activity is.

---

[1] There were, however, two later prominent Stoics, Panaetius and Posidonius, who are said to have denied the sufficiency of virtue for happiness (DL VII.128; cf. Cicero, *Fin.* IV.79), although this is said

The difference between what kind of good virtue is and what kind of activity it is can be seen in two very different arguments that Cicero gives for the Stoic sufficiency thesis. One we saw above: "Reason has shown that virtue is the only good. This being so, the wise person must always be happy." On this argument, only virtue is good, and so it follows that virtue is sufficient for happiness (so also *Fin.* V.83).[2] Elsewhere, however, Cicero gives a different argument:

You know not, madman, you know not how great is the strength that virtue possesses; you merely utter the name 'virtue', you do not know what virtue itself means. No one can fail to be supremely happy who relies solely on himself *and who places all his possessions within himself alone*... (PS 17, italics added)

This argument is different from the first because this one says not only that virtue is the only good, but also that virtue is something completely inward and internal[3]—and it is from this *pair* of claims, Cicero suggests here, that the Stoics' sufficiency thesis follows.

I argue in this chapter that it is this second kind of argument, not the first, that captures the Stoics' reasoning, and is valid to boot. That is to say, the Stoics' sufficiency thesis is not based solely on their belief that virtuous activity is the only good, and rightly so. Even if virtuous activity is the only good, whether it is sufficient for happiness depends on whether virtuous activity is embodied in vulnerable worldly pursuits and attachments. That is the idea at work in Cicero's second argument: since virtue is the only good (PS 6–15), the virtuous person is guaranteed happiness, *provided* that he "places all his possessions within himself alone." Provided, that is, that he draws the boundaries of the self so as to include only his faculty of choice. Indispensable for the Stoics' case for the sufficiency thesis is what I have called the formalized conception of the self.

I begin by outlining the Stoics' basic account of the good, which they say is exhausted by virtue and what "participates in" virtue (section 1). This notion of "participation" is crucial, since it expands the good to include things that on their own are not good at all but can nonetheless become constituents of virtuous activity. In fact, I argue that this is exactly what we see in the case of those types of emotion that

without any explanation why they would have held this unorthodox view. Kidd 1971a argues compellingly that there is good reason to be suspicious of this claim, and of claims in general that Posidonius differed sharply from Stoic orthodoxy about the nature of the good—which would have been shocking given Cicero's claim that it is that issue that defines all the different schools (see also Rist 1969, 7–10; Kidd 1971b; and my Chapter 6). Indeed, as Long and Sedley (1987, 410) are surely correct to observe, if any Stoic had denied the sufficiency of virtue for happiness, it is most surprising that Cicero made no mention of it. In any event, I shall confine my remarks to the orthodox Stoic view, as it was only that view that was taken as important in the Stoics' contribution to the sufficiency debate. (Indeed, that fact alone would make it very surprising if there were strong disagreement on the Stoic side on this point: why would the Stoics' critics, so eager to seize on *any* apparent in-house dispute, not have seized on a dispute as egregious as this one would have been.)

[2] See also *TD* V.18–19, 33–4, 83. For discussion of this type of argument, see Irwin 1986, 209–42; 2007, 288, 321–2, chap. 13 passim; Annas 1993a, 389–91.

[3] See Irwin 1986, 228–34; Lesses 1989, 100.

the Stoics say participate in virtue (section 2). In that case, if bodily and external things cannot be goods and important for happiness, this is not because virtuous activity alone is good but because virtuous activity is such that bodily and external things cannot participate in it (section 3). In other words, it is because of their view of the self.

1 Stoic values: good, bad, and indifferent

We have two main sources for Stoic value theory: the overview given by Diogenes Laertius in book VII of his *Lives of Eminent Philosophers*, and the more extensive synopsis from Arius Didymus, subsequently preserved in John Stobaeus' *Anthology* (5th century AD).[4] According to Diogenes, the Stoics say that what is good is "that which is perfectly in accord with nature for a rational being, qua rational" (DL VII.94). Since this is our nature, our fulfillment and happiness "is a life which is consistent and in agreement with nature," that is, our rational nature (AD II.6). This is why virtue is good, because it benefits us in that way that is distinctive of our nature (DL VII.94). As Arius Didymus puts the point, the virtues have the goal of living "consistently with nature," that is, with the practical rationality that it is our nature to have, so that what is natural for us is "to discover what is appropriate and to stabilize [one's] impulses and to stand firm and to distribute fairly" (AD II.5b3). So the good, and virtuous activity in particular, is understood in terms of human fulfillment, and in particular our fulfillment as practically rational creatures. Notice, then, that Stoic thought about the good begins from the perspective of our fulfillment as humans, and regards our humanity as defined by our practical rationality. In other words, they take our nature to be what I have called rational self-construction (Chapter 3).

If the good is what fulfills humans as rational creatures, and practical rationality is something active and creative, then the good should be not a property but a *power*—something active and creative that shapes our lives in an intelligent way. And this is just how the Stoics understand goodness, namely as a power "to benefit" us by fulfilling and actuating us as humans. In particular, the good is "that from which it characteristically results that one is benefited," or more generally, "that which is such as to benefit" (AD II.5d) and "that from which there is something beneficial" (DL VII.94; cp. Seneca, *Ep.* 117.2). Diogenes Laertius captures the idea of goodness as a power with the following analogy:

[J]ust as heating, not cooling, is a property of the hot, so benefiting, not harming, is a property of the good; but wealth and health do not benefit any more than they harm; therefore, neither wealth nor health is good. Again, they say that what can be used [both] well and badly is not

---

[4] For an excellent overview of the structure of Arius' discussion, see Long 1983. Long (pp. 41–3, 55) also discusses the difficult scholarly question of whether Arius Didymus is in fact the author of the synopsis preserved in Stobaeus. Like most scholars, I shall assume that he is; nothing in this book shall depend on this assumption, though.

good; but it is possible to use wealth and health [both] well and badly; therefore, wealth and health are not good. (DL VII.103)

This is quick, but it is actually very instructive. In characterizing the good as such as to benefit (sc. its possessor), as the hot is such as to heat, the Stoics seem to intend two basic points. First, the good is what is good all on its own, without requiring something else to make it good. The Stoics do not mean merely that the good is choice-worthy for its own sake as opposed to instrumentally: after all, health is valuable for its own sake and not (only) as a means. Rather, the idea is that the good does not need to be given a direction within one's life by something else before it can be of any benefit. To have the good as part of one's life, then, is *necessarily* to have it as a part of one's life in the right way, in a way that makes life better: it is such as to benefit.

And second, the good is what is responsible for the beneficial direction given to all other things: as the hot is what makes other things hot, so the good is what makes our use of other things good. This is why the Stoics think of the virtues as skills or crafts.[5] It is in our capacity to give ourselves and our lives direction, after all, that our rationality is active and creative. The Stoics put the point this way: humans and animals alike all have impulses—roughly, things they get it into their heads to do—but humans through the use of practical reason can direct their impulses intelligently, as a craftsman gives direction intelligently to the materials of his craft. "When reason has been given to rational animals," Diogenes reports, "as a more perfect governor of life, then for them the life according to reason properly becomes what is natural for them. For reason supervenes on impulse as a craftsman" (DL VII.86).[6]

So for the Stoics, the good is such as to occupy the right place in one's life, just in virtue of its very nature, and is such as to make other things occupy their right place as well. In other words, the Stoics make a fundamental distinction between what I have called a *fashioning* good and other things that need to be *fashioned* (see Chapter 4).

More precisely, the Stoics identify three basic value categories: what is good in virtue of fashioning things beneficially, what is bad because it fashions things harmfully, and what is neither of these but waits to be fashioned. First of all, the Stoics say that there are two things in the category of "good": virtue and whatever participates in virtue (AD II.5a–5b).[7] As we have seen, virtue for the Stoics is essentially an active power, and can be understood variously as a source of action, a mode in which one acts, and as the person acting (DL VII.94). Moreover, it is virtue that is good by its nature and impossible to use badly, and that makes one act well with respect to all other things. Specifically, Arius Didymus (II.5b) says that by "virtue" the Stoics mean two things. On the one hand, "virtues" in the strict sense are just the cardinal virtues—prudence or wisdom, justice, temperance or self-control, and courage. These, they say, are forms of

---

[5] *Technai, epistēmai*; see e.g. AD II.5b, 5b10; Sextus Empiricus, *M* XI.200. More on this below.

[6] "Impulse" is actually a technical notion in Stoic psychology; we shall look at it more carefully below.

[7] "Participates in virtue": *metechon aretēs*. See also Epictetus, *Diss.* II.9.15; II.19.13; Sextus Empiricus, *M* XI.22–23.

knowledge, that is, forms of skill or expertise that are practical, active, systematic, and correct. And on the other hand, there are also virtues that are not cardinal virtues or forms of knowledge, but attributes and capacities of a person with the virtues (or the "supervenient byproducts" of virtue), such as the health, soundness, strength, and beauty of the soul (AD II.5b4). The other sort of good besides virtue is what "participates in" virtue, which they identify as various forms of emotional soundness: joy, good spirits, confidence, and wish (AD II.5b; see also DL VII.96). All of these things count as good because virtue is good, and these are its parts and attributes.

Second, the bad is defined as what is such as to harm its possessor, considered as a rational creature, and the same two points that applied to the good now apply, *mutatis mutandis*, to the bad. One is that the bad is bad in its own right, without requiring anything else to make it bad, and the other is that it is responsible for the badness of other things. The bad, then, is also understood in terms of its causal power. And so Arius Didymus says that for the Stoics the only bad things are vice and what participates in vice (II.5a–5b1). This is because the vices—understood as sources of action, modes of action, and persons who act—fashion other things badly (or rather, fail to fashion them well) and therefore are by their nature impossible to use well (DL VII.95). The vices include, first, the "cardinal" vices (folly, intemperance, injustice, and cowardice), which are forms of ignorance, that is, lacks of skill and expertise; and second the attributes of a person having the cardinal vices, which are not forms of ignorance per se but are such things as pusillanimity, weakness, and powerlessness (AD II.5b). And what "participates in" vice are various forms of emotional unsoundness, such as distress and anxiety (AD II.5b).[8]

The third and final value category belongs to everything that can be put to either good or bad use, that is, can be good or bad depending on how they are used or what direction they are given. And this is everything else besides virtue, vice, and what participates in them: health, wealth, reputation, pleasure and pain, even life and death (DL VII.102–7; AD II.5a). None of these things differentiates a good person from a bad one (AD II.5b9),[9] and none of them has any fashioning power of the sort we have discussed, but rather must be fashioned before they can have a good place in one's life.[10]

The Stoics call such things *adiaphora* (literally "things without difference"), which is commonly rendered "indifferent things." However, I prefer to call them "undifferentiated things" instead, for two main reasons. One, calling these things "undifferentiated" emphasizes the idea that the *adiaphora* are neither good nor bad on their own, and take on a good or bad role only when someone does something with them, as opposed to the "differentiating" powers of good or bad use of such things. In themselves, that is,

---

[8] I.e., the "passions" or *pathē*. More on the emotions below and in Chapter 11.

[9] Cp. Sextus Empiricus, *M* XI.200–1, 207.

[10] We shall return below to the sense in which these things can become "good" or "bad."

they are not "differentiated" as either good or bad parts of one's life; that will depend on something else.[11]

And two, this labeling avoids the misleading idea that the *adiaphora* are "indifferent" in the sense that they just do not matter, as if one's health or parents (say) just do not matter.[12] This is a misunderstanding that the Stoics themselves actually take pains to ward off (AD II.7, 7c; DL VII.104). As with the English word 'indifferent,' *adiaphora* can refer to things that stimulate no impulse at all, that is, don't get us moving in one way or another about them, such as whether the hairs on one's head are odd or even in number (AD II.7c; DL VII.104). These are things that Arius Didymus calls "absolutely" *adiaphora*. But when the Stoics call things like health *adiaphora*, they understand that such things *do* naturally stimulate impulse one way or another—as health stimulates impulse toward it (so it is "preferred") and sickness stimulates impulse away (it is "dispreferred" or "rejected"; see AD II.7b, 7g; DL VII.104–7). Rather, their point is simply that such things, by their nature, are not such as to benefit or harm, and are not by their nature parts of either happiness or unhappiness. It is therefore important to keep in mind that indifferent or undifferentiated things are not indifferent as to pursuit and avoidance, but only as to happiness and unhappiness.[13]

The striking thing to notice about the Stoic account of the basic value categories, in broad outline anyway, is how *familiar* it is as a form of eudaimonist thinking about values. The Stoic account begins from the notion of human fulfillment, and is guided by a picture of our nature as defined by our agency and our capacity for practical reasoning. From this perspective, the Stoics observe a fundamental asymmetry between our active and creative rationality and the things upon which we exercise it, and it is in terms of that asymmetry that they differentiate between types of value. Accordingly, the Stoics also maintain that virtue—our creative potential exercised wisely—is a part of our fulfillment and happiness in a way that nothing else can be. "The particular value of virtue is distinct," as Cicero puts it: "a matter of kind, not degree" (*Fin.* III.34). In broad outline, then, this approach is exactly like the one I sketched in Chapters 3–4, even though my approach there was self-consciously Aristotelian. Surprisingly, the difference between Stoics and Aristotelians really doesn't lie here.

Of course, even if the Stoics' way of thinking about the *nature* of the good is familiar, their view about *what* things are good is most extraordinary: the only good things, they say, are virtue and what participates in virtue. However, that virtuous activity is the

---

[11] Calling these things "undifferentiated" thus has the further benefit of making it clear that the issue is not whether they are desirable for their own sake, but only whether they are such as to contribute to happiness just on their own. (See e.g. Lesses 1989, who conflates these two issues and thus concludes that preferred indifferents must have only instrumental value. For critique, see Barney 2003, 312–13.)

[12] See also Irwin 1998, 173–7, and 2007, 324–6, 331–3, who rightly points out the latter mistake. This is, however, a common misconception.

[13] See Sextus Empiricus, *M* XI.61–3. However, the "heterodox" Stoic Aristo is said to have held that while there is a distinction in value between virtue and vice, there is no distinction in value—not even this "selective" value, preferred vs. rejected—among undifferentiated things (Cicero, *Fin.* IV.43, 47; DL VII.160; Sextus Empiricus, *M* XI.64–7).

only good, I argue, is *exactly* the right thing to say—for them and for us. And crucially, it does not follow from that that virtue is sufficient for happiness. *That* depends on what kinds of things can be parts of virtuous activity. Or in the Stoics' terms, it depends on what things can "participate in" virtue.

2 Happiness and other good things

We suppose that all sorts of things are good things and important for our happiness: lovers, families, rewarding careers, things we love to do just because we can, and so on. According to the Stoics, it may be natural to prefer these things, but none of them is strictly speaking good. They are, rather, "undifferentiated" things, and such things are not part of happiness. So much we have seen so far. However, there is a further feature of the Stoic account that makes a crucial difference here: *the line between undifferentiated things and good things is actually permeable.*

This is not a point that has been made before, as far as I can see, and so it will be controversial. So to substantiate this point, I want to look at an important case in which that line between "good" and "undifferentiated" is in fact permeated: the emotional dimension of the virtues. As we saw above, the Stoics say that a person's emotional life can be a good thing, because some emotions (joy, good spirits, confidence, and wish) "participate in virtue" (AD II.5b). But of course, no emotional life ever starts out that way; every emotional life, by its nature, starts out as an undifferentiated thing. That means that undifferentiated things can become good things by becoming parts of—"participating in"—virtuous activity itself. In that case, the real question is *what sorts of things can become parts of virtuous activity.* But let's work our way towards that question by beginning with the Stoic account of these good emotions.

2.1 Good emotions[14]

According to the Stoics, there are certain types of emotion that are characteristic of virtuous persons. The Stoics call these emotions collectively the *eupatheiai* (Latin, *constantiae*), a term of art that means literally "good affections."[15] These are contrasted with what they call the *pathē* (Latin, *perturbationes*) or "passions," another term of art for disordered affective states, ones that do not participate in virtue.[16] It follows, obviously, that the virtuous person is "without *pathē*," or *apathēs*. Of course, they do not mean for

---

[14]   My discussion focuses on the Stoic analysis of emotion as a mental phenomenon, not on their analysis of emotion as a psycho-physical phenomenon. For the latter, see Samburski 1959, chap. 2; Inwood 1985, chap. 2; Annas 1992, chap. 2; Graver 2007, chap. 1.

[15]   See esp. DL VII.116; Cicero, *TD* IV.12–14.

[16]   Many scholars call only the *pathē* "emotions," but this suggests erroneously that the Stoics think people should be wholly dry, unemotional, and stony; con. DL VII.116–17; Epictetus, *Diss.* III.2.4; see Irwin 1998, 183–91; Cooper 2005; Long 2006, 380–2. It also highlights the fact that there is no easy English equivalent for *eupatheiai*. So for the sake of simplicity, I shall refer to both in English as "emotions" when speaking of them together (see also Long 2006, 380–1) and—compromising—call each by its Greek name when speaking of it specifically.

a minute that he is "apathetic" in the sense of affectless or cold: as Diogenes Laertius tells us (VII.117), the Stoics "say the wise man is also *apathē*, because he is not disposed to them [the *pathē*]. And the base man is '*apathē*' in a different sense, which means the same as hard-hearted and cold." What they mean, rather, is that a virtuous person does not have *disordered* emotions; or in our terms, such a person is emotionally sound.

The idea that there are disordered emotions, and that virtue is free of them, is obvious enough. What is much more controversial, however, is the Stoics' view that these disordered emotions all stem entirely from certain cognitive mistakes, in particular mistaken ways of thinking about what is important to your happiness: emotional disorder, they maintain, is the result of unreasonable beliefs about happiness and the good.[17] To understand what they mean, we actually need to begin with their broader account of action. Action, on the Stoic view, begins with "assenting" to certain thoughts of a distinctly practical kind—what they call "impulsive appearances" or "impressions," or just "impulses"—about what is to be done here and now. To assent to such an impulse or appearance is to agree that that action is the thing to be done, and the result is not merely a desire but the beginning of the act of doing what had appeared the thing to be done.[18] Now, the Stoics understand the emotions in terms of their analysis of impulse and assent as well; in fact, they think of emotional reactions as kinds of actions.[19] When the "action" in question is that of having an emotional response to something, there is the impulsive appearance that a certain response is the fitting one to have, here and now, and the emotion proper is the assent to that appearance, agreeing that the way to look at the situation really is as a sad or a joyful one, say.[20] This illustrates the sense in which the Stoics think that emotions depend on the particularities of the agent, such as his background values, assumptions, goals, and so on.[21]

Among the emotions, a *pathos* is distinctive in that the impulsive appearance in question is misguided and excessive, and thus is a distortion of reason—an "ailment"

---

[17] See AD II.10, 10b; Cicero, *TD* III.32–54, 60, 66–75; Seneca, *Ep.* 99. A further controversy surrounds their view about *which* emotions count as disordered and why. That view depends, of course, on their broader normative theory, to which we shall turn in Chapter 11.

[18] See Origen, *On Principles* 3.1.2–3 (= IG II-25); DL VII.86; Nemesius, *On Human Nature*, 291, 1–6 (= LS 53O); Philo, *Allegories of the Laws* 1.30 (= LS 53P); AD II.9 (= LS 53Q); Plutarch, *Contrad.* 1037f (= LS 53R), 1057a (= LS 53S). For a fuller discussion of the Stoic account of impulse and assent, and of emotion in general, see Annas 1992, chaps. 4 and 5; see also Inwood 1985, chap. 3; Frede 1986; Cooper 1999, chap. 21. Rather confusingly, the Stoics call both the initial impulse and the assent to it all just "impulses." For the sake of clarity, I shall call only the former "impulses."

[19] See also Inwood 1985, 100–1.

[20] It is in this sense that the Stoics take emotions to be kinds of judgments or beliefs. See DL VII.111–14; AD II.9–9b; Seneca, *On Anger* II.4; see also Sorabji 2000, 29–31. Galen (*Doctrines* 5.1.4, 4.3.2 [= IG II-120]) argues that this idea was Chrysippus' innovation and an aberration from the original Stoic view (in Zeno), but many scholars hold (rightly, I think) that this claim is spurious (see e.g. Inwood 1985, 13–1, 143; Long and Sedley 1987, 422; con. Sorabji 2000, 34–6, 55–65, 99–108; Gill 2005; Price 2005). It is important to note that the Stoics distinguished emotions as actions involving complex attitudes from the more visceral feelings, or what they called "pre-emotions" (*propatheiai*); see the note on *propatheiai* in Chapter 11.

[21] On the importance of these standing background attitudes, see Graver 2007, 41–6, 63–6.

or "affliction" in the psyche.[22] These *pathē* are of four main types, labeled with ordinary Greek and Latin words used by the Stoics as terms of art: 'pleasure' (Greek *hēdonē*, Latin *laetitia*), which is assent to an unreasonable "pro" impulse towards something present; 'distress' (*lupē, aegritudo*), assent to an unreasonable "con" impulse away from something present; 'longing' (*epithumia, libido*), assent to an unreasonable pro impulse towards something still in the future; and 'anxiety' (*phobos, metus*), assent to an unreasonable con impulse away from something still in the future.[23] The *eupatheiai*, by contrast, are forms of reasonable assent to impulsive appearances free of cognitive error: 'joy' (*chara, gaudium*) and 'wish' (*boulēsis, voluntas*) are assent to a reasonable pro impulse about something in the present or future, respectively, and 'caution' (*eulabeia, cautio*) is assent to a reasonable con impulse away from something in the future.[24]

This way of understanding the nature of the emotions has an important result. On the Stoic view, the *eupatheiai* that the virtuous person has are not merely alterations or moderations of the *pathē*, as if they were generically similar. Such a view stands in deliberate contrast with Aristotle's well-known view that (say) anger is the same thing in even-tempered people and hot-headed people, who differ only in that one hits the "mean" with respect to anger whereas the other one goes to "excess."[25] By contrast, the Stoics distinguish *pathē* from *eupatheiai* even in their very names, to emphasize their belief that virtuous and vicious persons have radically different emotional lives[26] rather than variations of some homogeneous state, as if it were possible to have mistaken and

---

[22] For the "excessiveness" of *pathos*, see esp. Galen, *Doctrines* 4.2.9–18. For *pathos* as distorted reason, see DL VII.110–116; AD II.10–10e; Cicero, *TD* III.15, IV.22; Galen, *Doctrines* 4.2.9–18, 4.4.16–18, 24–5. In treating *pathos* as an "ailment," it is worth noting that the Stoics take advantage of the fact that *pathos* in Greek can connote disturbance, suffering, and constitutional disorder (cf. English 'pathology' and cognates); cf. Gosling and Taylor 1982, 421. See DL VII.115; AD II.10e; Galen, *Doctrines* 4.5.21–5, 5.2.3–7. However, it is clear that were not employing anything like the modern notion of a mental illness; see Rhodes 1997.

[23] DL VII.111–14; AD II.10b; Cicero, *TD* III.24–5, IV.10–12, 47; *Fin.* III.35.

[24] DL VII.114–17; Cicero, *TD* IV.12–14; on caution in particular, Plutarch, *Contrad.* 1037f–1038a (= IG II-114).

Why there is no *eupatheia* in the case of impulses away from present things—a counterpart of "distress"—is an interesting and controversial question (see e.g. Sorabji 2000, 49–50). Cicero characterizes *pathē* and *eupatheiai* both as attitudes towards present and future good and bad things; if the terms 'good' and 'bad' are used in their strict technical sense, then the *eupatheiai* can have as their objects nothing but virtue and vice (so e.g. Inwood 1985, 174–5; Sorabji 2000, 53; Long 2002, 245; Brennan 2003, 270; Brennan 2005a, 93–8; Sellars 2006, 118–19;Graver 2007, 51–5); on this view, there is no *eupatheia* that is the counterpart of distress because the virtuous person is never presented with his own vice (see Cicero, *TD* III.77). But this seems needlessly austere to me; rather, like Diogenes Laertius, Plutarch, and Arius Didymus (II.7c), I prefer to characterize the *eupatheiai* as going "towards" or "away" from their objects, whether (in the technical sense) good, bad, or undifferentiated, differing from *pathē*, not in their objects, but only in their attitudes about their objects with respect to happiness (I have benefited here from discussion with Nancy Sherman). See Knuuttila 2004, 68–70, for discussion. Why there is no *eupatheia* corresponding to distress, I think, is based on one-by-one analyses of various forms of distress: e.g. anger in Seneca, *On Anger*, grief in Cicero, *TD* (see Chapter 11), etc. However, nothing in this chapter depends on this supposition.

[25] See Aristotle, *NE* II.6; III.6; IV.5. See also Seneca's critique of this view in *On Anger* I.

[26] See e.g. Cicero, *TD* III.22, 74, IV.38–57.

unreasonable attitudes in a better or worse way.[27] The Stoic account also contrasts with the Platonist view that anger is a sort of basic drive in one part of the soul that is to be controlled and harnessed by another part.[28] This is because the Stoics believe that the mind or soul is not a complex of separate motivational forces, but a single thing that acts in diverse ways,[29] so that emotions and desires are each identical to the whole mind looking at things now in this way and now in that—a "turning" of the whole mind.[30] And so Seneca speaks of anger as a "transformation" of the soul as it comes to see its object under certain sorts of descriptions (see *On Anger* I.8.3). On this view, then, emotional lives differ as people do, so it would be misleading to treat "our emotional life" as just one kind of thing, differently "tuned" from one person to the next.[31]

Here we come upon an important point for our purposes: just *having* an emotional life is an undifferentiated thing—it does not separate good people from bad, and can be given either a good or a bad direction ("used well or badly," as the Stoics say).[32] Now, as an emotional life—understood as a capacity to assent to certain kinds of practical appearances—takes on a good direction, it becomes a different *kind* of emotional life from one with a bad direction; the Stoics make it clear that the *eupatheiai* are not just redirected *pathē*.[33] In other words, the line between good things and *bad* things is not permeable. However, as one's raw emotional life takes shape under reasonable evaluative beliefs, it actually becomes part of virtue itself—it "participates" in virtue—and thus it *becomes differentiated* as one of the good things. Moreover, the Stoics go on to consider emotional reactions as kinds of action, and they classify joy and good spirits—the *eupatheiai*, broadly speaking—among the so-called "morally perfect actions" (*katorthōmata*), or what we might call virtue in action: such things as being prudent, being temperate, acting justly, being joyful (*chairein*), doing good works, being in good spirits (*euphrainesthai*), walking prudently, and everything which is done in accordance with right reason (AD II.11e). So joy and good spirits are among

---

[27] Chrysippus famously described the *eupatheiai* as being like walking but the *pathē* like running, movements he contrasted in their responsiveness to right reason: Galen, *Doctrines* 4.2.9–18 (= IG II-117); cp. *Doctrines* 4.4.24 (= IG II-118); Seneca, *On Anger* I.1, 3.

[28] See esp. Galen, *Doctrines* 3.3.13–24, and notes to Chapter 11.

[29] I.e. the so-called *hēgemonikon* or "controlling part" of the soul: DL VII.110; Iamblichus, *On the Soul* (= LS 53K); Seneca, *Ep.* 113.23 (= LS 53L).

[30] See Plutarch, *On Moral Virtue* 440e–441d, 446f–447a. It is therefore disappointing that Aristotle should be so cavalier about the different senses of "parts" in the context of moral psychology, as he is at *NE* I.13, 1102a26–32. Seneca takes Aristotle to task over this point, in *On Anger* I.7–13.

[31] See e.g. Cicero, *TD* IV.38–42, 48–55, 77–8; Seneca, *On Anger*, esp. I.1–3. It is an interesting question whether there are differences in how *pathē* and *eupatheiai* feel (see Graver 2007, chaps. 2–3); even so, I take no position on this question here.

[32] I would agree with Rist (1969, 49) that pleasure when treated as an indifferent (e.g. DL VII.102) is pleasure in this generic sense, of which the *pathos* and the *eupatheia* (joy) are species.

If just having an emotional life is an undifferentiated thing, then isn't exactly the same true about the capacity for choice as well—i.e. that just having the capacity to assent to appearances is an undifferentiated thing? (I thank James Warren for this question.) The answer is yes, as Epictetus himself makes clear when (at *Diss.* I.17) he says that reason makes a review of all of our faculties, including itself. See Dobbin 1998, 69–70.

[33] See Frede 1986 for discussion.

the *eupatheiai*, and being joyful and in good spirits are kinds of actions from virtue. So responding emotionally in accordance with the *eupatheiai* is a kind of "action" (cf. AD II.5k), and an action that is distinctive of those whose impulses are in line with right reason—including right reason about what kinds of things are such as to benefit with respect to happiness, and what things are not. It is for this reason, I think, that Arius Didymus understands "caution" both as grouped with such *eupatheiai* as joy and good spirits, *and* as a form of the virtue of courage (AD II.5b and 5b2, respectively).[34]

Not surprisingly, then, the Stoics say that the *eupatheiai* are parts of happiness: as Arius Didymus tells us, joy, good spirits, and confidence are goods that are "fulfilling" of happiness (AD II.5g).[35] To be sure, they are not parts of happiness in just the same way as the virtues, which are both "fulfilling" and "productive" of happiness. But this is what we should expect: the *eupatheiai* are parts of happiness because they are an emotional life under the direction of something else, namely right reason, and are parts of virtue itself, whereas virtue is part of happiness just because of its very nature. This is a very important idea: a differentiated thing—a fashioned good—can become part of happiness, *if* it can become a part of virtuous activity.[36]

2.2 The control thesis revisited

Notice that although the Stoics say that both virtuous activity and *eupatheiai* like joy are good things, this does not mean that they locate happiness in some *pair* of things; rather, the addition of joy here serves to amplify what sorts of things are parts of *virtue itself*. It is for this reason I think that Arius Didymus (II.6d) says that for the Stoics, joy and good spirits are not "necessary" for happiness. He certainly cannot mean that it is possible to have the virtues without having the *eupatheiai*; rather, he means that they are not things that have to be *added on* to virtue for the sake of happiness, as if virtue lacked something necessary.[37] The *eupatheiai* are necessary for happiness, then, not in the sense of being in addition to virtue, but because of their intimate relationship with virtue.

This means that the Stoics can locate happiness in a good like virtue and a good like joy *without* facing the difficulties that plagued their Aristotelian colleagues when they located happiness in both virtue and other goods (see Chapter 5). The Stoics and Aristotelians all agreed that virtuous activity is the unique and defining element in a happy human life, but unlike the Stoics the Aristotelians held that happiness involves

[34] See also Tsekourakis 1974, 91. Consequently, in one sense the wise person always has the *eupatheiai*—where his impulses are concerned, he is always wise—and in a sense he does not, since he is not always having this or that particular *eupatheia* (although Seneca's definition of joy [*Ep.* 23.4–5] makes it virtually constant). See AD II.5c.

[35] See also Cicero, *Fin.* III.55. The distinction between "fulfilling" and "productive" goods is a difficult one, but I will not pursue the matter here.

[36] I argue for a similar way of thinking about the sort of good that pleasure is in Plato's ethics in 2005. In thinking through the present argument, I have benefited from discussions with Tony Long, although he may still wish to talk me out of it.

[37] But con. Tsekourakis 1974, 96–7. I would understand Seneca, *On the Happy Life* 15.2–3 in a similar way (but con. Lesses 1989, 106).

other elements as well *besides* virtuous activity. As a result they kept running into the same dilemma: they could not make those other goods matter in a robust way without compromising the definitive role that virtuous activity is supposed to play. So in principle anyway, what the Stoics did was exactly what would have saved the Aristotelians: they made (for instance) joy a part of happiness by placing joy, not *alongside* virtuous activity, but *within* it. In other words, the Stoics were right to say that a happy human life is the same thing as a life of virtuous activity. In fact, that is *precisely* what we found Aristotle's thesis that virtue "controls" happiness—the control thesis—requires, in response to Aristotle's dilemma: *it is only insofar as things can be transformed into ongoing patterns of virtuous activity that we should think of them as potential parts of happiness in the first place.*

The Stoics made that approach work with joy and the other *eupatheiai*. In principle, it could work with other things, too: it all depends on what things can be understood as internal to virtuous activity. And *that* depends on the *boundaries of the self*. It certainly did in the Stoics' case, or so I argue now.

3 Happiness, virtue, and the boundaries of the self

For the Stoics, the "good affections" (*eupatheiai*) are genuine goods because virtue transforms these emotions and makes them part of itself—in the Stoics' terms, they participate in virtue. Of course, the Stoics believe that all emotions are forms of "assent," that is, exercises of the faculty of choice, and I argue now that for the Stoics, the line between what can and cannot participate in virtue lies exactly there: between what is and is not an exercise of the faculty of choice. In particular, I argue that this way of drawing that line is exactly what we see in the Stoics' thinking about virtue and practical reasoning when it comes to bodily and external things.

3.1 Making other things "good"

Epictetus says something surprising: virtue is a "magic wand" that turns whatever it touches not into gold, but into a good:

"This is the magic wand of Hermes. Touch with it whatever you please, and it will turn to gold." No; but bring whatever you please, and I will turn it into something good. (*Diss.* III.20.12)

So bodily health, for instance, is a good for a virtuous person (III.20.4); what is more, Arius Didymus tells us that for a virtuous person, such externals as children, friends, and acquaintances are goods too (AD II.5e, 5m; cp. DL VII.95). These claims are surprising because, as we also know—from Epictetus and Arius Didymus themselves—the only goods are virtue and what participates in virtue:

[S]ome things are good, some bad, and others undifferentiated: the good are virtue, and whatever participates in virtue; the evil, the contrary; and the undifferentiated, riches, health, reputation. (*Diss.* II.9.15, modifying Hard's translation)

Good are things like this: prudence, temperance, justice, courage, and everything which is either virtue or participates in virtue. Bad are things like this: imprudence, wantonness, injustice, cowardice and everything which either is vice or participates in vice. Undifferentiated are things like this: life and death, good and bad reputation, pleasure and pain, wealth and poverty, health and disease, and things similar to these. (AD II.5a, modifying Inwood and Gerson's translation)

Initially, then, the things that Epictetus and Arius Didymus say here are as confusing as Socrates' claim that virtue is the only good and that virtue makes other things good, too (see esp. *Ap.* 30b and *Euthd.* 281d-e, discussed in Chapter 6). Likewise, we might also complain—as Cicero tells us some ancient critics did—that when the Stoics say that virtue is "good" and health and wealth "preferred," this is really just mincing words because they are all just "good."[38]

Now, we have seen that it is possible for undifferentiated things to migrate, under the fashioning guidance of virtue, across the line and into the category of good things, as happens with the *eupatheiai*. If that is what is going on with these bodily and external goods as well, then that would explain how the Stoics could say all of these different things about goods at once. *Is* that what is going on here?

No, as the broader context of Epictetus' "magic wand" passage makes clear:

Is my neighbour a bad one? He is so to himself; but a good one to me. He trains me to be good-tempered and fair-minded. Is my father bad? To himself, but good to me. 'This is the magic wand of Hermes. Touch with it whatever you please, and it will turn to gold.' No; but bring whatever you please, and I will turn it into something good. Bring sickness, death, poverty, reproach, a trial for one's very life. All these, through the wand of Hermes, shall become beneficial. 'What will you make of death?'—Why, what else but an adornment to you; what but a means of your showing in action what kind of person a man is who follows the will of nature. 'What will you make of sickness?'—I will show its nature, I will excel in it, I will be serene and happy. I will not flatter my physician. I will not pray to die. What need you ask further? Whatever you give me, I will make it something blessed (*makarion*), and a source of happiness (*eudaimonikon*), something imposing and admirable. (*Diss.* III.20.11–15)

For Epictetus, health is a good, but in exactly the same way that sickness is also a good: in each case, the good is *how I conduct myself* in relation to whatever is presented to me (cf. *Diss.* III.20.4). In other words, it is not these undifferentiated things *themselves* that become good, it is *I* who become good in the way that I exercise choice in regards to them. In the same way, Epictetus says, an external thing like a relationship with a brother or father can become "good"—that is, *I* can become good in the choices I make with respect to my brother or father, even if he is a thieving, abusive creep (I.15; III.3.7–10; *Handbook* 30). This perspective stems from the long-standing Stoic belief that virtue is a skill or craft: "as the material of the carpenter is wood, and that of

---

[38] Cicero reports such complaints from the Academic skeptics Carneades (*Fin.* III.41) and Antiochus (V.22, 74, 78, 90, 93), a criticism that Cicero himself gives a good airing in *Fin.* IV. See Irwin 1990, 39, for discussion.

statuary bronze, so the subject-matter of the skill of living is each person's own life" (*Diss.* I.15.2; cf. III.3.1; DL VII.86).

Furthermore, Arius Didymus seems to have understood the Stoic notion of external "goods" in exactly the same way as Epictetus did:

> Only the virtuous man has good children, though not all have virtuous children since it is necessary for him who has children to use them as such. Only the virtuous man has a good old age and a good death; for a good old age is conducting oneself virtuously at a certain age, and a good death is to make one's end virtuously with a certain kind of death. (AD II.11q)

In technical parlance, Arius Didymus says, the point can be understood in terms of the Stoics' distinction between "mixed" and "unmixed" goods:

> Again, of good things, some are unmixed, such as knowledge, while others are mixed, such as having good children, a good old age, a good life. Having good children is the natural and virtuous possession of children; good old age is the natural and virtuous use of old age; and similarly for a good life. (AD II.5m)

The "unmixed" goods are the virtues, understood as forms of knowledge or expertise,[39] and they are called "unmixed" because they are not the mixture of undifferentiated materials and a differentiating force applied to them: they are themselves that very differentiating force. (As I put the point above, virtue is a "fashioning" good.) The "mixed" goods, on the other hand, are undifferentiated things—such as having children, being old, being alive—that one has "used" well, that is, in relation to which one is wise and virtuous; they are "fashioned" goods. But of course, in saying that such things become "goods," Arius Didymus makes it clear that it is not the *things* that become good, but the virtuous *person* in relation to them. We might say the usage of "good" in this context is "adverbial," so to speak (conceptually, not grammatically), modifying the doing or the having, and not "adjectival," modifying the thing done or had.[40]

So here is what the Stoics say about the line between undifferentiated things and good things. First of all, an undifferentiated thing can itself become a good thing only insofar as it can participate in virtuous activity (section 2). However, something can participate in virtuous activity only insofar as it is itself a kind of exercise of the faculty of choice (this section): that is why the *eupatheiai* can participate in virtue and things like health or relationships cannot. For undifferentiated things of the latter sort, then, the only sense in which they can be "good" and thus important for happiness is that one can be good in the choices one makes with respect to them. Therefore, on the Stoic view the virtuous activity in which happiness consists is strictly *formalized* virtuous

---

[39] According to the Stoics, all of the cardinal virtues and their subordinate types are forms of knowledge: AD II.5b–5b2, 5b5.

[40] I thank Mark LeBar for this way of putting the point. Con. Reydams-Schils (2005, chap. 2), who takes passages like AD II.5e to say that certain relationships are goods in the straightforward sense. However, she does not consider passages like AD II.5m, which understand that goodness strictly as one's virtuous conduct with respect to those relationships.

activity, that is, the virtuous exercise of the will. That is why they believe that virtue is sufficient for happiness—not just because virtuous activity is the only good, but because virtuous activity is *also* just the exercise of the faculty of choice.

3.2 The formalized self and practical reasoning

According to the Stoics, the only good thing is virtuous activity, which is just the wise exercise of the faculty of choice; and the only bad thing is the contrary of this. Consequently, virtuous activity and happiness are both invulnerable to circumstances: wisdom, Epictetus says, is the magic wand by which a virtuous person turns even sickness into happiness. Likewise, virtuous activity requires no special worldly resources, and losses of things like health or wealth are no threat to happiness.

What is more, we can see the Stoics' formalized conception of activity also in the ways in which the Stoics deal with a couple of puzzles that that conception raises about practical reasoning. One of the puzzles concerns the Stoics' claim that virtue is a skill or craft, one that works on the "materials" of one's life as carpenters work on wood (Epictetus, *Diss*. I.15.2). However, ultimately skills like carpentry have value only for the sake of their products; so how can the Stoics think both that virtue is a skill and that its value is entirely independent of everything else?[41] The other puzzle is related: if the only good or bad things are how we exercise the faculty of choice, then how could one choice rather than another count as wise or "skillful" in the first place? Typically, we think that choosing wisely is, if anything, a matter of choosing good things over bad things, but for the Stoics everything but choice itself is undifferentiated—neither good nor bad, so what could it mean to choose wisely from among those things? This is a problem we encountered in our discussion of Socrates in Chapter 6: since our reasons for choosing are ultimately for the sake of our happiness, then if virtue is the only thing that matters for happiness, we cannot explain what reasons there could be to prefer, say, a clean bed over a filthy bed (see Vlastos 1991, 203, 214–16). And yet clearly there *is* a reason to prefer clean beds.

The Stoics addressed each of these puzzles explicitly, although their responses in each case have been controversial. Some scholars have argued that the Stoics addressed the first puzzle by treating virtue as a stochastic skill rather than a productive one.[42] Stochastic skills, such as chess, have only one purpose, namely the very exercise and mastery of the skill itself. Of course, the game of chess has an *object*—to checkmate the opponent's king—but that is not the *purpose* of chess, which is to play well at something challenging and interesting. However, it is not likely that the reason that virtuous persons act for the sake of justice, for instance, is for the sake of being adept at doing so;

---

[41] See esp. Long and Sedley 1987, 408–10; see also N. White 1990; Barney 2003. Socrates raises the same query for his own view that wisdom is both a skill and the only good (*Euthd.* 288d-293a), without arriving at an answer that satisfies him. Instead, he poses the question as an invitation to undertake serious philosophical reflection.

[42] E.g. Irwin 1986, 230–1; Sorabji 2000, 8, 171 ("the game's the thing"; cf. Bonhöffer 1894/1996, 73).

there is, after all, something such persons hope to accomplish, not just as an "object" but because such an accomplishment *matters* to them. It is more likely, I think, that the Stoics thought of virtue as a skill in a sui generis way, combining the salient features of other, different kinds of skills.[43] Like all skills, virtue is something intelligent and practical, and it approaches its subject matter in a systematic and unified way.[44] But in some ways, the Stoics say, virtue is a skill like acting or dancing, because exercising the skill of virtue has its own point apart from any product (Cicero, *Fin.* III.24). In other ways it is like archery, where one aims at a strategically salient target but ultimately the real skill lies only in the aiming (*Fin.* III.22). There may be no one skill that virtue is exactly like, but thinking of virtue as a skill can still be illuminating.[45]

The archery analogy reveals something else as well: the Stoics must distinguish between the "target" of a virtuous act—which is something undifferentiated—and the "aiming" itself, which is the wise exercise of choice and a good (Cicero, *Fin.* III.22). This brings us to the second puzzle: how can we understand the idea of having a reason to choose in one way over another if the choosing itself is the only good there is? Seneca imagines someone asking, "If good health, rest, and freedom from pain are not likely to hinder virtue, shall you not seek all these?" And he answers as follows:

Of course I shall seek them, but not because they are goods—I shall seek them because they are according to nature and because they will be acquired through the exercise of good judgment on my part. What, then, will be good in them? This alone—that it is a good thing to choose them. For when I don suitable attire, or walk as I should, or dine as I ought to dine, it is not my dinner, my walk, or my dress that are goods, but the deliberate selection which I show in regard to them, as I observe, in each thing I do, a mean that conforms with reason. Let me also add that the selection of neat clothing is a fitting object of a man's efforts; for man is by nature a neat and well-groomed animal. Hence the selection of neat attire, and not neat attire in itself, is a good; since the good is not in the things selected, but in the quality of the selection. (*Ep.* 92.11–12)

Epictetus makes the same point more concisely:

What, then, are we to use these externals in a careless way? By no means; for this again is an evil for the faculty of choice (*prohairesei*) and hence unnatural to it. Rather, externals are to be used with care, because their usage is not an indifferent matter . . . (*Diss.* II.5.6–7)[46]

---

[43] Annas 1993a, 397–405. See also Blecher 2006; Brennan 2005a, 146–51; Irwin 2007, 324–5. N. White 1990, 51–5, argues that Stoic virtue is a disposition to choose acts under the description of fitting into a coherent pattern in accordance with cosmic nature; however, if the problem is how the highest good could be a disposition concerned wholly with indifferent things, it is unclear to me how shifting that concern to a *pattern* of indifferent things is supposed to solve it.

[44] See AD II.5b–5b5; see also DL VII.126. The systematic and unified nature of virtue is the basis of the Stoics' belief in the unity of the virtues: AD II.5b5; Plutarch, *Contrad.* 1046e–f.

[45] Moreover, Irwin 1990 argues that the Stoics' way of separating the exercise of skill from its outcome makes it easy to explain how a thwarted attempt to do something virtuous can still be a virtuous act, unlike Aristotelians who took external success to be a necessary condition of virtuous action.

[46] Cp. II.6.1; IV.2; Cicero, *Fin.* III.13 ff. See also Bonhöffer 1894/1996, 72–5, 86–108; Frede 2007, 165–6; Stephens 2007, 48–54. Con. Mitsis 2003, who assumes that if, say, another person's death is an indifferent thing, then so too are one's motives in trying to rescue him.

More precisely, the Stoics' response is to make the following distinction. When picking a bed to sleep in or clothes to wear, the relevant consideration is what it is natural to prefer: my body is for me to look after, so I should avoid a bed that would make me sick or fatigued, or strain my back; rational creatures have dignity, so I should present myself in clothes that are neat and clean, and suited to the occasion. Picking between undifferentiated things in this way is what the Stoics call "selection" (eklogē; AD II.7). In selection, *what* is selected has no bearing of its own on happiness, even though we select from among things that are naturally "preferred" or "dispreferred." However, the very *act* of selecting matters in a different way, because selecting according to the relevant considerations just is to exercise practical rationality. So while the *bed* that I select is neither good nor bad, my *selecting* it according to the relevant considerations—my natural concern for my health and hygiene—*is* good. More precisely, determining to make my selection in this way is a second kind of practical reasoning, which the Stoics call "choice" (hairesis, AD II.5i). Unlike selection, choice picks between things that are good and bad themselves. Choice picks between different modes of selection.

Now, it will come as no surprise that the Stoics' account of practical reasoning is controversial,[47] but what concerns us at present is not whether the account is correct, but the very fact that the Stoics need some account of this sort in the first place. The Stoics need such an account not because they maintain that virtuous activity is the only good. They need it because they maintain that it is *formalized* virtuous activity that is the only good. To see this, consider the advice that Epictetus gives a father who was so distraught over his child daughter's illness that he ran out of the house (*Diss.* I.11). The father was wrong to run out, Epictetus says, because the natural thing for a father to do is to care for his child. Given the distinction between selection and choice, Epictetus' advice can be put more precisely as follows:

While staying and leaving are undifferentiated things, staying in this case is nonetheless naturally "preferred" and leaving "dispreferred," considering a father's natural role; so it is staying that you should select in this case. Now, what is good is the choice to act in accordance with naturally appropriate selection. That is why what you had reason to do was to stay with your daughter.

---

[47] One difficulty concerns how to understand "natural" preference in the account of selection. If "natural" here is not normative, the worry goes, then the fact that something is naturally preferred gives no reason to select it; but if it is normative then calling a preference "natural" is just to say there is good reason for it, so our original question comes back: what is that reason? What is more, on either horn of the dilemma the Stoics would seem to require a *second* source of reasons for action, based on something other than eudaimonia. Cicero discusses this problem of "two highest ends" in *Fin.* IV, without being much impressed by the Stoics' answers. In fact, he says that this is why Aristo denied any differences in "selective" value between undifferentiated things (IV.43, 47); see the note on Aristo, above. My appreciation of this problem has been sharpened through discussions with Mark LeBar.

Now consider an alternative explanation of why the father should have stayed:

Being that girl's father is an end of yours—it is one of the things you have chosen to give your life to. That means that you have chosen to make your relationship with her a source of reasons for you to do all sorts of things. One of those things is staying and caring for her when she needs you—that just is the sort of activity that is your loving your daughter, and loving your daughter is one of the things that your happiness is. That is why what you had reason to do was to stay with your daughter.

For our purposes, the salient difference between these two explanations is this: the first one starts from the idea that the father's relationship with his daughter is *not* one of the activities that is identical to his happiness, whereas the second one starts from the idea that it *is*. For Epictetus, the only end that one can have reason to live for is the end of making wise choices; in that case nothing else is good, and so Epictetus requires exactly the sort of account of better and worse choices that the Stoic distinction between "choice" and "selection" is meant to provide. By contrast, on the second explanation, the father's end is not just *to handle* his relationship with his daughter well but *that relationship* itself, handled wisely. On Epictetus' approach, his wise handling of the relationship is virtuous activity and happiness; on the alternative approach, the relationship wisely handled is virtuous activity and happiness. Because the alternative approach does not make wise choosing the only good and thus the ultimate source of reasons for action, it does not require the same account of practical reasoning that we find in the Stoics. Of course, the difference between these two approaches is that the Stoic approach works with a *formalized* conception of virtuous activity, and the alternative with an *embodied* conception. Therefore, what accounts for the Stoics' distinctive approach to practical reasoning is not their belief that virtuous activity is the only good but, crucially, their belief in the formalized conception of the boundaries of the self.

At least since Cicero, the prevailing view has been that the ancient sufficiency debate was over whether or not virtuous activity is the only good. But I have argued that that is a red herring: even the Aristotelians had excellent reason to agree with that thesis, and from that thesis it does not follow that virtue is sufficient for happiness anyway. The real question is what "virtuous activity" includes. The issue, in a word, is the boundaries of the self.

The essence of the good is a certain disposition of our choice, and essence of evil likewise. What are externals, then? Materials for the faculty of choice, in the management of which it will attain its own good or evil. How, then, will it attain the good? If it does not admire the materials themselves: for its judgements about the materials, if they are correct, make our choice good, and if they are distorted and perverse, make it bad. (Epictetus, *Diss.* I.29.1–3)

I disagree. A life of virtuous activity may be the same thing as a life of human happiness, but virtuous activity is vulnerable because it is embodied in particular relationships and attachments that are vulnerable. And that makes a great difference in the kind of good that happiness is. On the Stoic view, we should love others as if our happiness depends on *loving*. I think we should love others as if our happiness depends on *the ones we love*. That sounds much more like the way I would want to find things to live for and then live for them.

However, neither of these views comes without a price. I have just hinted at what I think the price is for the Stoics. But my view comes at a price too—there is a *reason*, after all, why Epictetus and the other Stoics think of the appropriate place for the boundaries of the self in the way they do. Epictetus himself gives us a clue:

When people hold absurd opinions about things that lie outside the sphere of choice, regarding them as good and evil, it is quite inevitable that they will pay court to tyrants. And oh that it were tyrants only, and not their lackeys as well! (*Diss.* I.19.16–17)

The inevitability of such debasement is not yet obvious, but Epictetus' belief in it certainly fits with something we have seen already (Chapter 7), namely his conviction that identifying oneself with choice alone is indispensable for remaining truly *free*. So I undertake in Part 3 to articulate my own way of thinking about the self, and to consider whether I really must pay the price for that way of thinking that Epictetus argues I must and, if so, whether it is a price I can afford.

PART 3

Happiness now: rethinking the self

9

The Embodied Conception of the Self

Happiness is a life of embodied virtuous activity. So I say, anyway, and so far I have explained why I think happiness is a life of activity, and why I think that that activity must be wise and emotionally healthy (i.e. virtuous) in order for it to be happiness. What remains is to make more explicit what I mean by calling activity "embodied," something I have explained in only a provisional way so far. This is my task in this final part of the book.

By "embodiment" here I have in mind a certain way in which a person might understand himself and his happiness in relation to a world he ultimately cannot control. One way of putting the point is that *happiness is indexical*: I can speak of "my happiness," but I can also speak of "*this* happiness" of mine. When I speak of "my happiness," I merely mean mine as opposed to someone else's. But when I speak of "this happiness," I mean something more. My life is a life of activities—as a husband, as a father, as a worker, as a member of communities—and those activities are not just *in* my life: they *are* my life, and they are *this happiness* of mine, with all their particularity. This is what I mean by thinking of those activities as "embodied," which contrasts with thinking that my happiness consists in how I conduct myself with respect to those activities. Simply put, on the latter view, a person's happiness would be his life of the activity of *exercising wisdom* as he engages in those other activities (i.e. happiness is a life of "formalized" activity); on the embodied view, a person's happiness is his life of *those activities*, provided he exercises wisdom in them. The difference between these views is clearest in cases of significant change or loss. On the formalized view, the activity that is one's happiness can continue even when loss closes off those other activities. On the embodied view, the loss of *those activities* just is the loss of *that happiness*.

This contrast—a contrast between different views of what I have called "the boundaries of the self"—is the one that I argued in Part 2 has always been crucial for understanding how wisdom or virtue and other sorts of goods might be related to happiness. In this chapter I try to say more precisely what I mean by thinking of activity as embodied. In the next two chapters I ask whether it is a good idea, from the perspective of our happiness, to think of activity in that way.

My plan throughout is to focus on serious life-changes, and especially loss. This focus should aid in clarifying the embodied conception in the present chapter, since the loss of bodily function or a loved one is often experienced as changing who one is, and such an experience illuminates the idea of taking one's body or loved one to be within the boundaries of the self. In fact, as we shall see, self-conception is a major focus of much contemporary research on bodily change and bereavement. Then in the chapters to follow, this focus should also guide us in thinking about the dangers that might be involved in expanding the boundaries of the self to include things outside our control.

1 Bereavement, grief, and the boundaries of the self

I want to begin simply. In clarifying a conception of the self as embodied, the task is not so much to concoct a novel way of thinking of ourselves that we might take up as it is to draw our attention to a way in which I think we actually *do* think of ourselves (for better or worse). In other words, in laying out the "embodied conception of the self" I am really just trying to point to a normal and even familiar way of understanding oneself. Why then does it need pointing out? Because it is, we might say, hidden in plain sight. For the most part we just live our lives, not really noticing what makes our lives recognizable to us as "ours" in the first place. We notice the people and things that are important in our lives, but rarely do we notice how their presence makes possible the very thought, "*This* life is my life." When we do notice that thought, it is usually because of some change that makes the thought no longer possible. Losing someone dearly loved is exactly that kind of change. So I propose to point to the embodied conception first by pointing to a common way of experiencing bereavement, before venturing to explain why bereavement should be so commonly experienced that way.[1]

1.1 Grief observed

Grief psychologist Colin Murray Parkes has observed that while there is a distinction between one's view of oneself and one's view of the world, it is extremely difficult to know exactly where that distinction is to be drawn. Since many of the parts of one's identity are also shared with the world—one's body, language, possessions, loved ones—one must therefore ask, "What is the boundary of me?" (Parkes 1987, 113):

If the possessions and the roles by which we control, order, and predict the world can be shared, changed, and dissolved, then it may be that the self that depends so much upon these tools and tasks to provide an image is also capable of experiencing change. If I lose my ability to predict and to act appropriately, my world begins to crumble, and since my view of myself is inextricably

---

[1] Following the standard usage in the psychological literature, I take "bereavement" to be the state of affairs of having lost a loved one and "grief" to the broad pattern of subjective reactions to that loss (not a particular emotion but a complex bundle of emotions and other internal phenomena; see Bonanno 2001; Shaver and Tancredy 2001; Weiss 2001, 47–50). Both bereavement and grief should be distinguished from "mourning," which is the more overt and often public set of behaviors of the bereaved.

For the sake of simplicity, I shall focus exclusively on heterosexual conjugal bereavement, since it has been found to be the most likely to result in psychiatric care (Parkes 2006, 177), and because of the particularly extensive literature available on it. In other words, I'll be looking where there is the most light right now.

bound up with my view of the world, that too will begin to crumble. If I have relied on another person to predict and act in many ways as an extension to myself then the loss of that person can be expected to have the same effect upon my view of the world and my view of myself as if I had lost a part of myself. (Parkes 1987, 114)

Likewise, philosopher Thomas Attig observes that the loss of a loved one brings an experience of "loss of our wholeness. It is as if each of us were a web of connections to the things, places, other people, experiences, activities, and projects we care about."[2]

The thought that beloved others can be within the "boundary of me" is not just a theoretical postulate, but seems to be a common and even fundamental feature of how people typically grieve. This is nowhere clearer than in C. S. Lewis's account of his own grief at the loss of his wife, which he recorded with alarming candor and honesty in *A Grief Observed*. In his middle age Lewis married Joy Gresham, an American divorcee living in England. At first this was strictly a legal arrangement to save her from deportation; however, Joy was then suddenly diagnosed with cancer, and Lewis and Joy then had a religious marriage so that Lewis could care for her in his home with a clear conscience. Two events then followed: Joy's cancer went into remission, and meanwhile she and Lewis fell deeply in love and into a shared, effervescent happiness. Indeed, it is during this time that Lewis, inspired by his happiness with Joy, wrote what some consider the most profound and insightful works on love of his career (*Till We Have Faces* and *The Four Loves*). Then, two years later, Joy's cancer made an aggressive return and in a few months had finally taken her life.[3]

Lewis kept notes of his experience after Joy's death, in part with the aim of recording what he thought would be the "state" of grief, as if to map it like a terrain, but in fact what he found himself recording was a very long process of grief (1976, 68–9). Lewis's record is very instructive for our purposes, since it records his experience of the loss of another as a loss of himself, and which grows naturally into the process of rebuilding himself.

Lewis notes that a sort of torpor descended on him, in which time seemed to pass without his really living in it. The very first line in Lewis's notebook is that, quite unexpectedly, grief feels like fear, a feeling he articulates more fully later in his notes:

And grief still feels like fear. Perhaps, more strictly, like suspense. Or like waiting; just hanging about waiting for something to happen. It gives life a permanently provisional feeling. It doesn't seem worth starting anything. I can't settle down. I yawn, I fidget, I smoke too much. Up till this I always had too little time. Now there is nothing but time. Almost pure time, empty successiveness. (Lewis 1976, 38–9)

Lewis comes later to understand why time feels this way: time is where living goes on, but what makes being alive really living is a network of possibilities that the things in one's world—in this case, a loved one—make possible.

---

[2] Attig 2001, 36, also citing Attig 1996, 134–43.
[3] These events are described by Lewis's acquaintance Chad Walsh (1976); see also Attig 2001. They are also dramatized in the Richard Attenborough film *Shadowlands*, which I discuss in Chapters 1 and 10.

I think I am beginning to understand why grief feels like suspense. It comes from the frustration of so many impulses that had become habitual. Thought after thought, feeling after feeling, action after action, had [Joy] for their object. Now their target is gone. I keep on through habit fitting an arrow to the string; then I remember and have to lay the bow down. So many roads lead thought to [Joy]. I set out on one of them. But now there's an impassible frontier-post across it. So many roads once; now so many *culs de sac*. (Lewis 1976, 55)

Lewis goes on to describe his struggle to understand who he is and what his life is about now that Joy is gone. He wonders whether he might simply go back to being who he was before he met Joy, but he immediately realizes that his life with Joy has become a part of his identity that cannot be denied (1976, 69–71). That change in his identity, he soon realizes, is both what requires him to redefine himself now and what shapes how he must do so:

To say the patient is getting over it after an operation for appendicitis is one thing; after he's had his leg off it is quite another. After that operation either the wounded stump heals or the man dies. If it heals, the fierce, continuous pain will stop. Presently he'll get back his strength and be able to stump about on his wooden leg. He has "got over it." But he will probably have recurrent pains in the stump all his life, and perhaps pretty bad ones; and he will always be a one-legged man. There will be hardly any moment when he forgets it. Bathing, dressing, sitting down and getting up again, even lying in bed, will all be different. His whole way of life will be changed. All sorts of pleasures and activities that he once took for granted will have to be simply written off. Duties too. At present I am learning to get about on crutches. Perhaps I shall presently be given a wooden leg. But I shall never be a biped again. (1976, 61–2)

Lewis's experience of grief is just what we should expect it to be. As Martha Nussbaum has put the point, it is a difficult question whether one's life, were one imagined to go on alone, would be the life of an agent one could even recognize as oneself (Nussbaum 1986, 367). That is precisely Lewis's struggle: in feeling the loss of Joy he feels also the loss of a central part of himself. There is something of him that is gone, and it will always be gone. In this spirit, Lewis says that giving spiritual comfort to a bereaved mother is a "comfort to the God-aimed, eternal spirit within her. But not to her motherhood. The specifically maternal happiness must be written off" (1976, 30). That is, to capture what the mother has lost we must speak not just of *her* happiness but of *that* happiness of hers.

Lewis's experience of the loss of part of himself is one that he shares with very many bereaved persons (see Marris 1974, 37–8). In fact, it is very common for bereaved persons to describe their loss exactly as Lewis does: it is like amputation, like losing part of the body (see Parkes 1987, 202–9, for discussion). One widow expressed the point this way:

It seems that when we got married we were one, and I was much richer and stronger than what I am now. So I feel I'm in a way crippled. I have to learn to live this way . . . I feel like somebody that just lost their arm or a leg or something. I just have to live without it. I was quite touched the other day. I was in the savings bank, and I saw this girl who had lost a hand and not quite half an arm. And she was able to sign her name on a check and take the money out. I feel that she must have had quite a bit of adjustment to do. That is going to happen to me, in a way. In a way, it's the same because I just have to learn it. (Reported by Glick et al. 1974, 158–9)

Likewise, as one bereaved parent said, "It's like losing my right arm. I can't grow a new arm, but I'm learning to live as a one armed man."[4] In fact, this way of expressing the sense of losing part of oneself is such a common feature of grief that psychologists have dubbed it the "amputation metaphor," and it is a phenomenon whose clinical observation is about as old as the psychological study of grief itself.

However, the connection between bereavement and amputation is actually more than metaphorical. Since the 1970s psychologists have studied the nature of grief as a response to significant losses of all different sorts, and it is now widely accepted in the field that the experience of grief among the bereaved really *is* like grief among amputees.[5] On the one hand, amputees often describe their loss by comparing it to bereavement.[6] As one early theorist put the point, "The emotion most persons feel when told that they must lose a limb has been well compared with the emotion of grief at the death of a loved one. A part of one's body is to be irrevocably lost; the victim is 'incomplete', he is no longer a whole man."[7] And on the other hand, those who have experienced both amputation and bereavement sometimes perceive them as similar, as did a man who described the loss of his wife as like the previous loss of his leg.[8] Of course, the experiences of bereavement and amputation are not exactly the same, since the love for a spouse is not the same sort of bond one has with an arm or leg.[9] Nonetheless, comparisons of grieving in widows and amputees has shown that while there is more intense initial grief among widows than amputees, widows also improve more than amputees within the first year after the loss, so that levels of grief in the two groups are actually very similar after about a year.[10] The similarity between these kinds of losses, it seems, is due to the fact in each case the loss involves a perception of "internal loss of self": "You sometimes feel you've had part of your body taken away and you're no longer part of the world—they've taken part of your life away."[11]

These and other data have led to the conclusion that psychological reactions to serious losses all share the relevant characteristics of bereavement—including feelings of mutilation—so that grief has become a useful way of understanding reactions to a wide range of significant losses.[12] This was the central contention of Peter Marris'

---

[4] Klass 1984–5, 367.

[5] See Archer 1999, 89 and references.

[6] Parkes 1975 and references; 1987, 202–8.

[7] Kessler 1951, 107–8, cited in Parkes 1975, 204.

[8] M. J. Brown 1986, cited in Archer 1999, 89.

[9] See Parkes 2006, 30–1; Weiss 2008, 38.

[10] Parkes 1975, 205–7, 209–10.

[11] Patient testimony, reported by Parkes 1987, 205.

[12] See Marris 1974; Parkes 1987, 208–10; Archer 2008, 50–1. However, as Weiss (2008, 38–9) notes, there is still more work to be done in understanding the border between losses that are life-changing in this way and those that are not.

groundbreaking book *Loss and Change*, in which he argued that grief is a reaction not only to bereavement and amputation but also to such changes as relocation and even social mobility.[13] It is worth pointing out that grief in these cases is not confined to an "objective worsening" of one's situation, but is found even in people who leave the slums, or advance in their education, or move into a higher social class.

The upshot of these investigations is that a life-changing loss, such as bereavement of a loved one, "alters one's view of the world and more importantly, provides drastic alterations in one's view of himself."[14] To be sure, some of these alterations are mundane and quotidian: changes in who makes sure that the bills are paid, who does the driving, how many places to set at the breakfast table, and so on.[15] But even these changes in daily roles are part of larger and more profound changes in the overall plans that give our roles their meanings.[16] Grieving therefore involves more than responding to changed circumstances, as when one has to get used to the rearranged furniture in the front room. It involves nothing less than a gradual incorporation of environmental changes into a new conception of oneself.[17] "The fundamental crisis of bereavement," Marris observes, "arises, not from the loss of others, but the loss of self" (1974, 32–3). And it has become virtually a truism in contemporary bereavement literature that, in very close relationships anyway, the loss of another is experienced as a loss in the self.[18] As a result, the main research questions in this field today concern, not whether loss of another is experienced as loss of self, but how that sort of loss is best resolved.[19]

What I have in mind by the "embodied conception of the self" is just that way of understanding oneself and one's life that Lewis, Parkes, Marris, and the others are all talking about. This sort of self-understanding draws the boundaries of the self so as to include beloved others within the self. Again, this is not to say that one is aware of having drawn those boundaries in such a way, much less that one has done so deliberately; but the fact that they *are* so often drawn in that way explains why it is such a common feature of grief to experience the loss of a beloved as a loss of oneself as well.

1.2 Towards an understanding of grief

People who have suffered terrible loss sometimes say things like, "I feel as if a part of me has died." We might have thought that that was just a figure of speech, but it seems that often those who say such things mean exactly what they say. Such is the typical experience of grief; but *why* would grief be like that? How could the loss of someone

[13] Marris 1974. See also Parkes 1987, 208–10. On comparisons of bereavement to relocation, see also Klass 1984–5, 363.

[14] Cattell 1974, 153, cited in Hardt 1978–9, 279.

[15] See e.g. Glick et al. 1974, 149–54; Weiss 2008, 38.

[16] Parkes 1987, 109–11.

[17] See Archer 1999, 7, citing Parkes 1971.

[18] See e.g. Davis 2008; Mikulincer and Shaver 2008.

[19] I discuss some of this research in the next chapter.

else feel like a loss of part of *oneself*? As Parkes himself asks, "Why should the loss of someone 'out there' give rise to an experience of the loss of something 'in here'?"[20]

In his seminal 1971 paper "Psychosocial Transitions: A Field for Study," Parkes proposed a broad framework for thinking about major life changes and their psychological relevance. Parkes understood these changes—so-called "psychosocial transitions"—as involving three main factors. The first factor is change in "life space," which is a change in any of those parts of the environment with which one interacts and with respect to which one's behavior is organized. As an extremely simple example, think about walking into a familiar room after the furniture has been rearranged; the momentary feeling of surprise or disorientation is a reaction to a change in life space. Likewise, the loss of a loved one or a body part is a change in life space, but obviously of a much more profound sort. For instance, in Lewis's case it is because of the change in life space that "grief feels like suspense": "It comes from the frustration of so many impulses that had become habitual" (1976, 55).

Second, changes in life space have a psychological impact on a person by altering what Parkes called a person's "assumptive world": one's unique set of beliefs, attitudes, and assumptions on the basis of which one navigates the world and carries out one's purposes.[21] For instance, when a familiar room is rearranged, one realizes while bumping into the furniture how much one had come to rely on such background assumptions. As Parkes pointed out, one's assumptive world includes a number of things: awareness of one's body, its parts, and their location and movement; one's sense of what kind of physical presence one is in the world; and one's sense of what other persons, things, and projects are available. Consequently, he argued, significant changes in life space are stressors because they require substantial reorganization of one's assumptive world, which at the least is a difficult and challenging task. Lewis describes exactly this sort of difficulty as well: "So many roads lead thought to [Joy]. I set out on one of them. But now there's an impassible frontier-post across it" (1976, 55).

It is because major changes in life space are a shock to one's assumptive world, Parkes argued, that bereavement and amputation are both so stressful, as well as why they are so often stressful in such similar ways (Parkes 1975, 208). It is not difficult to see why one's assumptive world would be vulnerable to such profound shocks. An assumptive world has been well compared to a computer operating system on which other programs run (Parkes 2006, 31). It is an internal model of the environment for action that includes basic assumptions about one's relationships, one's abilities and roles, one's responsibilities and possessions, what problems one is likely to face and one's capacity to handle them, what one can expect from others, and so on. In short, it is the entire

---

[20] Parkes 1987, 108.

[21] It is important to note that these "assumptions" need not all be cognitive or available to conscious awareness (see Attig 2001, 41).

mental backdrop against which a person approaches the world in everyday life.[22] It seems plausible, then, that the reason the bereaved compare themselves to amputees (and vice versa) is because in the loss of another they are suddenly confronted with a radical shift in their understanding of their environment and how they fit into it (Parkes 1987, 114–17).[23]

However, it is in virtue of the third aspect of such major life changes or "psychosocial transitions" that they potentially challenge the understanding of the *self*: the things that change within the life space are often things within the boundaries of the self. As Parkes put the point, "Anything which I can call 'mine'—'my' job, 'my' home town, 'my' left arm, 'my' wife—can become, to some extent, part of myself" (1971, 104). This third idea is crucial for our purposes: the loss of a loved one, after all, is compared to the loss of a body part, not merely because they both involve a similarly *large* adjustment but because they involve a similar *kind* of adjustment—an adjustment to the loss of oneself and the challenge of reconsidering who one is.

The basic idea is this. One's assumptive world includes assumptions about what makes one who one is, or what I have called psychological identity;[24] consequently, some shocks to one's assumptive world can be experienced as threatening one's psychological identity. Now, central among those identity-shaping assumptions can be the continuity of certain features of one's life space, such as having certain physical opportunities, or being in certain relationships with particular others, and this is in fact very common. In that case, losses in those features of life space shock that aspect of one's assumptive world that is one's psychological identity, and as a result those changes are experienced as losses of one's very self. That is why, following such losses, one is challenged to redefine oneself with respect to a deeply changed life space—like learning to live as a one-legged man, as Lewis says.

Parkes' account of psychosocial transitions has become part of the basic framework of contemporary research into the nature of grief, and it does indeed give answers to the questions it set out to answer. It explains why such losses as bereavement and amputation are as stressful as they are, and why those two sorts of losses (as well as others) are often stressful in very similar ways. It also explains why losses like these can be so profound, upsetting one's very sense of oneself: that is, it explains how loss "out

---

[22] See Parkes 1971; 1975; 1987, 109–17; 2006, 31–5; 2008, 477. It would be worth considering how the notion of assumptive worlds relates to the notion of patterns of construing and encoding the practical environment in cognitive-affective personality theory (see Russell 2009, chap. 8; Snow 2009). But I cannot pursue the question here.

[23] The need to shape one's "assumptive world" so as to avoid unnecessary shock and dismay is a major Stoic theme: it is in this spirit, I think, that Cicero (*TD* III.30, 58) quotes Anaxagoras as saying when told of his son's death, "I knew that I had begotten a mortal." Epictetus' teachings are also full of exhortations to remember that all of one's attachments must be surrendered sooner or later: e.g. *Diss.* III.24.27–30, 84–8, 104–5; IV.1.110; IV.10.31–2; *Handbook* 3, 4, 11, 26. See also Seneca, *On Peace of Mind* 13.2–3 (= IG II-106). For discussion, see Irwin 1998, 189; Long 2002, 249.

[24] I define "psychological identity" in Chapter 4 as a person's sense of what person he or she is, including the totality of relationships, commitments, attachments, and projects that give one's life its unique shape as being one's own. See also Schechtman 1996.

there" can be experienced as loss "in here." And these answers are significant for our purposes, since they show how it is that an embodied conception of the self leads to certain ways of experiencing major life changes like bereavement.

However, it fell outside the purview of Parkes' account to offer a complete explanation of that conception of the self, so for our purposes there are still some important questions left to answer. One question concerns how it comes to happen that people take their bodies or loved ones to be part of psychological identity in the first place, and another question is why this is so common. So I want to take up these questions in the next section with respect to the body, and then in the final section I argue that the same account of the body's importance to psychological identity also explains why other people are important in that way too.

2 Embodied selves and bodily change

In order to understand why one's body can be such an important part of psychological identity, I want to focus on three main ideas. One is how deeply "physical" our experience of ourselves and our orientation towards the world are. Here the central idea is what philosophers and scientists call the "body schema," which is our basic awareness of ourselves as situated in a physical order. The second is "body image," which is one's sense of one's distinctive physical presence in the world and the practical possibilities it affords. And third, crucially, is the idea that one's sense of one's practical possibilities in the physical world is central to one's sense of who one is—what part of the world one is and what one can make of one's life in that world.

2.1 What in the world you are: body schema

Shaun Gallagher defines body schema as a system of processes that regulate bodily posture and motion without perceptual monitoring (Gallagher 2001, 149–51). These processes are automatic, but they are not reflexive (like a leg jerking when rapped on the kneecap). Rather, body schema involves various sensory processes that gather information about the body and its orientation. As such, body schema makes our experience of ourselves deeply "bodily" in a couple of main ways. First, it appears to be body schema that is the first sense of oneself as a physical thing separate from other physical things. For instance, when neonates "correct" their bodily movements to align with the movements of others, they evidently recognize a difference between their own gestures and another's gesture, thereby making "a rudimentary differentiation between self and non-self" (Gallagher 2001, 158).

Second, and more important for our purposes, body schema is also a sense of one's physical orientation, a kind of sensory processing known as proprioception. Proprioception takes a couple of forms. For one thing, each of us has proprioceptive awareness of his body and its parts. For instance, the neonatal behavior of imitating the facial expressions of others suggests that neonates connect visible body transformations in others with a strictly proprioceptive grasp of their own non-visible body transformations.[25] For another thing, we have proprioceptive awareness of the orientation of the body, such as where one's left arm is, or where on one's body one is being touched, or with what force one's hand is moving. For instance, think about what happens when a mosquito lands on your arm. Because of the mind's body schema, you can feel not only that something has landed on you, but also where on you it has landed; you can also slap that part of your arm accurately and with proper force, without having to look first or even think about what you are doing.

Body schema thereby has an enormous impact on one's experience of oneself and the world, but its impact is more noticeable by its absence than its presence. For instance, Maurice Merleau-Ponty developed the notion of body schema through his studies of early research on patients lacking a proprioceptive and kinesthetic grasp of their own bodies as a result of a condition now known as "deafferentation."[26] This is a rare and strange condition in which peripheral sensory fibers are interrupted and cannot carry certain sorts of sensory input from a body part to the brain. The result is that the brain cannot "update" its information about movement and posture automatically, so one must manipulate one's limbs deliberately and mechanically, often by visually checking limb movement and posture.[27] For instance, imagine putting your left hand in the air and then not being able to tell where it is, or feeling a mosquito land on you but not knowing where—worse, imagine having to work out how to use that wayward left arm to slap the right place with the right force. The patient experiences his body as a *thing*, something he moves as one might move objects on a table. As one patient is reported to have described it, "it's like the body's blind."[28]

One of the main impacts that body schema has on our experience, therefore, is that physical movement occurs as if it were a natural extension of the mind. Again, consider the difference it makes when body schema is absent. Patients suffering from deafferentation can become surprisingly dexterous in their movements: Merleau-Ponty (1962) mentions one patient who worked assembling wallets all day, and neurologist Oliver Sacks (1985) tells of a patient in his care who was eventually able to return to her job as a computer programmer after losing her proprioceptive abilities.[29] Nonetheless, what such patients cannot become is *fluid* in their movements, which are more like staging and posing than really moving.[30] Normally, when one intends to grab a cup,

---

[25] See Gallagher 2001 for discussion.

[26] See Merleau-Ponty 1962. Unfortunately, although Merleau-Ponty's discussion concerns body schema, his phrase '*schema corporel*' is often translated as 'body image'; see Gallagher 2001, 148.

[27] See Gallagher 2001, 153.

[28] Sacks 1985, 46.

[29] Sacks observed in the latter patient that her lack of proprioceptive feedback was rapidly replaced by visual and auditory feedback, enabling her to start moving around again with increasing facility. She also relearned to control her speech, as her loss of proprioception had deprived her of any natural "vocal posture."

[30] In fact, those suffering from deafferentation seem to lack even the fluidity of motion in their bodies that normal persons can develop in their manipulation of external objects, presumably because the latter consists in extending one's body schema outwards to incorporate those objects. See Merleau-Ponty 1962, 165–70; see also Toombs 2001, 256.

say, one formulates that goal and the body automatically reorients and rearranges itself towards that goal. One suffering from deafferentation, by contrast, lacks that fluidity of bodily orientation towards a goal, in two ways. First, the motion itself must go through a number of intermediary steps, and is not "all at once": to grab the cup, one must first determine the proximity of one's arm to the cup, move one's elbow like this, one's wrist like that, curl one's fingers just so, and so on. Or as Sacks noticed, his patient could grasp knife and fork, but struggled to grasp them with the right pressure; she either grasped them until her knuckles turned white, or they simply fell from her hands. And second, patients have difficulty with miming, so that one who has learned to salute while standing at attention may have great difficulty saluting without standing at attention, and one who can easily grab his coffee cup may struggle to put together the movements involved in "grabbing" an imaginary cup. In these cases, as Merleau-Ponty hypothesized, limb movements are learned and made as mechanical sequences, so that isolating some parts of a sequence presents, in effect, a new sequence—learning to salute-without-standing, say.[31]

Fortunately, for most of us bodily movement is not so much what the mind *causes* as what it *does*. Body schema is therefore significant for our purposes, as it suggests that a deep part of the sense of oneself is being a distinct part of the physical world whose physical movements are the direct forays of consciousness out into the world. Of course, body schema is a kind of sensory awareness and not any kind of conception of psychological identity (nor does it entail one). Even so, it is completely unsurprising that creatures with this kind of sensory awareness might go on to think of their lives in terms of how they might engage with parts of the physical world, and might do so commonly.

2.2 Who in the world you are: body image

To better understand why humans commonly take particular bodily goods to be important to psychological identity, we need to think next about "body image," which is a nexus of intentional attitudes about one's body and the broad range of meanings that one attaches to one's body as part of one's total existence. As such, body image involves attitudes and assumptions about one's place in a physical world, which in a human being—a physical creature—also provides a ready set of assumptions about just who one is.

One's body is one's presence in the world; unsurprisingly, one's attitudes and assumptions about that presence usually carry deep personal significance. For instance, research suggests that the most significant factors for depression in amputees are whether the patient is accepting of his altered body and how accepting he thinks others will be.[32] Moreover, there is also evidence that the likelihood of post-traumatic

---

[31] Merleau-Ponty 1962, part 1, chap. 3. For other cases of proprioceptive breakdown not arising from deafferentation, see Sacks 1985, chaps. 5 and 7.

[32] See Rybarczyk et al. 1995; Behel et al. 2002. It is especially worth noting that violent trauma is not a statistically relevant factor for depression in amputees, since the rate of depression does not differ significantly between surgical and accidental amputations (Fukunishi 1999).

stress disorder (PTSD) following a disfiguring incident also depends on body image. In one study, female patients were found to be especially prone to PTSD given a facial burn as opposed to burns elsewhere, regardless of how much total body surface had been burned. Likewise, females suffering a digital amputation were more prone to PTSD given a cosmetically disfigured or atrophied reattachment than with other reattachments, regardless of the degree of physical functionality in the reattached digit.[33] It seems likely, then, that although significant changes to the body often result from trauma, a major factor in the psychological impact of such changes is their impact on body image, or one's feelings about oneself as a particular body.

These examples illustrate the significance that people commonly attach to their physical presence: both what they present before others and what they present before themselves. Now, we may simply chalk this up to vanity, but that would be too quick. To be sure, a person usually cares whether the body he presents looks good, but he may care as much or more whether the body he presents actually represents *him*. It is no stretch of the imagination that many amputees may be less worried about the attractiveness of their bodies than about having bodies that seem alien and not recognizable as themselves. As is well known, such feelings can even lead to very strong desires for body alterations, from routine plastic surgery to sex change operations. In fact, in recent years there has been increased awareness of the desire of some persons to have even a normal, healthy limb amputated. These persons are not delusional about their limbs, yet they find them alienating: they feel they are in the "wrong body," and desire an amputation in order to restore a sense of wholeness and true identity.[34]

However, for our purposes body image is even more significant as a set of attitudes about one's unique menu of options for action in the physical environment. After all, our lives are lives of activity, and activity usually means manipulating parts of the physical world. How, then, might our attitudes about the activities available to us shape our very understanding of our lives and ourselves? I want to examine this question by thinking about the loss of limb control, and asking this pair of more specific questions: how does body image change as control of one's body deteriorates, and how does that change bear on psychological identity?

On both of these questions, philosopher S. Kay Toombs, who also suffers from MS, provides invaluable insights (Toombs 2001). Because Toombs suffers from a degenerative disease, she has experienced first-hand how bodily changes yield changes in body image that are also changes in one's deeper psychological identity. In particular, she argues that changes in body image have an impact on one's psychological identity precisely because those changes impact one's sense of one's possibilities for action in the world.

---

[33] See Fukunishi 1999, whose study concerned only female patients, and so does not provide data comparing females with males.

[34] See the groundbreaking study by First 2005. See also Bayne and Levy 2005 for discussion.

First of all, some changes in one's attitudes about one's physical possibilities are changes in one's sense of one's *present* self. Some of these are changes in how one physically relates to others. For instance, Toombs describes the experience of going to an airport ticket counter in a wheelchair, where her head just reaches the counter, so that people behind the counter must bend over the counter to speak to her, and she must shout over the counter in order to speak to them. Likewise, she reports that when she attends parties and receptions in a wheelchair, conversations all take place literally over her head. In these situations people will often speak to her standing husband about her instead of directly to her, and breaking into the conversation means talking up to others as a child would to adults. Such experiences, she says, foster a sense of isolation from others, a sense of oneself as living parallel to others, but not really *with* them.

Other changes come about because one's attitudes about one's capacities for bodily orientation are also attitudes about one's place in a causal nexus. Following Sartre, Toombs puts the point this way: one's legs are not just objects in the world to which one is specially attached, but are "the possibility of walking, running, playing tennis," so that loss of body function "represents a modification of the existential possibilities inherent in the lived body" (Toombs 2001, 254). There is no distinction between what one believes one can physically do and what place one takes oneself to occupy in the physical world, since having a certain place in the physical world just is to do and to be capable of doing certain things in it. And as we saw above, *thing-in-the-physical-world* seems to be our original and basic orientation.

Second, changes in body image can also amount to discontinuity with one's *past*. To see this, note that while we do experience our unique individuality in our cognitive styles, we also experience our individuality in a unique corporeal style, a style of moving through the physical world, and this style can change over time. For instance, Toombs says that when she sees herself walking in old home movies, the image seems foreign to her. It is difficult for her, not only to remember when she used to walk, but even to understand that any walking person could be she: "I find it hard to remember how it was to be that person," she says, "or, even *who* I was when I moved like that."[35] With the loss of her ability to walk, then, she has of course lost a certain mode of getting around the physical world, but more than that, she has lost any sense of herself as one who exists as part of the physical world in that previous kind of way. Interestingly, and tragically, Sacks' patient who suffered from deafferentation reported the very same experience while watching an old home movie:

"Yes, of course, that's me!" [She] smiles, and then cries: "But I can't identify with that graceful girl any more! She's gone, I can't remember her, *I can't even imagine her.* It's like something's been scooped right out of me, right at the centre . . . that's what they do with frogs, isn't it? They scoop

---

[35] Toombs 2001, 254, italics in original. Although I have never been a smoker, it seems to me that Stephen King hits on an interesting insight in his short story "Quitters, Inc.": to give up smoking is to give up not only cigarettes but also a wide range of bodily movements that go with cigarettes.

out the centre, the spinal cord, they *pith* them ... That's what I am, *pithed*, like a frog." (Sacks 1985, 50, italics in original)

Finally, changes in body image can also change one's sense of extending into the *future*. Toombs reports having a very different sense of time, since what is a moment's task for others becomes for her the focus of substantial planning and effort. As a result, her life centers far more around the "here and now," and so she is not the same sort of planning, continuing agent that others are or that she used to be. Likewise, because so much of her time is spent focusing on the small steps towards even very proximate goals, her goals and plans become spread over much greater spans of time.[36] In virtue of such changes, the entire structure of intentional agency changes as well.[37] In the case of a degenerative disease, one's ability to project oneself into the future is overshadowed by the realization that what one can do now may be something that one will never be able to do again (Toombs 2001, 259). Consequently, such change in one's body amounts to a change in one's sense of one's future—what goals one can reasonably adopt, what plans one can reasonably expect to execute, and the rate at which time marches on. Such changes impact one's expectations of one's future possibilities, and indeed the very ability to project possibilities onto one's future.

1.3 Bodily goods and psychological identity

We began by asking why one's body, its parts, and its movements are so often entwined with one's sense of what person one is. Now we have our answer: considering how we live, it would be surprising if things were otherwise! In both our sensory apparatus and our attitudes, we experience our bodies as *us*, our presence in a physical world. As such, our bodies are our mode of orientation towards our goals, and thus our lives of activity, out in the world. Our bodies are the very possibility of acting in the world: what we can do now, what expectations we can have, what plans we can realistically make, how much time we will need, how we extend into the future, and with what certainty we can rely on any of this. These *just are* those parts of the "assumptive world" by which a physically oriented creature understands what sort of future he might put together for himself. So it is no surprise at all that change in one's body is not only causally linked to changes in psychological identity, but is often *experienced as* a change in psychological identity itself.

I say it is no surprise that our experience should be like this; I have not said that it is inevitable, much less that it is a good thing. Consider Epictetus, who was lame himself: "Lameness is an impediment to one's leg, but not to the faculty of choice" (*Handbook* 9). Epictetus believed that his life of activity just was a life of exercising that faculty; I take him at his word that he experienced his lameness as changing his options without changing *him*, and for all that I have said he may have been the wiser for it. My point is

---

[36] Toombs 2001, 258. Stephen Hawking (1988) reports, with surprising good humor, having similar experiences as Lou Gehrig's disease began inhibiting his movements.

[37] I thank Mark LeBar for this way of putting the point.

simply that it is *that* sort of view that requires explanation and, as Epictetus himself acknowledged, deliberate effort to acquire. An outlook on oneself as a certain range of possibilities for engaging the physical world might be an outlook we should overcome, but it certainly is the default outlook that is there to *be* overcome in the first place. This is why I said above that the view I am trying to make clearer is hidden in plain sight.

3 Embodies selves and other selves

When people say that the loss of mobility or a body part is like a loss of self, they are *exactly* right. Serious bodily changes are a shock to one's assumptions about one's possibilities for action, and these are often among one's deepest assumptions about who one is. I argue now that when people say that bereavement is like losing a body part, they are *exactly* right too. At bottom, my argument for this is a very simple one: if my legs are part of my sense of my possibilities for action, then *for the very same reason*, so too is my spouse, or my career, or my friends. After all, my spouse and my career are as much a part of my sense of my possibilities for engaging the world as my legs are.

But now for the argument in more detail. As we saw in section 1, people go about their lives by relying on a host of background beliefs, assumptions, and other attitudes about their environment for action: in general, what possibilities it holds for one and what sorts of pursuits are available in it. Furthermore, a crucial part of that background is a set of beliefs, assumptions, and other attitudes about what person one is—which plans and projects and pursuits are central to what one's life is about. Now, what we saw in section 2 was that this self-defining background typically includes attitudes about one's physical being, which is experienced as the very possibility of continuing in a certain pursuit, undertaking a certain project, or executing a certain plan. That is why significant bodily changes are not merely stressful but threatening to one's identity: they upset one's sense of oneself as the one whose life involved making those plans and pursuing those projects. This is just what we mean in saying that one's physical being can be placed within the boundaries of the self.

Now, recall *why* it is that bodily goods can be within the boundaries of the self: because one's body can be the very possibility of those opportunities for action by which one understands who one is and what one's life is about. However, external goods can and usually do play exactly the same role for us: they too are the very possibility of loving this person, parenting this child, doing this work, living in this place. These too are possibilities for action in the physical world—and if any possibilities for action can define one's sense of oneself, surely these can. That is why losses in these areas of life are typically threatening to identity as well, leaving one to reconsider who one is going to be; and again, that is just what it means to say that such things are typically within the boundaries of the self. That is to say, typically the conception of the self is the one I have called the *embodied* conception.

So, to put it simply, if one's legs represent the possibility of an existence as a certain person, then so too do certain relationships and pursuits—*they just are the things one is doing in the world.* To lose a leg—or a spouse, or a career—is to lose forever a particular way of being in the world, leaving one to find a new self to be. As Eric Mack observes, human beings

live in and through a world of physical objects which extends beyond the space occupied by their respective bodies. . . . Nor is the activity in which human life consists merely a matter of recurrent excursions (or raids) into the world of extra-personal objects. Extra-personal objects enter into and help define the specific goals, ambitions, and commitments through which individuals compose their respective lives. Particular extra-personal objects become deeply incorporated into the specific strategies that individuals formulate for their life pursuits. Living in and through the extra-personal world may be merely contingently connected with the pure concept of goal-oriented activity. But it is surely necessarily connected with *human* life and the *human* pursuit of ends.[38]

If this is the way in which bodily and external goods matter for our happiness, then it is clear that they matter, not in addition to virtuous activity, or even for the sake of virtuous activity. They matter for happiness because they are the very form and mode of *this* activity that is *this* happiness. It is virtuous activity that controls happiness, but on the embodied conception of the self, there is no difference between virtuous activity and all the ways in which one interacts with unique parts of the physical world with practical wisdom and emotional soundness.

But of course, now the real questions for the embodied conception are *normative*. After all, there is nothing I have said in this chapter that the Stoics need deny. On the contrary, the Stoics believe that every animal has a natural awareness of itself that is from the first an awareness of its physical constitution—its body parts, proper posture, and so on; furthermore, as humans grow and age they are aware of themselves as having the bodies and physical opportunities characteristic of their age,[39] and even a bull after a long winter knows what it can do against an attacking lion.[40] More than that, the Stoics are perfectly aware that people do, and do very commonly, become closely attached to other persons, as well as to things and places, finding in those attachments possibilities that they take to be crucial for themselves. Rather, the Stoics' point is that such attachments are all *deeply problematic*, however common they may be. This is arguably *the* central idea in Epictetus' ethics:

For what is weeping and groaning? A judgement. What is misfortune? A judgement. What is sedition, discord, complaint, accusation, impiety, foolish talk? All these are judgements, and

---

[38] Mack 1990, 532–3; see also Mack 1995a, 199; 1995b. It is an important question, the question of central importance to Mack here, how these considerations should shape social institutions that define rights to control access to parts of the world (i.e. property rights) and access to schemes for acquiring such rights; see also Lomasky 1987 and Russell 2010. But it is one I must leave for another time.

[39] Seneca, *Ep.* 121. This is part of the process the Stoics call *oikeiōsis*, "familiarization" or "appropriation"; see Chapter 7.

[40] Epictetus, *Diss.* I.2.30–2.

nothing more; and judgements concerning things outside the sphere of choice, taking them to be good or evil. Let anyone transfer these judgements to things within the sphere of choice, and I will guarantee that he will preserve his constancy, whatever be the state of things about him.[41]

In a word, Epictetus' message about the boundaries of the self is, "Keep downsizing!"

So *is* the embodied conception a wise way of thinking about oneself? Is it compatible with emotional soundness? These are the normative questions I want to ask about the embodied conception now, judging it first against our own common-sense standards of emotional soundness and quality of life (Chapter 10), and then against the much more demanding standards we find among the Stoics (Chapter 11).

[41] *Diss.* III.3.18–19; see Sorabji 2006, 181–2, for discussion.

10

The Embodied Conception and Psychological Well-Being

If thinking about loss can reveal how the embodied conception of the self works, it can also reveal what might be dangerous about it. Increased vulnerability to loss is one of the risks of expanding the boundaries of the self—not surprisingly, since that is in fact part of the point. As I said in the very first chapter, to be vulnerable to loss is to be so closely connected to someone or something that there is something to *be* lost. I think that happiness is a life in which one invests enough in the world to have something to lose, so on my way of thinking about happiness, vulnerability just comes with the territory, because it has to. But this vulnerability is not just to *loss*—surely bad enough—but to loss of *self*. Nothing can make me invulnerable to losses *out there*— why make myself vulnerable to losses *in here*? Can we afford to be vulnerable in that way? Does expanding the boundaries of the self jeopardize our emotional well-being, making recovery from loss inordinately difficult? Does it jeopardize our freedom, making us the pawns of those who might control those parts of our happiness that we cannot?[1]

In the previous chapter we saw that C. S. Lewis's record of his grief at the loss of his wife is revealing about how we place others within the boundaries of the self. However, it is also revealing about the risks involved in doing so. In fact, that risk is at the center of the film *Shadowlands*, which dramatizes the story of "Jack" Lewis and his wife Joy. And as Jack makes clear, he thinks of his happiness not just as a life of activity but as *this* life of *this* activity, a life he shares with Joy:

Jack: No, I don't want to be somewhere else anymore, not waiting for anything new to happen, not looking round the next corner, no next hill. Here, now. That's enough.
Joy: That's your kind of happy, isn't it?
Jack: Yes. Yes it is.
Joy: It's not going to last, Jack.

Joy says this not to be unkind, but because she and Jack both know she is about to die; so she reminds Jack that he has *this* happiness at all only because it gives him something to lose: "The pain then," Joy tells him, "is part of the happiness now." But of course,

---

[1] These are the sorts of questions I raised at the end of Chapter 5.

there is the rest of the story: eventually there is *this pain now* which is part of *that happiness then*. How damaging might that pain be, if it is the pain, not just of loss, but of loss of self?

Such questions present a serious challenge for my way of thinking about happiness, and in this chapter I want to focus on grief and the resolution of grief, as a way of asking whether my way of thinking about happiness makes a person too vulnerable to psychological damage. It seems only natural, after all, to assume that the more one's identity is entwined with another person, the more devastating that person's loss would have to be.[2] That is an empirical claim, and I argue that empirical investigation suggests that that claim is actually *false*. More than that, empirical investigation suggests just the reverse: as long as he trusts in his own competence, a person bereaved of such a close relationship as that is probably *more* likely to handle grief well than anyone else.

In the first section, I examine different types of closeness in relationships and argue that close relationships like the one I just described put the bereaved at least risk of damage. However, even if that is true it could still be the case that avoiding such damage requires cutting off that closeness with the deceased. In the second section, I argue that that too is just the reverse of what the empirical literature suggests.

First, though, a brief word about what counts here as a good or bad grief outcome. Psychologists understand this normative concept operationally, in terms of quality of life.[3] For instance, we might say an outcome is worse to the extent that it involves more severe depression, or longer-lasting depression; greater physical pain, fatigue, or sleep-lessness; the abuse of alcohol or other substances; prolonged delays in returning to normal activities; and so on. Now, philosophers will notice that this approach just appeals to common-sense ideas about quality of life, which may involve little theoretical sophistication. Furthermore, even among psychologists the precise distinction between good and bad outcomes has been contested (we shall see one such controversy as we proceed). Nonetheless, this is certainly a serviceable way to begin, and in any case, whatever theoretical sloppiness this approach may have will not actually have much bearing on the conclusions we can draw.[4]

---

[2] See e.g. Moller 2007.

[3] The normativity of these concepts is crucial to appreciate. A cautionary tale: in a provocative 1961 article George Engel hypothesized that *all* grief is an illness or disorder, on the basis that it seemed to meet all of the standard criteria for illnesses. The field has never embraced this hypothesis, although versions of it still crop up occasionally in arguments over whether grief should be classified as a mental disorder, according to the criteria now standardized in the DSM-IV; see Wilkinson 2000 and references. However, there are two serious problems with this whole line of thinking. One, it makes the rather alarming assumption that the class of "mental disorders" must not be a vague class. And two, and more important, what counts as normal as opposed to disordered grief is above all a normative question, so such a distinction is precisely the sort that a diagnostic tool like the DSM-IV will be very unlikely to make, certainly not in any very philosophically satisfactory way. If there is an issue in this "debate" at all, it is not so much what grief is as how we define and diagnose disorders.

[4] Of course, the Stoics will disagree, since they reject most of our common-sense assumptions about quality of life. I consider their objections in the next chapter.

1 Closeness, coping, and grief

Grief is complex. We see this too in Lewis's record. He responded to Joy's death with a flurry of emotions, deep sorrows, and pains as well as warm recollections. Joy's death was the cause of much stress, in managing the details of his everyday life as well as in sorting out how to make sense of his loss and his future. Joy's death was difficult for him cognitively as well, as it made him re-examine some of his most basic attitudes about himself, the world, and even God. However, there is one aspect of grief that particularly interests us at the moment: with Joy's death, Lewis lost someone whose closeness had been the promise of a certain kind of future, and thus the security of his picture of what his life was about.[5] That is why he experienced her loss also as a loss of self. Our first question is whether that kind of bond with a loved one makes it more difficult to come through bereavement and grief all in one piece.

1.1 Attachment and resilience

The significance of the bonds between the bereaved and the deceased has been a major area of investigation in the modern study of grief. Psychologists typically call these bonds "attachments," and unsurprisingly they find that whether and how one will grieve the loss of another will depend on (among other things) the kind of attachment one has with the deceased. In the mid twentieth century, psychiatrist John Bowlby argued that a central feature of human psychology is the basic need to bond with others—"attachment figures"—for a sense of safety and security. Grief, on Bowlby's view, is a reaction to the loss of an attachment figure.[6]

Now, not all attachments are the same, and how one grieves the loss of an attachment figure will vary depending on the nature or "style" of the attachment. In particular, attachment styles vary along a pair of dimensions: one, the level of confidence in one's own coping skills and, two, the degree of closeness with the attachment figure. By "closeness" here, psychologists mean the degree of one's resistance to separation from the other person, one's reliance on his or her presence, and one's requiring that other person for the practicality, and indeed the very relevance, of one's roles and plans.[7]

Closeness therefore offers a useful way of thinking about the embodied conception of the self. Furthermore, since different attachment styles predict very different levels of success in grief resolution, attachment theory provides an excellent framework for our question about the embodied conception: it is clear that "embodied" attachments will be high along the dimension of closeness; so do the prospects of successful grief resolution vary more along the *closeness dimension* or along the *coping dimension*? The

---

[5] See also Weiss 2008, 36.

[6] See Weiss 2008, 36, for discussion. Bowlby developed the attachment theory in a magisterial trilogy: 1969, 1973, and 1980. On the biological basis of attachment and grief, a major theme in Bowlby's work, see Archer 1999; see also Parkes 1987; Worden 1991, 7–8; Archer 2008, 47–8.

[7] Parkes 1987, 138; see also Archer 1999, 166 and references.

psychological evidence, I argue, suggests that bad grief outcomes have much more to do with poor coping than with close attachment.

Let's begin by identifying some basic types of attachment relations.[8] As I said, attachment theorists distinguish these relations along two dimensions: how self-assured one is, and how close one is to the other. Each of these dimensions can be seen as a continuum of varying degrees, and the two dimensions cut across each other roughly as follows:

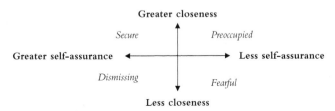

Moving north along the closeness dimension, one's identity is increasingly entwined with the attachment figure and the boundaries of the self are expanded; and moving west along the dimension of self-assurance, one's confidence in one's competence and ability to take care of oneself increases. Consequently, while the so-called "secure" (NW) and "preoccupied" (NE) attachments are both characterized by a high degree of closeness to another, the latter unlike the former attachment is characterized by clinging and over-dependence, looking to another to compensate for incompetence and other deficiencies one perceives in oneself. By contrast, "dismissing" (SW) and "fearful" (SE) attachments both put more distance between oneself and the attachment figure; however, the dismissing attachment is distant out of a heightened sense of self-reliance and the fearful out of distrust.

For purposes of understanding grief, these attachment styles are significant because they correspond to different levels of ability to resolve grief successfully, or what psychologists call "resilience."[9] There are two things to note about this correspondence. First, the evidence to date strongly suggests that *resilience varies primarily along the coping (horizontal) dimension*, increasing towards the western end—and *not* along the closeness dimension. For instance, R. Chris Fraley and George A. Bonanno (2004) found that bereaved patients with attachments towards the eastern end of the schema had significantly higher levels of depression and negative emotions than patients on the western end; they were also at greater risk of post-traumatic stress syndrome, and not

---

[8] In distinguishing and characterizing these types, I follow with small revisions the representative discussion of Fraley and Bonanno 2004. See also Archer 1999, 173, and Parkes 2006. It is important to note that these are types of relations, not types of persons, since attachment types can vary significantly both over time and between one relationship and another. See Archer 1999, 174. Nonetheless, it is possible and often useful to describe persons as having one sort of characteristic attachment style or another.

[9] Resilience is defined operationally: it is a placeholder for a bundle of personal attributes and strategies (to be identified by further empirical study) that tend towards good grief outcomes. Con. Moller 2007, 307, who treats resilience as a "disposition."

only had higher levels of anxiety but also tended to become more anxious within fifteen months of bereavement. Similarly, Colin Murray Parkes and Robert Weiss (1983) found that attachments that are characterized by preoccupation or "anxiety" (NE), as well as ambivalent or "fearful" attachments (SE), were powerful determinants of problematic reactions to bereavement, in stark contrast to "secure" attachments (NW).[10] And Parkes (2006) has also found that adults who recollected childhood attachments to parents towards the western end of the coping dimension tend to have better psychological and physical grief outcomes than those on the eastern end.

What might account for this? Fraley and Bonanno (2004, 887–8) hypothesize that those with dismissing attachments (SW) may be more resilient because they are more disposed to direct their attention away from uncomfortable thoughts, and of course may perceive less of a tie between their own identity and their relation to the deceased in the first place. Furthermore—and more important for our purposes—they suggest that persons in secure attachments (NW) probably do well at drawing on positive emotions and memories, and maintaining a sense of security by means of "continuing bonds" with the deceased, with the result that such persons have higher thresholds for experiencing anxiety and are better able to regulate the anxiety they do experience. Simply put, this evidence suggests that good grief outcomes are possible and likely among those whose identities include others they love, *provided* that such attachments are not substituting for insecurities about themselves.[11]

The second main point is that *secure attachments may even predict the best grief outcome of all.* The consensus in the field seems to be that no attachment style predicts a *better* outcome than the secure style (see Parkes 2006 and Mikulincer and Shaver 2008, 105–6, for discussion). It is less clear, however, whether dismissing styles have *as good* an expectation. On the one hand, Fraley and Bonanno (2004, 887) found that whereas fearful attachments are associated with increased levels of sorrow and distress, for the most part dismissing attachments are not. More than that, Bonanno et al. (2008) have shown that, although the absence of distress following bereavement (so-called "absent grief") has traditionally been assumed to be detrimental, many patients with absent grief actually cope very well with bereavement, provided that they are resilient rather than merely in "defensive denial" (see also Parkes 2006, 91–3).

But on the other hand, there is also reason to suspect that persons whose attachments are *characteristically* dismissing may not cope with bereavement as well over all as persons whose attachments are characteristically secure. For instance, Parkes has

---

[10]   See Parkes 2006, 27–8, for discussion; see also Shaver and Tancredy 2001, 77–80; Bonanno et al. 2008, 299. There is general consensus that persons in fearful attachments (SE) fare the worst in bereavement and overall; see e.g. Mikulincer and Shaver 2008, 106.

[11]   Notice, then, that it would be far too quick to conclude from the phenomenon of resilience that in such cases the death of another has a "comparatively minor impact" on one's life (*pace* Moller 2007, 308). Rather, resilience seems usually a way of living with the loss of someone whose impact on one's life really was major; we do not, e.g., maintain continuing bonds with persons whose impact on our life was only comparatively minor. Someone may be an important figure in my life even if I am able to go on pretty well after his or her loss, provided that how I go on is deeply shaped by my having had that person in my life.

found that when bereaved, characteristically dismissing adults are more likely than others to wish they could cry more than they do, and are likely to experience feelings of regret, guilt, and self-blame.[12] There may also be reason to think that such adults may not actually avoid but only ignore the stress of bereavement, since there seems to be a correlation between dismissing attachments and increased somatic symptoms in bereavement.[13]

Finally, there are also questions about the overall well-adjustment of characteristically dismissing persons. Parkes has found that children in dismissing attachments to their parents tend to grow into adults who generally express little affection, love, or grief, and we may think that this greater emotional detachment and extreme self-reliance is itself maladaptive (Parkes 2006, 94, 121). Furthermore, it may be for this reason that there is also a correlation between a dismissing attachment style and marital conflict (pp. 91, 93, 97). Indeed, Parkes goes so far as to conclude that persons who form secure attachments cope with bereavement, relationships, and the stresses of life in general better than those with any other attachment style, including the dismissing style (p. 75).

So the empirical evidence about grief strongly suggests that closeness and devastation absolutely do not go hand in hand. On the contrary, provided that one trusts in one's own competence, being very closely connected to the people one loves is probably the best bet for psychological well-being. At the very least, there is no bet that's better.

1.2 Complicated grief

So far I have focused on grief as we think of it in common, familiar cases of bereavement. However, some forms of grief are problematic and pathological. For instance, a case of highly problematic grief is at the center of Mike Binder's film *Reign Over Me*, which tells the story of Charlie Fineman, a once successful man who for years has utterly failed to cope with the sudden and tragic loss of his wife and children in an airplane crash. After the loss, Charlie finds it terrifying to think about who he had been before the loss, and finds it almost impossible to think about starting a new life, so much so that the mere suggestion that he might start dating or return to his previous line of work is enough to make him violent. As a result, Charlie virtually ceases to exist: he avoids almost all human contact; he lets himself run down, so that he seems lost beneath an overgrowth of hair, stubble, and rumpled clothing; and he spends his days playing video games, aimlessly riding his scooter, and endlessly remodeling his kitchen. Charlie keeps busy but he has stopped living; there's really no one that he is any more.[14]

---

[12] Parkes 2006, 91, 99–100. Parkes speculates that this may show that it is not the case that those in dismissing attachments do not care about others, but that they both care and struggle to express it.

[13] Mikulincer and Shaver 2008, 104–6.

[14] A similar reaction to traumatic loss is depicted in Terry Gilliam's film *The Fisher King*, where the reaction to loss results in serious mental illness and homelessness.

Charlie is an example of what I shall call "complicated" as opposed to "normal" grief.[15] In contemporary grief research, the normal/complicated distinction is drawn in terms of good or bad functioning: simply put, grief is complicated to the extent that it seriously interferes with somatic, psychological, and/or practical functioning.[16] Complicated grief takes very many forms, but what they all have in common is distress that is so intense, long-lasting, or both, that the bereaved finds it extremely difficult to return to a normal human life. In a word, the distinction between normal and complicated grief is a quality of life issue.[17]

Now, I have argued that in cases of normal grief, closeness of attachment does not increase the risk of a poor outcome. But what about cases like Charlie's? When a loss is as tragic and horrific as Charlie's is, does close attachment tend to complicate grief?

The factors that lead to complicated grief are varied and extremely complex.[18] Some of these factors are psychological attributes of the bereaved person. These can include pre-existing psychological and emotional maladjustment, such as intense separation anxiety or a diminished sense of one's abilities and worth outside the relationship;[19] feelings of hopelessness and despair about oneself;[20] an inhibited ability to express emotion;[21] and in general a prior history of affective disorders and insecurities.[22] However, closeness of attachment per se has not been identified as a psychological determinant of complicated grief. On the contrary, as we saw above, secure attachments are types of extremely intimate attachments, and yet it is clear from this list of maladjustments that secure attachments are the least likely to manifest the psychological factors that tend to complicate grief. So we can set these factors aside.

However, there are other factors for complicated grief that are no respecters of persons. Some of these have to do with the events surrounding the loss itself. For instance, a death that follows a protracted illness can be especially difficult to accept,[23] especially if the bereaved has become identified with care-giving.[24] On the other hand, a lack of any forewarning of death can also make grief more difficult, because the death is more shocking.[25] Other factors arise after the loss, such as social isolation, which

[15] Different psychologists use different labels for this distinction; my labels are borrowed from Therese Rando (1992–3, 44–5). The basic distinction itself seems to have been made first in Lindemann's (1944) groundbreaking empirical study of bereavement.

[16] See Stroebe et al. 2008, 6–8.

[17] Weiss 2008, 35. It is important for us to notice the ineliminable normativity of the normal/complicated distinction. This represents a point at which psychiatry and eudaimonism intersect, since drawing the line between problematic and non-problematic grief ultimately rests on a conception of what it is for humans to live well; see also Leavy 1997; Nordenfelt 1997, 289.

[18] For a careful classification of types of risk factors, see Stroebe and Schut 2001.

[19] Parkes 1987, 129, 144–6.

[20] Mikulincer and Shaver 2008, 101–2.

[21] Parkes 2006, 91, 99–100.

[22] Parkes 1987, 153; Parkes 2006, 27; Bonanno et al. 2008, 298–9.

[23] Rando 1992–3, 47; Bonanno and Kaltman 1999, 764.

[24] Parkes 1987, 143.

[25] Parkes 1987, 149; Archer 2008, 51; Bonanno et al. 2008, 299–300. The consensus about suddenness as a factor is that it is not the suddenness of death per se that is problematic, but its cognitive impact stemming

sometimes results from a long time spent caring for the deceased, and other lacks of social support, as well as failed attempts to avoid grieving or, by contrast, a sense of a duty to the dead to protract mourning.[26] But perhaps the most severe forms of complicated grief arise from traumatic deaths, such as violent deaths, especially when the violence is horrific[27] or when the body of the deceased is either unrecovered or mutilated.[28] Trauma can be further compounded when one believes the death may have been preventable,[29] and can lead to feelings of blame, shame, and guilt[30] or even post-traumatic stress disorder.[31]

Traumatic grief is especially relevant for our purposes, since there is little reason to expect that any sort of psychological well-adjustment could make one immune to shocks of this magnitude. In fact, Charlie Fineman himself is a clear case of traumatic grief. He had witnessed the violent and horrific destruction of the airplane carrying his family, whose bodies were never recovered.[32] Charlie also feels guilt and shame because he had snapped at his wife the last time they had spoken (as it happens, about plans to remodel the kitchen). And the event that claimed Charlie's family— the 11 September 2001 attacks on the World Trade Center—is one that changed forever the basic assumptions about the safety of the world for people around the globe; how much more it must have changed the assumptions of someone like Charlie.

However, even in cases of trauma, there is some evidence that persons who tend to form close, secure attachments generally pull through better than those who form other sorts of attachments. According to Parkes, his research indicates that both trauma and non-secure attachments contribute to overall distress in bereavement; not surprisingly, those who tend to form fearful (or "disorganized") attachments do worst of all in coping with trauma. But even those who tend to form dismissing attachments appear to have disproportionate tendencies to abuse alcohol when faced with traumatic circumstances (Parkes 2006, 141–2). If all this is correct, then distress tends to be highest for people facing trauma within *non*-secure attachments.

Now, let me repeat: surely it would be too much to suppose that any sort of attachment style or form of psychological adjustment can eliminate risk of complicated

---

from a lack of preparation for the shock to one's "assumptive world" (I discuss this concept in Chapter 9, and below).

[26] See Parkes 1987, 126, 129, 143; 2006, 27.

[27] Parkes 2006, 29–30; 2008, 463; Rando 1992–3, 47.

[28] Parkes 2008, 463.

[29] Rando 1992–3, 47.

[30] Parkes 2006, 29–30; 2008, 463.

[31] See e.g. Bonanno and Kaltman 1999, 767. Traumatic events are especially difficult for the bereaved, because they typically involve sudden and radical changes in their assumptive worlds and thus pose deep threats to one's sense of security. The connection between trauma and disruption of assumptive worlds is a central theme in the research of Janoff-Bulman (e.g. 1992). See also Bonanno and Kaltman 1999, 767; Parkes 2006, 29–30, 33–4; 2008, 477; Archer 2008, 51. I shall return to this below.

[32] Likewise, Perry in *The Fisher King* witnesses his wife being shot through the head in the middle of a conversation while the two of them are on a date.

grief.[33] In particular, it is not clear whether bereavement can be anything *but* complicated, to some extent or other, when the loss is a particularly traumatic one. Even so,
what does seem clear is that even in these cases, persons who form close, secure
attachments have prospects for successful grief resolution that are at least as good as
anyone else's.

2 Coping with grief: how they do it

Grief is always distressful, but it is not always disastrous, not even for those who are
deeply attached to those they lose—in fact, *especially* not for them. Most of the time
people find that life goes on, and that life can even be happy again. Of course, the
happiness of a life shared with the loved one now lost—*that* happiness—is gone for ever.
Life can be happy again, but the deal is: new life, new happiness. A good outcome is to
close that deal. But just what does such an outcome look like, and how is the deal closed?

These are important questions for us to consider. I have argued that the primary
predictor of a bad grief outcome is inability to cope with the emotions and stresses of
bereavement, and not how closely attached one was to the deceased. But for all that, it
may still be the case that part of successful coping is the ability to weaken or even
completely sever one's attachment to the deceased as part of the grieving process. In
fact, many psychologists have believed that closely attached persons best cope with
bereavement by focusing on that closeness as part of their *problem*. On the contrary, our
best current evidence, I argue, suggests that holding on to that closeness is often part of
the solution.

2.1 Is closeness a problem to solve?

Beginning with Freud, for much of the twentieth century the dominant view about
grief resolution consisted of two main ideas: one, the way to resolve grief is to directly
confront painful memories and emotions, a process often described in terms of various
stages of "grief work"; and two, the successful outcome of this work is psychological
"detachment" from the deceased.[34] On this view, attachment is the problem, so
detachment is the solution. In fact, some have even identified complicated grief as
any failure to do the required work to detach oneself from the deceased.

However, this approach to grief resolution has proven problematic in both of its
main theses.[35] First, there is no evidence that people who directly confront and focus

---

[33] See Rando 1992–3, 44. Indeed, as Parkes (2006, 145–6) notes, too idyllic a background may actually
leave one, even a "secure" person, more vulnerable to distress in adulthood, because their assumptive worlds
are correspondingly too idyllic.

[34] This Freudian approach is most commonly associated with Elisabeth Kübler-Ross (1969, 2005), and
often appears in grief counseling texts (e.g. Worden 1982, 1991). However, nowadays "grief work" is often
just the generic label for any process of resolving grief; see e.g. Field 2008, 114–16.

[35] For discussion and review of the "grief work" paradigm, see Stroebe and Stroebe 1991; Stroebe 1992–3;
Bonanno and Kaltman 1999, 760, 761–3; Stroebe and Schut 1999, 199–204; Stroebe and Schut 2001; Field
2008, 114–16.

on their pain have better grief outcomes—for example, suffer less depression—than those who do not make such a focus.[36] This is because the experience of grief is highly individualized, and although it has long been assumed that those who avoid confronting and "working through" their pain must be only hiding, delaying, and perhaps worsening their inevitable distress, the experimental evidence has not borne this assumption out.[37] Likewise, although it has long been assumed that expressing one's painful emotions, verbally or in writing, is a necessary and useful part of grief resolution, this assumption lacks any conclusive support.[38] And even among those who *do* directly confront the pain of bereavement, those who make that pain their focus actually have poorer grief outcomes than those whose confrontations are balanced with more positive emotions.[39]

The second major problem for the "grief work" approach, and the one that is especially relevant for our purposes, is that there is no reason to think that detachment from the deceased should be the goal of grief resolution in the first place. Now, the disagreement here is not over whether the bereaved should continue to be attached to the deceased as if the deceased were *still alive*. Rather, the greatest challenge to the "grief work" approach is the fact that it can be positively healthy for the bereaved to form a continuing attachment to the deceased as a loved one *now absent*. Psychologist Nigel P. Field argues that, contrary to the Freudian "grief work" approach, the question of the bereaved person's attachment to the deceased is not a one-dimensional question—whether to relinquish that attachment or not. Rather, it is multi-dimensional, a matter of separating what should be relinquished—namely, the unrealistic goal of maintaining the relationship as it was—on the one hand, and on the other retaining that relationship in a way that does not interfere with getting on with life.[40] In other words, so far from being the problem, close attachment can be a big part of the solution.[41] In the remainder of this chapter I explain how.

2.2 *"The next figure in the dance"*

Lewis records his grief over the loss of his wife, and he records its resolution too. When we lose someone we dearly love, Lewis writes, at first "we think of this as love cut short; like a dance stopped in mid-career or a flower with its head unluckily snapped

---

[36] Stroebe and Stroebe 1991; Bonanno 2001; Archer 2008, 52–3.

[37] Stroebe and Schut 2001; Bonanno et al. 2008.

[38] Bonanno and Kaltman 1999, 771; Pennebaker et al. 2001; Stroebe et al. 2002; Archer 2008, 53–6. On the benefits of written expression in stressful contexts besides bereavement, see Pennebaker 1997.

[39] See Stroebe 1992–93, 24; see also Bonanno 2001; Nolen-Hoeksema 2001.

[40] See Field 2008; see also Rando 1993.

[41] On this point see Worden 1991, 87; Rando 1992–3;1993; Stroebe 1992–93, 32–3; Attig 1996; 2000; 2001, 46; Bonanno and Kaltman 1999, 764–5, 770; Shaver and Tancredy 2001, 81–2; Weiss 2001; 2008, 36–7; Fraley and Bonanno 2004, 887; Field 2008, 116–19; Mikulincer and Shaver 2008, 94–5. It is worth noting that on this point, Worden has revised his task-based approach between his 1982 and 1991 editions.

off—something truncated and therefore, lacking its due shape." But Lewis comes to reconsider:

I wonder. . . . [B]ereavement is a universal and integral part of our experience of love. It follows marriage as normally as marriage follows courtship or as autumn follows summer. It is not a truncation of the process but one of its phases; not the interruption of the dance, but the next figure. We are "taken out of ourselves" by the loved one while she is here. Then comes the tragic figure of the dance in which we must learn to be still taken out of ourselves though the bodily presence is withdrawn, to love the very Her, and not fall back to loving our past, or our memory, or our sorrow, or our relief from sorrow, or our own love. (Lewis 1976, 58–9)

Having been Joy's partner and lover is part of Lewis's being, and from this a couple of points follow. First, now that Joy is gone Lewis has to begin a *new* life for himself: he cannot keep that part of his being intact by wallowing in the past or living a lifelong, Victorian sorrow (Lewis 1976, 65).[42] The point, after all, is to move on to the *next* figure in the dance, not to get stuck in the figure before. To take on his grief itself as his identity—the identity of "Joy's widower"—would be a kind of suicide, truly the end of the man who is Joy's lover.

The second point is that, as Lewis rightly perceives, his new life cannot begin *from nowhere*. The end of his life with Joy means beginning a new life without her, but that new life is best understood as the natural next step in the long process of being Joy's lover—the next figure in *that dance*. Now, Lewis confesses that it did occur to him to make a clean break, to go back to his earlier bachelor life and thus to "a past kind of happiness, my pre-[Joy] happiness" (1976, 69–70). However, he immediately realizes that that too would be to deny who he now is:

[T]he invitation seemed to me horrible. The happiness into which it invited me was insipid. I find that I don't want to go back again and be happy in that way. It frightens me that a mere going back should even be possible. For this fate would seem to me the worst of all; to reach a state in which my years of love and marriage should appear in retrospect a charming episode— like a holiday—that had briefly interrupted my interminable life and returned me to normal, unchanged. And then it would come to seem unreal—something so foreign to the usual texture of my history that I could almost believe it had happened to someone else. Thus [Joy] would die to me a second time; a worse bereavement than the first. Anything but that.

Did you ever know, dear, how much you took away with you when you left? You have stripped me even of my past, even of the things we never shared. (pp. 70–1)

Lewis's efforts to recover, then, are shaped by a pair of perspectives: on the one hand, the need to move on to what lies ahead, in order to keep himself intact; and on the other, the need to deal with what lies behind, also in order to keep himself intact. Between those two perspectives, Lewis finds there is only one option: to create a new self *out of* the old self, finding the best way to go on as the person he has

---

[42] On the sorrow of Queen Victoria, see e.g. Marris 1974, 28; Parkes 1987, 126.

become—a person shaped by both his love for Joy and her death. What that meant for Lewis on a daily basis he does not share. But it seems clear that Lewis found a healthy way to cope, lifelong, with his grief.

Since change is inevitable, so too is the need to adapt to it. But adaptation must also preserve a sense of continuity by which one's existence can remain recognizable as one's own.[43] Or to put it simply, coping is "both conservative and revolutionary" (Neimeyer 2001, 266). These are the two perspectives that Lewis discovers he needs to balance: staying in the "dance" while moving to the next "figure." As it turns out, he was ahead of his time.

2.3 Good grief

The idea of balancing these "conservative" and "revolutionary" perspectives is the foundation of Margaret Stroebe and Henk Schut's highly influential "Dual Process Model" of grief resolution (Stroebe and Schut 1999). On this model, successful grief resolution is the result of a balance of attention given to these two perspectives within grief, or what Stroebe and Schut call a pair of "orientations." In the loss-orientation, the bereaved is involved in coming to terms with the loss and especially with the irrevocable change in the relationship with the deceased. It is here that one may confront one's emotions and attitudes about the deceased, and undertake the work of accepting that the deceased is gone for ever. On the other hand, in the restoration-orientation, the bereaved focuses on coping with new tasks, roles, and in general the new reality that has been created by the departure of the deceased. Here one can explore new possibilities, do new things, acquire new skills, and form new relation-ships, in the process sometimes gaining some needed distance from the more painful tasks of the loss-orientation.

The need for this distance illustrates a further point: just as important as these two orientations is the process of "oscillation" between them, so as to balance attention between mourning one's loss and exploring one's future.[44] The process of oscillation is dynamic, insofar as progress made within one orientation can also help one progress within the other. For instance, finding that one is capable of completing new tasks can help one feel less dependent on the deceased, and likewise gains in understanding one's new relationship with the deceased can help one envision new relationships and projects.

Balancing the two orientations is critical to successful grief resolution. There is considerable evidence suggesting that too great a focus on either orientation makes a

---

[43] See Marris 1974, 5–6, 19–22. Neurologist Oliver Sacks (1985, chap. 2) tells of a patient who remembered being in the Navy during World War II as if it were yesterday (literally!) but had no awareness of the intervening decades. There is a very real sense in which it was just not clear who he was, or the extent to which he was anyone at all. In fact, when shown his gray-headed reflection in a mirror, he became extremely upset and quite unsure who he was, because the present image was severed from the past he remembered for himself.

[44] Stroebe and Schut 1999, 115–16.

good grief outcome less likely.[45] Moreover, a plausible hypothesis put forward by the Dual Process Model is that failures to resolve grief can be understood as resulting from a breakdown of oscillation and a fixation on one orientation or the other.[46] Consider first a fixation on the restoration-orientation. Such a fixation involves the denial or suppression of grief, and evidence suggests "that it may be impossible to avoid grieving unremittingly without severe costs to mental and physical well-being" (Stroebe and Schut 1999, 216). For instance, one study found a greater correlation between suppression and increased distress among widowers than among widows in a rather "traditional" society, arguably because men in such societies are more likely to be distracted by work and are generally expected to grieve less. If that is so, then it may be that these widowers were more prone to distress because their avoidance of grief emotions was more extreme.[47] This hypothesis is supported by findings that widowers can benefit from confronting the pain of loss, even if this means ignoring social expectations.[48]

At the other extreme is fixation on the loss-orientation. This is typically character-ized by ruminating on negative feelings and memories, which has been shown to make grief more severe and in some cases complicated. Although it is within the loss-orientation that the pain of grief is primarily confronted, such confrontation can be detrimental unless balanced with positive emotion, as in the case of rumination.[49] In fact, even though confiding in others has been shown to predict better physical health in the outcome of grief, ruminating has been shown to predict just the opposite.[50] Consequently, balance between the two orientations is crucial in order for the loss-orientation to be effective.[51] This hypothesis is also consistent with evidence that, while parents bereaved by sudden infant death syndrome are very likely to seek for a meaning to attach to the loss, they are not very likely to find it, and those who give up the search for meaning, or perhaps find something positive in the loss instead, show lower levels of distress.[52]

It is important to note that while a proper balance of these two perspectives is critical to successful grief resolution, there is no single balance that is the proper one in every case. For one thing, we have seen that attachments to the deceased vary greatly from one bereaved person to the next, and so it is not surprising that a proper balance for one person may give more weight to one of the orientations than that orientation would have in a proper balance for someone else.[53] For another, there is much evidence—and it is hardly surprising—that grief is experienced differently in different cultures and

---

[45] See ibid. 216.   [46] Ibid. 217–18.
[47] Ibid. 480–1.   [48] Stroebe 1992–3, 34.
[49] Stroebe and Schut 2001, 63–4, 65–6; see also Bonanno and Kaltman 1999, 766.
[50] Stroebe 1992–3, 24, discussing Pennebaker and O'Heeron 1984.
[51] Bonanno and Kaltman 1999, 766–7, 771; Stroebe and Schut 1999, 220; Stroebe and Schut 2001, 64–5, 67.
[52] Davis 2001, 147–8.
[53] See e.g. Stroebe and Schut 2001; Bonanno et al. 2008.

even between genders.[54] Furthermore, ways of coping with grief that may be pathological in one person or circumstance—for instance, a sense of the lost person's presence—may be quite appropriate in another.[55]

However, even if the balance might look different in different places, why should coping with grief involve balancing these two perspectives in the first place? The answer is this: the reason that bereavement is so distressful in the first place is that it is shocking in both a backward-looking and a forward-looking way. In other words, bereavement is what psychologists call a "psychosocial transition." As we saw in the previous chapter, a psychosocial transition involves three things: (1) a change in one's usual circumstances ("life space") which (2) interrupts the attitudes and assumptions that form the backdrop against which one makes and carries out plans (one's "assumptive world"), in such a way that (3) one is forced to reconsider one's possibilities for action and thus what one's life is to be about (the "boundaries of the self").[56] Now, the shock involved in bereavement is the interruption it causes in one's "assumptive world," in two ways. One, the loss of a loved one is itself highly disorienting, because it is the loss of a person whose presence had been the basis of one's plans and assumptions about one's practical possibilities. And two, the consequent changes in plans and possibilities require one to re-envision one's future. This two-fold shock, after all, is why the loss of a loved one that had been central to one's self-understanding is experienced as a loss of self.

Consequently, the process of coping with grief—that two-fold shock—involves integrating these two sets of changes into one's assumptive world, including one's sense of self. That is to say, grief resolution is the process of constructing a new assumptive world that both integrates the reality of one's loss and defines a new relationship to a world devoid of the deceased loved one.[57] And of course, these two parts of the process are what is meant by the loss-orientation and the restoration-orientation.

Therefore, our best understanding of the success of persons in secure attachments to cope with grief is that they activate both sides of the "oscillation" cycle successfully. Even though their identity is entwined with the deceased, persons in secure attachments are sufficiently assured of their own competence to avoid getting stuck in the loss-orientation, while also giving that orientation its due on account of the strength of their attachment.[58] Indeed, this seems true of Lewis's experience, who undeniably experienced the loss of Joy as a loss of self, but who also undeniably determined to reconstruct himself as continuing in a bond with Joy after her death.

And that is precisely the point: successfully coping does not require *removing* the deceased from one's identity. Rather than assuming that attachment is the problem and prescribing a regimen for detaching oneself from the deceased, psychologists now focus

---

[54] E.g. Stroebe and Stroebe 1991, 480–1; Stroebe 1992–3, 28–30 and references.

[55] Rando 1992–3, 44–5.

[56] The notion of psychosocial transitions was first introduced by Parkes 1971; see also 1975, 1987.

[57] See Field 2008, 117–18, summarizing Rando 1993.

[58] Mikulancer and Shaver 2008, 98–9.

on what a good outcome looks like, in terms of quality of life, and investigate the coping strategies of those who resolve grief well.[59] What they have found is that the best outcomes are balanced outcomes: giving the lost relationship a personal meaning that one can live with. In fact, for many people that balance involves creating a "continuing bond" with the deceased, as Lewis did with Joy.[60] Of course, sheer closeness with the deceased is not necessarily beneficial; as we saw above, some (non-secure) forms of closeness are dysfunctional, and in such cases weakening the bond may be the best compromise.[61] But for persons who are better able to balance the two perspectives on loss, often the best way forward is to *remain* close to the deceased, retaining the deceased as part of one's identity while arriving at a new understanding of *what part* of one's identity the deceased is now to be. Such persons do not sever their attachment to the deceased but "reorganize" it, exploring the meaning of the relation-ship while also exploring the new reality.[62] Psychologists Mario Mikulincer and Phillip R. Shaver put the point this way:

Psychologically successful mourners can integrate elements of their identity that were related to the lost relationship into a new reality, maintain a symbolic bond to the deceased while adjusting to real circumstances, and restore and even enhance their sense of security and well-being on the basis of both the continuing attachment bond with the deceased and new attachment bonds with living companions. (2008, 94)

2.4 Resolving complicated grief

What about complicated grief? In order to understand what role close attachment might play in the resolution of complicated grief, we need to know a bit more about what causes grief to become complicated. We saw in section 1 that there are all sorts of factors that contribute to grief complication: some of them are forms of psychological maladjustment on the part of the bereaved, and some are particularly difficult circum-stances surrounding the bereavement, including trauma in more extreme cases. All of these factors can complicate grief, but how do they come to do so?

As we have seen, grief resolution can be understood as the process of rebuilding one's assumptive world when it has been shocked by bereavement, by balancing a perspective on what one has lost and a perspective on the changes to come. Now, in cases of complicated grief, and especially traumatic grief, the shock to one's assumptive world is unusually great, and as a result, these shocking circumstances are extremely difficult to integrate into one's assumptive world.[63] Since that integration just is the process of coping with grief, coping breaks down and grief becomes complicated.

[59] On this operational approach to grief resolution, see e.g. Stroebe 1992–3; Field 2008, 115–16.

[60] On "continuing bonds" as part of grief resolution, see Bonanno and Kaltman 1999, 764–5, 770; Fraley and Shaver 1999; Attig 2001, 46; Mikulincer and Shaver 2008.

[61] Bonanno and Kaltman 1999, 770.

[62] See Mikulincer and Shaver 2008; see also Stroebe and Schut 1999; Stroebe, Schut, and Stroebe 2005.

[63] See Janoff-Bulman 1992; Bonanno and Kaltman 1999, 767; Parkes 2006, 33–4; Archer 2008, 51.

More specifically, Therese Rando, a specialist on complicated grief, argues that coping breakdowns in cases of complicated grief fall into two broad categories: failures to realize the loss fully, and failures to accept change in one's relation to the deceased (Rando 1992–3, 45). In the terms of the Dual Process Model, failing to realize the loss represents a failure to activate the loss-orientation, and failing to accept change a failure to activate the restoration-orientation. In that case, the general cause of complicated grief is the presence of any aspect of bereavement that frustrates balanced oscillation between the loss-orientation and the restoration-orientation.[64]

This frustration is especially pronounced in cases of traumatic grief, such as Charlie Fineman's. Charlie is utterly terrified of his past; he spends most of his time busying himself (riding his scooter, playing video games, shopping for records) in order to avoid thinking about his past, and when he cannot keep those thoughts at bay he goes into a destructive fit. What we see in Charlie's grief is the loss of voluntary control over oscillation, where periods of extreme avoidance of the loss-orientation are punctuated by invasive, uncontrollable, and even violent thoughts about the loss.[65] Because the traumatic events he has experienced are extremely difficult to integrate into his assumptive world, he is caught in cycles of compulsive rehearsal of the loss and attempts to suppress the memory of it altogether.[66]

For our purposes, there are a couple of things we should notice at this point. One is that normal grief and complicated grief are not different *kinds* of grief. Resolution in each case involves a similar process, and grief becomes complicated when extraordinary stressors complicate that process.[67] The other point, which follows from the first, is that detachment from the deceased is *not* part of the resolution of complicated grief, any more than in the case of normal grief. In both cases, what is needed is a successful rebuilding of one's background understanding of who one is and what one's life is about. Where the bond to the deceased is extremely close, the solution is not to sever that bond. On the contrary, the solution is to preserve that bond as part of one's identity while moving forward into a new life—dancing the *next* figure in the *same* dance.

To summarize: having an embodied conception of oneself is not only consistent with a good grief outcome, but may even be the key to the very *best* outcomes, as well as overall well-adjustment. So here's a piece of advice: the person with the best chance for a happy life is the one who can cope with change, finds people to love, and then loves them as if his happiness, his very identity, depended on them. On my view, doing all of that wisely is just what happiness *is*.

---

[64] See Stroebe and Schut 1999, 217.
[65] See Stroebe and Schut 1999, 218.
[66] See Archer 2008, 52.
[67] See Rando 1992–3, 44; Parkes 2006, 136; Mikulincer and Shaver 2008, 100–2; Weiss 2008, 35.

11

The Stoics' Case Against the Embodied Conception

I argued in the previous chapter that as long as they are secure with themselves, people who entwine their identity with the people they love are the most likely to bear grief well when they are bereaved of their loved ones. Perhaps that is all there is to say about grief: life just does make victims of us from time to time, and the best we can do is to pursue the greatest *vulnerable* happiness we can hope for. I have focused on certain sorts of losses, but of course we are victims of fortune in other ways as well. Consider tragic dilemmas, cases in which circumstances present us with a set of options every one of which is awful and regrettable. Think for instance of Agamemnon, faced with a choice between either sacrificing his daughter or else leading his army to ruin. In such cases, there may be reasons to take one option over another, but neither of them could be considered "the right thing to do"—neither of them could be an occasion for anything but sorrow and regret, even devastation, perhaps even a ruined life.[1]

But there is another way to think about our vulnerability: we are vulnerable to becoming not only victims but *perpetrators* of evil. From this perspective, our question becomes the following: if I cherish something as if my happiness depends on it, so that I will grieve sorely at its loss, mightn't I also be vulnerable to falling into wrongdoing in order to protect it?

In this chapter I want to look at both kinds of vulnerability—to loss and to wrongdoing—and how the dangers they involve bear on the reasonableness of the embodied conception of the self. In doing so, I shall concentrate on Cicero and especially Epictetus, in whom this focus is especially vivid. A central theme in Cicero's *Tusculan Disputations*, we shall see, is that in attaching to anything outside one's control as if one's happiness depended on it, one sets one's own trap and falls into wrongdoing. But it is Epictetus in the *Discourses* who offers such a sobering perspective on just *what* that wrongdoing is: it is abnegation of one's freedom and autonomy, and thus of one's very humanity. In a word, Cicero and Epictetus argue that attachments of that sort are ones that we cannot afford to make. And they both have a point.

---

[1] See Nussbaum 1986, chap. 2; Hursthouse 1999, chap. 3.

1 Cicero on being susceptible to grief

The idea from the previous chapter that some people "bear grief well" would do little to impress the Stoics. People grieve because they take bereavement to be a serious threat to happiness; but as Cicero tells us, the Stoics argue that this way of looking at bereavement—or for that matter, at any loss—is seriously mistaken (*TD* III.2–3, 13, 84).[2] In that case, there is no such thing as "grieving well" in the first place (III.7–10). On the contrary, the ideas that make us susceptible to grief should be pulled up like weeds by their very roots and fibers (III.13; cf. Epictetus, *Diss.* III.19). Here the Stoics do not mean by grief the visceral pangs and feelings of stress that follow bereavement; these, they agree, we can't do very much about.[3] But when the Stoics speak of grief as something to be uprooted, they mean not this "gut reaction" but grief as a complex response to loss, the sort of thing that leads to mourning and can be considered an outlook on one's situation.[4]

Cicero's discussion of Stoic views on grief comes in the third and fourth books of his *Tusculan Disputations*. There he focuses on two central Stoic theses about "distress," of which grief is a species (see IV.16). The first thesis is that distress is up to us and is mistaken; this is the topic of book III, where Cicero focuses on the cognitive basis of distress and its mistakenness.[5] Much of the discussion concerns the idea that distress is dependent on our attitudes and assumptions about events, not on the events themselves. In particular, he argues, grief stems not from bereavement per se, but from our attitudes about bereavement as making us seriously worse off, and in particular the judgment that grieving is the right thing to do.[6] However, on the Stoic view, these attitudes are mistaken: some circumstances are worth avoiding, but none is a threat to

---

[2] See also Galen, *Doctrines* 4.5.21–5.

[3] These feelings the Stoics called "pre-emotions" (*propatheiai*), which work on a visceral, biological level: see e.g. Aulus Gellius, *Attic Nights* 19.1.17–18 (= LS 65Y); Epictetus, *Diss.* I.12.20–1; *Handbook* 5; fragment 9. For discussion, see Annas 1992, 110 and references, esp. to *TD* III.83 and Seneca, *On Anger* II.1–4.; Inwood 1985, 176; Knuuttila 2004, 63–7; Graver 2007, chap. 4. It is presumably in this sense that Seneca (*Ep.* 9.3) says that the bereaved Stoic sage "feels his troubles" (for Seneca on grief, see Olberding 2005). Interestingly, the *propatheiai* raised an important in-house controversy as to whether there must be a sub-rational part of the soul, which "mainstream" Stoicism had denied; see Kidd 1971b; Nussbaum 1994, 373-4.

[4] See also Graver 2007, 183. However, Nancy Sherman has suggested to me that Epictetus sometimes seems to exhort us to insulate ourselves even against *propatheiai*, as when he says that one should train so as not to feel awe at the sight of a soldier's sword (*Diss.* IV.7.25–6).

[5] On this theme in Stoicism, see Engberg-Pedersen 1990b, chap. 7.

[6] See esp. Cicero, *TD* III.28–79, IV.14–15, 79–84; Seneca, *Ep.* 63; Epictetus, *Diss.* I.11.28–33, I.12.20–1, III.3.18–19; *Handbook* 5, 16; fragment 9. For discussion, see Inwood 1985, 147–53; Strange 2004. The Stoics call this aspect of *pathos* "freshness" (Cicero, *TD* III.55–61), which is both its being recent rather than "faded" and, more significantly, its "greenness" and vigor, such that its object is seen as worth getting worked up about (III.75; see also AD II.10b; Andronicus, *On Passions* 1 [= LS 65B]). It is this "greenness" of one's attitudes about loss that prompts distress, not the event or even its suddenness per se (Cicero, *TD* III.55–61, 67). For remarkably similar ideas about grief in modern psychology, see e.g. Bonanno and Kaltman 1999, 763; Stroebe and Schut 1999, 204–5.

happiness (III.36–7) or even a genuine evil (III.75–9, IV.60, 74); so there is never cause for distress (IV.58–64), and no duty to mourn (III.61–6, 76, 79).[7]

The second thesis, the focus of book IV, is that distress is necessarily excessive. Not surprisingly, these two theses are connected: it is because distress is part of a deeply mistaken outlook on the world that it is necessarily excessive.[8] Because grief, like distress generally, is out of line with right reason, Cicero says, it is a "disorder"—*pathos* in Greek, *perturbatio* in Latin—"and contrary to nature" (*TD* IV.11). In that case, there can no more be a correct way to grieve than there can be a correct way to refuse to obey reason (IV.39).

Obviously, the Stoics are correct to say that any emotional response that is deeply mistaken has gone too far already. Imagine someone who hoards junk that he finds it emotionally difficult to part with, thinking it is somehow important to his well-being. Clearly such a person has a deeply mistaken outlook on his well-being, and the emotions that go with that outlook are seriously unhealthy. In a similar way, the Stoics say that emotions that are part of a deeply mistaken outlook have *already* gone too far— they are by their very nature unreasonable (*TD* IV.23–4), dangerous (IV.41–2), and therefore excessive (see IV.38–40).

But of course, the big question is whether *grief* is one of those emotions—whether it really is mistaken, every time and in every form.[9] The received view reconstructs the Stoics' argument for this as follows: virtue is sufficient for happiness, therefore virtue is the only good and vice the only bad; and that is why it is mistaken to grieve a loss as if it were bad.[10] Cicero is sometimes said to argue this way at *TD* V.40–1,[11] where he says that because it is important for "the happy man to be safe, impregnable, fenced and fortified," we must deny the Aristotelian claim that there are goods besides virtue. Now, the received view takes this to say that virtue is sufficient for happiness, understanding "fortified" here to mean fortified against any kind of loss that could threaten happiness. But there are at least two serious problems with this way of taking

---

[7] Although the Stoics urge us to eradicate such emotions, they are not naïve about how difficult that would be: different people are predisposed towards or away from certain kinds of emotional patterns, e.g. naturally hot-headed or bold (Cicero, *TD* IV.27–8; DL VII.111; AD II.10e); emotions become habitual over time (Cicero, *TD* IV.23–33; DL VII.115; AD II.10e; Galen, *Doctrines* 4.5.21–5 [= LS 65L], 5.2.3–7 [= LS 65R]); and (*pace* Sherman 2005, chap. 7) the Stoics seem to have appreciated the importance of social support: e.g. Epictetus' *Discourses* show daily work with developing students, Cicero's treatises are written as dialogues addressed to friends, and of course there are Seneca's many letters to friends.

[8] It is important to note that the Stoics consider emotions "excessive" insofar as they are mistaken; they do not mean that they are "overpowering," as if a passionate part of the soul overpowered a rational part. Cf. Inwood 1985, 158–9, 167–73; Long and Sedley 1987, 422; Knuuttila 2004, 59.

[9] Indeed, recall two things we saw in Chapter 8: one, distress is one of the cardinal *pathē* (*TD* III.25) and grief is a species or form of distress (IV.16–19; AD II.10b); and two, there is no "good affection" or *eupatheia* that is a counterpart of distress (*lupē*). So neither grief nor anything even *like* it is an acceptable reaction to loss.

[10] Nussbaum (1994, 361, 362–3) takes this sort of argument to be the basis, not only of the Stoics' thesis that grief is mistaken (p. 390), but also of their theory of the emotions in general (p. 367). See also Brennan 2005a, 121–2; Sellars 2006, 111; N. White 2006, 97. I argue against the received view in a forthcoming paper.

[11] Brennan 2005a, note to page 122. See also *TD* V.28.

Cicero's argument. One, Cicero usually argues in precisely the opposite direction: the thesis that virtue is the only good is a *premise* that supports the sufficiency thesis as a *conclusion*.[12] And two, reconstructed in this way, the argument is utterly hopeless. Suppose we were to challenge the standard Stoic line that grief is mistaken. On the received view, the Stoics' response is to remind us that virtue is the only good—*because otherwise* virtue would not be sufficient for happiness. Nonplussed, we would presumably reply, "But virtue *isn't* sufficient for happiness." Now, on the received view, the Stoics will answer: "But it must be—*because otherwise* we would be vulnerable to loss!" Well, what should we say to *that*? Vulnerability comes at a price, but why should we think it's just a deal-breaker?[13] Surely *this* is not the idea that kept the Stoics in the sufficiency debate for a few hundred years—a debate that by and large they were *winning*.

Fortunately, a better reconstruction of the Stoics' case against grief is already there in *Tusculan Disputations* itself. The Stoics were indeed keen to make the happy person "fortified," but as Cicero makes clear in *TD* III, this fortification was against any possible *degradation of character*: those beliefs that make us prone to grieve also obstruct our ability to act virtuously, so the happy person must be fortified against those degrading beliefs. Cicero summarizes no fewer than seven Stoic arguments for this claim:

1) If one is susceptible to distress, then one will not be disdainful of bad circumstances but will instead be susceptible to excessive fear, dejection, and despair. Each of these is incompatible with courage. But practical wisdom (*sapientia*) requires courage. Therefore, practical wisdom is incompatible with susceptibility to distress (III.14–15).

2) A brave person must be "great-souled" (*esse magni animi*), and a great-souled person must disdain bad fortune. No one can disdain what distresses him; therefore, courage is incompatible with susceptibility to distress. Since practical wisdom requires courage, practical wisdom is incompatible with susceptibility to distress (III.15).

3) A mind upset by distress is unable to do its proper work. Since its proper work is the use of right reason (*ratione bene uti*) and practical wisdom is always ready to carry out that work, practical wisdom is incompatible with distress (III.15).

4) A temperate person must stand firm in all circumstances, and thus must remain calm, and therefore must not be susceptible to distress. Since practical wisdom requires temperance, practical wisdom is incompatible with susceptibility to distress (III.18).

---

[12] See the texts cited at the beginning of Chapter 8. See also *TD* V.33–4, and even V.83 which Nussbaum (1994, 362–3) cites in favor of her reading.

[13] Indeed, proponents of the received view go on to reject the Stoic position on *exactly* these grounds. See Brennan 2005a, 122; see also Nussbaum 1994, 399–401.

5) Susceptibility to distress makes one also susceptible to anger, but practical wisdom is incompatible with anger (III.19).[14]

6) An angry person desires and enjoys the misfortunes of others (namely those he thinks have done him wrong), but practical wisdom is incompatible with this. Someone who is susceptible to distress is also susceptible to anger. Therefore, practical wisdom is incompatible with susceptibility to distress (III.19).

7) Susceptibility to distress makes one susceptible to pity (*misericordia*, pain at another's misfortunes), and pity makes one susceptible to envy (*invidentia*, pain at another's good fortune). But practical wisdom is incompatible with envy. Therefore, practical wisdom is incompatible with susceptibility to distress (III.20–1).

"This," Cicero says, "is how the Stoics state the case" (III.22), and he concludes from all of these considerations that susceptibility to distress makes one prone to vice (IV.75), diseased (III.22, 74), degraded, hideous, and craven (IV.35, 64, 68). It is in this spirit that he criticizes the Aristotelian Theophrastus, who held that happiness requires goods of the soul and body as well as external goods, for being "low" and "mean" in his thinking (V.24).[15]

Now, there are two things we should notice about these arguments. First, although Cicero is drawing on much fuller Stoic arguments, he presents them only in the quickest outline sketches, and in their highly compressed form we probably won't find them terribly convincing.[16] Of course, the Stoics do place a rather lower threshold on what counts as vice than we would—they say, after all, that there is no space between vice and complete virtue (DL VII.127). But of course that only pushes the question back: why put that threshold so low?[17]

But second, and more important at present, Cicero's discussion is highly revealing of the basic *structure* of the Stoic case against susceptibility to grief: an outlook on our happiness that would make us susceptible to grief is an outlook we cannot live with, because such an outlook is *ethically perilous*.[18] We cannot *both* hold on to the assumptions that make grief seem a reasonable response to loss, the Stoics argue, *and* be ever

---

[14] See *TD* IV.48–55, 77–8; and of course Seneca, *On Anger*, esp. I.2, II.5.

[15] On Theophrastus, see Chapter 5.

[16] Nor does he do much to unpack or buttress those arguments in *TD*; on the contrary, he takes the point that grief is a defect of character as having been made, and focuses in book III on the voluntariness of grief and in book IV on the awfulness of such defects.

[17] Indeed, as Graver (2007, 110–12, 116–22) reminds us, the Stoics would say that everyone who is not a sage, and thus everyone who is susceptible to distress, is "insane"—not in a medical sense, but in the sense of being prone to being "carried away" (in Chrysippus' metaphor: Galen, *Doctrines* 4.2.9–18) and forgetting themselves (see e.g. AD II.5b13).

[18] See also Sorabji 2000, 169–84, who argues that although the Stoics make virtue the only good in order to guarantee the tranquility of the virtuous person, this is because the loss of that tranquility is ethically perilous, as e.g. when love leads to jealousy and hate in one who fails to regard the beloved as indifferent with respect to happiness.

ready to live with practical wisdom and emotional soundness. Think of their view this way: once a person has made something important for his *individual* fulfillment that he cannot control, he is susceptible to grief over its loss—and that comes at the expense of *human* fulfillment. And that leaves exactly two options: either downsize the boundaries of the self to include only the faculty of choice that makes one human, or else upsize those boundaries and compromise that very humanity. Their argument against grief, then, is an argument *for* the formalized conception of the self.

So the structure of the Stoics' arguments is extremely intriguing, but so far we have not seen much in the way of its central contention: namely that susceptibility to grief *is* susceptibility to degradation. Why think so? That is where Epictetus comes in.

2 Epictetus' objection: an overview

Epictetus' argument is surprisingly simple: since people will do what they judge necessary to preserve their happiness, a person who chooses to make things outside his control important for his happiness thereby turns those things into tools by which he can be manipulated. I begin in this section with an overview of Epictetus' broad approach, before turning in the next section to the specific premises of his argument. Throughout, I shall move between Epictetus' texts and Tom Wolfe's arresting novel *A Man in Full*, which is a deliberate illustration of exactly how, according to Epictetus, one's attachments to externals can become a source of manipulative power for others.

If there is one theme that binds the *Discourses* together (as well as the shorter *Handbook*), it is this: one must learn above all else that one's happiness lies entirely in doing well those things that are completely within one's control to do. In life, Epictetus says,

this is the chief business: distinguish things and weigh them one against another, and say, 'Externals are not within my power, choice is. Where shall I seek good and evil? Within; in what is my own.' But in regard to what belongs to others, never use the words good, or evil, or benefit, or injury, or any word of that kind.[19]

As we saw in Chapter 7, for Epictetus everything is divided into two groups where happiness is concerned: the power of choice, and everything else. It is only in how I exercise my choice—in how I do the one thing it is within my power to do—that any good or benefit, or evil or injury, is to be found:

Where lies the good? In choice. Where evil? In choice. Where lies that which is neither good nor evil? In things that lie outside the sphere of choice.[20]

This is a most radical view, and it is one that Epictetus' students are constantly forgetting—not surprisingly, since (as he is fully aware) it clearly flies in the face of our ordinary beliefs. Why then does Epictetus hold such a startling view? This view just

---

[19] *Diss.* II.5.4–5. On "choice" in Epictetus, see Chapter 7.
[20] *Diss.* II.16.1; see also III.10.18; *Handbook* 19.

is the formalized conception of the self, and Epictetus' reason for embracing it is simply this: you will do what you think your happiness requires, and so if you think your happiness requires things that you cannot control, then you will become a target for coercion by anyone who does have control over those things, and even by circumstances themselves. In other words, pinning your happiness on anything outside your control means abandoning the very autonomy that is crucial to your humanity, and therefore to your real prospects for human happiness.

Epictetus illustrates this point with many stories. One of these is the myth of Medea, who murdered her two young sons to spite their father Jason for his betrayal of her. Even this most outrageous act, Epictetus says, is really just a case of her doing what she thinks is her best option (*Diss.* I.28.7; II.17.19–22). As long as Medea thinks that revenge is her best option, there is no other course for her to seek; and so as long as she has the attitudes she has about her husband and her situation—that is, about these "externals"—there is nothing else for her to do, and in this way she affords her circumstances a terrible control over her actions.

Another story concerns a Stoic conversing with a man who has been summoned by Nero to perform in one of his degrading stage plays (*Diss.* I.2.12–18). Surprisingly, the Stoic tells the man that he may as well go ahead and do as Nero asks: since he has already begun to consider it, weighing up the value of things outside his control, he has already given Nero all the power over him that Nero needs.

This central theme in Epictetus' lectures is depicted with particular vividness in *A Man in Full*. The novel's central character is Charlie Croker, an aging commercial real estate developer in Atlanta whose empire is on the verge of collapse owing to a debt of over half a billion dollars (in mid-nineties dollars), money he had used to build a massive office building—Croker Concourse, named in an apparent fit of megalomania—that now sits mostly empty. Charlie's creditors have begun seizing his assets and are moving in closer. What hits Charlie the hardest is their threat to seize his country plantation home—complete with its multi-million-dollar horses and private jets, but mainly with all the other things that prop up Charlie's perception of himself as a "real man," a man of power and wealth, but most of all an old-time brand of American deep-South masculinity. In fact, the book's title is taken from a line in a folk song passed down through generations of the plantation's workers about a mythical "Cap'n Charlie," whose surname, coincidentally, was also Croker: "Charlie Croker was a man in full / He had a back like a jersey bull." So the workers call Croker "Cap'n Charlie" too, and appropriately enough Charlie is also particularly proud of the massive back he developed in his university days as a football star. It is to this plantation that Charlie regularly invites potential clients, hoping to win their business by putting them under the spell of the "real man" world of the plantation, with its quail hunts, thoroughbred studs, and general masculine atmosphere of the antebellum South, a spell by which Charlie himself is irretrievably charmed. It is here on his plantation, of all places in the world, that Charlie most feels that he, Cap'n Charlie, is a man in full. And it is all of this, and everything else too, that Charlie now stands on the brink of losing.

So when a young lawyer comes to Charlie and tells him that there are powerful people just waiting to pressure his creditors to restructure Charlie's debt, Charlie is ready to listen. In exchange for this generous assistance, the lawyer explains, Charlie would have to make a statement on behalf of the lawyer's client, whose potentially explosive case is of particular interest to the mayor of Atlanta, among other powerful persons. The trouble is, Charlie finds this client despicable, and even worse, to speak on his behalf would be, in Charlie's eyes, to betray a friend and business associate whose daughter it is that the lawyer's client is accused of having sexually assaulted. For a while Charlie tries to avoid the problem, going in for a knee operation he had been putting off and consequently being laid up in bed, incapacitated. But eventually the lawyer and the city's power-brokers corner him, and ultimately he has no choice but to make his statement, since otherwise he will lose everything he owns, and with it everything that makes him the man he is.

Charlie's predicament is exactly the sort of predicament that Epictetus has in mind, and it is about people like Charlie that Epictetus wrote,

If I place value on my body, I have given myself up as a slave; if on my miserable property, I am a slave likewise; for I immediately show to my own detriment how I may be taken. (*Diss.* I.25.23–4)

By pinning his happiness on things outside his control, Charlie announces to everyone the means by which they can take him. As long as he takes his happiness to lie in those things, there is nothing else he can do: he has no choice but to do what others would manipulate him into doing. This puts him at the mercy of circumstance, and so Charlie becomes anxious, sleepless, and extremely depressed, as he stands to lose his entire fortune. Consequently, he is also at the mercy of anyone who might be able to work those circumstances against him, which is precisely why the city's power-brokers come after him in the first place.

This, according to Epictetus, is exactly what happens when we cling to things outside our control, and he says that a man's master is

[w]hoever has authority over the things that a man desires, to get them for him or to take them away. "Have we so many masters, then?"—We have. For, prior to all human masters, circumstances are our masters—and they are many. It necessarily follows, then, that those who have power over any of these circumstances are also our masters ... When we love and hate and fear these things, those who have the disposal of them must necessarily be our masters. (*Diss.* IV.1.59, 60)

And so Epictetus warns his students, again and again:

[He] who desires, or is averse to, things outside his own power can neither be faithful nor free, but must necessarily be changed and tossed back and forth with them; must necessarily too be subject to others, who can procure or prevent what he desires or wants to avoid. (I.4.19)

[W]hen you have subjected what is your own to externals, submit to slavery from that time forth, and do not struggle, and at one time be willing to be a slave, and at another time not willing, but simply, and wholeheartedly, be one or the other... [I]f you gape after externals you must necessarily be tossed up and down, according to the inclination of your master. And who is your master? He who has authority over any of the things that you strive to acquire, or want to avoid. (II.2.12–13, 25–6)

Be aware who your masters are, and as long as you allow them this hold on your body, follow everyone who is stronger than you are. (II.13.23)

[T]he value you place on an external object, whatever it may be, makes you subservient to another. (IV.4.1)[21]

Ultimately, this is the philosophical motivation for Epictetus' choice of the formalized over the embodied conception of the self. For if Epictetus is right and strong attachment to things outside the power of choice is incompatible with autonomy, then he identifies a most serious problem for the embodied conception of the self. On that view, a person—the very subject of whom happiness is either predicated or not—includes not only the power of choice that one controls, but also a number of things that one cannot control. But if people do what they think is their best option where their happiness is concerned, then their attachment to things outside their control becomes a means by which those people can be controlled. Such attachments, then, threaten one's autonomy—tragically, since autonomy is crucial to a person's humanity and thus to human happiness. In that case, for the sake of one's humanity and happiness one has reason not to allow anything outside one's control within the boundaries of the self. For the sake of one's happiness, one has reason to reject the embodied conception of the self and embrace the formalized conception.

Epictetus' case rests on three claims which we have glimpsed already: that people tend to do what they judge is their best option; that autonomy is crucial to our humanity and thus to our happiness; and that making happiness depend on things outside one's control threatens one's autonomy. Since Epictetus' case, if successful, would be a powerful argument against the embodied view of the self, we should examine each of these claims in more detail.[22]

3 Epictetus' argument

3.1 The first premise: doing what we think best

A crucial premise for Epictetus is the thesis that *people tend to do what they judge to be their best option*, "best" here being best *for the sake of their happiness*.[23] This thesis is not the vacuous claim that whatever a person does just has to be what he thought was his best

---

[21] On enslavement in Epictetus, see Stephens 2007, 14–15.

[22] While I do not pretend that this is the only argument that Epictetus offers (see Stephens 2007, 10–15, for discussion of others), I do believe that it is the main argument on which his others ultimately depend. However, I shall not argue for this strong claim here, and nothing in this chapter will hang on it.

[23] This is a point he takes himself to share with Socrates; see e.g. *Diss.* II.1.22–8, rehearsing the argument of Plato, *Gorg.* 466d–468e.

option. Rather, it comes down to a pair of substantive claims, one about the form of practical rationality and one about the role of practical rationality in human action.

The first claim about practical rationality is this: part of the very form of practical rationality is choosing to do what one judges to be one's best option. This is surely correct. The act of doing what one judges to be the best option calls for no explanation, whereas ignoring one's judgment about the best option is as clear a lapse of practical rationality as there can be. Of course, the claim as I have put it here is very weak, mainly because it says nothing about criteria for judging one option to be better or worse than another. But of course Epictetus believes that practical rationality, in virtue of its very form, is such as to choose what one judges to be the best option where one's final end, eudaimonia, is concerned.

As we saw above, Epictetus says that we can observe such practical rationality even in the case of Medea. Even her outrageous act of infanticide, Epictetus argues, was ultimately a case of her doing what she thought was her best option. As such, he argues, Medea's act is not crazed or irrational, but an ordinary case of practical rationality: *given* her priorities, she arrived at a *correct* judgment of her best option, and it is precisely that option that she chose.

It was because she was unable to endure [not getting what she desired] that Medea came to murder her own children, the action of a noble spirit in this regard at least, that she had a proper impression of what it means to be disappointed in one's desire. (*Diss.* II.17.19)

Of course, as Epictetus points out, Medea's judgment was also deeply incorrect in the sense that it began from the wrong priorities, and more realistic priorities would have led her to a completely different judgment about her options:

This is the error of a soul endued with great vigour. For she knew not where the power to do what we wish lies; that it is not to be acquired from outside ourselves, nor by altering or disarranging things. (II.17.21)

If we insist on calling her "irrational," it must be on the grounds that she was mistaken in the substance of her beliefs about what her happiness required. She made no mistake at all in perceiving what follows from those beliefs.

We observe the very same practical rationality in Charlie Croker as well. While Charlie recovers from his knee operation, he encounters Connie, a young in-home therapy worker who has recently begun trying to live his life according to Epictetus' teachings as he understands them. Charlie asks Connie in the abstract about a dilemma such as his, and Connie replies that Epictetus would consider it "selling out" to let others manipulate one in order to avoid some catastrophe (reading out passages from *Diss.* I.2). Charlie finds this a fine sentiment in the abstract, but in real life he is terrified by the very vivid prospect of total bankruptcy, and so he asks Connie what Epictetus could possibly have to say about a catastrophe like that:

"This is all very noble, in the abstract, all this your man is saying, but what does it have to do with real life? Let's think about real life for a second. Let's think about a situation in which you lose everything... you *lose everything!* You see what I'm saying? You lose *everything*, the house where you live, your income, your cars—*everything*. You're out on the street. You don't know where your next meal's coming from. What good do a lot of high-sounding ideals mean then?"

The boy said, "Many of Epictetus' disciples asked him that exact same thing, and you know what he told them?"

"No, what?"

"Have you ever seen an old beggar?" The kid's eyes were boring right into him.

"You're asking *me*?"

"Yes."

"Sure I have," said Charlie, "plenty of them."

"See? *They've* gotten by," said the boy. "*They've* managed to get food to eat, 365 days a year, probably. *They're* not starving. What makes you think they can all find food, and you wouldn't be able to?"

"What kinda consolation is that supposed to be? I'd rather die than go around with a cup in my hand."

The boy smiled, and his eyes brightened. "Epictetus talks about exactly that, Mr. Croker. He says, 'You're not afraid of starving, you're afraid of losing face.'... And yet if it happened, it wouldn't be nearly as bad as you think, Mr. Croker."[24]

Connie's point is that the reason Charlie would rather die than go bankrupt has nothing to do with survival and everything to do with pride. In fact, this is just what Charlie had said at the beginning of their conversation about his dilemma, when he had asked Connie this question:

"[W]hat does Epictetus have to say about bankruptcy?—or is that something too mundane for a philosopher to think about?"

"Not too mundane for Epictetus, Mr. Croker. One place he says, 'You are all nervous and you can't sleep at night for fear you're going to run out of money. You say, "How will I even get enough to eat?" But what you are really afraid of is not starvation but the prospect of not having a cook or somebody to wait on you at the dinner table or somebody to take care of your clothes and your shoes and the laundry and make up the beds and clean up the house. In other words, you are afraid you may no longer be able to lead the life of an invalid.' "[25]

And that is exactly what Charlie is afraid of. Charlie thinks that he cannot live without his servants and minions and private jets and racehorses and mansions and plantation, not because he would literally die without them but because no life without them would be a life *for him*. In other words, Charlie's worry is not that there might not be life after bankruptcy but that bankruptcy would destroy the Charlie Croker that he takes himself to be. So Charlie is in the same situation as Medea was: he may well be

---

[24] Wolfe 1998, 685, 686, italics in original. See *Diss.* III.26.6–7.

[25] Ibid. 682. See *Diss.* III.26.21–3; see also I.9.8. This makes a great impact on Charlie, who had knee surgery precisely so as to be bedridden and thus duck the lawyer and the mayor.

mistaken about how he weighs up good and bad options, but he makes no mistake at all about what follows from how he weighs his options up. In that sense, in Charlie as in Medea we see a "noble spirit" and "great vigor": he understands what his best option is *given* the things that he cares about. And Medea is worth keeping in mind here for another reason too. For Epictetus, the problem with someone like Charlie is not that he wants *so much*; after all, what did Medea want but for her husband not to run out on her? The problem is *how* he wants it—for the sake of his very happiness, *this* happiness of *this* Charlie Croker.

Epictetus' second point about practical rationality is this: because doing what one judges one's best option is part of the very form of action that is intelligible as having been done for reasons, doing what one judges one's best option is utterly typical of creatures like us. This, of course, is why akrasia is such a difficult phenomenon to understand: how is it that doing what one judges one's best option could be *both* part of the very form of human action *and* something that humans apparently fail to do when acting? Famously, the Stoics denied that there is any such thing as akrasia (e.g. *Diss.* I.28.6), arguing that the soul is a single power—reason—whereas akrasia would require another power in the soul to oppose reason.[26] Consequently, for the Stoics this claim about practical rationality was an absolutely universal principle of human action: people always, and necessarily, do what they judge to be their best option.[27] According to the Stoics, people are "irrational" only in the sense of being substantively mistaken about what their best option is, as in the case of Medea or Charlie Croker, but never in the sense of failing to do what they judge to be their best option (I.28.7–8). For this reason, Marcus Aurelius once wrote,

Whoever you meet, say to yourself at once: "What are his doctrines concerning good and bad things?" For if he has doctrines of a certain sort concerning pleasure and pain and their sources, and fame and its absence, and death and life, I shall not think it remarkable or strange if he acts as he does. I shall remember that he is *compelled* to act in this way.[28]

However, Epictetus' objection does not require anything as robust as the impossibility of akrasia and the necessity of doing what one judges one's best option (or being

---

[26] On this point the Stoics explicitly rejected Plato's view (*Rep.* IV, 439e–440a), explaining apparent akrasia as vacillation between impulses and indecision about to which impulse to give one's assent (Plutarch, *On Moral Virtue* 446f–447a [= IG II-119]); this led to a long debate with Platonists: see Galen, *Doctrines* 3.1.25 (= LS 65H), 4.3.2–5 (= LS 53K), 4.4.16–18, 24–5 (= IG II-118), 4.5.21–5 (= LS 53M), 5.1.4, 4.3.2 (= IG II-120), 5.2.49–5.3.8 (= IG II-121), 5.6.34 (= LS 65I); see also Inwood 1985, 132–9; Cooper 1999, chap. 21. Interestingly, this debate often focused on Medea: see Galen, *Doctrines* 3.3.13–24; Epictetus, *Diss.* I.28 and II.17; see Gill 1983 for discussion.

[27] See esp. *Diss.* I.3.4; I.18.2; I.28.10; III.3.3–4; III.7.5, 33; *Handbook* 42.

[28] *Med.* VIII.14, italics added. The Greek word here rendered 'compelled' is *anangkazetai*. Cp. Epictetus, *Diss.* I.3.4: "of necessity (*anangkē*) each man must deal with each thing according to the opinion that he holds about it." This idea is central to the Stoics' analysis of anger, which they say is never justified since the target of one's anger is always someone who, like oneself, simply does what seems best to him. Such a person may be guilty of a mistake but not intentional wrongdoing, which is impossible. See *Diss.* I.28.1–10; *Handbook* 42; Seneca, *On Anger*.

"compelled" by that judgment, in Marcus' phrase). If, for instance, Charlie allows himself to be manipulated by others, this is precisely because his choice *is* practically rational and he *does* do what he judges his best option; it is neither here nor there whether human action is *necessarily* like this. Moreover, such a choice on Charlie's part is worrisome because it would stem from a *typical* and *successful* exercise of practical rationality, regardless of whether such exercises of practical rationality are what *always* happen. In the end, Epictetus' worry does not turn on whether or not practical rationality might *fail* to function normally. His worry is about precisely those cases in which practical rationality *succeeds*, showing a noble spirit with great vigor.

3.2 The second premise: externals and manipulation

Epictetus' second premise is a corollary of the first. Since humans tend to do what they judge to be their best option for preserving their happiness, *humans can be manipulated by whatever or whoever can dispose of things they take to be important for their happiness which they cannot control themselves.* This is how pressure comes to be exerted on Charlie Croker in the first place. It is taken as given that Charlie will do what he must to preserve his happiness, and it is taken as given that he judges keeping his property and social position to be necessary for his happiness. However, someone else is now in control of Charlie's property (and with it his social position), namely his creditors and those who can control them. The city's power-brokers therefore deduce that because they can control Charlie's property they can also control Charlie himself. And they are correct in that, *as long* as Charlie lacks control over something he cannot do without and is rational enough to see what follows from that.

Ironically, it is Charlie's very autonomy and rationality that get him into this trap. It is up to no one but Charlie to decide what sort of importance he will attach to his property and position; as Epictetus asks, rhetorically, "Can anyone compel you to have any opinion contrary to your will?" (*Diss.* II.6.21) And because he is rational Charlie can appreciate that he must do whatever it takes to preserve whatever he gives that importance. In such cases, Epictetus says that "choice compels choice":

Can anyone restrain you from assenting to truth? No one. Can anyone compel you to admit a falsehood? No one. You see, then, that you have in this area a choice incapable of being restrained or compelled or hindered. Well, is it any otherwise with regard to impulse and desire? What can overpower one impulse but another impulse? What can overpower desire and aversion but another desire and aversion? 'But if a person inflicts the fear of death upon me', someone says, 'he compels me.' No, it is not what is inflicted upon you that compels you, but your own judgement that it is better to do such and such a thing than to die. Here, again, you see it is your own judgement that compelled you—that is, *choice compelled choice.*[29]

---

[29] I.17.22–26, italics added. See also I.19.16; I.25.4; I.29.12; II.23.19; III.3.11–13; III.19.2; IV.4.23; IV.10.19; *Handbook* 9.

Consequently, the choice to bind one's happiness to something outside one's control ultimately leaves one trapped into doing whatever one must do to keep hold of it.[30] Now, this means that a person who binds his happiness only to the use of right reason is also compelled to do whatever he must do to keep hold of it, but of course what he is thereby "compelled" to do is only to act in accordance with right reason. Such a person cannot become anyone's tool—and that's the point.[31]

3.3 The third premise: autonomy, humanity, and happiness

Epictetus' third and final premise is one that we also encountered in Chapter 2, namely that *autonomy is crucial for our humanity and therefore our happiness.* As I argued there, a human being (unlike many other animals) needs to live a life that is genuinely his own, and thus needs the freedom to live by exercising practical reasoning, experiencing complex emotions, making choices, and living with the implications of his choices. Moreover, whatever human happiness is, it must be something distinctly human, and so must be the happiness of a creature that is such as to live autonomously.

Epictetus constantly reminds his students that to be human is to be capable of giving and withholding "assent" in accordance with norms we recognize, norms for believing and norms for acting. He describes this distinctly human process as "making use of one's impressions." For instance, one may have the impression now that such and such a thing is the case, or that such and such an act is the thing to do. Such impressions we may share with animals, Epictetus says, but what is distinctive of humanity is that we have the option—indeed, the burden—of choosing whether or not to agree that such and such really is the case or really is the thing to do.[32] Even our emotions, Epictetus argues, are not merely things that happen to us,[33] but a use of our impressions, that is, an agreement that a way it seems fitting to feel really is fitting. For instance, he says, it is not inevitable that one should fear even the sword of a tyrant's soldier: deadly things by themselves do not frighten us—we don't go around flinching at roof tiles, but they are deadly too. Rather, they frighten us only if we agree that they and death itself are things worth fearing (*Diss.* IV.7.1–4, 16, 25–8; cp. *Handbook* 5, 16).

Epictetus' constant reminders of our "making use of the impressions" serve to draw an important contrast between humans and all other things and creatures in the world. To use an image that Epictetus could not have used, we might say that all the world's contents can be divided into things that are input/output devices and things that are not. Input/output devices are things without reason that can therefore only react,

---

[30] As Long (2002, 217) puts the point, in such cases "we have hindered and constrained ourselves by our own voluntary abrogation of autonomy."

[31] So for Epictetus, being compelled is not a matter of whether one made a choice—one always makes a choice, on his view—but whether one chose in accordance with right reason. Cf. Bobzien 1998, 339–43. As Inwood 2005, 490, puts the point, for Epictetus the important point is not to be pushed around by any tyrant, even if that tyrant is one's own emotions or desires.

[32] See esp. *Diss.* I.6.10–17. See also, e.g., I.1.7; I.20.5; II.1.4; II.8.20; III.1.25–6. Christine Korsgaard (1996, 93) has well described this burden as "the problem of the normative."

[33] As the Greek *pathos* naturally suggests, deriving from *paschein,* "to suffer" or "undergo."

whether to physical forces or (in the case of sentient creatures) to sensible stimuli: exert pressure upon an object in this way, and the object moves in that way; present such-and-such a stimulus and the organism behaves thus-and-so. Such things lack autonomy—literally, a power of ruling themselves. Such things, like pencils or pack animals, are so constituted that input pressures or stimuli of one kind translate into output reactions of another kind, and it is for precisely this reason that they can be so readily used as instruments. With the possession of reason, however, a creature can *make use* of pressures and stimuli, a process that keeps input from merely, mechanically, translating into a kind of output. Their "output" can now be described appropriately as something *they do*.[34] Epictetus often calls this human possession a gift from Zeus, but as I said above, that gift is also a burden: because of that possession we cannot simply make do with sensory input and appetites, since we must always ask whether such impressions give us *reasons* to believe or to desire. This point Epictetus sometimes makes by noting that whereas most capacities comprehend just their own area of concern—carpentry, for instance, concerns building, but not when or whether to build—reason is a unique capacity that comprehends every capacity, including itself (*Diss.* I.1.1–6; II.23.7–15).

Now, for the Stoics themselves these claims about human autonomy are supported by their robust compatibilism about the will,[35] but we need not go that far to appreciate the force of Epictetus' point. That point is that the very form of human life is acting by way of responding to what reasons to act one takes oneself to have.[36] To abandon that autonomy is therefore to abandon that very form of life that makes our life distinctly human, and as such something awesome and precious. This sense of awe and preciousness is conveyed by Epictetus' constant references to reason as a gift from Zeus that is so liberating that Zeus himself cannot even take it back (e.g. *Diss.* I.6.40).

This third premise sinks in for Charlie Croker as well. Until his encounter with Connie, and through Connie Epictetus, Charlie had assumed with those putting pressure on him that he really had no choice: if it takes making a statement for Charlie to keep from losing everything and no attempts at evasion will succeed, then he has no choice but to make a statement. And as Connie points out, this is exactly the sort of predicament that Epictetus supposes his listeners are usually in—trapped. However, Epictetus argues that although people are often enslaved and trapped, no one is ever trapped *unless* he is complicit. Those who are pressuring Charlie can trap him only as long as Charlie remains attached to the things they threaten to take away from him, and that attachment is ultimately up to Charlie. As Epictetus would put the point, those who pressure Charlie can only present him with certain impressions, and it remains up to Charlie what use he will make of those impressions. Charlie is awestruck by the

---

[34] Not coincidentally, this broad contrast is one that Kant also makes at the beginning of *Groundwork* 1.

[35] See Dobbin 1998, 65–8.

[36] On this point, see Strawson 1962 and, following Strawson, Darwall 2006, chap. 1.

realization that even here, in the midst of all of this pressure and impending financial and social ruin, he might still have the option of living on his own terms.[37]

For Epictetus, that kind of realization is the first step towards living a life that can properly be called human—and not just on Epictetus' view of happiness, but on the very view of human happiness I have put forward in this book. Since happiness is something distinctly human, to surrender autonomy is to forgo anything that could count as human happiness.

3.4 The conclusion: happiness, autonomy, and things outside our control

This is where Epictetus' objection bares its teeth: since autonomy is crucial for our happiness (premise 3), it follows that *we must make nothing outside our control necessary for our happiness*. Or, as I have represented the argument here,

1) Humans tend to do what they judge to be their best option for preserving their happiness; so, as a corollary,
2) Humans can be manipulated by whatever or whoever can dispose of things they take to be important for their happiness which they cannot control themselves. But since
3) Human happiness requires autonomy, it follows that
4) Happiness requires that we not take things we cannot control to be important for our happiness.

And this is *exactly* what Epictetus tells us:

You must, I adjure you by the gods, cease to admire material things, *cease to make yourselves slaves*, first of things, and then, on their account, of the men who have the power either to bestow them or take them away. (*Diss.* III.20.8, italics added)

[T]his is in my power, to be free from all compulsion; no one can hinder or force me to use [the impressions] any otherwise than I please. Who after this has any power over me? Philip, or Alexander, or Perdiccas, or the Persian king? How should they have it? For *he that can be subjected by man must, long before, let himself be subjected by things.* He, therefore, whom neither pleasure nor pain, nor fame nor riches, can get the better of, and who is able, whenever he thinks fit, to spit his whole body into his tormentor's face and depart from life, whose slave can he ever be? To whom is he subject? (III.24.69–71, italics added)

The man who is not subject to hindrance and has things ready at hand he wants them is free; but the man who can be hindered or compelled or propelled into anything against his will is a slave. And who can never be hindered? The man who sets his desire on nothing that is not his own. And what are those things that are not our own? Those that are not in our own power, either to have or not to have, or to have them of a particular nature, or under specific conditions. (IV.1.128–9)[38]

---

[37] See Wolfe 1998, 667.
[38] See also I.9.21; I.18.17, 21; I.29.5–8; II.8.27–9; III.24.56; III.26.38–9; IV.4.38–40; *Handbook* 1. On what is "your own," see *Diss.* I.22.9–11; II.15.1; II.19.32; III.1.40; III.24.3, 69; IV.1.77; *Handbook* 1; see also Chapter 7.

Since the only thing that is ultimately within our control is the exercise of the will, human happiness must consist in the good exercise of the will *and nothing else*. That is why, for the Stoics, only virtuous activity is good, *and* virtuous activity must be separable from all bodily and external things. That is to say, virtuous activity must be *formalized* activity, in order for that activity to count as a life of *human* happiness.

Consequently, the only way for Charlie to free himself from his trap is to undo his ensnaring choices about what his happiness requires and be prepared instead to lose anything he cannot control—that is the only way to remain truly autonomous. In the end, this is what Charlie does, shocking everyone by handing his property over to his creditors and thereby eliminating the means by which they or anyone else might try to manipulate him. He chooses to be strong—to "be a bull," as he puts it—and not to be anyone's instrument.[39]

4 The significance of Epictetus' objection

Epictetus thinks we have much to lose by allowing anything we cannot control within the boundaries of the self. But how serious is Epictetus' worry? Does he overstate his case? To assess his objection, I want to focus on two related ways in which circumstances can impact those who pin their happiness on them, both of which are of concern to Epictetus and, we shall see, to Cicero as well. One of these is how making happiness vulnerable to circumstances affects our emotional reactions to circumstances (4.1), and the other is how such vulnerability affects our own virtuousness (4.2). These two points are related, in that emotional soundness is part of virtuousness.

4.1 The bad things that befall us

On the formalized conception of the self, actions as they bear on one's happiness are limited to how one exercises one's will, whereas on the embodied view actions as they bear on happiness also include the impact one has on the world through exercising the will.[40] This difference is significant for thinking about a particularly heinous sort of misfortune, namely the misfortune of having to do some awful but unavoidable thing oneself, such as sending others to their likely death, or making the choice to end another's life. It is obvious that in such cases what one does is something that, in its own right, no one—certainly no virtuous person—would ever want to do. This is not where the formalized and embodied views differ. Rather, they diverge over just what one takes oneself to have done in such cases, and thus over how it is appropriate to feel about what one has done. On the formalized view, there is room for sorrow over the

---

[39] Charlie resonates with Epictetus' comparison of a free man to a bull that knows it is prepared for any lion that might attack (*Diss.* I.2.30–2).

[40] The phrase "as they bear on happiness" is an important one: where one draws the boundaries of an action as bearing on one's happiness need not be where one draws the boundaries for metaphysical purposes or for moral assessment as "right" or "wrong" (cf. Russell 2009, 61–5).

awful thing that has *transpired*,[41] but on the embodied view, it is also appropriate to feel regret for the awful thing that one has *done*.

Martha Nussbaum discusses an example of that kind of regret (1986, chap. 2). She considers the tragic dilemma in Euripides' play *Agamemnon*: as Agamemnon is preparing to lead the Greek army to war against Troy, the gods reveal to him that his army shall fail unless he makes a sacrifice of his daughter Iphigenia. As Euripides' play makes clear, Agamemnon slides terribly from thinking that sacrificing his daughter is what he ought to do to feeling satisfied with himself for doing it. Agamemnon's failure, Nussbaum argues, is not just that he fails to feel the appropriate sorrow and regret: he should also feel devastated by the terrible thing he has done. This, she argues, is because in doing such an awful thing, Agamemnon has lost not only his daughter but also his own goodness (1986, 41–3). Such a deep emotional reaction, Nussbaum says, is part of the very reaction that it is appropriate and humane to have to such a heinous action (pp. 45–50). This is because action, for Nussbaum, is more than the "exercise of reason or intellect, narrowly conceived" (p. 47). Indeed, she holds that a virtue is a "preparation" for virtuous activity construed as including the impact one has on the world (pp. 324–5).[42]

Or consider a different example from Rosalind Hursthouse, in which one must choose between prolonging one's unconscious parent's life by extraordinary medical means and discontinuing the medical treatment currently keeping him or her alive (1999, 69–70; cf. 1995, 62). In such a case, there may well be considerations favoring discontinuing care over prolonging it, but even so it is still appropriate to feel devastated by such a choice. Such a choice may even be morally appropriate and virtuously made, but, Hursthouse argues, "it is surely right to insist that the mere fact that one had intentionally done [such a thing] *should* haunt the rest of one's life if [that thing] were very terrible, even granted that one was blameless" (1999, 77, italics in orig.). As such, one's action is a serious blow to one's happiness: even if one resolves the dilemma appropriately, even virtuously, nonetheless "a virtuous agent cannot emerge [from such a dilemma] with her life unmarred."[43]

Evidently, for the purpose of thinking about how an action bears on the agent's happiness, Nussbaum and Hursthouse draw the boundaries of an action just where the embodied conception draws them. On such a view, grief and devastation are appropriate responses, not only to the losses that fortune inflicts on us, but also to the ways in which fortune restricts our options for action, whatever option we take.

---

[41] Here again one wonders why for the Stoics there is no "good affection" or *eupatheia* that is a negative reaction to a present situation, regarded not as an evil but as something not to be preferred (see notes to Chapter 8).

[42] In fact, Nussbaum argues not only that Agamemnon's action is an awful thing and a cause for regret, but also that such an action is *morally wrong* and a cause for *remorse*. Evidently, she draws the boundaries of action in the same place, both for assessing its relation to happiness and for assessing its moral quality.

[43] Even so, Hursthouse says, one's action will not be *wrong* provided that it is virtuously chosen.

However, the Stoics argue that becoming emotionally invested in something outside our control—invested as if our happiness depends on it—is too costly, and in some cases anyway it is obvious that it is. To extend Nussbaum's example, think about a military commander in wartime who must choose whom he will send to their almost certain death on a daily basis. Or to extend Hursthouse's example, consider those who must deal with end-of-life choices all the time, such as doctors and administrators in intensive care units, or people in societies without adequate healthcare for newborns or the elderly (which, in the not too distant past, was every society). In cases like these, being devastated by doing what one must do is just not an option. The people themselves clearly cannot afford the devastation, for the sake of their own mental and emotional well-being. And the people who will need them to be ready to make the next difficult choice—perhaps later the same day—cannot afford to have them be devastated over an earlier choice, either.

Thankfully, people in these positions often manage to keep the boundaries of the self in a safe place. To be sure, persons who do awful but unavoidable things do need to register the awfulness of what they do, in order to keep their humaneness intact, as Agamemnon failed to do. And yet we recognize that even this *has* to have a limit. There is value in appreciating awfulness for what it is, but there is also value in one's own peace of mind—and no reason that the former should just trump the latter. Furthermore, there is value in having some control over where one sets the limit, rather than being at the mercy of fortune in one's emotional response.

These considerations support several of the Stoics' main points about our attitudes about things outside our control. For one thing, when and how we grieve depends on where we place the boundaries of the self, including where we place the boundaries of our actions. For another, we can do something about where we place those boundaries and therefore about when and how we grieve. Furthermore, and importantly, where it is appropriate to place those boundaries depends on a couple of crucial ethical considerations. One, in placing the boundaries we must take into consideration our own need and the need of those who depend on us to maintain our emotional and mental well-being, as well as our related preparedness to choose and act virtuously. This, of course, is the sort of risk that Cicero has in mind in *Tusculan Disputations*: being susceptible to grief can make one prone to levels of emotional distress and rational impairment that threaten our capacity for virtuous activity. And two, we must avoid losing our autonomy by giving our circumstances too much power to dictate our emotional responses and our preparedness to act well. This is the risk that worries Epictetus.

Cicero and Epictetus have a point. It is for these very reasons that people who are in the business of handling tragic dilemmas owe it to themselves and everybody else to draw a line between the awfulness in which they are involved and what actions they put down on their own personal ledgers. But the same point clearly holds for everyone else as well. We all face circumstances we cannot control and we all have reason to avoid the immense ethical perils of pinning our happiness on our circumstances when it costs too much to do so.[44]

Even so, these considerations do not take us all the way to the Stoic thesis that it is *always* too costly to allow *anything* outside our control within the boundaries of the self. On the contrary, never letting anything outside—family, friends, projects—within those boundaries must surely have a cost as well (more on this below). And if it can be appropriate to expand the boundaries of the self in this way, then feeling devastated by unavoidably awful circumstances is an *appropriate* way of registering such awfulness, so far from being an ethical *peril*. At most, then, the Stoics show that we must be careful, that there is a line between being appropriately vulnerable to circumstances and being *so* vulnerable or fragile as to become rationally or emotionally impaired or unfree.

This reply assumes that the Stoics intend the extreme view that there just is no line between appropriate vulnerability and ethical peril. However, I think that the Stoics' point can be put much more subtly than that. Even granting that there is such a line, surely it matters how good we *actually are* at keeping our balance along that line. This question is all the more challenging when we remind ourselves that staying on the right side of that line is not at all like just solving a problem: it is a matter of holding on to our wisdom, our emotional balance, and our freedom when what is at stake are things to which we are attached as if our happiness depends on them. It is exactly this sort of struggle that we see in Charlie Croker—and, Epictetus says, in Medea: what is it to attach to something in that way but to risk being emotionally distraught about losing it, rationally impaired about what to do about it, and at the mercy of circumstances that threaten it? The Stoics' point, I think, can be put, not as the absolute certainty that from such attachments it follows as a matter of logic that one must fall into ethical peril, but as a point about human psychology that such attachments expose us to risks of ethical peril that just *are* where most of our suffering, impairment, and unfreedom come from.

4.2 The bad things that we become

Epictetus writes in, and for, a culture in which a person's prospects routinely are down to the discretion of some patron or autocrat. In such a world, it is clear that the surrender of one's autonomy is an ever-present threat and that it is always dangerous to stake very much happiness on things outside one's control. It is in this spirit that Admiral James Stockdale said to himself, as he found himself parachuting into enemy captivity in Vietnam, that he was leaving his own world and entering the world of Epictetus.[45] But perhaps the strength of Epictetus' outlook in desperate circumstances is its weakness everywhere else. Epictetus' objection might have teeth in Stockdale's

---

[44] I remember being told when I was first entering the job market in philosophy that advisors would never be as emotionally invested in their students' employment prospects as the students were. At first I found this news unsettling, and I even resented it a bit. But then I was given the explanation, which even then I could see had to be right: neither the advisors themselves nor next year's group of candidates could afford such an investment in my situation now.

[45] Stockdale 1994, cited by Sherman 2005, 1.

circumstances, or Charlie Croker's, but most of *us* will never be in circumstances remotely like those. Why should *we* take Epictetus' objection seriously?

Epictetus addresses this question directly. Suppose, he imagines someone saying, that my ambition is to become a senator or to hold some other public office. In that case, Epictetus, you may have a point: it's clear how present the danger is of losing my freedom in pursuing something so far outside my control. But suppose that I *don't* want to go to Rome and be a senator. Suppose instead that all I want is to stay in my hometown and live a quiet life of study, reading my books and leaving the rest of the world to itself. What danger could I possibly be in then? Surprisingly, Epictetus says that the danger has not changed at all:

[T]he value you place on an external object, whatever it may be, makes you subservient to another. What difference does it make, then, whether you desire to be a senator or not to be a senator?...[I]f you attach value to anything outside the sphere of choice, you destroy that choice. (*Diss.* IV.4.1–2, 23)

Anything that we stake our happiness on can become a source of unfreedom, Epictetus says, if that thing is something we cannot control. We can lose our freedom to other people who threaten or offer what we desire for happiness, and we can lose our freedom even to circumstances. If you have your heart set on a life of quiet study, what else can you do but be upset when you cannot get books, or cannot find the time to read, or are faced with distractions (*Diss.* IV.4.2, 5, 8)? Likewise for staying at home rather than going to Rome: if you make your happiness depend on staying home, what can you do but be upset when you find yourself having to go to Rome anyway (IV.4.34–8)? Such attachments, then, can make us slaves in how we act and even in how we feel. As a result, those attachments threaten to overturn practical wisdom and emotional balance—and those sorts of attachments are absolutely everywhere.

But here we are likely to wonder, again, whether Epictetus is making such attachments too extreme. It is one thing to think that living in a certain city, say, is part of one's happiness, and another to think that it is part of one's happiness to live in that city *at any cost*. Indeed, on my view nothing can be part of happiness that is not internal to virtuous activity, that is, activity that is both practically wise and emotionally sound. In that case, one cannot take one's happiness to be something fixed and independent of the practical wisdom and emotional soundness with which one acts. And that means that becoming attached to staying in a certain city *at all costs* for the sake of one's happiness is necessarily self-defeating, since how one chooses concerning those costs will be part of either happiness or its opposite. So for all that Epictetus has said, there can still be a line between rationally fighting for one's happiness and losing one's happiness in the very act of fighting for it.

However, here too I think that there is a much subtler way of taking Epictetus' point. To see it, recall one of the defining features of the embodied conception of the self, namely that the life of activity that is one's happiness is always particular, or as I said in Chapter 9, "indexical": one's happiness is always *this* happiness, consisting in *this* activity in relation to *this* person or *this* place or *this* project. This is because the objects of one's activity, on the embodied view, are not merely those things in relation to which one acts but part of the very form and substance of the activity. Put another way, those activities and attachments and loves in which one's happiness consists take on a life of their own—that's what it is for something "out there" to become something "in here." That, after all, is the point of the embodied conception—precisely that we should let those attachments take on a life of their own: happiness is finding *those* kinds of things to live for, and then *living for them.* And here is what follows: part of what it is for one to have *this* attachment, be part of *this* happiness, is for one to be unwilling to let go of that attachment without one hell of a fight.

Now, all of this is still consistent with the idea that there is a point at which holding on to and fighting for an attachment ceases to be practically wise and emotionally sound, and thus where continuing to fight costs too much with respect to happiness. However, even if there is such a point, again: doesn't it matter how good we actually are at finding it? Indeed, comparing the task to "finding a point" gives far too much credit to our abilities. Striking a balance here is not like solving a problem in geometry. It is a matter of struggling to be wise and balanced about things we are utterly passionate about, things to which we are committed as if our happiness depends on them, things for which we cannot but fight, things whose loss would be a loss within the very boundaries of the self.

This, I think, is Epictetus' point, and we see it in his treatment of Medea. Epictetus quotes Medea's line in Euripides' play, "Yes, I understand what terrible things I am about to do, but anger takes charge of my deliberations."[46] Notice, then, that Medea recognizes that somewhere there is a line between acting for the sake of something and acting for its sake at all costs, and that one way of describing her impending act is that it crosses that line. However, anger offers another way of describing her act—to "take vengeance on one who has injured and wronged me" (*Diss.* II.17.20)—and that is the description with which she agrees. What else could she have done, Epictetus' asks, since she sees the loss of her husband as such a very great loss? This, he says, is just what it is to desire something and be disappointed in losing it (II.17.19, 22).

It is important to remember, as we saw above, that Epictetus does not treat Medea's action as a case of akrasia, as if she had assented to one description of her situation but then did something else anyway. On the contrary, Epictetus offers her as an example supporting his thesis that people *always* do what they take to be their best option (*Diss.* I.28.6). His point, therefore, is that even when one knows there is a line to be crossed and akrasia does not interfere, there is *still* the very real danger of crossing the line—and that danger is just part of what it is to set one's heart on something as if one's happiness depends on it.

---

[46] *Diss.* I.28.7, my translation. The translation of this line is difficult, because in Greek it is (deliberately?) ambiguous between the rendering I have given and Hard's rendering, "passion overwhelms my resolutions." I have chosen the former because I don't see how to preserve that ambiguity in English, and this rendering better captures the Stoic interpretation of the line.

Of course, we should not think by extremes here, as if anyone who loves another as if his or her happiness depends on it will therefore be capable of murder. I don't think that is Epictetus' point, though. He does not mean that the grave things we see in tragedies will also happen to us, but he does want us to see in tragedies a basic human problem: the difficulty of sticking to right reason when we are committed to things we cannot control. That is a problem we face every single day.

Nor does Epictetus' point rest on extreme thinking about how we fare when we face that problem. Most days are simply not worth writing a tragedy about. But anxieties and failures to act virtuously also tend to be part of our daily experience, and how many of those failures are down to our assumptions about what our happiness depends on? We protect and cling to persons and things as if our happiness depends on them, and so we also worry and fear as if our happiness depends on them (recall Cicero, *TD* III.14–15). We see how much control our circumstances and other people have over the things we want as if our happiness depends on them, and we feel powerless and small (III.15). We worry about what others might do to keep us from those things, and we become suspicious and resentful (III.19). We need to be ready to exercise right reason, but we find it difficult to see our way clearly because our attachment to things outside our control has taken on a life of its own (III.15). We become upset over things we cannot control, and are not at our best when we need to be (III.18). We will not be parted from these things, and we become possessive, jealous, and spiteful of others (III.20–1). These are ways in which we fall short every day in practical wisdom and emotional balance. According to Epictetus, they are not failures or lapses of practical reasoning; on the contrary, they are just how practical reasoning works when we adopt certain assumptions about our happiness.

The Stoic case against grief, therefore, is that one who will grieve is attached to things outside his control in a way that he cannot afford to be, for two main reasons. One of these is Cicero's focus, namely the threat to wisdom and emotional health that such attachments represent. The other is Epictetus' focus: even if none of us would be willingly bad in any of these ways, still by choosing to attach our happiness to things outside our control we leave little room for ourselves to do otherwise. No wonder Epictetus insists that of all the philosophical disciplines, the proper handling of emotion is by far the most important (*Diss.* III.2.1–3).

Cicero's and Epictetus' objections have implications for the embodied conception of the self that should now be very clear. It takes virtuous activity and human autonomy to live a happy life, but bringing things outside one's control within the boundaries of the self threatens virtue and autonomy alike. The Stoics are not unaware that people *could* place the boundaries of the self in this way; on the contrary, they seem to recognize that people usually do *exactly* that. Their point is that the ethical cost to the agent of doing so—the cost in terms of practical wisdom and emotional sound-ness—is simply too high. And they do have a point.

◊ ◊ ◊

We have explored the costs of the increased vulnerability that the embodied conception of the self brings. Those costs are not merely uneasiness at the very idea of vulnerability—that we could live with—although the Stoics are sometimes read as threatening us with little more than that. Rather, those costs are ones that even I—and even an ancient Aristotelian—have to take very seriously, since they threaten the capacities for practical wisdom, emotional balance, and personal autonomy on which human happiness ultimately depends.

However, there are costs on the side of the formalized conception as well. If we see the risks of the embodied conception in Charlie Croker, then we can also see the costs of the formalized conception by imagining a subtle change in Charlie's situation. Charlie's willingness to forgo his property maybe is inspiring, but we should ask ourselves how inspired we would be if what Charlie had forgone had been his loved ones, and not just his plantation. Charlie, after all, is a man of great wealth, but as it happens, he also has no personal relationships that do not depend completely on his wealth. Charlie frees himself by giving up every*thing*, but not by giving up any*one*.[47] If, by contrast, Charlie's life had been full of rich and intimate closeness with others, and the price of extricating himself from his dilemma had been to walk away from those relationships, we might still admire his courage, but perhaps we would also mourn the fact that his courage cost him his happiness.

In fact, this is precisely the situation that young *Connie* is in, who, unlike Charlie, is very close to his two children.[48] Wolfe does not advertise the point, but as far as Epictetus is concerned, making *people* important for one's happiness is every bit as corrosive of autonomy as making *things* important for one's happiness—either way, one binds one's happiness to something one cannot control. To be sure, many of Epictetus' warnings about attachments to other people serve simply to remind us— quite rightly—that we cannot wish that those we love might live for ever: just as one cannot expect to have figs whether they are in season or not, so one cannot expect that one can always have the people one loves (*Diss.* III.24.85–8).[49] But Epictetus goes well beyond this reminder, urging us to be prepared to let go of our loved ones *readily*:

[Right judgments are] the things that a man ought to study all day long, so that, unaffected by all that is not his own, whether friend or place or gymnasia or even, indeed, his own body, he remembers the law and has that constantly before his eyes. And what is the divine law? To preserve what is one's own, not to claim what is another's; to use what is given us, and not desire what is not given us; and, when anything is taken away, to give it up readily, and to be thankful for the time you have been permitted the use of it, and not cry after it, like a child for its nurse and its mamma.[50]

---

[47] To be sure, Charlie eventually loses his young trophy wife when he loses his property, but he had already become alienated from her long before his encounter with Epictetus.

[48] Here I have benefited from discussion with Mark LeBar.

[49] See also III.24.58–60; *Handbook* 3.

[50] *Diss.* II.16.27–8. See also *Handbook* 7.

The Greek phrase here rendered "readily" is *eulutōs kai autothen*: quite literally, "easily untied (*eulutōs*) and all at once (*kai autothen*)."[51] To keep such bonds always easy to untie all at once, Epictetus recommends the practice of telling oneself that external things are not essential to one, beginning with things like cups and shirts, progressing to things like dogs, horses, and land, and finally to one's body, one's siblings, one's spouse, one's children (*Diss.* IV.1.110–12). In this way, he promises, one can become like Diogenes the Cynic, for whom everything was "easily untied" (*euluta*) and "only tacked on" (*monon prosērtēmena*; IV.1.152–3). Consequently, although it would be the result of madness in most people to regard one's property, spouse, or children as mere pieces in a child's game, in the Stoics this is actually the result of "learning, through reason and demonstration" (IV.7.5–11). One who has learned this, Epictetus says, is prepared to say that his father means nothing for his happiness, only the good, and that the death of a child means nothing for his happiness, only the good (III.3.5, 15; III.8.1–3). As I said, Wolfe does not emphasize this point; however, Epictetus does, praising such readiness to be parted from loved ones in the heroic exemplars of Diogenes and Heracles (III.24.13–15), and of course Socrates (IV.1.159).

Therefore, if Charlie's attachments expose him to manipulation and loss of autonomy, then so do Connie's, and for exactly the same reason. And so if Charlie must keep his attachments to his property "easily untied" and "only tacked on," and in the end nothing to his happiness, then so too must Connie with respect to his attachments to his children. However, once close attachments like Connie's must be *eliminated* from a happy life and replaced with attachments that are only loose and easily untied, one begins to wonder whether it is correct to call such a life "happy" in the first place. This is the difference between loving others and loving others as if one's happiness depends on them.[52] There is no denying that happiness requires autonomy, but here too we can ask: at what cost?

So, where does this leave us? Unfortunately, we are left with a tragic conflict. I have argued that whether or not we take virtue to be sufficient for happiness depends on our choice between two conceptions of the self, what I have called the formalized and the embodied conceptions. But I have also argued that either way, the stakes are very high. Simply put, as embodied vulnerability increases, one kind of loss follows, and as formalized invulnerability increases, a different kind of loss follows. The Stoics have a point. We would not choose to live without intimate connections, but we cannot live without virtue and autonomy either; and yet, if Cicero and Epictetus are right, then chances are that we cannot have it both ways. But there is also a point to thinking that it is in our relationships with others and our investments in meaningful projects that our happiness is *found*, and so it must be rational for the sake of our happiness to include such things within the boundaries of the self.

---

[51] In fragment 4 Epictetus says that such things should be yielded up "gladly" (*asmenous*).

[52] See e.g. Stephens 1996, who argues that Epictetus treated eros as a *pathos*, understanding love as a type of external behavior, but in "emotional isolation" from others.

I would be lying if I said I knew how to resolve this dilemma. And it would be not just a lie but an arrogant, outrageous lie, pretending that I could argue away the possibility that for humans, this kind of dilemma just comes with the territory. I cannot see any way to dissolve it, either, although I am sure others will offer suggestions. Some will say that this shows why we should leave virtue out of our thinking about happiness in the first place; but I cannot accept that wisdom and a healthy emotional life have nothing to do with happiness for creatures whose entire existence is so deeply transformed by their creative power of practical rationality. Others will say that that is exactly the problem—we shouldn't think of happiness in terms of *human* nature in the first place. But to say that would be to misconstrue even the importance of individual fulfillment for happiness, since it is only because of a shared humanity that each of us so deeply needs to grow, flourish, and express himself as a unique, self-governing individual in the first place.[53] To say that individual fulfillment is all there is to happiness is just to hide the fact that to say even that much is *already* to think of happiness as happiness *for humans*.

So the upshot is: I am stuck with this dilemma. In fact, if I am right about this dilemma, we are *all* stuck with it. Now, I have argued in this book that happiness for humans is a life of embodied virtuous activity: a life of activity that is both wise and inextricable from the relationships that define each of us. That is still my thesis here at the book's end. But I don't believe it because I suppose that somehow I have proved it is true. I believe it because I have chosen to accept the risks on this side of the dilemma over those on the Stoics' side. It is a choice I have made with some faith and much trepidation, which is I think the most that anyone can do here. In fact, if I am right in my thinking about happiness in this final chapter, then no *proof* as to what happiness is, on either side, will ever be in the offing.

Making up our minds about happiness turns out to be a matter of dealing with a tragic conflict, and as with any tragic conflict, the best we can hope for is to make a choice we can live with. I hope that my readers will be persuaded of the central claims of this book—that happiness is eudaimonia, that happiness is a life of virtuous activity, and that the activity in which happiness consists is embodied activity in the way I have characterized it. Of course, that is what every philosopher hopes for—that people will be impressed by arguments and persuaded of theses—even though that hope is almost always dashed. But my even deeper hope may also be a more realistic one. The position we take on what virtue has to do with happiness is inextricably bound to how we define ourselves and our relations to persons and things in the world around us, and however attractive we may find the position we take, it always has a cost that we cannot afford to ignore. If I can move others to recognize what is at stake, my hope will be thoroughly satisfied.

---

[53] As Jean Hampton (1993, 149) puts the point, "One of the traits that mark us out as human beings is our capacity to develop distinctive personalities."

Works Cited

Ackrill, J., "Aristotle on Eudaimonia," in N. Sherman, ed., *Aristotle's Ethics: Critical Essays* (New York: Rowman and Littlefield, 1999).

Annas, J., "Naturalism in Greek Ethics: Aristotle and After," *Proceedings of the Boston Area Colloquium in Ancient Philosophy* 4 (1988), 149–71.

—— *Hellenistic Philosophy of Mind* (Berkeley: University of California Press, 1992).

—— *The Morality of Happiness* (Oxford: Oxford University Press, 1993a).

—— "Virtue as the Use of Other Goods," *Apeiron* 26 (1993b), 53–66.

—— "Is Plato a Stoic?" *Méthexis* 10 (1997), 23–38.

—— *Platonic Ethics, Old and New* (Ithaca, New York: Cornell University Press, 1999).

—— "Should Virtue Make You Happy?" in R. Shiner and L. Jost, eds., *Eudaimonia and Well-Being: Ancient and Modern Conceptions* (Kelowna, BC: Academic Press, 2002).

—— "Marcus Aurelius: Ethics and its Background," *Rhizai* 2 (2004), 103–19.

—— "Ethics in Stoic Philosophy," *Phronesis* 52 (2007a), 58–87.

—— "Carneades' Classification of Ethical Theories," in A. M. Ioppolo and D. N. Sedley, eds., *Pyrrhonists, Patricians, Platonizers: Hellenistic Philosophy in the Period 155–86 BC* (Naples: Bibliopolis, 2007b).

—— *Intelligent Virtue* (Oxford: Oxford University Press, 2011).

—— ed. and R. Woolf, trans., *Cicero: On Moral Ends* (Cambridge: Cambridge University Press, 2001).

Anscombe, G. E. M., *The Collected Philosophical Papers of G. E. M. Anscombe, vol. 3: Ethics, Religion and Politics* (Oxford: Blackwell, 1981).

Archer, J., *The Nature of Grief* (London: Routledge, 1999).

—— "Theories of Grief: Past, Present, and Future Perspectives," in M. S. Stroebe et al., eds., 2008.

Attig, T., *How We Grieve: Relearning the World* (Oxford: Oxford University Press, 1996).

—— "Relearning the World: Making and Finding Meanings," in R. A. Neimeyer, ed., 2001.

Audi, R., "Acting for Reasons," in A. R. Mele, ed., *The Philosophy of Action* (Oxford: Oxford University Press, 1997).

—— *The Heart of Grief: Death and the Search for Lasting Love* (Oxford: Oxford University Press, 2000).

Barnes, J., "Antiochus of Ascalon," in M. Griffin and J. Barnes, eds., *Philosophia Togata: Essays on Philosophy and Roman Society* (Oxford: Oxford University Press, 1989).

Barney, R., "A Puzzle in Stoic Ethics," *Oxford Studies in Ancient Philosophy* 24 (2003), 303–39.

Bartsch, S., *The Mirror of the Self* (Chicago: University of Chicago Press, 2006).

Bayne, T. and N. Levy, "Amputees by Choice: Body Integrity Identity Disorder and the Ethics of Amputation," *Journal of Applied Philosophy* 22 (2005), 75–86.

Behel, J. M., B. Rybarczyk, T. R. Elliott, J. J. Nicholas, and D. L. Neyenhuis, "The Role of Perceived Vulnerability in Adjustment to Lower Extremity Amputation," *Rehabilitation Psychology* 47 (2002), 92–105.

Bentham, J., *The Rationale of Reward* (London: John and H. L. Hunt, 1830).

Bett, R., "Nietzsche, the Greeks, and Happiness (with Special Reference to Aristotle and Epicurus)," *Philosophical Topics* 33 (2005), 45–70.

Blecher, I., "The Stoic Method of Happiness," *Apeiron* 39 (2006), 157–76.

Bobzien, S., *Determinism and Freedom in Stoic Philosophy* (Oxford: Oxford University Press, 1998).

Bonanno, G., "Grief and Emotion: A Social-Functional Perspective," in M. S. Stroebe et al., eds., 2001.

—— K. Boerner, and C. B. Wortman, "Trajectories of Grieving," in M. S. Stroebe et al., eds., 2008.

Bonanno, G. and S. Kaltman, "Toward an Integrative Perspective on Bereavement," *Psychological Bulletin* 125 (1999), 760–76.

Bonhöffer, A. F., *The Ethics of the Stoic Epictetus*, trans. W. O. Stephens (orig. 1894; New York: Peter Lang, 1996).

Bostock, D., *Aristotle's Ethics* (Oxford: Oxford University Press, 2000).

Bowlby, J., *Attachment and Loss, vol. 1: Attachment* (New York: Basic Books, 1969).

—— *Attachment and Loss, vol. 2: Anxiety and Anger* (London: Hogarth 1973).

—— *Attachment and Loss, vol. 3: Loss: Sadness and Depression* (London: Hogarth 1980).

Brennan, T., "Stoic Moral Psychology," in B. Inwood, ed., *The Cambridge Companion to the Stoics* (Cambridge: Cambridge University Press, 2003).

—— *The Stoic Life* (Oxford: Oxford University Press, 2005a).

—— "Brennan on Mitsis on Long," *Southern Journal of Philosophy* 43 (2005b), 250–6.

—— "Socrates and Epictetus," in S. Ahbel-Rappe and R. Kamtekar, eds., *A Companion to Socrates* (Oxford: Blackwell, 2006).

Brickhouse, T. and N. Smith, *Plato's Socrates* (Oxford: Oxford University Press, 1994).

—— *The Philosophy of Socrates* (Boulder, CO: Westview Press, 2000a).

—— "Making Things Good and Making Good Things in Socratic Philosophy," in T. Robinson and L. Brisson, eds., *Plato: Euthydemus, Lysis, Charmides* (Sankt Augustin: Academia Verlag, 2000b).

Broadie, S., *Ethics with Aristotle* (Oxford: Oxford University Press, 1991).

—— and C. Rowe, *Aristotle, Nicomachean Ethics: Translation, Introduction, and Commentary* (Oxford: Oxford University Press, 2002).

Brown, E., "Socrates in the Stoa," in S. Ahbel-Rappe and R. Kamtekar, eds., *A Companion to Socrates* (Oxford: Blackwell, 2006).

Brown, M. J., *Loss and Grief, Part 1: Experiences Shared*, videocassette (Tavistock Publications, 1986).

Cattell, J. P., "Psychiatric Implications in Bereavement," in A. H. Kutscher, ed., *Death and Bereavement* (Springfield, IL: Charles C. Thomas, 1974).

Cooper, J., ed., *The Complete Works of Plato* (Indianapolis/Cambridge: Hackett, 1997).

—— *Reason and Emotion* (Princeton: Princeton University Press, 1999).

—— "Plato and Aristotle on 'Finality' and '(Self-)Sufficiency,'" in R. Heinaman, ed., 2003.

—— "The Emotional Life of the Wise," *Southern Journal of Philosophy* 43 (2005), 176–218.

Crisp, R., *Reasons and the Good* (Oxford: Oxford University Press, 2006).

—— "Well-Being," *Stanford Encyclopedia of Philosophy* (Stanford: Stanford University Press revised 2008).

Cullity, G. and B. Gaut, eds., *Ethics and Practical Reason* (Oxford: Oxford University Press, 1997).

Darwall, S., *Welfare and Rational Care* (Princeton: Princeton Umiversity Press, 2002).

—— *The Second-Person Standpoint* (Cambridge, MA: Harvard University Press, 2006).

Davis, C. G., "The Tormented and the Transformed: Understanding Responses to Loss and Trauma," in R. Neimeyer, ed., *Meaning Reconstruction and the Experience of Loss* (Washington, DC: American Psychological Association, 2001).

—— "Redefining Goals and Redefining Self: A Closer Look at Posttraumatic Growth Following Loss," in M. S. Stroebe et al., eds., 2008.

Denis, L., "A Kantian Conception of Human Flourishing," in L. Jost and J. Wuerth, eds., *Perfecting Virtue: New Essays on Kantian Ethics and Virtue Ethics* (Cambridge: Cambridge University Press, 2011).

Dimas, P., "Happiness in the *Euthydemus*," *Phronesis* 47 (2002), 1–27.

Dobbin, R., "Προαίρεσις in Epictetus," *Ancient Philosophy* 11 (1991), 111–35.

—— *Epictetus:* Discourses *Book 1*, trans. and comm. (Oxford: Oxford University Press, 1998).

Dodds, E. R., *Plato: Gorgias*, text and comm. (Oxford: Oxford University Press, 1959).

Driver, J., *Uneasy Virtue* (Cambridge: Cambridge University Press, 2001).

Dyson, H., "The God Within: The Normative Self in Epictetus," *History of Philosophy Quarterly* 26 (2009), 235–53.

Engberg-Pederson, T., *Aristotle's Theory of Moral Insight* (Oxford: Oxford University Press, 1983).

—— "Stoic Philosophy and the Concept of a Person," in Gill, ed., 1990a.

—— *The Stoic Theory of Oikeiosis* (Aarhus, Denmark: Aarhus University Press, 1990b).

Engel, G., "Is Grief a Disease? A Challenge for Medical Research," *Psychosomatic Medicine* 23 (1961), 18–22.

Erskine, A., *The Hellenistic Stoa: Political Thought and Action* (Ithaca, NY: Cornell University Press, 1990).

Farquharson, A. S. L., trans., *Marcus Aurelius: Meditations* (Oxford: Oxford University Press, 1989).

Feldman, F., *Pleasure and the Good Life* (Oxford: Oxford University Press, 2004).

—— *What is This Thing Called Happiness?* (Oxford: Oxford University Press, 2010).

Ferejohn, M., "Socratic Thought Experiments and the Unity of Virtue Paradox," *Phronesis* 29 (1984), 105–22.

Field, N. P., "Whether to Relinquish or Maintain a Bond with the Deceased," in M. S. Stroebe et al., eds., 2008.

First, M. B., "Desire for Amputation of a Limb: Paraphilia, Psychosis, or a New Type of Identity Disorder," *Psychological Medicine* 35 (2005), 919–28.

Foot, P., *Natural Goodness* (Oxford: Oxford University Press, 2001).

Fortenbaugh, W. W., ed., *On Stoic and Peripatetic Ethics: The Work of Arius Didymus* (New Jersey: Transaction, 1983).

—— P. Huby, R. Sharples, and D. Gutas, eds., *Theophrastus of Ereseus: Sources for his Life, Writings, Thought and Influence*, vol. 2 (Leiden: Brill, 1992).

—— and S. White, eds., *Lyco of Troas and Hieronymus of Rhodes: Text, Translation, and Discussion* (New Jersey: Transaction, 2004).

Fraley, R. C. and G. A. Bonanno, "Attachment and Loss: A Test of Three Competing Models of the Association between Attachment-Related Avoidance and Adaptation to Bereavement," *Personality and Social Psychology Bulletin* 39 (2004), 878–90.

—— and P. R. Shaver, "Loss and Bereavement: Attachment Theory and Recent Controversies Concerning 'Grief Work' and the Nature of Detachment," in J. Cassidy and

P. R. Shaver, eds., *Handbook of Attachment: Theory, Research, and Clinical Applications* (New York, 1979).

Frede, M., "The Stoic Theory of the Affections of the Soul," in M. Schofield and G. Striker, eds., *The Norms of Nature* (Cambridge: Cambridge University Press, 1986).

—— "On the Stoic Conception of the Good," in K. Ierodiakonou, ed., *Topics in Stoic Philosophy* (Oxford: Oxford University Press, 1999).

—— "A Notion of a Person in Epictetus," in T. Scaltsas and A. S. Mason, eds., *The Philosophy of Epictetus* (Oxford: Oxford University Press, 2007).

Fukunishi, I., "Relationship of Cosmetic Disfigurement to the Severity of Posttraumatic Stress Disorder in Burn Injury or Digital Amputation," *Psychotherapy and Psychosomatics* 68 (1999), 82–6.

Gallagher, S., "Dimensions of Embodiment: Body Image and Body Schema in Medical Contexts," in S. K. Toombs, ed., *Handbook of Phenomenology and Medicine* (Dordrecht, the Netherlands: Kluwer, 2001).

Gill, C., "Did Chrysippus Understand Medea?" *Phronesis* 28 (1983), 136–49.

—— ed., *The Person and the Human Mind* (Oxford: Oxford University Press, 1990).

—— "Is There a Concept of Person in Greek Philosophy?" in S. Everson, ed., *Companions to Ancient Thought, 2: Psychology* (Cambridge: Cambridge University Press, 1991).

—— *Personality in Greek Epic, Tragedy, and Philosophy* (Oxford: Oxford University Press, 1996).

—— "Protreptic and Dialectic in Plato's *Euthydemus*," in T. M. Robinson and L. Brisson, eds., *Plato: Euthydemus, Lysis, Charmides* (Sankt Augustin: Academia Verlag, 2000).

—— "Competing Readings of Stoic Emotions," in R. Salles, ed., 2005.

—— *The Structured Self in Hellenistic and Roman Thought* (Oxford: Oxford University Press, 2006).

—— "The Ancient Self: Issues and Approaches," in P. Remes and J. Sihvola, eds., 2008a.

—— "The Self and Hellenistic-Roman Philosophical Therapy," in A. Arweiler and M. Moller, eds., *Vom Selbst-Verstandnis in Antike und Neuzeit: Notions of the Self in Antiquity in Beyond* (Berlin: De Gruyter, 2008b).

—— "The Ancient Self: Where Now?" *Antiquorum Philosophia* 2 (2008c), 77–99.

—— ed., and R. Hard, trans., *Epictetus: The Discourses, The Handbook, Fragments* (London: Everyman, 1995).

Glick, I. O., C. M. Parkes, and R. S. Weiss, *The First Year of Bereavement* (New York: Robert Wiley & Sons, 1974).

Görgemanns, H., "*Oikeiōsis* in Arius Didymus," in W. W. Fortenbaugh, ed., 1983.

Gosling, J. C. B. and C. C. W. Taylor, *The Greeks on Pleasure* (Oxford: Oxford University Press, 1982).

Graver, M. R., *Stoicism and Emotion* (Chicago: University of Chicago Press, 2007).

Griffin, J., *Well-Being: Its Meaning, Measurement and Moral Importance* (Oxford: Oxford University Press, 1986).

—— "Replies," in R. Crisp and B. Hooker, eds., *Well-Being and Morality: Essays in Honour of James Griffin* (Oxford: Oxford University Press, 2000).

Gummere, R. A., trans., *Seneca ad Lucilium Epistulae Morales* (Cambridge, MA: Loeb/Harvard, 1917).

Hampton, J., "Selflessness and Loss of Self," *Social Philosophy and Policy* 10 (1993), 135–65.

Hardt, D. V., "An Investigation of the Stages of Bereavement," *Omega* 9 (1978–9), 279–85.

Hawking, S., *A Brief History of Time* (New York: Bantam, 1988).

Haybron, D. M., *The Pursuit of Unhappiness* (Oxford: Oxford University Press, 2008).

—— "Happiness," *Stanford Encyclopedia of Philosophy* (Stanford: Stanford University Press, 2011).

Heinaman, R., "*Eudaimonia* and Self-Sufficiency in the *Nicomachean Ethics*," *Phronesis* 33 (1988), 31–53.

—— "Rationality, *Eudaimonia* and *Kakodaimonia* in Aristotle," *Phronesis* 38 (1993), 31–56.

—— "The Improvability of Eudaimonia in the *Nicomachean Ethics*," *Oxford Studies in Ancient Philosophy* 23 (2002), 99–145.

—— ed., *Plato's and Aristotle's Ethics* (Aldershot: Ashgate, 2003).

—— "Eudaimonia as an Activity in *Nicomachean Ethics* I.8–12," *Oxford Studies in Ancient Philosophy* 33 (2007), 221–53.

Huby, P., "Peripatetic Definitions of Happiness," in W. W. Fortenbaugh, ed., 1983.

Hurka, T., *Perfectionism* (Oxford: Oxford University Press, 1993).

Hursthouse, R., *Beginning Lives* (Oxford: Oxford University Press, 1987).

—— "Applying Virtue Ethics," in R. Hursthouse et al., eds., 1995.

—— *On Virtue Ethics* (Oxford: Oxford University Press, 1999).

—— G. Lawrence, and W. Quinn, eds., *Virtues and Reasons: Philippa Foot and Moral Theory* (Oxford: Oxford University Press, 1995).

Inwood, B., "Hierocles: Theory and Argument in the Second Century AD," *Oxford Studies in Ancient Philosophy* 2 (1984), 151–83.

—— *Ethics and Human Action in Early Stoicism* (Oxford: Oxford University Press, 1985).

—— "Seneca on Freedom and Autonomy," in R. Salles, ed., 2005.

—— *Seneca: Selected Philosophical Letters* (Oxford: Oxford University Press, 2007).

—— and L. Gerson, eds., *Hellenistic Philosophy*, 2nd ed. (Indianapolis/Cambridge: Hackett, 1997).

Irwin, T., *Aristotle: Nicomachean Ethics* (Indianapolis/Cambridge: Hackett, 1985).

—— "Stoic and Aristotelian Conceptions of Happiness," in M. Schofield and G. Striker, eds., *The Norms of Nature* (Cambridge: Cambridge University Press, 1986).

—— "Virtue, Praise, and Success: Stoic Responses to Aristotle," *Monist* 73 (1990), 59–79.

—— "Aristippus against Happiness," *Monist* 74 (1991), 55–82.

—— "Socrates the Epicurean," in H. Benson, ed., *Essays on the Philosophy of Socrates* (Oxford: Oxford University Press, 1992).

—— *Plato's Ethics* (Oxford: Oxford University Press, 1995).

—— "Kant's Criticisms of Eudaemonism," in S. Engstrom and J. Whiting, eds., *Aristotle, Kant, and the Stoics: Rethinking Happiness and Duty* (Cambridge: Cambridge University Press, 1996).

—— "Socratic Paradox and Stoic Theory," in S. Everson, ed., *Companions to Ancient Thought, 4: Ethics* (Cambridge: Cambridge University Press, 1998).

—— "Permanent Happiness: Aristotle and Solon," in N. Sherman, ed., *Aristotle's Ethics: Critical Essays* (New York: Rowman & Littlefield, 1999).

—— *The Development of Ethics*, vol. 1 (Oxford: Oxford University Press, 2007).

Jacobs, J., *Aristotle's Virtues: Nature, Knowledge, and Human Good* (New York: Peter Lang, 2004).

Janoff-Bulman, R., *Shattered Assumptions: Towards a New Psychology of Trauma* (New York: Free Press, 1992).

Kahn, C., "Discovering the Will: From Homer to Augustine," in J. Dillon and A. A. Long, eds., *The Question of 'Eclecticism': Studies in Later Greek Philosophy* (Berkeley: University of California Press, 1988).

Karamanolis, G., "Transformations of Plato's Ethics: Platonist Interpretations of Plato's Ethics from Antiochus to Porphyry," *Rhizai* 1 (2004), 73–105.

Kekes, J., *The Examined Life* (New York: Associated University Presses, 1988).

—— *Moral Wisdom and Good Lives* (Ithaca, NY: Cornell University Press, 1995).

—— *The Art of Life* (Ithaca, NY: Cornell, 2002).

Kessler, H. H., "Psychological Preparation of the Amputee," *Industrial Medicine and Surgery* 20 (1951), 107–8.

Kidd, I. G., "Stoic Intermediates and the End for Man," in A. A. Long, ed., *Problems in Stoicism* (London: Athlone, 1971a).

—— "Posidonius on Emotions," in A. A. Long, ed., *Problems in Stoicism* (London: Athlone, 1971b).

King, J. E., trans., *Cicero: Tusculan Disputations* (Cambridge, MA: Harvard/Loeb, 1927).

Klass, D., "Bereaved Parents and the Compassionate Friends: Affiliation and Healing," *Omega* 15 (1984–5), 353–73.

Knuuttila, S., *Emotions in Ancient and Medieval Philosophy* (Oxford: Oxford University Press, 2004).

Korsgaard, C., "Two Distinctions in Goodness," *The Philosophical Review* 92 (1983), 169–95.

—— "Aristotle on Function and Virtue," *History of Philosophy Quarterly* 3 (1986), 259–79.

—— "The Reasons We Can Share: An Attack on the Distinction between Agent-Relative and Agent-Neutral Values," *Social Philosophy and Policy* 10 (1993), 24–51.

—— *The Sources of Normativity* (Cambridge: Cambridge University Press, 1996).

Kraut, R., "Two Conceptions of Happiness," *The Philosophical Review* 88 (1979), 167–97.

—— *Aristotle on the Human Good* (Princeton: Princeton University Press. 1989).

—— "Aristotle on the Human Good: An Overview," in N. Sherman, ed., *Aristotle's Ethics: Critical Essays* (Lanham, Maryland: Rowman & Littlefield, 1999).

—— *What is Good and Why* (Cambridge, MA: Harvard, 2007).

Kübler-Ross, E., *On Death and Dying* (London: Routledge, 1969).

—— *On Grief and Grieving* (London: Simon & Schuster, 2005).

Leavy, S. A., "Commentary on 'The Stoic Conception of Mental Disorder,'" *Philosophy, Psychiatry, and Psychology* 4 (1997), 295–6.

LeBar, M., "Good For You," *Pacific Philosophical Quarterly* 85 (2004), 195–217.

—— "Eudaimonist Autonomy," *American Philosophical Quarterly* 42 (2005), 171–84.

—— "Development and Reasons," *Philosophical Quarterly* 58 (2008), 711–19.

—— "Virtue Ethics and Deontic Constraints," *Ethics* 119 (2009), 642–71.

Lesses, G., "Virtue and the Goods of Fortune in Stoic Moral Theory," *Oxford Studies in Ancient Philosophy* 7 (1989), 95–127.

Lewis, C. S., *A Grief Observed* (New York: Bantam, 1976).

Lindemann, E., "Symptomatology and Management of Acute Grief," *American Journal of Psychiatry* 101 (1944), 141–8.

Lomasky, L., *Persons, Rights, and the Moral Community* (Oxford: Oxford University Press, 1987).

Long, A. A., "Arius Didymus and the Exposition of Stoic Ethics," in W. W. Fortenbaugh, ed., 1983.

—— "Socrates in Hellenistic Philosophy," *Classical Quarterly* 38 (1988), 150–71.

—— "Representation and the Self in Stoicism," in S. Everson, ed., *Companions to Ancient Thought, 2: Psychology* (Cambridge: Cambridge University Press, 1991).

Long, A. A., *Stoic Studies* (Cambridge: Cambridge University Press, 1996).

——"The Socratic Legacy," in K. Algra, J. Barnes, J. Mansfield, and M. Schofield, eds., *The Cambridge History of Hellenistic Philosophy* (Cambridge: Cambridge University Press, 1999).

——*Epictetus: A Stoic and Socratic Guide to Life* (Oxford: Oxford University Press, 2002).

——*From Epicurus to Epictetus* (Oxford: Oxford University Press, 2006).

——and D. N. Sedley, *The Hellenistic Philosophers*, 2 vols. (Cambridge: Cambridge University Press, 1987).

McCabe, M. M., "Indifference Readings: Plato and the Stoa on Socratic Ethics," in T. P. Wiseman, ed., *Classics in Progress: Essays on Ancient Greece and Rome* (Oxford: Oxford University Press, 2002).

McDowell, J., "The Role of *Eudaimonia* in Aristotle's Ethics," in A. O. Rorty, ed., *Essays on Aristotle's Ethics* (Berkeley: University of California Press, 1980).

——"Two Sorts of Naturalism," in R. Hursthouse et al., eds., 1995a.

——"Eudaimonism and Realism in Aristotle's Ethics," in R. Heinaman, ed., *Aristotle and Moral Realism* (London: University College, 1995b).

——*Mind and World* (Cambridge, MA: Harvard University Press, 1996).

——"Some Issues in Aristotle's Moral Psychology," in S. Everson, ed., *Companions to Ancient Thought, 4: Ethics* (Cambridge: Cambridge University Press, 1998).

MacIntyre, A., *After Virtue* (Notre Dame, IN: Notre Dame Press, 1981).

Mack, E., "Self-Ownership and the Right of Property," *Monist* 73 (1990), 519–43.

——"The Self-Ownership Proviso: A New and Improved Lockean Proviso," *Social Philosophy and Policy* 12 (1995a), 186–218.

——"Self-Ownership, Marxism, and Egalitarianism, Part II: Challenges to the Self-Ownership Thesis," *Politics, Philosophy and Economics* 1 (1995b), 237–76.

McKenzie, C., "Personal Identity, Narrative Integration and Embodiment," in S. Campbell, L. Meynell, and S. Sherwin, eds., *Embodiment and Agency* (Pennsylvania: Pennsylvania State University Press. 2009).

Marris, P., *Loss and Change* (London: Pantheon Books, 1974).

Merleau-Ponty, M., *Phenomenology of Perception*, trans. C. Smith (London: Routledge, 1962).

Mikulincer, M. and P. R. Shaver, "An Attachment Perspective on Bereavement," in M. S. Stroebe et al., eds., 2008.

Mill, J. S., "Bentham," in *Dissertations and Discussions* (London, 1859).

——*Utilitarianism* (London, 1863).

Mitsis, P., "Stoicism," in C. Shields, ed., *The Blackwell Guide to Ancient Philosophy* (Oxford: Blackwell, 2003).

——"The Stoics on Property and Politics," *Southern Journal of Philosophy* 43, supp. (2005), 230–49.

Moller, D., "Love and Death," *Journal of Philosophy* 104 (2007), 301–16.

Neimeyer, R. A., "The Language of Loss: Grief Therapy as a Process of Meaning Reconstruction," in R. A. Neimeyer, ed., *Meaning Reconstruction and the Experience of Loss* (Washington, DC: American Psychological Association, 2001).

Nolen-Hoeksema, S., "Ruminative Coping and Recovery from Loss," in M. S. Stroebe et al., eds., 2001.

Nordenfelt, L., "The Stoic Conception of Mental Disorder: The Case of Cicero," *Philosophy, Psychiatry, and Psychology* 4 (1997), 285–91.

Nozick, R., *Anarchy, State, and Utopia* (New York: Basic Books, 1974).

Nussbaum, M., *The Fragility of Goodness* (Cambridge: Cambridge University Press, 1986).

—— "Nature, Function, and Capability," *Oxford Studies in Ancient Philosophy*, supp. 1 (1988), 145–84.

—— "Aristotelian Social Democracy," in R. B. Douglass, G. M. Mara, and H. S. Richardson, eds., *Liberalism and the Good* (New York: Routledge, 1990).

—— "Human Functioning and Social Justice: In Defense of Aristotelian Essentialism," *Political Theory* 20 (1992), 202–46.

—— "Non-Relative Virtues: An Aristotelian Approach," in M. Nussbaum and A. Sen, eds., *The Quality of Life* (Oxford: Oxford University Press, 1993).

—— *The Therapy of Desire* (Princeton: Princeton University Press, 1994).

—— "Aristotle on Human Nature and the Foundations of Ethics," in J. E. J. Altham and R. Harrison, eds., *World, Mind, and Ethics: Essays on the Ethical Philosophy of Bernard Williams* (Cambridge: Cambridge University Press, 1995).

—— "Kant and Stoic Cosmopolitanism," *Journal of Political Philosophy* 5 (1997), 1–25.

Olberding, A., "The 'Stout Heart': Seneca's Strategy for Dispelling Grief," *Ancient Philosophy* 25 (2005), 141–54.

Parfit, D., *Reasons and Persons* (Oxford: Oxford University Press, 1984).

Parkes, C. M., "Psychosocial Transitions: A Field for Study," *Social Science and Medicine* 5 (1971), 101–15.

—— "Psychosocial Transitions: Comparison Between Reactions to Loss of a Limb and Loss of a Spouse," *British Journal of Psychiatry* 127 (1975), 204–10.

—— *Bereavement*, 2nd American ed. (Washington, DC: International Universities Press, 1987).

—— *Love and Loss* (London and New York: Routledge, 2006).

—— "Bereavement Following Disasters," in M. S. Stroebe et al., eds., 2008.

—— and R. S. Weiss, *Recovery from Bereavement* (New York: Basic Books, 1983).

Pennebaker, J. W., "Writing about Emotional Experiences as a Therapeutic Process," *Psychological Science* 8 (1997), 162–6.

—— and R. C. O'Heerong, "Confiding in Others and Illness Rate among Spouses of Suicide and Accidental Death Victims," *Journal of Abnormal Psychology* 93 (1984), 473–6.

—— E. Zech, and B. Rimé, "Disclosing and Sharing Emotion: Psychological, Social, and Health Consequences," in M. S. Stroebe et al., eds., 2001.

Price, A. W., "Were Zeno and Chrysippus at Odds in Analyzing Emotion?" in R. Salles, ed., 2005.

Purinton, J., "Aristotle's Definition of Happiness (*NE* 1.7, 1098a16–18)," *Oxford Studies in Ancient Philosophy* 16 (1998), 259–97.

Rackham, H., trans., *Cicero: de Oratore Book III, de Fato, Paradoxa Stoicorum, de Partitione Oratoria* (Cambridge, MA: Harvard/Loeb, 1942).

Ramelli, I., *Hierocles the Stoic: Elements of Ethics, Fragments, and Excerpts*, trans. D. Konstan (Atlanta: Society of Biblical Literature, 2009).

Rando, T., "The Increasing Prevalence of Complicated Mourning," *Omega* 26 (1992–3), 43–60.

—— *Treatment of Complicated Mourning* (Champaign, IL: Research Press, 1993).

Reeve, C. D. C., *Practices of Reason: Aristotle's Nicomachean Ethics* (Oxford: Oxford University Press, 1992).

Remes, P. and J. Sihvola, eds., *Ancient Philosophy of Self* (Berlin: Springer, 2008).

Reshotko, N., "Virtue as the Only Unconditional—But not Intrinsic—Good: Plato's *Euthydemus* 278e3–281e5," *Ancient Philosophy* 21 (2001), 325–34.

—— *Socratic Virtue* (Oxford: Oxford University Press, 2006).

Reydams-Schils, G., *The Roman Stoics* (Chicago: University of Chicago Press, 2005).

Rhodes, R., "Commentary on 'The Stoic Conception of Mental Disorder,'" *Philosophy, Psychiatry, and Psychology* 4 (1997), 303–4.

Richardson, H. S., *Practical Reasoning about Final Ends* (Cambridge: Cambridge University Press, 1994).

Richardson Lear, G., *Happy Lives and the Highest Good: An Essay on Aristotle's Nicomachean Ethics* (Princeton: Princeton University Press, 2004).

Ridge, M., "Reasons for Action: Agent-Neutral vs. Agent-Relative," *Stanford Encyclopedia of Philosophy*, revised 2011.

Rist, J. M., *Stoic Philosophy* (Cambridge: Cambridge University Press, 1969).

Roche, T., "Commentary on Russell," *Proceedings of the Boston Area Colloquium in Ancient Philosophy* 24 (2008), 113–22.

Roopen, M., "On the Eudemian and Nicomachean Conceptions of Eudaimonia," *American Catholic Philosophical Quarterly* 79 (2005), 365–88.

Ross, D., trans., *Aristotle: The Nicomachean Ethics*, revised by J. L. Ackrill and J. O. Urmson (New York: Oxford University Press, 1980).

Rudebusch, G., *Socrates, Pleasure, and Value* (Oxford: Oxford University Press, 1999).

Russell, D., review of Rudebusch 1999, *Ancient Philosophy* 20 (2000), 468–72.

—— "Locke on Land and Labor," *Philosophical Studies* 117 (2004), 303–25.

—— *Plato on Pleasure and the Good Life* (Oxford: Oxford University Press, 2005).

—— "Happiness and Agency in the Stoics and Aristotle," *Proceedings of the Boston Area Colloquium in Ancient Philosophy* 24 (2008), 83–112.

—— *Practical Intelligence and the Virtues* (Oxford: Oxford University Press, 2009).

—— "Embodiment and Self-Ownership," *Social Philosophy and Policy* 27 (2010), 135–67.

—— "Two Mistakes about Stoic Ethics," forthcoming among the proceedings of the 2011 Keeling Colloquium in Ancient Philosophy.

—— and M. LeBar, "Well-Being and Eudaimonia: A Reply to Haybron," in J. Peters, ed., *Virtue and Vice* (London: Routledge, forthcoming).

Rybarczyk, B., D. L. Neyenhuis, J. J. Nicholas, S. M. Cash, and J. Kaiser, "Body Image, Perceived Social Stigma, and the Prediction of Psychological Adjustment to Leg Amputation," *Rehabilitation Psychology* 40 (1995), 95–110.

Sacks, O., *The Man Who Mistook His Wife for a Hat* (New York: Summit, 1985).

Salles, R., ed., *Metaphysics, Soul, and Ethics in Ancient Thought: Themes from the Work of Richard Sorabji* (Oxford: Oxford University Press, 2005).

Sambursky, S., *Physics of the Stoics* (London: Hutchinson & Co., 1959).

Sanders, J. T., "Projects and Property," in D. Schmidtz, ed., *Robert Nozick* (Cambridge: Cambridge University Press, 2002).

Santas, G., "Socratic Goods and Socratic Happiness," *Apeiron* 26 (1993), 37–52.

Schechtman, M., *The Constitution of Selves* (Ithaca, NY: Cornell University Press, 1996).

Scheffler, S., "Agent-Centred Restrictions, Rationality, and the Virtues," in S. Scheffler, ed., *Consequentialism and its Critics* (Oxford: Oxford University Press, 1988).

—— *Human Morality* (Oxford: Oxford University Press, 1992).

Schmidtz, D., "Choosing Ends," *Ethics* 104 (1994), 226–251.

Schofield, M., *The Stoic Idea of the City* (Cambridge: Cambridge University Press, 1991).

—— "Epictetus on Cynicism," in T. Scaltsas and A. S. Mason, eds., *The Philosophy of Epictetus* (Oxford: Oxford University Press, 2007).

Sellars, J., *Stoicism* (Berkeley: University of California Press, 2006).

—— "Stoic Cosmopolitianism and Zeno's *Republic*," *History of Political Thought* 28 (2007), 1–29.

—— *The Art of Living*, 2nd ed. (London: Bristol Classical Press, 2009).

Sen, A., *On Ethics and Economics* (Oxford: Blackwell, 1987).

Sharples, R., "Aspasius on Eudaimonia," in A. Alberti and R. Sharples, eds., *Aspasius: The Earliest Extant Commentary on Aristotle's Ethics* (Berlin: de Gruyter, 1999).

Shaver, P. R. and C. M. Tancredy, "Emotion, Attachment, and Bereavement: A Conceptual Commentary," in M. S. Stroebe et al., eds., 2001.

Sherman, N., "Aristotle on Friendship and the Shared Life," *Philosophy and Phenomenological Research* 47 (1987), 589–613.

—— *The Fabric of Character* (Oxford: Oxford University Press, 1989).

—— *Stoic Warriors* (Oxford: Oxford University Press, 2005).

Slote, M., *Morals from Motives* (Oxford: Oxford University Press, 2001).

Smith, M., "A Theory of Freedom and Responsibility," in G. Cullity and B. Gaut, eds., 1997.

Snow, N., *Virtue as Social Intelligence* (New York: Routledge, 2009).

Sorabji, R., *Emotion and Peace of Mind* (Oxford: Oxford University Press, 2000).

—— *Self* (Chicago: University of Chicago Press, 2006).

—— "Epictetus on *proairesis* and Self," in T. Scaltsas and A. S. Mason, eds., *The Philosophy of Epictetus* (Oxford: Oxford University Press, 2007).

—— "Graeco-Roman Varieties of Self," in P. Remes and J. Sihvola, eds., 2008.

Stephens, W. O., "Epictetus on How the Stoic Sage Loves," *Oxford Studies in Ancient Philosophy* 14 (1996), 192–210.

—— *Stoic Ethics: Epictetus and Happiness as Freedom* (London: Continuum, 2007).

Stockdale, J., *Courage Under Fire: Testing Epictetus' Doctrines in a Lab of Human Behavior* (Stanford, Calif.: Hoover Institution Press, 1994).

Strange, S. K., "The Stoics on the Voluntariness of the Passions," in S. K. Strange and J. Zupko, eds., *Stoicism: Traditions and Transformations* (Cambridge: Cambridge University Press, 2004).

Strawson, P. F., "Freedom and Resentment," *Proceedings of the British Academy* 48 (1962), 1–25.

Striker, G., "Plato's Socrates and the Stoics," in P. A. Vander Waerdt, ed., *The Socratic Movement* (Ithaca, New York: Cornell University Press, 1994).

Stroebe, M. S., "Coping with Bereavement," *Omega* 26 (1992–3), 19–42.

—— and H. Schut, "The Dual Process Model of Coping with Bereavement: Rationale and Description," *Death Studies* 23 (1999), 197–224.

—— —— "Meaning Making in the Dual Process Model of Coping with Bereavement," in R. Neimeyer, ed., *Meaning Reconstruction and the Experience of Loss* (Washington, DC: American Psychological Association, 2001).

—— and W. Stroebe, "Does 'Grief Work' Work?" *Journal of Consulting and Clinical Psychology* 59 (1991), 479–82.

———R. O. Hansson, and W. Stroebe, eds., *Handbook of Bereavement Research: Consequences, Coping, and Care* (Washington, DC: American Psychological Association, 2001).

——— ———H. Schut, E. Zech, and J. van den Bout, "Does Disclosure of Emotions Facilitate Recovery from Bereavement? Evidence from Two Prospective Studies," *Journal of Consulting and Clinical Psychology* 70 (2002), 169–79.

———H. Schut, and W. Stroebe, "Attachment in Coping with Bereavement," *Review of General Psychology* 9 (2005), 48–66.

———R. O. Hansson, H. Schut, and W. Stroebe, eds., *Handbook of Bereavement Research and Practice: Advances in Theory and Intervention* (Washington, DC: American Psychological Association, 2008).

Sumner, L. W., *Welfare, Happiness, and Ethics* (Oxford: Oxford University Press, 1996).

——— "Something in Between," in R. Crisp and B. Hooker, eds., *Well-Being and Morality: Essays in Honour of James Griffin* (Oxford: Oxford University Press, 2000).

——— "Happiness Now and Then," in L. J. Jost and R. A. Shiner, eds., *Eudaimonia and Well-Being: Ancient and Modern Conceptions* (Kelowna, BC: Academic, 2002).

Swanton, C., *Virtue Ethics: A Pluralistic View* (Oxford: Oxford University Press, 2003).

Telfer, E., *Happiness* (London: St Martin's Press, 1980).

Thomson, J. J., "The Right and the Good," *Journal of Philosophy* 94 (1997), 273–98.

Tiberius, V., "Well-Being: Psychological Research for Philosophers," *Philosophy Compass* 1 (2006), 493–505.

——— *The Reflective Life* (Oxford: Oxford University Press, 2008).

——— and A. Plakias, "Well-Being," in J. Doris and the Moral Psychology Research Group, eds., *The Moral Psychology Handbook* (Oxford: Oxford University Press, 2010).

Toner, C. H., "Aristotelian Well-Being," *Utilitas* 18 (2006), 218–31.

Toombs, S. K, "Reflections on Bodily Change," in S. K. Toombs, ed., *Handbook of Phenomenology and Medicine* (Dordrecht, the Netherlands: Kluwer, 2001).

Tsekourakis, D., *Studies in the Terminology of Early Stoic Ethics*, *Hermes Einzelschriften* 32 (Wiesbaden: Franz Steiner, 1974).

Tsouna McKirahan, V., "The Socratic Origins of the Cynics and Cyrenaics," in P. A. Vander Waerdt, ed., *The Socratic Movement* (Ithaca, NY: Cornell University Press, 1994).

Van Cleemput, G., "Aristotle on *Eudaimonia* in *Nicomachean Ethics* I," *Oxford Studies in Ancient Philosophy* 30 (2006), 127–57.

Vlastos, G., *Socrates: Ironist and Moral Philosopher* (Ithaca, NY: Cornell University Press, 1991).

Wallace, R. J., "Reason and Responsibility," in G. Cullity and B. Gaut, eds., 1997.

Walsh, C., "Afterword" to Lewis 1976.

Weiss, R. S., "Grief, Bonds, and Relationships," in M. S. Stroebe et al., eds., 2001.

——— "The Nature and Causes of Grief," in M. S. Stroebe et al., eds., 2008.

White, N., "Stoic Values," *Monist* 73 (1990), 42–58.

——— *Individual and Conflict in Greek Ethics* (Oxford: Oxford University Press, 2002).

——— *A Brief History of Happiness* (Oxford: Blackwell, 2006).

White, S., *Sovereign Virtue* (Stanford: Stanford University Press, 1992).

——— "Happiness in the Hellenistic Lyceum," *Apeiron* 35, supp. (2002), 69–93.

——— "Lyco and Hieronymus on the Good Life," in W. W. Fortenbaugh and S. White, eds., 2004.

Wilkinson, S., "Is 'Normal Grief' a Mental Disorder?" *Philosophical Quarterly* 50 (2000), 289–304.

Williams, B., *Ethics and the Limits of Philosophy* (Cambridge, MA: Harvard University Press, 1985).

Wolfe, T., *A Man in Full* (New York: Farrar, Straus, and Giroux, 1998).

Worden, W., *Grief Counseling and Grief Therapy* (New York: Springer, 1982).

—— *Grief Counseling and Grief Therapy*, 2nd ed. (New York: Springer, 1991).

Index Locorum

General Index